Table of Conter

MW00377863

Operations and Algebraic Thinking

▶ **Use the four operations with whole numbers to solve problems.**

▶ **Gain familiarity with factors and multiples.**

▶ **Generate and analyze patterns.**

Number and Operations in Base Ten

▶ **Generalize place value understanding for multi-digit whole numbers.**

▶ Use place value understanding and properties of operations to perform multi-digit arithmetic.

Number and Operations – Fractions

▶ **Extend understanding of fraction equivalence and ordering.**

▶ **Build fractions from unit fractions by applying and extending previous understandings of operations on whole numbers.**

▶ **Understand decimal notation for fractions, and compare decimal fractions.**

Measurement and Data

▶ Solve problems involving measurement and conversion of measurements from a larger unit to a smaller unit.

▶ Represent and interpret data.

▶ Geometric measurement: understand concepts of angle and measure angles.

Geometry

▶ **Draw and identify lines and angles, and classify shapes by properties of their lines and angles.**

Introduction

Core Standards for Math offers two-page lessons for every content standard in the *Common Core State Standards for Mathematics*. The first page of each lesson introduces the concept or skill being taught by providing step-by-step instruction and modeling and checks students' understanding through open-ended practice items. The second page includes multiple-choice practice items as well as problem-solving items.

Common Core State Standards for Mathematics: Content Standards

Content Standards define what students should understand and be able to do. These standards are organized into clusters of related standards to emphasize mathematical connections. Finally, domains represent larger groups of related standards. At the elementary (K–6) level, there are ten content domains. Each grade addresses four or five domains. The table below shows how the domains are placed across Grades K–6.

Domains	K	1	2	3	4	5	6
Counting and Cardinality (CC)	●						
Operations and Algebraic Thinking (OA)	●	●	●	●	●	●	
Numbers and Operations in Base Ten (NBT)	●	●	●	●	●	●	
Measurement and Data (MD)	●	●	●	●	●	●	
Geometry (G)	●	●	●	●	●	●	●
Numbers and Operations—Fractions (NF)				●	●	●	
Ratios and Proportional Relationships (RP)							●
The Number System (NS)							●
Expressions and Equations (EE)							●
Statistics and Probability (SP)							●

The lessons in **Core Standards for Math** are organized by content standard. The content standard is listed at the top right-hand corner of each page. The entire text of the standards is provided on pages 259–264. The lesson objective listed below the content standard number indicates what part of the standard is emphasized in the lesson. You may choose to have students complete all the lessons for a particular standard or select lessons based on the more focused objectives.

Algebra • Multiplication Comparisons

Tara has 3 times as many soccer medals as Greg. Greg has 4 soccer medals. How many soccer medals does Tara have?

Step 1 Draw a model.

Greg ◯◯◯◯

Tara ◯◯◯◯ ◯◯◯◯ ◯◯◯◯

Step 2 Use the model to write an equation.

$n = \underline{\ 3\ } \times \underline{\ 4\ }$ **Think:** n is how many soccer medals Tara has.

Step 3 Solve the equation.

$n = \underline{\ 12\ }$

So, Tara has $\underline{\ 12\ }$ soccer medals.

Draw a model and write an equation.

1. 4 times as many as 7 is 28.

2. 16 is 8 times as many as 2.

_____

_____

3. 3 times as many as 6 is 18.

4. 10 is 2 times as many as 5.

_____

_____

Core Standards for Math, Grade 4

Name _____

Thurs. RTI
Lesson 1
CC.4.OA.1

1. Mei has 32 shells. This is 4 times as many shells as Rob has. Mei made a model to compare the numbers of shells.

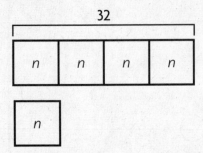

Which equation represents how to find the value of n?

(A) $32 = n + 4$ (C) $32 + 4 = n$

(B) $32 = 4 \times n$ (D) $32 \times 4 = n$

2. Julia has 24 baseball cards. This is 4 times as many as Chad has. How many baseball cards does Chad have?

(A) 4   (C) 20

(B) 6   (D) 96

3. Kirin has 28 books. This is 7 times as many books as Gail has. Kirin made a model to compare the numbers.

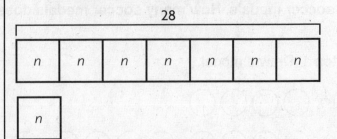

Which equation represents how to find the value of n?

(A) $28 = n + 7$ (C) $28 + 7 = n$

(B) $28 \times 7 = n$ (D) $28 = 7 \times n$

4. Robin bought 40 flowers. This is 8 times as many as the number of vases that she has. How many vases does Robin have?

(A) 3   (C) 5

(B) 4   (D) 8

Problem Solving

5. Alan is 14 years old. This is twice as old as his brother James is. How old is James?

6. There are 27 campers. This is nine times as many as the number of counselors. How many counselors are there?

Name _____

Algebra • Comparison Problems

Jamie has 3 times as many baseball cards as Rick. Together, they have 20 baseball cards. How many cards does Jamie have?

Step 1 Draw a box with the letter *n* in it to show that Rick has an unknown number of cards. Jamie has 3 times as many cards as Rick, so draw three identical boxes to represent Jamie's cards.

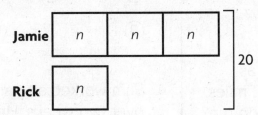

Step 2 Use the model to write an equation.
   Think: There are 4 equal bars. The number in each bar is
      represented by *n*.

There are a total of 20 cards. So, ___4___ × *n* = ___20___.

Step 3 Solve the equation to find the value of *n*.
   Think: 4 times what number is 20?
Since 4 × ___5___ = 20, the value of *n* is ___5___.

Rick has ___5___ cards.

Step 4 Find how many cards Jamie has.
   Think: Jamie has 3 times as many cards as Rick.

So, Jamie has 3 × ___5___ = ___15___ baseball cards.

Draw a model. Write an equation and solve.

1. Maddie has 2 times as many stickers on her notebook as Meg. Together, they have 15 stickers. How many stickers are on Maddie's notebook?

2. How many more stickers are on Maddie's notebook than on Meg's notebook?

_____   _____

1. Maria has 4 times as many necklaces as Sheila. Together, they have 25 necklaces. How many necklaces does Maria have?

   Ⓐ 4   Ⓒ 15

   Ⓑ 5   Ⓓ 20

2. Fernando ran 3 times as far as Aaron. They ran a total of 12 miles. How many miles did Fernando run?

   Ⓐ 9 miles

   Ⓑ 6 miles

   Ⓒ 3 miles

   Ⓓ 2 miles

3. Mr. Anson made a walkway using 4 times as many red bricks as gray bricks. He used a total of 80 bricks. How many red bricks did Mr. Anson use?

   Ⓐ 5   Ⓒ 16

   Ⓑ 8   Ⓓ 64

4. Sam worked a total of 36 hours over two weeks. He worked twice as many hours in the second week as the first. How many hours did he work in the first week?

   Ⓐ 6   Ⓒ 24

   Ⓑ 12   Ⓓ 36

Problem Solving  REAL WORLD

5. Rafael counted a total of 40 white cars and yellow cars. There were 9 times as many white cars as yellow cars. How many white cars did Rafael count?

   _____

6. Sue scored a total of 35 points in two games. She scored 6 times as many points in the second game as in the first. How many more points did she score in the second game?

   _____

Name _____

Lesson 3
COMMON CORE STANDARD CC.4.OA.3
Lesson Objective: Use the *draw a diagram*
strategy to solve multistep problems.

Problem Solving • Multistep Multiplication Problems

Use the strategy *draw a diagram* to solve a multistep
multiplication problem.

Amy planted 8 rows with 18 tulips in each row. In each of
the 4 middle rows, there are 4 red tulips. All of the other
tulips are yellow. How many of the tulips are yellow tulips?

Read the Problem	Solve the Problem
What do I need to find? I need to find the total number of <u>yellow</u> tulips.	I drew a diagram for each color of tulip. 18 tulips 4 rows — R R R R / R R R R / R R R R / R R R R — 8 rows 4 tulips
What information do I need to use? There are <u>8</u> rows of tulips with <u>18</u> tulips in each row. There are <u>4</u> rows of tulips with <u>4</u> red tulips in each row.	Next, I found the number in each section. **All Tulips**　　　　**Red Tulips** 8 × 18 = 144　　　4 × 4 = 16
How will I use the information? I can <u>multiply</u> to find the total number of tulips and the number of red tulips. Then I can <u>subtract</u> to find the number of yellow tulips.	Last, I subtracted the number of red tulips from the total number of tulips. <u>144</u> – <u>16</u> = <u>128</u> So, there are <u>128</u> yellow tulips.

1. A car dealer has 8 rows of cars with
   16 cars in each row. In each of the first
   3 rows, 6 are used cars. The rest of the
   cars are new cars. How many new cars
   does the dealer have?

2. An orchard has 4 rows of apple trees
   with 12 trees in each row. There are
   also 6 rows of pear trees with 15 trees
   in each row. How many apple and
   pear trees are in the orchard?

_____　　_____

　　　　Core Standards for Math, Grade 4

1. All the seats in two sections of a movie theater are occupied. In one section, there are 8 rows with 18 seats in each row. In the other section, there are 12 rows with 6 seats in each row. How many people are seated in these two sections of the theater?

   (A) 44   (C) 144

   (B) 72   (D) 216

2. Savannah makes 18 gift baskets to sell in her store. She puts 4 peaches in 10 of the baskets and 2 peaches in the remaining 8 baskets. How many peaches does Savannah place in the gift baskets?

   (A) 24   (C) 56

   (B) 40   (D) 108

3. All the seats in two sections of a concert hall are occupied. In one section, there are 18 rows with 9 seats in each row. In the other section, there are 14 rows with 8 seats in each row. How many people are seated in these two sections of the concert hall?

   (A) 274   (C) 112

   (B) 162   (D) 49

4. Mrs. Klein delivered 3 books to 11 classrooms and 4 books to 6 classrooms. How many books did Mrs. Klein deliver to all the classrooms?

   (A) 24   (C) 57

   (B) 33   (D) 119

5. Peter baked 5 pies for a bake sale. He cut each pie into 12 slices. He sold 9 slices from each of the 5 pies. How many slices of pie did Peter get to take home? Explain how you found your answer.

   _____

   _____

   _____

   _____

   _____

Name _____

Lesson 4
COMMON CORE STANDARD CC.4.OA.3
Lesson Objective: Represent and solve
multistep problems using equations.

Algebra • Solve Multistep Problems Using Equations

The **Order of Operations** is a special set of rules which gives the order in which calculations are done in an expression. First, multiply and divide from left to right. Then, add and subtract from left to right.

Use the order of operations to find the value of _n_.

$$6 \times 26 + 3 \times 45 - 11 = n$$

Step 1 Circle the first multiplication expression in the equation.

$$(6 \times 26) + 3 \times 45 - 11 = n$$

Step 2 Multiply 6×26.

$$\underline{156} + 3 \times 45 - 11 = n$$

Step 3 Circle the next multiplication expression in the equation.

$$156 + (3 \times 45) - 11 = n$$

Step 4 Multiply 3×45.

$$156 + \underline{135} - 11 = n$$

Step 5 There are no more multiplication or division expressions. Circle the first addition expression in the equation.

$$(156 + 135) - 11 = n$$

Step 6 Add $156 + 135$.

$$\underline{291} - 11 = n$$

Step 7 Subtract $291 - 11$.

$$\underline{280} = n$$

Find the value of _n_.

1. $5 \times 43 + 9 \times 24 + 25 = n$

_____ $= n$

2. $7 \times 29 + 4 \times 46 - 56 = n$

_____ $= n$

1. In his stamp book, Dane has 6 pages with 15 stamps on each and 9 pages with 20 stamps on each. He gives 25 stamps away. Which equation can Dane use to find how many stamps he has left?

   (A) $6 \times 15 \times 9 \times 20 - 25 = n$

   (B) $6 \times 15 + 9 \times 20 - 25 = n$

   (C) $6 + 15 \times 9 + 20 - 25 = n$

   (D) $6 + 15 \times 9 \times 20 + 25 = n$

2. Tim has 5 boxes with 18 sports cards in each. He buys 7 packs of sports cards with 13 cards in each. If Tim buys another 10 sports cards, how many sports cards will he have?

   (A) 53   (C)   191

   (B) 181   (D) 1,271

3. Latisha has 7 boxes with 21 shells in each. She has 6 bags with 17 shells in each. She gives away 18 shells. Which equation can Latisha use to find how many shells she has left?

   (A) $7 + 21 \times 6 + 17 - 18 = n$

   (B) $7 \times 21 + 6 \times 17 + 18 = n$

   (C) $7 + 21 + 6 + 17 - 18 = n$

   (D) $7 \times 21 + 6 \times 17 - 18 = n$

4. Sara has 6 albums with 15 photos in each. Maya has 8 albums with 13 photos in each. If Sara adds 12 more photos, how many photos will Sara and Maya have in all?

   (A) 54   (C) 206

   (B) 182   (D) 404

Problem Solving  REAL WORLD

5. A bakery has 4 trays with 16 muffins on each tray. The bakery has 3 trays of cupcakes with 24 cupcakes on each tray. If 15 cupcakes are sold, how many muffins and cupcakes are left?

   _____

6. Katy bought 5 packages of stickers with 25 stickers in each package. She also bought 3 boxes of markers with 12 markers in each box. If she receives 8 stickers from a friend, how many stickers and markers does Katy have now?

   _____

Name _____

Lesson 5
COMMON CORE STANDARD CC.4.OA.3
Lesson Objective: Use the strategy *draw a diagram* to solve multistep multiplication problems.

Problem Solving • Multiply 2-Digit Numbers

A library ordered 17 cases with 24 books in each case. In 12 of the cases, 18 books were fiction books. The rest of the books were nonfiction. How many nonfiction books did the library order?

Read the Problem	Solve the Problem
What do I need to find? I need to find <u>how many nonfiction books</u> were ordered.	• First, find the total number of books ordered. $\underline{17} \times \underline{24} = \underline{408}$ books ordered • Next, find the number of fiction books. $\underline{12} \times \underline{18} = \underline{216}$ fiction books • Last, draw a bar model. I need to subtract.
What information do I need to use? <u>17</u> cases of <u>24</u> books each were ordered. In <u>12</u> cases, <u>18</u> books were fiction books.	 ┌────────────────────────┐ │ 408 books ordered │ └────────────────────────┘ ┌──────────────┐ │ 216 fiction books │ └──────────────┘──────── ?
How will I use the information? I can find the <u>total number of books ordered</u> and the <u>number of fiction books ordered</u>. Then I can draw a bar model to compare the <u>total number of books</u> to the <u>number of fiction books</u>.	$408 - 216 = \underline{192}$ So, the library ordered <u>192</u> nonfiction books.

1. A grocer ordered 32 cases with 28 small cans of fruit in each case. The grocer also ordered 24 cases with 18 large cans of fruit in each case. How many more small cans of fruit did the grocer order?

2. Rebecca rode her bike 16 miles each day for 30 days. Michael rode his bike 25 miles for 28 days. Who rode farther? How much farther?

_____

_____

_____

_____

1. In July, traffic officers wrote an average of 34 tickets each day. In August, they wrote an average of 47 tickets each day. How many more tickets did traffic officers write in August than in July? (Hint: July and August have 31 days each.)

   (A) 403

   (C) 1,457

   (B) 1,045

   (D) 2,511

3. A concert hall has seats on a main floor and in a balcony. The main floor has 24 rows of 28 seats in each row. The balcony has 9 rows of 22 seats in each row. How many more seats are on the main floor than in the balcony?

   (A) 870

   (C) 474

   (B) 672

   (D) 198

2. An arena's lower-level section has 32 rows with 50 seats in each row. The upper-level section has 28 rows with 42 seats in each row. How many more seats are in the lower-level section than in the upper-level section?

   (A) 400

   (C) 1,176

   (B) 424

   (D) 1,600

4. Jevonne lives in a large apartment complex. Building A has 17 floors with 8 apartments on each floor. Building B has 12 floors with 8 apartments on each floor. How many more apartments are in Building A than in Building B?

   (A) 40

   (C) 136

   (B) 96

   (D) 204

5. A chess club orders a T-shirt and a notebook for each of its 24 members. Each T-shirt costs $13, and each notebook costs $2 each. How much more do the T-shirts cost in all than the notebooks? Explain how you found your answer.

   _____

   _____

   _____

   _____

Interpret the Remainder

When you solve a division problem with a remainder, the way you interpret the remainder depends on the situation and the question.

Way 1: Write the remainder as a fraction.

Callie has a board that is 60 inches long. She wants to cut 8 shelves of equal length from the board and use the entire board. How long will each shelf be?

Divide. 60 ÷ 8 $\underline{7\ r4}$

The remainder, 4 inches, can be divided into 8 equal parts.

$$\frac{4}{8} \begin{matrix}\leftarrow \text{remainder} \\ \leftarrow \text{divisor}\end{matrix}$$

Write the remainder as a fraction.

Each shelf will be $\underline{7\frac{4}{8}}$ inches long.

Way 2: Drop the remainder.

Callie has 60 beads. She wants to make 8 identical bracelets and use as many beads as possible on each bracelet. How many beads will be on each bracelet?

Divide. 60 ÷ 8 $\underline{7\ r4}$

The remainder is the number of beads left over. Those beads will not be used. Drop the remainder.

Callie will use $\underline{7}$ beads on each bracelet.

Way 3: Add 1 to the quotient.

Callie has 60 beads. She wants to put 8 beads in each container. How many containers will she need?

Divide. 60 ÷ 8 $\underline{7\ r4}$

The answer shows that Callie can fill 7 containers but will have 4 beads left over. She will need 1 more container for the 4 leftover beads. Add 1 to the quotient.

Callie will need $\underline{8}$ containers.

Way 4: Use only the remainder.

Callie has 60 stickers. She wants to give an equal number of stickers to 8 friends. She will give the leftover stickers to her sister. How many stickers will Callie give to her sister?

Divide. 60 ÷ 8 $\underline{7\ r4}$

The remainder is the number of stickers left over. Use the remainder as the answer.

Callie will give her sister $\underline{4}$ stickers.

---

1. There are 35 students going to the zoo. Each van can hold 6 students. How many vans are needed?

2. Sue has 55 inches of ribbon. She wants to cut the ribbon into 6 equal pieces. How long will each piece be?

_____

_____

1. A group of 40 people takes the swan boat ride. Each boat can carry 6 people. If the guide fills as many boats as possible, how many people will ride in the last boat?

   Ⓐ 34

   Ⓑ 7

   Ⓒ 6

   Ⓓ 4

2. Vanna uses thank-you notes that come in packs of 8. She has to write 29 thank-you notes. How many packs of thank-you notes should she buy?

   Ⓐ 3

   Ⓑ $3\frac{5}{8}$

   Ⓒ 4

   Ⓓ 5

3. Nolan divides his 88 toy cars into boxes. Each box can hold 9 cars. How many boxes can Nolan fill?

   Ⓐ 7

   Ⓑ 9

   Ⓒ 10

   Ⓓ 12

4. Selim puts 30 ounces of trail mix equally into 9 bags. How many ounces will be in each bag?

   Ⓐ 4 ounces

   Ⓑ $3\frac{1}{3}$ ounces

   Ⓒ 3 ounces

   Ⓓ $2\frac{1}{2}$ ounces

Problem Solving REAL WORLD

5. Joanna has 70 beads. She uses 8 beads for each bracelet. She makes as many bracelets as possible. How many beads will Joanna have left over?

6. A teacher wants to give 3 markers to each of her 25 students. Markers come in packages of 8. How many packages of markers will the teacher need?

Name _____

Lesson 7
COMMON CORE STANDARD CC.4.OA.3
Lesson Objective: Solve problems by using the strategy *draw a diagram.*

Problem Solving • Multistep Division Problems

There are 72 third graders and 84 fourth graders going on a field trip. An equal number of students will ride on each of 4 buses. How many students will ride on each bus?

Read the Problem	Solve the Problem
What do I need to find? I need to find the number of <u>students</u> who will ride on each bus.	I can model the number of students in all using a bar diagram. 	72	84	 _____ 156
What information do I need to use? There are <u>72</u> third graders and <u>84</u> fourth graders. There will be <u>4</u> buses.	I can model the number of buses and divide to find the number of students on each bus. | 39	39	39	39 | _____ 156
How will I use the information? I will make a bar diagram for each step. I will add <u>72 and 84</u> to find the total number of students. I will divide by <u>4</u> to find how many students will ride on each bus.	So, <u>39</u> students will ride on each bus.

1. Miranda has 180 beads for making jewelry. She buys 240 more beads. She wants to store the beads in a case with 6 sections. She wants to put the same number of beads in each section. How many beads should Miranda put in each section?

_____

2. All 203 students at Polk School eat lunch at the same time. One day 19 students were absent. If 8 students sit at each table in the lunchroom, how many tables were used that day at lunch?

1. There are 112 seats in a school auditorium. There are 7 seats in each row. There are 70 people seated. They filled all the seats in a row before starting to sit in a new row. How many rows are empty?

   (A) 6

   (B) 10

   (C) 16

   (D) 28

2. Ursula bought 9 dozen gauze pads for the health office. The gauze pads were divided equally into 4 boxes. How many gauze pads are in each box?

   (A) 108

   (B) 36

   (C) 27

   (D) 24

3. The school choir has 48 singers with high voices, 53 singers with middle voices, and 39 singers with low voices. The singers stand in 4 equal rows at concerts. How many singers are in each row?

   (A) 140

   (B) 45

   (C) 35

   (D) 34

4. The are 126 seats in a meeting room. There are 9 seats in each row. There are 90 people seated. They filled all the seats in a row before starting to sit in a new row. How many rows are empty?

   (A) 36   (C) 9

   (B) 10   (D) 4

5. An orchestra has 18 string players, 9 percussion players, 15 brass players, and 12 woodwind players. If all the players sit in rows of 9 chairs each, how many rows of chairs are needed? Explain your answer.

   _____

   _____

   _____

Mon. RTI

Lesson 8

COMMON CORE STANDARD CC.4.OA.4
Lesson Objective: Find all the factors of a number by using models.

Name _____

Model Factors

Use tiles to find all the factors of 25. Record the arrays and write the factors shown.

Step 1 Record the array and list the factors. **Think:** Every whole number greater than 1 has at least two factors, that number and 1.	$1 \times 25 = 25$ Factors: <u>1</u> , <u>25</u>

Step 2 Make an array to see if 2 is a factor of 25. **Think:** An array has the same number of tiles in every row and the same number of tiles in every column.	 You cannot use all 25 tiles to make an array that has 2 rows. There is 1 tile left. So, <u>2</u> is not a factor of 25.

Step 3 Continue making arrays, counting by 1, to find all the other factors of 25.

Is 3 a factor?

3 rows, 1 tile left
<u>No, 3 is not a factor of 25.</u>

Is 4 a factor?

4 rows, 1 tile left
<u>No, 4 is not a factor of 25.</u>

Is 5 a factor?

<u>5</u> rows, all tiles used.
$5 \times 5 = 25$

There are the same number of tiles in each row and column. <u>Yes, 5 is a factor of 25.</u>

If you continue to make arrays up to 24, you will find there are no additional factors of 25.

So, the factors of 25 are <u>1, 5, and 25.</u>

Two factors that make a product are sometimes called a factor pair.
What are the factor pairs for 25? <u>1 and 25, 5 and 5</u>

Use tiles to find all the factors of the product. Record the arrays and write the factors shown.

1. 35

_____

2. 36

_____

1. Sean helps his coach at the end of the game. He needs to put away 24 baseballs. He puts the same number of baseballs into each box. Which list shows how many baseballs could be in each box?

   (A) 2, 3, 4, or 7

   (B) 2, 4, 6, or 7

   (C) 2, 6, 8, or 10

   (D) 3, 4, 6, or 8

2. Jenn will use 18 connecting cubes to make a model of a park. The model will be in the shape of a rectangle and will have a height of one cube. In how many different ways can Jenn make the model of the park?

   (A) 1

   (B) 2

   (C) 3

   (D) 17

3. Elaine uses 19 connecting cubes to make a model of a house. The house model is in the shape of a rectangle and is one cube high. How many different ways could Elaine make the model of the house?

   (A) 1

   (B) 2

   (C) 4

   (D) 19

4. Which list shows the factors of 16?

   (A) 1, 2, 3, 8, 16

   (B) 1, 3, 4, 8, 16

   (C) 1, 2, 4, 8, 16

   (D) 1, 2, 4, 6, 16

Problem Solving REAL WORLD

5. Brooke has to set up 70 chairs in equal rows for the class talent show. But, there is not room for more than 20 rows. What are the possible number of rows that Brooke could set up?

   _____

6. Eduardo thinks of a number between 1 and 20 that has exactly 5 factors. What number is he thinking of?

   _____

Name _____

Lesson 9
COMMON CORE STANDARD CC.4.OA.4
Lesson Objective: Determine whether a number is a factor of a given number.

Factors and Divisibility

A number is divisible by another number if the quotient is a counting number and the remainder is 0.
You can decide if a number is divisible by 2, 3, 5, 6, or 9 by using divisibility rules instead of dividing. Divisibility rules help you decide if one number is a factor of another.

Is 39 divisible by 2, 3, 5, 6, or 9?

	Result	Conclusion	Divisibility Rules
39 ÷ 2	19 r1	39 is not divisible by <u>2</u>.	The last digit, 9, is not even, so 39 is not divisible by 2.
39 ÷ 3	13 r0	39 is divisible by <u>3</u>.	The sum of the digits, 3 + 9 = 12, is divisible by 3, so 39 is divisible by 3.
39 ÷ 5	7 r4	39 is not divisible by <u>5</u>.	The last digit, 9, is not a 0 or 5, so 39 is not divisible by 5.
39 ÷ 6	6 r3	39 is not divisible by <u>6</u>.	39 is not divisible by both 2 and 3, so it is not divisible by 6.
39 ÷ 9	4 r3	39 is not divisible by <u>9</u>.	The sum of the digits, 3 + 9 = 12, is not divisible by 9, so 39 is not divisible by 9.

39 is divisible by <u>3</u>.
So, 3 is a factor of 39.

Use the chart to tell whether 30 is divisible by each divisor. Explain.

		Result	Conclusion (yes/no)	Explanation
1.	30 ÷ 2			
2.	30 ÷ 3			
3.	30 ÷ 5			
4.	30 ÷ 6			
5.	30 ÷ 9			

Is 4 a factor of the number? Write *yes* or *no*.

6. 81   **7.** 24   **8.** 56

_____   _____   _____

1. Mariska was decorating her room. She arranged 63 picture tiles on a wall in the shape of a rectangle. How many rows of tiles could be on the wall?

   (A) 2

   (B) 5

   (C) 6

   (D) 9

2. Janice spent $54 to buy some pairs of pants. Each pair of pants cost the same whole-dollar amount. How many pairs of pants could she have bought?

   (A) 3   (C) 5

   (B) 4   (D) 7

3. Jorge gives an equal number of marbles to 6 friends. Which could be the total number of marbles he gave to his friends?

   (A) 15

   (B) 33

   (C) 56

   (D) 60

4. Lee and 4 friends want to play marbles. Lee has 40 marbles to share among them. All players must have the same number of marbles to start the game. How many marbles should each player get?

   (A) 5   (C) 10

   (B) 8   (D) 20

Problem Solving REAL WORLD

5. Bryson buys a bag of 64 plastic miniature dinosaurs. Could he distribute them equally into six storage containers and not have any left over? **Explain.**

6. Lori wants to distribute 35 peaches equally into baskets. She will use more than 1 but fewer than 10 baskets. How many baskets does Lori need?

_____

_____

Problem Solving • Common Factors

Susan sorts a collection of beads. There are 35 blue, 49 red, and 21 pink beads. She arranges all the beads into rows. Each row will have the same number of beads, and all the beads in a row will be the same color. How many beads can she put in each row?

Read the Problem	Solve the Problem

Read the Problem

What do I need to find?

I need to find _the number of beads in each row, if each row is equal and has only one color_

What information do I need to use?

Susan has _35 blue, 49 red, and 21 pink beads_

How will I use the information?

I can make a list to find all of the factors of _35, 49, and 21_

Then I can use the list to find the _common factors_

Solve the Problem

Factors of 35	Factors of 49	Factors of 21
1	1	1
5	7	3
7	49	7
35		21

The common factors are _7_ and _1_.

So, Susan can put _1_ or _7_ beads in each row.

1. Allyson has 60 purple buttons, 36 black buttons, and 24 green buttons. She wants to put all of the buttons in bins. She wants each bin to have only one color and all bins to have the same number of buttons. How many buttons can Allyson put in one bin?

2. Ricardo has a marble collection with 54 blue marbles, 24 red marbles, and 18 yellow marbles. He arranges the marbles into equal rows. The marbles in each row will be the same color. How many marbles can he put in one row?

_____

1. Miles has 36 engines, 54 boxcars, and 18 cabooses. He wants to arrange the train cars in equal rows, with just one type of car in each row. How many train cars can he put in each row?

Ⓐ 1 or 18

Ⓑ 1, 2, 9, or 18

Ⓒ 1, 2, 3, 6, 9, or 18

Ⓓ 1, 2, 3, 4, 6, 8, 9, 12, 18, 24, 36, or 72

2. Gina made a list of all the common factors of 24 and 36. Which list shows the common factors of 24 and 36?

Ⓐ 1, 2, 3, 4, 6, 8, 12, 24

Ⓑ 1, 2, 4, 6, 8, 9, 12, 24

Ⓒ 1, 2, 3, 4, 6, 12

Ⓓ 1, 6, 8, 12

3. Kendall has 45 dolphin stickers, 15 shark stickers, and 20 whale stickers. She wants to put an equal number of stickers into bags, with only one type of sticker in each bag. How many stickers can Kendall put in each bag?

Ⓐ 1

Ⓑ 1 or 5

Ⓒ 1, 3, 4 or 5

Ⓓ 1, 2, 3, 4, 5, 9, 10, 15, 20 or 45

4. Which of the following is **not** a common factor of 24, 32, and 64?

Ⓐ 12

Ⓑ 8

Ⓒ 4

Ⓓ 2

5. Karen is making two displays. One display has 57 red mugs. The other display has 76 sports mugs. The rows of each display must have the same number of mugs. What would be the greatest number of mugs possible to have in a row? Explain your answer.

_____

_____

_____

_____

Name _____

Lesson **11**
COMMON CORE STANDARD CC.4.OA.4
Lesson Objective: Understand the relationship between factors and multiples, and determine whether a number is a multiple of a given number.

Factors and Multiples

You know that $1 \times 10 = \underline{10}$ and $2 \times 5 = \underline{10}$.

So, 1, 2, 5, and 10 are all **factors** of $\underline{10}$.

You can skip count to find **multiples** of a number:

Count by 1s: 1, 2, 3, 4, 5, 6, 7, 8, 9, **10**, . . .

Count by 2s: 2, 4, 6, 8, **10**, 12, . . .

Count by 5s: 5, **10**, 15, 20, 25, . . .

Count by 10s: **10**, 20, 30, 40, . . .

Note that **10** is a multiple of 1, 2, 5, and 10. A number is a multiple of all of its factors.

A **common multiple** is a multiple of two or more numbers. So, 10 is a common multiple of 1, 2, 5, and 10.

1. Multiply to list the next five multiples of 3.

$\underline{\quad 3 \quad}$, _____, _____, _____, _____, _____

2. Multiply to list the next five multiples of 7.

$\underline{\quad 7 \quad}$, _____, _____, _____, _____, _____

Is the number a factor of 8? Write *yes* or *no*.

3. 2

_____

4. 8

_____

5. 15

_____

6. 20

_____

Is the number a multiple of 4? Write *yes* or *no*.

7. 2

_____

8. 12

_____

9. 16

_____

10. 18

_____

1. Paula is counting by 9s. Peter is counting by 4s. They pace the counting so that they will say the first common number together. What is the first number they both will say?

   (A) 16   (C) 45

   (B) 36   (D) 64

2. Ms. Ayers wrote a bonus problem on the board. If Jason correctly answers, he will get extra computer time. Jason must write a statement that correctly relates the numbers 5 and 10. Which statement should Jason write?

   (A) 5 is a multiple of 10.

   (B) 10 is a factor of 5.

   (C) 10 is a common multiple of 5 and 10.

   (D) 15 is a common multiple of 5 and 10.

3. Roger bought some boxes of pencils. There were 3 pencils in each box. Which could be the number of pencils he bought?

   (A) 16   (C) 25

   (B) 21   (D) 32

4. Manny makes dinner using 1 box of pasta and 1 jar of sauce. If pasta is sold in packages of 6 boxes and sauce is sold in packages of 3 jars, what is the least number of dinners that Manny can make without any supplies left over?

   (A) 3

   (B) 6

   (C) 9

   (D) 18

Problem Solving REAL WORLD

5. Ken paid $12 for two magazines. The cost of each magazine was a multiple of $3. What are the possible prices of the magazines?

6. Jodie bought some shirts for $6 each. Marge bought some shirts for $8 each. The girls spent the same amount of money on shirts. What is the least amount they could have spent?

Name _____

Thurs. RTI

Lesson 12

COMMON CORE STANDARD CC.4.OA.4
Lesson Objective: Determine whether a
number is prime or composite.

Prime and Composite Numbers

A **prime number** is a whole number greater than 1 that has
exactly two factors, 1 and the number itself.

A **composite number** is a whole number greater than 1 that has
more than two factors.

You can use division to find the factors of a number and
tell whether the number is prime or composite.

Tell whether 55 is *prime* or *composite*.	**Tell whether 61 is *prime* or *composite*.**
Use division to find all the numbers that divide into 55 without a remainder. Those numbers are the factors of 55.	Use division to find all the numbers that divide into 61 without a remainder. Those numbers are the factors of 61.
$55 \div 1 = 55$, so __1__ and __55__ are factors.	$61 \div 1 = 61$, so __1__ and __61__ are factors.
$55 \div 5 = 11$, so __5__ and __11__ are factors.	There are no other numbers that divide into 61 evenly without a remainder.
The factors of 55 are __1__, __5__, __11__, and __55__.	The factors of 61 are __1__ and __61__.
Because 55 has more than two factors, 55 is a composite number.	Because 61 has exactly two factors, 61 is a prime number.

Tell whether the number is *prime* or *composite*.

1. 44   Think: Is 44 divisible   **2.** 53   Think: Does 53 have
                 by any number other   other factors besides
                 than 1 and 44?   1 and itself?

_____   _____

3. 12   **4.** 50   **5.** 24   **6.** 67

_____   _____   _____   _____

7. 83   **8.** 27   **9.** 34   **10.** 78

_____   _____   _____   _____

1. Ms. Chan asked Dwight if 6 is a prime number or a composite number. How should he answer?

    (A) 6 is composite.

    (B) 6 is prime.

    (C) 6 is neither prime nor composite.

    (D) 6 is both prime and composite.

2. In a math game, Rob reads four statements about the number 51. He has to pick the true statement to win the game. Which statement should Rob choose?

    (A) 51 is divisible by 2.

    (B) 51 is divisible by 3.

    (C) 51 is divisible by 5.

    (D) 51 is a prime number.

3. Elina used 10 tiles in the shape of a rectangle to make a design. She drew a model of the design.

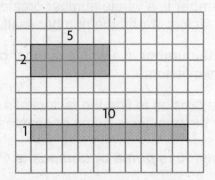

    What can Elina conclude about the number 10 from her model?

    (A) 10 is a prime number.

    (B) 10 is a composite number.

    (C) 10 is neither prime nor composite.

    (D) 10 is both prime and composite.

4. Maria's friend wrote 4 numbers and asked Maria to identify the prime number. Which is the prime number?

    (A) 21   (C) 23

    (B) 22   (D) 27

5. Ramon tells his friend that he is learning about prime numbers in math class. His friend asks him to name all the prime numbers between 20 and 30. What numbers should Ramon name? Explain how you know.

    _____

    _____

    _____

Name _____

Lesson 13

COMMON CORE STANDARD CC.4.OA.5

Lesson Objective: Generate a number pattern and describe features of the pattern.

Algebra • Number Patterns

**A pattern is an ordered set of numbers or objects, called terms.
The numbers below form a pattern. The first term in the pattern is 2.**

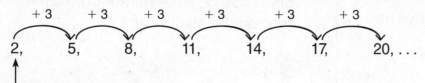

↑
First term

A rule is used to describe a pattern. The rule for this pattern is _add 3._

You can describe other patterns in the numbers. Notice that the terms in the pattern shown alternate between even and odd numbers.

For some patterns, the rule may have two operations.

$$
\overset{-2}{\frown}\ \overset{\times 2}{\frown}\ \overset{-2}{\frown}\ \overset{\times 2}{\frown}\ \overset{-2}{\frown}\ \overset{\times 2}{\frown}
$$

8,   6,   12,   10,   20,   18,   36, . . .

The rule for this pattern is _subtract 2, multiply by 2._ The first term is 8.
Notice that all of the terms in this pattern are even numbers.

Use the rule to write the numbers in the pattern.

1. Rule: Add 7.   First term: 12

12, ____, ____, ____, ____, . . .

2. Rule: Multiply by 3, subtract 1.   First term: 2

2, ____, ____, ____, ____, . . .

**Use the rule to write the numbers in the pattern.
Describe another pattern in the numbers.**

3. Rule: Subtract 5.   First term: 50

50, ____, ____, ____, ____, . . .

_____

_____

4. Rule: Multiply by 2, add 1.   First term: 4

4, ____, ____, ____, . . .

_____

_____

1. Caitlin's teacher wrote a row of numbers following a pattern.

   75, 68, 70, 63, 65, 58, 60

   What should the next number be?

   Ⓐ 51　　　Ⓒ 55

   Ⓑ 53　　　Ⓓ 62

2. Roberto wrote the number 60. If the rule is *subtract* 3, what is the fifth number in Roberto's pattern?

   Ⓐ 75　　　Ⓒ 48

   Ⓑ 72　　　Ⓓ 45

3. Julie wrote numbers on chairs for field day. She wrote the number 4 on the first chair. Her rule is *add* 5. What number did she write on the sixth chair?

   Ⓐ 28　　　Ⓒ 25

   Ⓑ 29　　　Ⓓ 34

4. Ben and Irie made a secret code. They wrote some numbers of the code so they could remember the pattern.

   7, 12, 10, 15, 13, 18, 16, 21

   What should the next number be?

   Ⓐ 18　　　Ⓒ 23

   Ⓑ 19　　　Ⓓ 26

Problem Solving REAL WORLD

5. Barb is making a bead necklace. She strings 1 white bead, then 3 blue beads, then 1 white bead, and so on. Write the numbers for the first eight beads that are white. What is a rule for the pattern?

   _____

   _____

6. An artist is arranging tiles in rows to decorate a wall. Each new row has 2 fewer tiles than the row below it. If the first row has 23 tiles, how many tiles will be in the seventh row?

   _____

   _____

Lesson 14
COMMON CORE STANDARD CC.4.OA.5

Lesson Objective: Use the strategy *act it out* to solve problems.

Problem Solving • Shape Patterns

Use the strategy *act it out* to solve pattern problems.

What might be the next three figures in the pattern below?

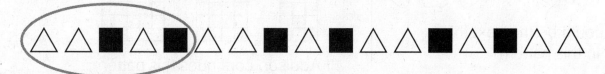

Read the Problem		
What do I need to find? I need to find the next three ___figures___ in the pattern.	**What information do I need to use?** I need to look for ___a group of figures___ that repeat.	**How will I use the information?** I will use pattern blocks to model the ___pattern___ and act out the problem.

Solve the Problem
Look for a group of figures that repeat and circle that group.   The repeating group is ___triangle___ , ___triangle___ , ___square___ , ___triangle___ , ___square___ .   I used ___triangles___ and ___squares___ to model and continue the pattern by repeating the figures in the group.   These are the next three figures in the pattern: 

1. Describe the pattern shown at right. Draw
   what might be the next figure in the pattern.

   _____

   _____

   _____

2. Use the pattern. How many circles will be in
   the sixth figure?

   _____

Name _____

1. Gloria painted this pattern on the wall of her bedroom.

Which could be the next three figures in this pattern?

Ⓐ 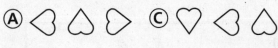 Ⓒ

Ⓑ  Ⓓ

2. Martha used counters to make this pattern.

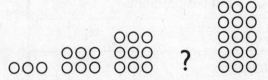

How many counters should she use in the missing figure?

Ⓐ 10   Ⓒ 14

Ⓑ 12   Ⓓ 18

3. Addison made this pattern by shading squares.

If Addison continues this pattern, how many squares should she shade in the next figure?

Ⓐ 13   Ⓒ 25

Ⓑ 20   Ⓓ 36

4. Ramona made this pattern with stickers.

Which could be the next three figures in this pattern?

Ⓐ   Ⓒ

Ⓑ   Ⓓ

5. Barb used square tiles to make this pattern.

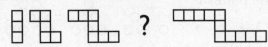

Tell how many tiles Barb should use in the missing figure. Explain how you found the answer.

_____

_____

_____

Name _____

RTI

Lesson 15

COMMON CORE STANDARD CC.4.NBT.1
Lesson Objective: Model the 10-to-1 relationship among place-value positions in the base-ten number system.

Model Place Value Relationships

A hundred grid can help you understand place-value relationships.

- One small square has been shaded to represent 1.

- Shade the rest of the first column. Count the number of small squares. There are <u>10</u> small squares. The model for 10 has <u>10</u> times as many squares as the model for <u>1</u>.

- Shade the remaining 9 columns. Count the number of small squares. There are <u>100</u> small squares. The model for 100 has <u>10</u> times as many squares as the model for <u>10</u>.

- If you shade ten hundred grids, you will have shaded 1,000 squares. So, the model for 1,000 has <u>10</u> times as many squares as the model for <u>100</u>.

A place-value chart helps you find the value of each digit in a number.

THOUSANDS			ONES		
Hundreds	Tens	Ones	Hundreds	Tens	Ones
		8,	5	1	6

In the number 8,516:

The value of the digit 8 is 8 thousands, or <u>8,000</u>.

The value of the digit 5 is 5 hundreds, or <u>500</u>.

The value of the digit 1 is 1 ten, or <u>10</u>.

The value of the digit 6 is 6 ones, or <u>6</u>.

Find the value of the underlined digit.

1. <u>7</u>56   2. 1,0<u>2</u>5   3. <u>4</u>,279   4. <u>3</u>5,703

_____   _____   _____   _____

Compare the values of the underlined digits.

5. <u>7</u>00 and <u>7</u>0

The value of 7 in _____ is _____ times the value of 7 in _____.

6. <u>5</u>,000 and <u>5</u>00

The value of 5 in _____ is _____ times the value of 5 in _____.

1. Darla copies her uncle's address and phone number into her contact list. His area code is 775. His ZIP code is 89507. Which statement about the value of the 5 in 77<u>5</u> and 89,<u>5</u>07 is true?

Ⓐ It is the same in both numbers.

Ⓑ It is 10 times as great in the ZIP code than it is in the area code.

Ⓒ It is 100 times as great in the ZIP code than it is in the area code.

Ⓓ It is 10 times as great in the area code than it is in the ZIP code.

2. On Monday, a music site sold 96,527 downloads of the new song by a popular band. What is the value of the digit 6 in 96,527?

Ⓐ 60,000

Ⓑ 6,000

Ⓒ 600

Ⓓ 60

3. Mario fills out an information card. His ZIP code is 83628. His area code is 208. Which statement about the value of the 2 in 83,6<u>2</u>8 and <u>2</u>08 is true?

Ⓐ It is 10 times as great in the area code than it is in the ZIP code.

Ⓑ It is 10 times as great in the ZIP code than it is in the area code.

Ⓒ It is 100 times as great in the area code than it is in the ZIP code.

Ⓓ It is the same in both numbers.

4. The attendance at a rock concert was 79,408 people. What is the value of the digit 4 in 79,408?

Ⓐ 40

Ⓑ 400

Ⓒ 4,000

Ⓓ 40,000

5. Compare the values of the underlined digits in 4,<u>3</u>12 and 1,4<u>3</u>2. Explain how you know.

_____

_____

_____

_____

Name _____

Lesson 16
RTI
COMMON CORE STANDARD CC.4.NBT.1
Lesson Objective: Rename whole numbers by regrouping.

Rename Numbers

You can use place value to rename whole numbers.
Here are different ways to name the number 1,400.

- **As thousands and hundreds**

  Think: 1,400 = <u>1</u> thousand <u>4</u> hundreds.
  You can draw a quick picture to help.

- **As hundreds**

  Think: 1,400 = <u>14</u> hundreds.
  You can draw a quick picture to help.

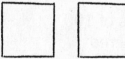

- **As tens**

  Think: 1,400 = <u>140</u> tens.

- **As ones**

  Think: 1,400 = <u>1,400</u> ones.

Rename the number. Draw a quick picture to help.

1. 180 = _____ tens

2. 1,600 = _____ hundreds

3. 6,000 = _____ thousands

4. 2,700 = 27 _____

5. 2 hundreds 6 tens = _____ tens

6. 71 thousands = _____

1. What is a way to rename 1 thousand 2 hundreds?

   Ⓐ 12 thousands

   Ⓑ 23 hundreds

   Ⓒ 12 hundreds

   Ⓓ 12 tens

2. Which renaming matches the number shown in the model?

   Ⓐ 123 thousands

   Ⓑ 123 tens

   Ⓒ 123 ones

   Ⓓ 1,203 ones

3. The computer lab provides blank CDs for students to use. The CDs come on spindles of 100. The lab ordered 25 spindles. How many CDs were ordered in all?

   Ⓐ 2,500

   Ⓑ 250

   Ⓒ 125

   Ⓓ 25

4. Pencils come in boxes of 100. The Zoller School ordered 30,000 pencils to start the school year. How many boxes were ordered?

   Ⓐ 30,000

   Ⓑ 3,000

   Ⓒ 300

   Ⓓ 20

Problem Solving

5. For the fair, the organizers ordered 32 rolls of tickets. Each roll of tickets has 100 tickets. How many tickets were ordered in all?

6. An apple orchard sells apples in bags of 10. The orchard sold a total of 2,430 apples one day. How many bags of apples was this?

Name _____

Lesson 17
COMMON CORE STANDARD CC.4.NBT.2
Lesson Objective: Read and write whole numbers in standard form, word form, and expanded form.

Read and Write Numbers

Look at the digit 6 in the place-value chart below. It is in the hundred thousands place. So, its value is <u>6 hundred thousands</u> .

In **word form**, the value of this digit is six hundred thousands.

In **standard form**, the value of the digit 6 is 600,000.

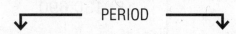
PERIOD

THOUSANDS			ONES		
Hundreds	Tens	Ones	Hundreds	Tens	Ones
6	5	9,	0	5	8

Read the number shown in the place-value chart. In word form, this number is written as six hundred fifty-nine thousand, fifty-eight.

Note that when writing a number in words, a comma separates periods.

You can also write the number in **expanded form**:
600,000 + 50,000 + 9,000 + 50 + 8

Read and write each number in two other forms.

1. 40,000 + 1,000 + 300 + 70 + 8

_____

2. twenty-one thousand, four hundred

_____

3. 391,032

_____

_____

1. Members of a stamp-collecting club have 213,094 stamps altogether. What is 213,094 written in word form?

   Ⓐ two hundred thirteen, ninety-four

   Ⓑ two hundred thirteen thousand, ninety-four

   Ⓒ two hundred thirteen thousand, nine hundred four

   Ⓓ two hundred thirteen thousand, four

2. Two hundred three thousand, one hundred ten people watched the fireworks display in town. What is that number written in standard form?

   Ⓐ 200,010

   Ⓑ 203,101

   Ⓒ 203,110

   Ⓓ 230,110

3. In 2010, an animal shelter found new homes for one hundred thirty thousand, six hundred nine dogs and cats. What is that number written in standard form?

   Ⓐ 136,309

   Ⓑ 130,690

   Ⓒ 130,609

   Ⓓ 130,069

4. The tollbooth records show that 105,076 cars passed through the toll plaza on Saturday. What is the expanded form of 105,076?

   Ⓐ 10,000 + 5,000 + 70 + 6

   Ⓑ 100,000 + 5,000 + 60 + 7

   Ⓒ 100,000 + 50,000 + 7 + 6

   Ⓓ 100,000 + 5,000 + 70 + 6

5. The expanded form of a number is 50,000 + 2,000 + 800 + 6. Write this number in standard form. Then explain how you know if any of the digits in standard form are zero.

   _____

   _____

   _____

COMMON CORE STANDARD CC.4.NBT.2
Lesson Objective: Compare and order whole numbers based on the values of the digits in each number.

Compare and Order Numbers

Compare 31,072 and 34,318. Write <, >, or =.

Step 1 Align the numbers by place value using grid paper.

Step 2 Compare the digits in each place value. Start at the greatest place.

Are the digits in the ten thousands place the same?
<u>Yes.</u> Move to the thousands place.
Are the digits in the thousands place the same?
<u>No.</u> 1 thousand is less than 4 thousands.

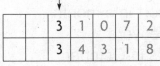 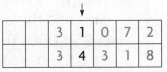

3 = 3   1 < 4

Step 3 Use the symbols <, >, or = to compare the numbers.

< means *is less than.*   > means *is greater than.*   = means *is equal to.*

There are two ways to write the comparison.

31,072 ⟨<⟩ 34,318   or   34,318 ⟨>⟩ 31,072

---

1. Use the grid paper to compare 21,409 and 20,891.
Write <, >, or =.

21,409 ◯ 20,891

Compare. Write <, >, or =.

2. $53,621 ◯ $53,760

3. 82,550 ◯ 80,711

Order from greatest to least.

4. 16,451; 16,250; 17,014

5. 561,028; 582,073; 549,006

---

1. A theme park had 674,989 visitors in June and 812,383 visitors in July. In August, the park had more visitors than in June, but fewer visitors than in July. Which of the following could be the number of visitors in August?

   (A) 544,989   (C) 765,124

   (B) 646,844   (D) 820,486

2. Brenda used number tiles to make the number 735,512. Frank used number tiles to make the number 734,512. Which statement about these numbers is correct?

   (A) 735,512 < 734,512

   (B) 735,512 > 734,512

   (C) 735,512 = 734,512

   (D) 734,512 > 735,512

3. During summer vacation, a state park had 248,368 visitors and a water park had 214,626 visitors. The zoo had more visitors than the water park, but fewer than the state park. Which of the following could be the number of visitors at the zoo?

   (A) 201,369   (C) 244,321

   (B) 212,729   (D) 263,023

4. The typical number of travelers who use the airport in a month is 250,000. There were 221,829 travelers in October, 283,459 in November, and 282,999 in December. Which number is **less** than the typical number of travelers?

   (A) 283,459   (C) 250,000

   (B) 282,999   (D) 221,829

5. Mr. Lee got 11,302 votes. Ms. Miller got 11,298 votes. Jana said that Ms. Miller won the election. Is Jana correct? Explain how you know.

   _____

   _____

   _____

   _____

   _____

Name _____

Round Numbers

When you round a number, you replace it with a number that is easier to work with but not as exact. You can round numbers to different place values.

Round 478,456 to the place value of the underlined digit.

Step 1 Identify the underlined digit.
The underlined digit, 4, is in the <u>hundred thousands place</u>.

Step 2 Look at the number to the right of the underlined digit.

If that number is 0–4, the underlined digit stays the same.

If that number is 5–9, the underlined digit is increased by 1.

The number to the right of the underlined digit is <u>7</u>, so the underlined digit, 4, will be increased by one; 4 + 1 = <u>5</u>.

Step 3 Change all the digits to the right of the hundred thousands place to zeros.

So, 478,456 rounded to the nearest hundred thousand is <u>500,000</u>.

1. In 2010, the population of North Dakota was 672,591 people. Use the number line to round this number to the nearest hundred thousand.

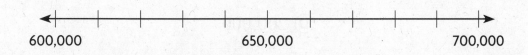

600,000   650,000   700,000

672,591 is closer to _____ than _____,

so it rounds to _____.

Round to the place value of the underlined digit.

2. 3,<u>4</u>52	3. <u>1</u>80	4. $<u>7</u>2,471	5. <u>5</u>72,000
_____	_____	_____	_____

6. <u>9</u>50	7. <u>6</u>,495	8. 83<u>5</u>,834	9. 96,<u>6</u>25
_____	_____	_____	_____

1. The population of Miguel's hometown is 23,718. What is 23,718 rounded to the nearest ten thousand?

   Ⓐ 20,000

   Ⓑ 23,700

   Ⓒ 24,000

   Ⓓ 30,000

2. A DVD rental business has 12,468 different movies. What is 12,468 rounded to the nearest thousand?

   Ⓐ 10,000

   Ⓑ 12,000

   Ⓒ 12,500

   Ⓓ 13,000

3. Last week, about 456,900 viewers watched a television show on the Egyptian pyramids. What is the **greatest** whole number that rounds to 456,900?

   Ⓐ 456,850

   Ⓑ 456,949

   Ⓒ 460,000

   Ⓓ 466,000

4. An office mailroom sorted 182,617 pieces of mail last year. What is 182,617 rounded to the nearest hundred thousand?

   Ⓐ 100,000

   Ⓑ 180,000

   Ⓒ 183,000

   Ⓓ 200,000

5. Flora says that she can round 72,586 at least four different ways, and all of them will be correct. Felix says that Flora's idea is impossible. What do you think? Use examples to support your thinking.

   _____

   _____

   _____

   _____

Name _____

Lesson 20

COMMON CORE STANDARD CC.4.NBT.4

Lesson Objective: Add whole numbers and determine whether solutions to addition problems are reasonable.

Add Whole Numbers

Find the sum. 63,821 + 34,765

Step 1 Round each addend to estimate.
60,000 + 30,000 = 90,000

Step 2 Use a place-value chart to line up the digits by place value.

Hundred Thousands	Ten Thousands	Thousands	Hundreds	Tens	Ones
		1			
6	3,	8	2	1
+ 3	4,	7	6	5
9	8,	5	8	6

Step 3 Start with the ones place. Add from right to left. Regroup as needed.

The sum is 98,586. Since 98,586 is close to the estimate 90,000, the answer is reasonable.

Estimate. Then find the sum.

1. Find 238,503 + 341,978. Use the grid to help.

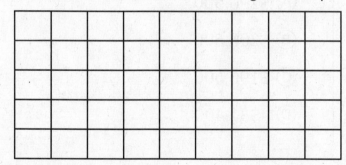

Estimate: _____

2. Estimate: _____

    52,851
+ 65,601

3. Estimate: _____

    54,980
+ 24,611

4. Estimate: _____

  604,542
+   87,106

5. Estimate: _____

  147,026
+ 106,792

6. Estimate: _____

  278,309
+ 422,182

7. Estimate: _____

  540,721
+ 375,899

1. The surface area of Lake Superior is 31,700 square miles. The surface area of Lake Michigan is 22,278 square miles. What is the total surface area of both lakes?

   (A) 9,422 square miles

   (B) 22,595 square miles

   (C) 53,278 square miles

   (D) 53,978 square miles

2. Last season, 57,690 fans went to football games at Oneida High School. This season 54,083 fans went to the games. What is the total number of fans who went to Oneida High School football games in both seasons?

   (A) 59,852

   (B) 110,673

   (C) 111,773

   (D) 112,673

3. A car wash cleaned 97,612 cars last year and 121,048 cars this year. What is the total number of cars washed in the two years?

   (A) 218,660

   (B) 118,650

   (C) 109,760

   (D) 109,716

4. Mrs. Torres paid $139,000 for her house. Eight years later, she built an addition for $67,500. How much did Mrs. Torres pay for her house and the addition?

   (A) $296,500

   (B) $206,500

   (C) $196,500

   (D) $81,400

5. The table shows the number of visitors to a cave over four years. In which two years did the cave have a total of about 90,000 visitors? Explain how you found the solution.

Year	Visitors
1	52,753
2	55,168
3	37,047
4	61,590

_____

_____

_____

Name _____

Lesson 21
COMMON CORE STANDARD CC.4.NBT.4
Lesson Objective: Subtract whole numbers and determine whether solutions to subtraction problems are reasonable.

Subtract Whole Numbers

Find the difference. 5,128 − 3,956

Estimate first.
Think: 5,128 is close to 5,000. 3,956 is close to 4,000.
So, an estimate is 5,000 − 4,000 = 1,000.

Write the problem vertically. Use grid paper to align digits by place value.

Step 1 Subtract the ones.

	5,	1	2	8	
−	3,	9	5	6	
				2	

8 − 6 = 2

Step 2 Subtract the tens.

		0	12		
	5,	~~1~~	2	8	
−	3,	9	5	6	
			7	2	

There are not enough tens to subtract. Regroup 1 hundred as 10 tens.
12 tens − 5 tens = 7 tens

Step 3 Subtract the hundreds.

	4	10	12		
	5,	~~0~~ ~~1~~	2	8	
−	3,	9	5	6	
		1	7	2	

There are not enough hundreds to subtract. Regroup 1 thousand as 10 hundreds.
10 hundreds − 9 hundreds = 1 hundred

Step 4 Subtract the thousands.

	4	10	12		
	5,	~~0~~ ~~1~~	2	8	
−	3,	9	5	6	
	1	1	7	2	

4 thousands − 3 thousands = 1 thousand

The difference is ___1,172___. Since 1,172 is close to the estimate of 1,000, the answer is reasonable.

Estimate. Then find the difference.

1. Estimate: _____

```
  6,253
− 3,718
```

2. Estimate: _____

```
 74,529
− 38,453
```

3. Estimate: _____

```
 232,318
− 126,705
```

1. A total of 3,718 tickets were sold for a skating show. Of that total, 1,279 were adult tickets. The remaining tickets were child tickets. How many child tickets were sold?

   (A) 2,439   (C) 3,439

   (B) 2,561   (D) 4,997

2. The number of people who took the subway to work in Sean's city one day was 31,426. The number of people who took the bus was 8,317. How many **more** people took the subway?

   (A) 39,743   (C) 23,119

   (B) 33,109   (D) 23,109

3. Michigan State and Wayne State are two large colleges in Michigan. Michigan State has 45,166 students enrolled. Wayne State has 32,160 students enrolled. How many **fewer** students are enrolled in Wayne State?

   (A) 3,006   (C) 13,006

   (B) 13,000   (D) 13,326

4. A desktop computer that Ryan likes costs $1,275. A laptop model of the same computer costs $1,648. How much **more** does the laptop cost?

   (A) $473   (C) $373

   (B) $433   (D) $333

Problem Solving REAL WORLD

Use the table for 5 and 6.

5. How many more people attended the Magic's games than attended the Pacers' games?

   _____

6. How many fewer people attended the Pacers' games than attended the Clippers' games?

   _____

Season Attendance for Three NBA Teams	
Team	**Attendance**
Indiana Pacers	582,295
Orlando Magic	715,901
Los Angeles Clippers	670,063

Problem Solving • Comparison Problems with Addition and Subtraction

For a community recycling project, a school collects aluminum cans and plastic containers. This year the fourth grade collected 5,923 cans and 4,182 containers. This is 410 more cans and 24 more containers than the fourth grade collected last year. How many cans did the fourth grade collect last year?

Read the Problem		
What do I need to find?	**What information do I need to use?**	**How will I use the information?**
I need to find the number of <u>cans the fourth grade</u> <u>collected last year.</u>	The fourth grade students collected <u>5,923</u> cans this year. They collected <u>410</u> more cans this year than the fourth grade collected last year.	I can draw a <u>bar model</u> to find the number of cans the fourth grade collected last year.

Solve the Problem
I can draw a bar model and write an equation to represent the problem.

```
+---------------------------------------+
|                 5,923                 |
+---------------------------------------+

+-----+---------------------------------+
| 410 |                                 |
+-----+---------------------------------+
            5,513
```

5,923 − 410 = ____5,513____

So, the fourth grade collected ____5,513____ aluminum cans last year.

Use the information above for 1 and 2.

1. Altogether, how many aluminum cans and plastic containers did the fourth grade collect this year?

_____

_____

2. This year the fifth grade collected 216 fewer plastic containers than the fourth grade. How many plastic containers did the fifth grade collect?

_____

_____

1. The number of inner tubes rented at the river this year increased by 1,009 over last year. The number of inner tubes rented last year was 4,286. How many inner tubes were rented this year?

1,009	4,286

Ⓐ 3,277   Ⓒ 5,285

Ⓑ 4,395   Ⓓ 5,295

3. A science museum has collected a total of 8,536 plant fossils. They have also collected 3,855 animal fossils. Use the bar model to find the total number of fossils the museum has.

8,536	3,855

Ⓐ 12,481   Ⓒ 11,381

Ⓑ 12,391   Ⓓ 4,681

2. Mr. Rey and Ms. Klein both took long car trips. Mr. Rey drove 2,178 miles. Ms. Klein drove 1,830 miles. How much farther did Mr. Rey drive on his trip?

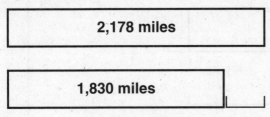

2,178 miles

1,830 miles

Ⓐ 348 miles   Ⓒ 1,348 miles

Ⓑ 748 miles   Ⓓ 4,008 miles

4. Volunteers worked for a total of 10,479 hours at the science center this year. Last year, they worked 8,231 hours. How many hours did the volunteers work in both years combined?

10,479	8,231

Ⓐ 18,710 hours   Ⓒ 2,648 hours

Ⓑ 18,600 hours   Ⓓ 2,248 hours

5. Mr. Dimka drove his truck 9,438 miles last year. This year he drove his truck 3,479 fewer miles. How many miles did Mr. Dimka drive this year? Draw a bar model to solve. Show your work.

Lesson 23

COMMON CORE STANDARD CC.4.NBT.5

Lesson Objective: Multiply tens, hundreds, and thousands by whole numbers through 10.

Multiply Tens, Hundreds, and Thousands

You can use a pattern to multiply with tens, hundreds, and thousands.

Count the number of zeros in the factors.

$4 \times 6 = 24$ ← basic fact

$4 \times 6\underline{0} = 24\underline{0}$ ← When you multiply by tens, the last digit in the product is 0.

$4 \times 6\underline{00} = 2,4\underline{00}$ ← When you multiply by hundreds, the last __two__ digits in the product are 0.

$4 \times 6,\underline{000} = 24,\underline{000}$ ← When you multiply by thousands, the last __three__ digits in the product are 0.

When the basic fact has a zero in the product, there will be an extra zero in the final product:

$5 \times 4 = \mathbf{20}$, so $5 \times 4,\underline{000} = 20,\underline{000}$

Complete the pattern.

1. $9 \times 2 = 18$

$9 \times 20 =$ _____

$9 \times 200 =$ _____

$9 \times 2,000 =$ _____

2. $8 \times 4 = 32$

$8 \times 40 =$ _____

$8 \times 400 =$ _____

$8 \times 4,000 =$ _____

3. $6 \times 6 = 36$

$6 \times 60 =$ _____

$6 \times 600 =$ _____

$6 \times 6,000 =$ _____

4. $4 \times 7 = 28$

$4 \times 70 =$ _____

$4 \times 700 =$ _____

$4 \times 7,000 =$ _____

Find the product.

5. $7 \times 300 = 7 \times$ _____ hundreds

      $=$ _____ hundreds

      $=$ _____

6. $5 \times 8,000 = 5 \times$ _____ thousands

      $=$ _____ thousands

      $=$ _____

1. Hideki is collecting pennies. Each month in May, June, and July, he put 200 pennies in a jar. How many pennies did Hideki put in the jar during these 3 months?

   (A) 60   (C) 6,000

   (B) 600   (D) 60,000

2. A factory produced 4,000 crayons every hour during an 8-hour shift. How many crayons were produced during the shift?

   (A)   320

   (B)   3,200

   (C)   32,000

   (D) 320,000

3. Maria wrote this pattern in her math notebook.

   $8 \times 5 = 40$
   $8 \times 50 = 400$
   $8 \times 500 = 4,000$
   $8 \times 5,000 = \blacksquare$

   What is the unknown number in Maria's pattern?

   (A) 40,000   (C) 400

   (B) 4,000   (D) 4

4. Ling wrote this problem on his paper.

   $9 \times 300 = \blacksquare$ hundreds

   What is the unknown number in Ling's problem?

   (A) 27   (C) 2,700

   (B) 270   (D) 27,000

Problem Solving REAL WORLD

5. A bank teller has 7 rolls of coins. Each roll has 40 coins. How many coins does the bank teller have?

6. Theo buys 5 packages of paper. There are 500 sheets of paper in each package. How many sheets of paper does Theo buy?

Lesson 24

COMMON CORE STANDARD CC.4.NBT.5

Lesson Objective: Estimate products by rounding and determine if exact answers to multiplication problems are reasonable.

Estimate Products

You can use rounding to estimate products.

Round the greater factor. Then use mental math to estimate the product.

6 × 95

Step 1 Round 95 to the nearest hundred.

95 rounds to 100.

Step 2 Use patterns and mental math.

$6 \times 1 = 6$

$6 \times 10 = 60$

$6 \times 100 = 600$

Find two numbers the exact answer is between.

7 × 759

Step 1 Estimate by rounding to the lesser hundred.

7 × 759

↓

$7 \times 700 = 4{,}900$

Think: $7 \times 7 = 49$

$7 \times 70 = 490$

$7 \times 700 = 4{,}900$

Step 2 Estimate by rounding to the greater hundred.

7 × 759

↓

$7 \times 800 = 5{,}600$

Think: $7 \times 8 = 56$

$7 \times 80 = 560$

$7 \times 800 = 5{,}600$

So, the product is between 4,900 and 5,600.

Estimate the product by rounding.

1. 6 × 316

2. 5 × 29

3. 4 × 703

_____

_____

_____

Estimate the product by finding two numbers the exact answer is between.

4. 3 × 558

5. 7 × 252

6. 8 × 361

_____

_____

_____

1. In one hour, 1,048 cars stopped at a traffic light. Which is the best estimate of how many cars will stop in 8 hours?

   Ⓐ 800   Ⓒ 8,000

   Ⓑ 1,000   Ⓓ 10,000

2. Beth travels 244 miles every week. Which expression shows the best estimate for the number of miles she would travel in 9 weeks?

   Ⓐ 200×9

   Ⓑ 200×10

   Ⓒ 300×9

   Ⓓ 300×10

3. A black bear has a mass of about 135 kilograms. Which is the best estimate of the mass of 3 black bears?

   Ⓐ less than 300 kilograms

   Ⓑ between 300 and 600 kilograms

   Ⓒ between 600 and 900 kilograms

   Ⓓ more than 900 kilograms

4. The youth center sold 62 raffle tickets for $8 each. Mrs. Sosa says they collected about $480. Which statement best describes why Mrs. Sosa's estimate is reasonable?

   Ⓐ 10×70 is 700.

   Ⓑ 8×60 is 480.

   Ⓒ 480 is not the product of 8×62.

   Ⓓ 8×500 is 4,000.

5. Every package of chicken nuggets contains 48 nuggets. Is it reasonable to estimate that 6 packages contain over 300 chicken nuggets? Explain your answer.

   _____

   _____

   _____

Name _____

Lesson 25

COMMON CORE STANDARD CC.4.NBT.5

Lesson Objective: Use the Distributive Property to multiply a 2-digit number by a 1-digit number.

Multiply Using the Distributive Property

You can use rectangular models to multiply 2-digit numbers by 1-digit numbers.

Find 9×14.

Step 1 Draw a 9 by 14 rectangle on grid paper.

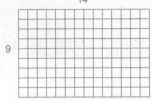

Step 2 Use the Distributive Property and products you know to break apart the model into two smaller rectangles.
Think: $14 = 10 + 4$.

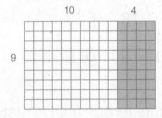

Step 3 Find the product each smaller rectangle represents.

$9 \times 10 = 90$

$9 \times 4 = 36$

Step 4 Find the sum of the products. $90 + 36 = 126$

So, $9 \times 14 = 126$.

Model the product on the grid.
Record the product.

1. 3×13

_____

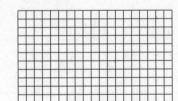

2. 6×16

_____

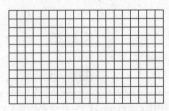

3. 5×17

_____

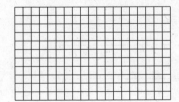

4. 4×14

_____

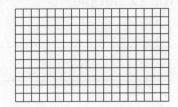

1. William models a product on grid paper. He asks Irie what product he modeled.

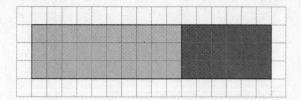

What should Irie's answer be?

Ⓐ 3 × 6 = 18 Ⓒ 3 × 16 = 48

Ⓑ 3 × 10 = 30 Ⓓ 6 × 13 = 78

2. Barney wants to buy 5 CDs that cost $15 each. He models 5 × 15 on grid paper to see if he can buy the CDs.

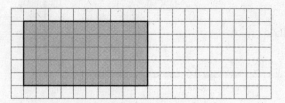

How many more squares must he shade to find the total cost?

Ⓐ 5 Ⓒ 25

Ⓑ 10 Ⓓ 75

Use the figure for 3–4.

Malia modeled 7 × 14 using base-ten blocks.

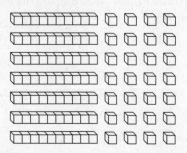

3. How many tens will there be in the final product?

Ⓐ 10 Ⓒ 8

Ⓑ 9 Ⓓ 4

4. What is the final product?

Ⓐ 98

Ⓑ 94

Ⓒ 90

Ⓓ 84

5. Thea will serve 8 ounces of punch to each friend at her party. Explain how to use grid paper to find much punch she will need for 12 people.

_____

_____

_____

Name _____

Lesson 26

COMMON CORE STANDARD CC.4.NBT.5

Lesson Objective: Use expanded form to multiply a multidigit number by a 1-digit number.

Multiply Using Expanded Form

You can use expanded form or a model to find products.

Multiply. 3×26

Think and Write	**Use a Model**
Step 1 Write 26 in expanded form.	**Step 1** Show 3 groups of 26.

$26 = 20 + 6$

$3 \times 26 = 3 \times (20 + 6)$

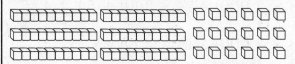

Step 2 Use the Distributive Property.

Step 2 Break the model into tens and ones.

$3 \times 26 = (3 \times 20) + (\underline{}\,3 \times \underline{}\,6)$

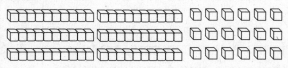

Step 3 Multiply the tens. Multiply the ones.

$(3 \times 2\ \text{tens})$ $(3 \times 6\ \text{ones})$

$3 \times 26 = (3 \times 20) + (3 \times 6)$

(3×20) (3×6)

$ = \underline{}\,60\, + \underline{}\,18$ $\begin{array}{r} 60 \\ +18 \end{array}$

$\underline{}\,60$ $\underline{}\,18$

Step 4 Add the partial products.   78

Step 3 Add to find the total product.

$\underline{}\,60\, + \underline{}\,18\, = \underline{}\,78$

So, $3 \times 26 = \underline{}\,78$.

Record the product. Use expanded form to help.

1. $6 \times 14 =$ _____

_____

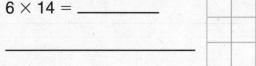

2. $4 \times 52 =$ _____

_____

3. $5 \times 162 =$ _____

_____

4. $3 \times 279 =$ _____

_____

1. A factory produces 2,354 hammers every hour. Which expression can be used to find how many hammers the factory produces in 3 hours?

   (A) $(3 \times 2,000) + 354$

   (B) $(3 \times 2,000) + (3 \times 300) + 54$

   (C) $(3 \times 2,000) + (3 \times 300) +$ $(3 \times 50) + (3 \times 4)$

   (D) $(3 \times 2,000) + (300 + 50 + 4)$

2. A large truck that can carry up to 168 boxes in a single trip will make 6 trips in one day. Which expression shows how to multiply 6×168 by using place value and expanded form?

   (A) $(6 \times 100) + (6 \times 60) + (6 \times 8)$

   (B) $(6 \times 800) + (6 \times 60) + (6 \times 1)$

   (C) $(6 \times 100) + (6 \times 60)$

   (D) $(6 \times 168) + (6 \times 16) + (6 \times 1)$

3. A grocery store has 367 cans of vegetables on each of 4 shelves. Which expression can be used to find how many cans of vegetables are on the four shelves?

   (A) $(4 \times 300) + (6 \times 10) + (1 \times 7)$

   (B) $(4 \times 300) + (4 \times 60) + 7$

   (C) $(4 \times 300) + (4 \times 60) + (4 \times 7)$

   (D) $(4 \times 300) + 60 + 7$

4. Suki uses place value and the expanded form $(7 \times 2,000) +$ $(7 \times 800) + (7 \times 90)$ to help solve a multiplication problem. Which is Suki's multiplication problem?

   (A) $7 \times 289 = 2,023$

   (B) $7 \times 2,089 = 14,623$

   (C) $7 \times 2,809 = 19,663$

   (D) $7 \times 2,890 = 20,230$

Problem Solving REAL WORLD

5. The fourth-grade students at Riverside School are going on a field trip. There are 68 students on each of the 4 buses. How many students are going on the field trip?

6. There are 5,280 feet in one mile. Hannah likes to walk 5 miles each week for exercise. How many feet does Hannah walk each week?

Name _____

Lesson 27

COMMON CORE STANDARD CC.4.NBT.5

Lesson Objective: Use place value and partial products to multiply a multidigit number by a 1-digit number.

Multiply Using Partial Products

Use partial products to multiply.

Multiply. 7 × $332

Step 1 Estimate the product.   332 rounds to 300; 7 × $300 = $2,100.

Step 2 Multiply the 3 hundreds, or 300, by 7.

$$\begin{array}{r} \$332 \\ \times\ \ 7 \end{array}$$ or $$\begin{array}{r} \$300 \\ \times\ \ 7 \\ \hline \$2,100 \end{array}$$

Step 3 Multiply the 3 tens, or 30, by 7.

$$\begin{array}{r} \$332 \\ \times\ \ 7 \end{array}$$ or $$\begin{array}{r} \$30 \\ \times\ \ 7 \\ \hline \$210 \end{array}$$

Step 4 Multiply the 2 ones, or 2, by 7.

$$\begin{array}{r} \$332 \\ \times\ \ 7 \end{array}$$ or $$\begin{array}{r} \$2 \\ \times\ \ 7 \\ \hline \$14 \end{array}$$

Step 5 Add the partial products. $2,100 + $210 + $14 = $2,324

So, 7 × $332 = $2,324. Since $2,324 is close
to the estimate of $2,100, it is reasonable.

Estimate. Then record the product.

1. Estimate: _____

$$\begin{array}{r} 181 \\ \times\ \ 2 \end{array}$$

2. Estimate: _____

$$\begin{array}{r} 156 \\ \times\ \ 4 \end{array}$$

3. Estimate: _____

$$\begin{array}{r} \$210 \\ \times\ \ 5 \end{array}$$

4. Estimate: _____

$$\begin{array}{r} 303 \\ \times\ \ 6 \end{array}$$

5. Estimate: _____

$$\begin{array}{r} \$427 \\ \times\ \ 2 \end{array}$$

6. Estimate: _____

$$\begin{array}{r} \$367 \\ \times\ \ 5 \end{array}$$

1. Zac will make 3 payments of $135 to buy a mountain bike. He used partial products to find the total cost of the bike. Which shows the sum of the partial products?

   Ⓐ $300 + $90 + $15 = $405

   Ⓑ $300 + $90 + $5 = $395

   Ⓒ $300 + $30 + $15 = $345

   Ⓓ $3 + $9 + $15 = $27

2. A theater has 8 sections. There are 168 seats in each section. Which sum of partial products shows the total number of seats in the theater?

   Ⓐ 800 + 60 + 8 = 868

   Ⓑ 800 + 48 + 64 = 912

   Ⓒ 800 + 480 + 8 = 1,288

   Ⓓ 800 + 480 + 64 = 1,344

3. A parking garage has 5 levels. There are 256 parking spaces on each level. Which sum of partial products shows the total number of parking spaces?

   Ⓐ 1,000 + 50 + 6 = 1,056

   Ⓑ 1,000 + 25 + 30 = 1,055

   Ⓒ 1,000 + 250 + 30 = 1,280

   Ⓓ 1,000 + 250 + 300 = 1,550

4. A company received 329 orders for a DVD set that contains 3 movies. Which sum of partial products shows the total number of DVDs the company will ship?

   Ⓐ 900 + 60 + 9 = 969

   Ⓑ 900 + 60 + 27 = 987

   Ⓒ 900 + 600 + 27 = 1,527

   Ⓓ 900 + 600 + 270 = 1,770

Problem Solving REAL WORLD

5. A maze at a county fair is made from 275 bales of hay. The maze at the state fair is made from 4 times as many bales of hay. How many bales of hay are used for the maze at the state fair?

   _____

6. Pedro gets 8 hours of sleep each night. How many hours does Pedro sleep in a year with 365 days?

   _____

Lesson 28

COMMON CORE STANDARD CC.4.NBT.5

Lesson Objective: Use mental math and properties to multiply a multidigit number by a 1-digit number.

Multiply Using Mental Math

Use addition to break apart the larger factor.	Use subtraction to break apart the larger factor.
Find 8 × 214.	**Find 6 × 298.**
Think: 214 = 200 + 14	**Think:** 298 = 300 − 2
8 × 214 = (8 × 200) + (8 × 14)	6 × 298 = (6 × 300) − (6 × 2)
= <u>1,600</u> + <u>112</u>	= <u>1,800</u> − <u>12</u>
= <u>1,712</u>	= <u>1,788</u>
Use halving and doubling.	When multiplying more than two numbers, use the Commutative Property to change the order of the factors.
Find 14 × 50.	**Find 2 × 9 × 50.**
Think: 14 can be evenly divided by 2.	**Think:** 2 × 50 = <u>100</u>
14 ÷ 2 = <u>7</u>	2 × 9 × 50 = 2 × <u>50</u> × 9
7 × 50 = <u>350</u>	= <u>100</u> × 9
2 × 350 = <u>700</u>	= <u>900</u>

Find the product. Tell which strategy you used.

1. 5 × 7 × 20

2. 6 × 321

_____

_____

3. 86 × 50

4. 9 × 399

_____

_____

1. An art store has 5 boxes of brushes. Each box contains 298 brushes. Which expression shows a strategy for finding the product of 5 × 298?

   Ⓐ 5 × (300 + 2) = 1,150

   Ⓑ 5 × (300 − 2) = 1,490

   Ⓒ 5 × (300 × 3) = 4,500

   Ⓓ 5 × (200 − 98) = 510

2. Carl plans to use a strategy to find 28 × 250. Which expression shows a strategy he could use?

   Ⓐ 5 × 6 × 250 = 7,500

   Ⓑ 4 × 7 × 25 = 700

   Ⓒ 7 × 4 × 250 = 7,000

   Ⓓ 28 × 2 × 50 = 2,800

3. Samantha has 4 boxes of action figures. Each box contains 198 figures. Which expression shows a strategy Samantha can use to find the product of 4 × 198?

   Ⓐ 4 × (200 + 2) = 808

   Ⓑ 4 × (200 − 2) = 792

   Ⓒ 4 × (200 × 3) = 2,400

   Ⓓ 4 × (200 + 98) = 1,192

4. Gino wants to multiply 4 × 125. Which is the best mental math strategy for him to use?

   Ⓐ halving and doubling

   Ⓑ use addition

   Ⓒ Commutative Property

   Ⓓ use subtraction

Problem Solving REAL WORLD

5. Section J in an arena has 20 rows. Each row has 15 seats. All tickets cost $18 each. If all the seats are sold, how much money will the arena collect for Section J?

6. At a high-school gym, the bleachers are divided into 6 equal sections. Each section can seat 395 people. How many people can be seated in the gym?

Name _____

Lesson 29

COMMON CORE STANDARD CC.4.NBT.5

Lesson Objective: Use regrouping to multiply a 2-digit number by a 1-digit number.

Multiply 2-Digit Numbers with Regrouping

Use place value to multiply with regrouping.

Multiply. 7×63

Step 1 Estimate the product.

$7 \times 60 = 420$

Step 2 Multiply the ones. Regroup 21 ones as 2 tens 1 one. Record the 1 one below the ones column and the 2 tens above the tens column.

$$\begin{array}{r} \overset{2}{6}3 \\ \times\ 7 \\ \hline 1 \end{array}$$

7×3 ones $= 21$ ones

Step 3 Multiply the tens. Then, add the regrouped tens. Record the tens.

$$\begin{array}{r} \overset{2}{6}3 \\ \times\ 7 \\ \hline 441 \end{array}$$

44 tens = 4 hundreds
4 tens

7×6 tens $= 42$ tens

Add the 2 regrouped tens.

42 tens + 2 tens = 44 tens

So, $7 \times 63 = 441$. Since 441 is close to the estimate of 420, it is reasonable.

Estimate. Then record the product.

1. Estimate: _____

$$\begin{array}{r} 42 \\ \times\ 6 \\ \hline \end{array}$$

2. Estimate: _____

$$\begin{array}{r} \$98 \\ \times\ 6 \\ \hline \end{array}$$

3. Estimate: _____

$$\begin{array}{r} 37 \\ \times\ 8 \\ \hline \end{array}$$

4. Estimate: _____

$$\begin{array}{r} \$54 \\ \times\ 9 \\ \hline \end{array}$$

5. Estimate: _____

$$\begin{array}{r} 37 \\ \times\ 5 \\ \hline \end{array}$$

6. Estimate: _____

$$\begin{array}{r} 93 \\ \times\ 4 \\ \hline \end{array}$$

7. Estimate: _____

$$\begin{array}{r} 86 \\ \times\ 9 \\ \hline \end{array}$$

8. Estimate: _____

$$\begin{array}{r} 59 \\ \times\ 7 \\ \hline \end{array}$$

1. Ava can text 44 words each minute. How many words can she text in 8 minutes?

   (A) 352

   (B) 322

   (C) 320

   (D) 36

2. Sara's mom bought tickets to the Philadelphia Zoo. She bought 6 tickets. Each ticket cost $18. What was the total cost of the tickets?

   (A) $32

   (B) $68

   (C) $108

   (D) $114

3. Gordon's heart beats 72 times in one minute. If it continues beating at the same rate, how many times will it beat in 7 minutes?

   (A) 79

   (B) 494

   (C) 504

   (D) 604

4. Antonio and his friends bought tickets for a play. They bought 8 tickets in all. Each ticket cost $23. What was the total cost of the tickets?

   (A) $31

   (B) $164

   (C) $171

   (D) $184

Problem Solving REAL WORLD

5. Sharon is 54 inches tall. A tree in her backyard is 5 times as tall as she is. The floor of her treehouse is at a height that is twice as tall as she is. What is the difference, in inches, between the top of the tree and the floor of the treehouse?

6. Mr. Diaz's class is taking a field trip to the science museum. There are 23 students in the class, and a student admission ticket is $8. How much will the student tickets cost?

Name _____

Lesson 30

COMMON CORE STANDARD CC.4.NBT.5
Lesson Objective: Use regrouping to
multiply a multidigit number by a 1-digit
number.

Multiply 3-Digit and 4-Digit Numbers with Regrouping

When you multiply 3-digit and 4-digit numbers, you may need to regroup.

Estimate. Then find the product.

$$\begin{array}{r} \$1,324 \\ \times \quad\ 7 \end{array}$$

Step 1 Estimate the product. $1,324 rounds to $1,000; $1,000 × 7 = $7,000.

Step 2 Multiply the 4 ones by 7.
Regroup the 28 ones as 2 tens 8 ones.

$$\begin{array}{r} ^{2} \\ \$1,324 \\ \times \quad\ 7 \\ \hline 8 \end{array}$$

Step 3 Multiply the 2 tens by 7.
Add the regrouped tens.
Regroup the 16 tens as 1 hundred 6 tens.

$$\begin{array}{r} ^{1\ 2} \\ \$1,324 \\ \times \quad\ 7 \\ \hline 68 \end{array}$$

Step 4 Multiply the 3 hundreds by 7.
Add the regrouped hundred.
Regroup the 22 hundreds as 2 thousands
2 hundreds.

$$\begin{array}{r} ^{2\ 1\ 2} \\ \$1,324 \\ \times \quad\ 7 \\ \hline 268 \end{array}$$

Step 5 Multiply the 1 thousand by 7.
Add the regrouped thousands.

$$\begin{array}{r} ^{2\ 1\ 2} \\ \$1,324 \\ \times \quad\ 7 \\ \hline \$9,268 \end{array}$$

So, 7 × $1,324 = $9,268.
Since $9,268 is close to the estimate of $7,000, the answer is *reasonable*.

Estimate. Then find the product.

1. Estimate: _____   **2.** Estimate: _____   **3.** Estimate: _____   **4.** Estimate: _____

$$\begin{array}{r} 3,184 \\ \times \quad 2 \end{array}$$
$$\begin{array}{r} \$828 \\ \times \quad 4 \end{array}$$
$$\begin{array}{r} 2,637 \\ \times \quad 5 \end{array}$$
$$\begin{array}{r} \$6,900 \\ \times \quad 7 \end{array}$$

1. Mr. Karros is buying 2 digital cameras for the yearbook club. The price of each camera is $259. What is the total price of the cameras?

   Ⓐ $408

   Ⓑ $418

   Ⓒ $508

   Ⓓ $518

2. Mr. Richards travels 163 miles each week for work. How far does he travel in 4 weeks for work?

   Ⓐ 442 miles

   Ⓑ 452 miles

   Ⓒ 642 miles

   Ⓓ 652 miles

3. Brandon has 4,350 digital photos saved on his computer. Linda has 3 times as many photos saved on her computer as Brandon has. How many digital photos does Linda have saved on her computer?

   Ⓐ 12,050

   Ⓑ 12,250

   Ⓒ 12,950

   Ⓓ 13,050

4. Jack has 2,613 songs saved on his MP3 player. Dexter has 4 times as many songs saved on his MP3 player as Jack has. How many songs does Dexter have saved on his MP3 player?

   Ⓐ 8,442   Ⓒ 10,452

   Ⓑ 10,442   Ⓓ 10,542

Problem Solving REAL WORLD

5. Lafayette County has a population of 7,022 people. Columbia County's population is 8 times as great as Lafayette County's population. What is the population of Columbia County?

6. A seafood company sold 9,125 pounds of fish last month. If 6 seafood companies sold the same amount of fish, how much fish did the 6 companies sell last month in all?

Lesson 31
COMMON CORE STANDARD CC.4.NBT.5
Lesson Objective: Use place value and
multiplication properties to multiply by tens.

Multiply by Tens

One section of seating at an arena has 40 rows. Each row has 30 seats.
How many seats in all are in that section?

Multiply. 30 × 40

Step 1 Think of each factor as a multiple
of 10 and as a repeated addition.

$40 = \underline{4} \times \underline{10}$ or $\underline{10} + \underline{10} + \underline{10} + \underline{10}$

$30 = \underline{3} \times \underline{10}$ or $\underline{10} + \underline{10} + \underline{10}$

Step 2 Draw a diagram to show
the multiplication.

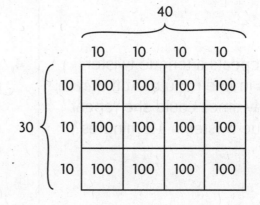

Step 3 Each small square in the diagram
shows 10 × 10, or $\underline{100}$. Count the
squares.

There are $\underline{12}$ squares of $\underline{100}$.

Step 4 Use patterns and mental math to
find 12 × 100.

$12 \times 1 = \underline{12}$

$12 \times 10 = \underline{120}$

$12 \times 100 = \underline{1,200}$

There are $\underline{1,200}$ seats in that section.

Choose a method. Then find the product.

1. 20 × 90 = _____

2. 40 × 40 = _____

3. 60 × 70 = _____

4. 50 × 30 = _____

5. 80 × 60 = _____

6. 90 × 40 = _____

1. Mrs. Yang types 80 words in one minute. At that rate, how many words can she type in 15 minutes?

   (A) 120

   (B) 800

   (C) 1,200

   (D) 1,600

2. Teneka repeats a tongue twister 20 times in one minute. At that rate, how many times could she repeat the tongue twister in 12 minutes?

   (A) 24

   (B) 32

   (C) 120

   (D) 240

3. Ben swam laps in a pool nonstop for 11 minutes. There are 60 seconds in 1 minute. What is the total number of seconds Ben swam?

   (A) 6,600 seconds

   (B) 710 seconds

   (C) 660 seconds

   (D) 600 seconds

4. People can join a skating club by paying $40 a year. The club had 67 members this year. How much money in all did the skating club collect from members this year?

   (A) $268

   (B) $2,680

   (C) $3,220

   (D) $26,800

Problem Solving  REAL WORLD

5. Kenny bought 20 packs of baseball cards. There are 12 cards in each pack. How many cards did Kenny buy?

6. The Hart family drove 10 hours to their vacation spot. They drove an average of 48 miles each hour. How many miles did they drive in all?

Lesson **32**

COMMON CORE STANDARD CC.4.NBT.5

Lesson Objective: Estimate products by rounding or by using compatible numbers.

Estimate Products

You can use rounding and compatible numbers to estimate products.

Use mental math and rounding to estimate the product.

Estimate. 62 × $23

Step 1 Round each factor to the nearest ten.

62 rounds to 60.
$23 rounds to $20.

Step 2 Rewrite the problem using the rounded numbers.

60 × $20

Step 3 Use mental math.

6 × $2 = $12
6 × $20 = $120
60 × $20 = $1,200

So, 62 × $23 is about __$1,200__.

Use mental math and compatible numbers to estimate the product.

Estimate. 24 × 78

Step 1 Use compatible numbers. 25 × 80

Step 2 Use 25 × 4 = 100 to help find 25 × 8.
25 × 8 = 200

Step 3 Since 80 has 1 zero, write 1 zero to the right of the product.

24 × 78
↓   ↓
25 × 80 = 2,000

So, 24 × 78 is about __2,000__.

Estimate the product. Choose a method.

1. 78 × 21

2. 59 × $46

3. 81 × 33

4. 67 × 21

_____

_____

_____

_____

5. 88 × $42

6. 51 × 36

7. 73 × 73

8. 99 × $44

_____

_____

_____

_____

9. 92 × 19

10. 26 × 37

11. 89 × 18

12. 58 × 59

_____

_____

_____

_____

Name _____

Lesson 32
CC.4.NBT.5

1. Doug rents a kayak for 12 days. The rental charge is $18 per day. Which is the **best** estimate for the total cost of the kayak rental?

Ⓐ about $400

Ⓑ about $200

Ⓒ about $160

Ⓓ about $120

2. Mr. Yu travels 44 miles for work every week. He worked 42 weeks last year. Which is the **best** estimate of the number of miles Mr. Yu traveled for work last year?

Ⓐ about 2,000 miles

Ⓑ about 3,000 miles

Ⓒ about 8,000 miles

Ⓓ about 10,000 miles

3. Cat cages cost $27 each. A cat hospital bought 12 new cages. Which is the **best** estimate of the total cost of the new cages?

Ⓐ $600

Ⓑ $300

Ⓒ $270

Ⓓ $200

4. On Friday, 17 buses left the bus station. Each bus carried a full load of 53 passengers. Which is the **best** way to estimate the total number of passengers who left the bus station that day?

Ⓐ $7 \times 50 = 350$

Ⓑ $10 \times 50 = 500$

Ⓒ $10 \times 60 = 600$

Ⓓ $20 \times 50 = 1,000$

Problem Solving REAL WORLD

5. A dime has a diameter of about 18 millimeters. About how many millimeters long would a row of 34 dimes be?

6. A half-dollar has a diameter of about 31 millimeters. About how many millimeters long would a row of 56 half-dollars be?

© Houghton Mifflin Harcourt Publishing Company

64

Core Standards for Math, Grade 4

Name _____

Lesson 33
COMMON CORE STANDARD CC.4.NBT.5
Lesson Objective: Use area models and partial products to multiply 2-digit numbers.

Area Models and Partial Products

You can use area models to multiply 2-digit numbers by 2-digit numbers.

Use the model and partial products to solve.

Draw a rectangle to find 19 × 18.

The rectangle is 19 units long and 18 units wide.

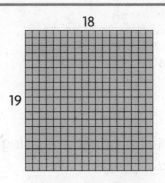

Step 1 Break apart the factors into tens and ones. Divide the area model into four smaller rectangles to show the factors.

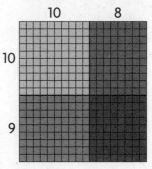

Step 2 Find the products for each of the smaller rectangles.

$$10 \times 10 = 100 \qquad 10 \times 8 = 80 \qquad 9 \times 10 = 90 \qquad 9 \times 8 = 72$$

Step 3 Find the sum of the products. $100 + 80 + 90 + 72 = 342$

So, 19 × 18 = 342.

Draw a model to represent the product. Then record the product.

1. 21 × 25

2. 16 × 14

3. 24 × 15

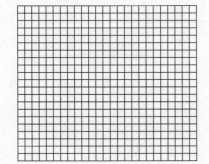

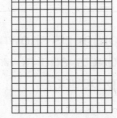

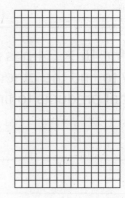

_____   _____   _____

Use the model for 1–2.

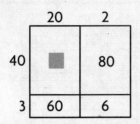

1. What partial product is missing from the model?

   (A) 60

   (B) 80

   (C) 600

   (D) 800

2. What is the product?

   43 × 22

   (A) 172

   (B) 846

   (C) 946

   (D) 1,286

Use the model for 3–4.

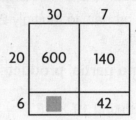

3. What partial product is missing from the model?

   (A) 36

   (B) 120

   (C) 180

   (D) 300

4. What is the product?

   26 × 37

   (A) 962

   (B) 782

   (C) 780

   (D) 260

5. This model for 45 × 34 has two partial products shown. Explain how to find the other partial products, and how to use the partial products to find the final product.

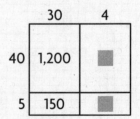

_____

_____

_____

Name _____

Lesson 34
COMMON CORE STANDARD CC.4.NBT.5
Lesson Objective: Use place value and partial products to multiply 2-digit numbers.

Multiply Using Partial Products

Multiply 25 × 43. Record the product.

Think: I can use partial products to find 25 × 43.

Step 1 Multiply the tens by the tens.
20 × 4 tens = 80 tens, or 800.

Step 2 Multiply the ones by the tens.
20 × 3 ones = 60 ones, or 60.

Step 3 Multiply the tens by the ones.
5 × 4 tens = 20 tens, or 200.

Step 4 Multiply the ones by the ones.
5 × 3 ones = 15 ones, or 15.

Step 5 Add the partial products.
800 + 60 + 200 + 15 = 1,075.

So, 25 × 43 = __1,075__.

```
      tens ones
        4   3
    ×   2   5
    _____
    8   0   0
        6   0
    2   0   0
    +   1   5
    _____
    1,  0   7   5
```

Record the product.

1.
$$
\begin{array}{r}
25 \\
\times\ 62 \\
\hline
\end{array}
$$

2.
$$
\begin{array}{r}
59 \\
\times\ 38 \\
\hline
\end{array}
$$

3.
$$
\begin{array}{r}
85 \\
\times\ 72 \\
\hline
\end{array}
$$

4.
$$
\begin{array}{r}
46 \\
\times\ 52 \\
\hline
\end{array}
$$

5.
$$
\begin{array}{r}
76 \\
\times\ 23 \\
\hline
\end{array}
$$

6.
$$
\begin{array}{r}
38 \\
\times\ 95 \\
\hline
\end{array}
$$

1. Lisa jumps rope at a rate of 86 jumps per minute. At this rate, what is the total number of times Lisa will jump in 15 minutes?

   Ⓐ 1,200

   Ⓑ 1,275

   Ⓒ 1,290

   Ⓓ 1,740

2. Students arranged 13 chairs in each of 32 rows for the school play. What is the total number of chairs the students arranged?

   Ⓐ 300

   Ⓑ 320

   Ⓒ 384

   Ⓓ 416

3. Rosa's vegetable garden has 15 rows of 32 corn plants each.

   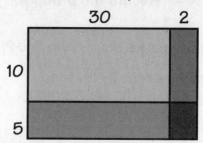

   How many corn plants are in Rosa's vegetable garden?

   Ⓐ 480   Ⓒ 450

   Ⓑ 465   Ⓓ 300

4. Some students are reorganizing supplies in the art room. They put 25 crayons in each of 24 boxes. What is the total number of crayons the students put into boxes?

   Ⓐ 760

   Ⓑ 600

   Ⓒ 582

   Ⓓ 200

Problem Solving REAL WORLD

5. Evelyn drinks 8 glasses of water a day, which is 56 glasses of water a week. How many glasses of water does she drink in a year? (1 year = 52 weeks)

6. Joe wants to use the Hiking Club's funds to purchase new walking sticks for each of its 19 members. The sticks cost $26 each. The club has $480. Is this enough money to buy each member a new walking stick? If not, how much more money is needed?

Multiply with Regrouping

Estimate. Then use regrouping to find 28 × 43.

Step 1 Round to estimate the product. $\qquad$ 30 × 40 = 1,200

Step 2 Think: 28 = 2 tens 8 ones.
Multiply 43 by 8 ones.
8 × 3 = 24. Record the 4. Write the
regrouped 2 above the tens place.
8 × 40 = 320. Add the regrouped
tens: 320 + 20 = 340.

$$\begin{array}{r} \overset{2}{43} \\ \times\ 28 \\ \hline 344 \end{array} \longleftarrow 8 \times 43$$

Step 3 Multiply 43 by 2 tens.
20 × 3 = 60 and 20 × 40 = 800.
Record 860 below 344.

$$\begin{array}{r} \overset{2}{43} \\ \times\ 28 \\ \hline 344 \\ 860 \end{array} \longleftarrow 20 \times 43$$

Step 4 Add the partial products. $\qquad$ 1,204 ⟵ 344 + 860

So, 28 × 43 = __1,204__. 1,204 is close to 1,200. The answer is **reasonable**.

Estimate. Then find the product.

1. Estimate: _____

2. Estimate: _____

3. Estimate: _____

$$\begin{array}{r} 36 \\ \times\ 12 \\ \hline \end{array}$$

$$\begin{array}{r} 43 \\ \times\ 29 \\ \hline \end{array}$$

$$\begin{array}{r} 51 \\ \times\ 47 \\ \hline \end{array}$$

1. A farmer planted 29 rows of apple trees. There are 27 trees in each row. How many apple trees did the farmer plant altogether?

(A) 261

(B) 723

(C) 783

(D) 1,881

2. Maria packed 24 bags of dog treats for the animal shelter. She put 16 dog treats in each bag. What is the total number of dog treats Maria packed?

(A) 168

(B) 240

(C) 384

(D) 624

3. Keiko can text 55 words each minute. At this rate, how many words will Keiko text in 15 minutes?

(A) 825

(B) 805

(C) 705

(D) 330

4. There are 96 word search puzzles in a puzzle book. Each puzzle has 22 words. How many words in all does the puzzle book have?

(A) 384

(B) 2,002

(C) 2,012

(D) 2,112

Problem Solving  REAL WORLD

5. Baseballs come in cartons of 84 baseballs. A team orders 18 cartons of baseballs. How many baseballs does the team order?

6. There are 16 tables in the school lunch room. Each table can seat 22 students. How many students can be seated at lunch at one time?

_____

_____

Name _____

Lesson 36
COMMON CORE STANDARD CC.4.NBT.5
Lesson Objective: Choose a method to
multiply 2-digit numbers.

Choose a Multiplication Method

Estimate. Then use regrouping to find 47 × 89.

$$
\begin{array}{r}
89 \\
\times\ 47 \\
\end{array}
$$

Step 1 Estimate the product. $50 \times 90 = 4{,}500$

Step 2 Multiply the 9 ones by the 7 ones.
Regroup the 63 ones as 6 tens 3
ones.

$$
\begin{array}{r}
{}^{6}\ \\
89 \\
\times\ 47 \\
\hline
3 \\
\end{array}
$$

Step 3 Multiply the 8 tens, or 80, by the 7
ones, or 7. Add the regrouped tens.
Regroup the 62 tens as 6 hundreds
2 tens.

$$
\begin{array}{r}
{}^{6}\ \\
89 \\
\times\ 47 \\
\hline
623 \\
\end{array}
$$

Step 4 Multiply the 9 ones by the 4 tens,
or 40. Regroup the 36 tens as 3
hundreds 6 tens.

$$
\begin{array}{r}
{}^{3}\ \\
{}^{\not{8}}\ \\
89 \\
\times\ 47 \\
\hline
623 \\
60 \\
\end{array}
$$

Step 5 Multiply the 8 tens, or 80, by the
4 tens, or 40. Add the regrouped
tens. Regroup the 35 hundreds as 3
thousands 5 hundreds.

$$
\begin{array}{r}
{}^{3}\ \\
{}^{\not{8}}\ \\
89 \\
\times\ 47 \\
\hline
623 \\
3{,}560 \\
\end{array}
$$

Step 6 Add the partial products.

$$
\begin{array}{r}
{}^{3}\ \\
{}^{\not{8}}\ \\
89 \\
\times\ 47 \\
\hline
623 \\
+\ 3{,}560 \\
\hline
4{,}183 \\
\end{array}
$$

So, $47 \times 89 = 4{,}183$. Since 4,183 is close to
the estimate of 4,500, it is reasonable.

Estimate. Then choose a method to find the product.

1. Estimate: _____   **2.** Estimate: _____   **3.** Estimate: _____   **4.** Estimate: _____

$$
\begin{array}{r}
76 \\
\times\ 31 \\
\end{array}
\qquad
\begin{array}{r}
24 \\
\times\ 35 \\
\end{array}
\qquad
\begin{array}{r}
14 \\
\times\ 28 \\
\end{array}
\qquad
\begin{array}{r}
64 \\
\times\ 56 \\
\end{array}
$$

1. Gabe runs on a treadmill for 45 minutes every morning. His body uses about 12 calories per minute to keep him moving. How many calories does Gabe use during his run?

(A) 135

(B) 440

(C) 540

(D) 580

2. A youth center sold raffle tickets to raise money for supplies. They sold 62 books of raffle tickets for $18 each. How much money did the youth center raise?

(A) $1,116

(B) $1,016

(C) $816

(D) $558

3. A store sold 52 shirts on Saturday for $28 each. What is the total amount customers paid for the shirts?

(A) $1,040

(B) $1,046

(C) $1,440

(D) $1,456

4. There are 68 students in the book club. Each student reads 14 books during summer vacation. How many books do the students read in all during summer vacation?

(A) 340

(B) 922

(C) 952

(D) 1,020

Problem Solving REAL WORLD

5. A movie theatre has 26 rows of seats. There are 18 seats in each row. How many seats are there in all?

6. Each class at Briarwood Elementary collected at least 54 cans of food during the food drive. If there are 29 classes in the school, what was the least number of cans collected?

Estimate Quotients Using Multiples

Find two numbers the quotient of 142 ÷ 5 is between. Then estimate the quotient.

You can use multiples to estimate. A **multiple** of a number is the product of a number and a counting number.

Step 1 Think: What number multiplied by 5 is about 142?
Since 142 is greater than 10 × 5, or 50, use counting numbers 10, 20, 30, and so on to find multiples of 5.

Step 2 Multiply 5 by multiples of 10 and make a table.

Counting Number	10	20	30	40
Multiple of 5	50	100	150	200

Step 3 Use the table to find multiples of 5 closest to 142.

$20 \times 5 = \underline{100}$
                ← 142 is between $\underline{100}$ and $\underline{150}$.
$30 \times 5 = \underline{150}$

142 is closest to $\underline{150}$, so 142 ÷ 5 is about $\underline{30}$.

Find two numbers the quotient is between. Then estimate the quotient.

1. 136 ÷ 6

between _____ and _____

about _____

2. 95 ÷ 3

between _____ and _____

about _____

3. 124 ÷ 9

between _____ and _____

about _____

4. 238 ÷ 7

between _____ and _____

about _____

1. There are 9 showings of a film about endangered species at the science museum. A total of 458 people saw the film. About how many people were at each showing?

   (A) about 40

   (B) about 50

   (C) about 60

   (D) about 90

2. Kelli and her family went to the beach for a vacation. They drove 293 miles in 7 hours to get there. About how many miles did they drive each hour?

   (A) about 40 miles

   (B) about 30 miles

   (C) about 20 miles

   (D) about 10 miles

3. Between which two numbers is the quotient of 87 ÷ 5?

   (A) between 5 and 10

   (B) between 10 and 15

   (C) between 15 and 20

   (D) between 20 and 25

4. Between which two numbers is the quotient of 93 ÷ 5?

   (A) between 20 and 25

   (B) between 15 and 20

   (C) between 10 and 15

   (D) between 5 and 10

Problem Solving REAL WORLD

5. Joy collected 287 aluminum cans in 6 hours. About how many cans did she collect per hour?

6. Paul sold 162 cups of lemonade in 5 hours. About how many cups of lemonade did he sell each hour?

Name _____

Lesson 38
COMMON CORE STANDARD CC.4.NBT.6
Lesson Objective: Use models to divide
whole numbers that do not divide evenly.

Remainders

Use counters to find the quotient and remainder.

$$9\overline{)26}$$

- Use 26 counters to represent the dividend, 26.

- Since you are dividing 26 by 9, draw 9 circles.
  Divide the 26 counters into 9 equal-sized groups.

- There are 2 counters in each circle, so the quotient is 2.
  There are 8 counters left over, so the remainder is 8.

$$9\overline{)26}^{\;2\;r8}$$

Divide. Draw a quick picture to help.

$$7\overline{)66}$$

- Use 66 counters to represent the dividend, 66.

- Since you are dividing 66 by 7, draw 7 circles.
  Divide 66 counters into 7 equal-sized groups.

- There are 9 counters in each circle, so the quotient is 9.
  There are 3 counters left over, so the remainder is 3.

$$7\overline{)66}^{\;9\;r3}$$

Use counters to find the quotient and remainder.

1. $6\overline{)19}$

2. $3\overline{)14}$

Divide. Draw a quick picture to help.

3. $39 \div 4$

4. $29 \div 3$

_____   _____

Name _____

1. Look at the model. What division does it show?

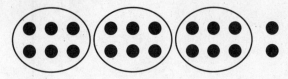

(A) $6 \div 3$ (C) $18 \div 3$

(B) $6 \div 4$ (D) $20 \div 3$

2. Ed used counters to model $4\overline{)19}$. What quotient and remainder did he find?

(A) quotient: 5 remainder: 1

(B) quotient: 4 remainder: 3

(C) quotient: 4 remainder: 2

(D) quotient: 3 remainder: 7

3. Margie arranged 40 counters into 6 groups of 6. There were 4 counters left over. What quotient and remainder did she model?

(A) quotient: 7 remainder: 2

(B) quotient: 6 remainder: 5

(C) quotient: 6 remainder: 4

(D) quotient: 6 remainder: 2

4. Look at the model. What division does it show?

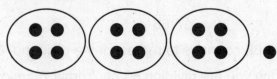

(A) $4 \div 3$ (C) $12 \div 3$

(B) $12 \div 4$ (D) $13 \div 3$

5. Stefan says this quick picture shows $31 \div 4$. Is he correct? What other division does the picture model? Explain.

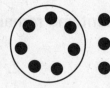

_____

_____

_____

_____

Divide Tens, Hundreds, and Thousands

You can use base-ten blocks, place value, and basic facts to divide.

Divide. $240 \div 3$

Use base-ten blocks.		Use place value.
Step 1 Draw a quick picture to show 240.		**Step 1** Identify the basic fact to use. Use $\underline{24 \div 3}$.
Step 2 You cannot divide 2 hundreds into 3 equal groups. Rename 2 hundreds as tens. $240 = \underline{24}$ tens		**Step 2** Use place value to rewrite 240 as tens. $240 = \underline{24}$ tens
Step 3 Separate the tens into 3 equal groups to divide. There are 3 groups of $\underline{8}$ tens. Write the answer. $240 \div 3 = \underline{80}$		**Step 3** Divide. $24 \text{ tens} \div 3 = \underline{8}$ tens $= \underline{80}$ Write the answer. $240 \div 3 = \underline{80}$

Use basic facts and place value to find the quotient.

1. $280 \div 4$

What division fact can you use?

_____

$280 = \underline{}$ tens

$28 \text{ tens} \div 4 = \underline{}$ tens

$280 \div 4 = \underline{}$

2. $1,800 \div 9$

What division fact can you use?

_____

$1,800 = \underline{}$ hundreds

$18 \text{ hundreds} \div 9 = \underline{}$ hundreds

$1,800 \div 9 = \underline{}$

3. $560 \div 7 = \underline{}$

4. $180 \div 6 = \underline{}$

5. $1,500 \div 5 = \underline{}$

6. $3,200 \div 4 = \underline{}$

1. Taylor took 560 photographs while on summer vacation. She wants to place an equal number of photos in each of 7 albums. How many photos will Taylor place in each album?

   Ⓐ 7

   Ⓑ 8

   Ⓒ 70

   Ⓓ 80

2. Which number sentence is **not** true?

   Ⓐ $200 \div 5 = 50$

   Ⓑ $400 \div 8 = 50$

   Ⓒ $2,000 \div 4 = 500$

   Ⓓ $4,000 \div 4 = 1,000$

3. A crayon factory packs 5 crayons in a sample pack. The factory gives sample packs to visitors under 12. How many sample packs can be made with 2,500 crayons?

   Ⓐ 5

   Ⓑ 50

   Ⓒ 500

   Ⓓ 5,000

4. Bayshore Elementary students collected $3,200 for new library books. Each of the 8 classes collected the same amount. How much did each class collect?

   Ⓐ $4,000

   Ⓑ $400

   Ⓒ $40

   Ⓓ $4

5. A factory packs 6 bars of soap into each family pack. Explain how to use basic facts and place value to find how many family packs can be made with 5,400 bars of soap.

   _____

   _____

   _____

   _____

Estimate Quotients Using Compatible Numbers

Compatible numbers are numbers that are easy to compute mentally. In division, one compatible number divides evenly into the other. Think of the multiples of a number to help you find compatible numbers.

Estimate. $6\overline{)216}$

Step 1 Think of these multiples of 6:

| 6 | 12 | 18 | 24 | 30 | 36 | 42 | 48 | 54 |

Find multiples that are close to the first 2 digits of the dividend. __18__ tens and __24__ tens are both close to __21__ tens. You can use either or both numbers to estimate the quotient.

Step 2 Estimate using compatible numbers.

$216 \div 6$ $216 \div 6$
$\downarrow$ $\downarrow$
$180 \div 6 = 30$ $240 \div 6 = 40$

So, $216 \div 6$ is between __30__ and __40__.

Step 3 Decide whether the estimate is closer to 30 or 40.

$216 - 180 = 36$ $240 - 216 = 24$

216 is closer to 240, so use __40__ as the estimate.

Use compatible numbers to estimate the quotient.

1. $3\overline{)252}$

2. $6\overline{)546}$

3. $4\overline{)2,545}$

4. $5\overline{)314}$

5. $2\overline{)1,578}$

6. $8\overline{)289}$

1. On Friday, 278 fourth graders went on a field trip to the Arizona State Museum. The staff divided them into 7 tour groups. Which is the **best** estimate of the number of students in each tour group?

   (A) 50

   (B) 40

   (C) 20

   (D) 7

2. Amanda and her four sisters divided 1,021 stickers equally. About how many stickers did each girl receive?

   (A) about 300

   (B) about 250

   (C) about 200

   (D) about 100

3. Use compatible numbers to estimate the quotient $531 \div 6$. Which is the **best** estimate?

   (A) 9

   (B) 90

   (C) 900

   (D) 9,000

4. For Earth Day, 264 students helped out at a tree farm. The staff divided the students into 9 teams. Which is the **best** estimate of the number of students on each team?

   (A) 30

   (B) 36

   (C) 40

   (D) 50

Problem Solving REAL WORLD

5. A CD store sold 3,467 CDs in 7 days. About the same number of CDs were sold each day. About how many CDs did the store sell each day?

   _____

6. Marcus has 731 books. He puts about the same number of books on each of 9 shelves in his a bookcase. About how many books are on each shelf?

   _____

Division and the Distributive Property

Divide. 78 ÷ 6

Use the Distributive Property and quick pictures to break apart numbers to make them easier to divide.

Step 1 Draw a quick picture to show 78.

Step 2 Think about how to break apart 78. You know 6 tens ÷ 6 = 10, so use 78 = 60 + 18. Draw a quick picture to show 6 tens and 18 ones.

Step 3 Draw circles to show 6 tens ÷ 6 and 18 ones ÷ 6. Your drawing shows the use of the Distributive Property.

$$78 ÷ 6 = \underline{(60 ÷ 6)} + \underline{(18 ÷ 6)}$$

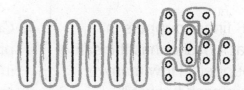

Step 4 Add the quotients to find 78 ÷ 6.

$$78 ÷ 6 = (60 ÷ 6) + (18 ÷ 6)$$

$$= \underline{10} + \underline{3}$$

$$= \underline{13}$$

Use quick pictures to model the quotient.

1. 84 ÷ 4 = _____

2. 54 ÷ 3 = _____

3. 68 ÷ 2 = _____

4. 65 ÷ 5 = _____

5. 96 ÷ 8 = _____

6. 90 ÷ 6 = _____

1. Lakya is using the Distributive Property to divide 128 by 4. Which does **not** show a way she could break apart the dividend?

   Ⓐ $128 \div 4 = (100 \div 4) + (28 \div 4)$

   Ⓑ $128 \div 4 = (120 \div 4) + (8 \div 4)$

   Ⓒ $128 \div 4 = (64 \div 4) + (64 \div 4)$

   Ⓓ $128 \div 4 = (12 \div 4) + (28 \div 4)$

2. Dawn has 48 finger puppets in 3 baskets. Each basket has the same number of puppets. How many puppets are in each basket?

   Ⓐ 14

   Ⓑ 15

   Ⓒ 16

   Ⓓ 18

3. The Distributive Property can help you divide. Which is **not** a way to break apart the dividend to find the quotient of $132 \div 6$?

   Ⓐ $(120 \div 6) + (12 \div 6)$

   Ⓑ $(100 \div 6) + (32 \div 6)$

   Ⓒ $(90 \div 6) + (42 \div 6)$

   Ⓓ $(72 \div 6) + (60 \div 6)$

4. Gordon took batting practice with a pitching machine. He hit 104 pitches in 8 minutes. If Gordon hit the same number of pitches, how many pitches did he hit each minute?

   Ⓐ 12

   Ⓑ 13

   Ⓒ 14

   Ⓓ 15

5. Steve has 68 tulips to divide into vases. There will be 4 tulips in each vase. Explain a way to use the Distributive Property to find the number of vases Steve will need.

   _____

   _____

   _____

   _____

Name _____

Lesson **42**
COMMON CORE STANDARD CC.4.NBT.6
Lesson Objective: Use repeated
subtraction and multiples to find quotients.

Divide Using Repeated Subtraction

You can use repeated subtraction to divide. Use repeated subtraction to solve the problem.

Nestor has 27 shells to make bracelets. He needs 4 shells for each bracelet. How many bracelets can he make?

Divide. 27 ÷ 4

Write $4\overline{)27}$.

Step 1

Subtract the divisor until the remainder is less than the divisor. Record a 1 each time you subtract.

$$
\begin{array}{r}
4\overline{)27} \\
-4 \quad 1 \\
\hline
23 \\
-4 \quad 1 \\
\hline
19 \\
-4 \quad 1 \\
\hline
15 \\
-4 \quad 1 \\
\hline
11 \\
-4 \quad 1 \\
\hline
7 \\
-4 \quad 1 \\
\hline
3
\end{array}
$$

Step 2

Count the number of times you subtracted the divisor, 4.

4 is subtracted six times with 3 left.

$$27 \div 4$$

$$\underline{6\ r3}$$

So, Nestor can make 6 bracelets.
He will have 3 shells left.

Use repeated subtraction to divide.

1. 30 ÷ 4

_____

2. 24 ÷ 5

_____

3. 47 ÷ 7

_____

1. There are 60 people waiting for a river raft ride. Each raft holds 15 people. Which number sentence can be used to find how many rafts will be needed?

Ⓐ $60 - 15 - 15 - 15 - 15 = 0$

Ⓑ $60 - 15 = 45$

Ⓒ $60 + 15 = 75$

Ⓓ $60 - 30 - 15 = 15$

2. There are 48 people waiting for a fishing tour. Each tour boat holds 12 people. Which number sentence can be used to find how many boats will be needed?

Ⓐ $12 + 48 = 60$

Ⓑ $48 - 12 = 36$

Ⓒ $48 - 24 = 24$

Ⓓ $48 - 12 - 12 - 12 - 12 = 0$

3. Jessie has 80 rubber bracelets. She arranges the bracelets in piles of 4. Which model shows $80 \div 4$?

Ⓐ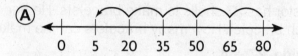

Ⓑ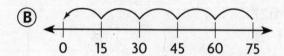

Ⓒ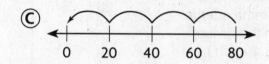

Ⓓ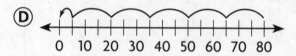

Problem Solving REAL WORLD

4. Gretchen has 48 small shells. She uses 2 shells to make one pair of earrings. How many pairs of earrings can she make?

5. James wants to purchase a telescope for $54. If he saves $3 per week, in how many weeks will he have saved enough to purchase the telescope?

_____

Divide Using Partial Quotients

You can use partial quotients to divide.

Divide. 492 ÷ 4

Partial quotients

Step 1 Subtract greater multiples of the divisor. Repeat if needed.

$$4)\overline{492}$$
$$-400 \quad 100 \times 4 \quad 100$$

Step 2 Subtract lesser multiples of the divisor. Repeat until the remaining number is less than the divisor.

$$92$$
$$-80 \quad 20 \times 4 \quad 20$$

$$12$$
$$-12 \quad 3 \times 4 \quad +3$$

Step 3 Add the partial quotients.

$$0 \qquad \qquad 123$$

Use rectangular models to record partial quotients.

100	80	12
4	400	

492
− 400
92

100	20	
4	400	80	12

92
− 80
12

100	20	3
4	400	80	12

12
− 12
0

$$\underline{100} + \underline{20} + \underline{3} = \underline{123}$$

Divide. Use partial quotients.

1.
$$3)\overline{6\,5\,7}$$

_____ 100 × _____ 100

_____ 100 × _____ _____

_____ _____ × _____

_____ _____ _____ × _____ + _____

Divide. Use rectangular models to record the partial quotients.

2. 852 ÷ 6 = _____

Core Standards for Math, Grade 4

1. Keith wants to fill 9 pages of his photo album with the same number of photographs on each page. If Keith has 117 photographs, how many photographs will he put on each page?

Ⓐ 8

Ⓑ 13

Ⓒ 17

Ⓓ 23

2. Diego bought 488 frozen yogurt bars in 4 different flavors for a party. If he bought the same number of each flavor, how many of each flavor did Diego buy?

Ⓐ 221

Ⓑ 211

Ⓒ 122

Ⓓ 62

3. Three popcorn stores donated a total of 636 bags of popcorn for the school fair. If each store donated the same number of bags, how many bags of popcorn did each store donate?

Ⓐ 112

Ⓑ 202

Ⓒ 210

Ⓓ 212

4. Sam filled 6 toy boxes with the same number of toys in each box. If he had 144 toys, how many toys did he put in each toy box?

Ⓐ 150

Ⓑ 24

Ⓒ 22

Ⓓ 14

Problem Solving REAL WORLD

5. Allison took 112 photos on vacation. She wants to put them in a photo album that holds 4 photos on each page. How many pages can she fill?

_____

6. Hector saved $726 in 6 months. He saved the same amount each month. How much did Hector save each month?

_____

Name _____

Lesson 44

COMMON CORE STANDARD CC.4.NBT.6

Lesson Objective: Use base-ten blocks to model division with regrouping.

Model Division with Regrouping

You can use base-ten blocks to model division with regrouping.

Use base-ten blocks to find the quotient 65 ÷ 4.

Step 1 Show 65 with base-ten blocks.

Step 2 Draw 4 circles to represent dividing 65 into 4 equal groups. Share the tens equally among the 4 groups.

Step 3 Regroup leftover tens as ones.

Step 4 Share the ones equally among the 4 groups.

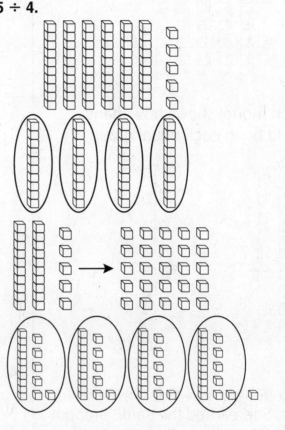

There are __1__ ten(s) and __6__ one(s) in each group with __1__ left over.

So, the quotient is ___16 r1___.

Divide. Use base-ten blocks.

1. 37 ÷ 2

_____

2. 74 ÷ 3

_____

3. 66 ÷ 5

_____

Name _____

1. Zack needs to divide these base-ten blocks into 3 equal groups.

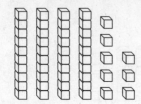

Which model shows how many should be in each equal group?

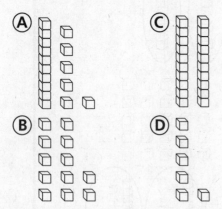

2. Emily earned $72 in 6 days walking dogs. She earned the same amount each day. How much did she earn each day?

Ⓐ $22   Ⓒ $13

Ⓑ $14   Ⓓ $12

3. Ethan needs to divide these base-ten blocks into 3 equal groups.

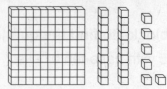

Which model shows how many should be in each equal group?

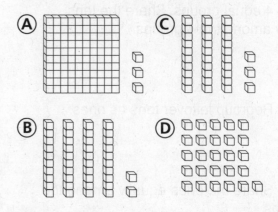

4. Zora blinked her eyes 96 times in 4 minutes. She blinked the same number of times each minute. How many times did Zora blink in one minute?

Ⓐ 22   Ⓒ 24

Ⓑ 23   Ⓓ 25

Problem Solving

5. Tamara sold 92 cold drinks during her 2-hour shift at a festival food stand. If she sold the same number of drinks each hour, how many cold drinks did she sell each hour?

_____

6. In 3 days Donald earned $42 running errands. He earned the same amount each day. How much did Donald earn from running errands each day?

_____

Name _____

Lesson **45**

COMMON CORE STANDARD CC.4.NBT.6
Lesson Objective: Use place value to determine where to place the first digit of a quotient.

Place the First Digit

Divide. 763 ÷ 3 = ■

Step 1 Estimate. Then divide the hundreds.

Think: 3 × 1 hundred = 3 hundreds
　　　3 × 2 hundreds = 6 hundreds
　　　3 × 3 hundreds = 9 hundreds

3 × 3 **hundreds** is too large.
Use 2 **hundreds** as an estimate.

```
    2    ← Divide 7 hundreds by 3.
3)763
  - 6    ← Multiply. 3 × 2 hundreds
    1    ← Subtract.
```

Step 2 Bring down the tens digit. Then divide the tens.

```
    2
3)763
  -6↓
   16    ← Bring down the 6.
```

```
   25    ← Divide 16 tens by 3.
3)763
  - 6
   16
 - 15    ← Multiply. 3 × 5 tens
    1    ← Subtract.
```

Step 3 Bring down the ones digit. Then divide the ones.

```
   25
3)763
  - 6
   16
 - 15↓
   13    ← Bring down the 3.
```

```
  254    ← Divide 13 ones by 3.
3)763
  - 6
   16
 - 15
   13
 - 12    ← Multiply. 3 × 4 ones
    1    ← Subtract.
```

Step 4 Check to make sure that the remainder is less than the divisor. Write the answer.

```
  254 r1    1 < 3
3)763
```

Divide.

1. 2)531　　　**2.** 4)628　　　**3.** 9)349　　　**4.** 7)794

1. Jake writes a division problem to find out how he can distribute 543 marbles among 7 of his friends. In what place is the first digit of the quotient?

   (A) thousands

   (B) hundreds

   (C) tens

   (D) ones

2. Sylvia plans to place 617 stamps in an album. Each page of the album holds 5 stamps. She uses division to find out how many full pages she will have. In what place is the first digit of the quotient?

   (A) hundreds   (C) tens

   (B) ones   (D) thousands

3. Jim will use division to find out how he can distribute 750 coupon books among 9 stores. In what place is the first digit of the quotient?

   (A) ones

   (B) tens

   (C) hundreds

   (D) thousands

4. Hilda wants to save 825 digital photographs in an online album. Each folder of the online album can save 6 photographs. She uses division to find out how many full folders she will have. In what place is the first digit of the quotient?

   (A) ones   (C) hundreds

   (B) tens   (D) thousands

Problem Solving  REAL WORLD

5. There are 132 projects in the science fair. If 8 projects can fit in a row, how many full rows of projects can be made? How many projects are in the row that is not full?

6. There are 798 calories in six 10-ounce bottles of apple juice. How many calories are there in one 10-ounce bottle of apple juice?

Divide by 1-Digit Numbers

Divide. 766 ÷ 6 = ■

Step 1 Use place value to place the first digit.
Think: 7 hundreds can be shared among 6 groups without regrouping.

$$
\begin{array}{r} 1 \\ 6)\overline{766} \end{array}
$$

Step 2 Bring down the tens digit. Then divide the tens.

$$
\begin{array}{r} 1 \\ 6)\overline{766} \\ -6\downarrow \\ \hline 16 \end{array}
$$

← Bring down the 6.

$$
\begin{array}{r} 12 \\ 6)\overline{766} \\ -6 \\ \hline 16 \\ -12 \\ \hline 4 \end{array}
$$

← Divide 16 tens by 6.

← Multiply. 6 × 2 tens

← Subtract.

Step 3 Bring down the ones digit. Then divide the ones.

$$
\begin{array}{r} 12 \\ 6)\overline{766} \\ -6 \\ \hline 16 \\ -12 \\ \hline 46 \end{array}
$$

← Bring down the 6.

$$
\begin{array}{r} 127 \\ 6)\overline{766} \\ -6 \\ \hline 16 \\ -12 \\ \hline 46 \\ -42 \\ \hline 4 \end{array}
$$

← Divide 46 ones by 6.

← Multiply. 6 × 7 ones

← Subtract.

Step 4 Check to make sure that the remainder is less than the divisor. Write the answer.

$$
\begin{array}{r} 127 \text{ r4} \\ 6)\overline{766} \end{array}
$$

4 < 6

Step 5 Use multiplication and addition to check your answer.

$$
\begin{array}{r} 127 \\ \times\ 6 \\ \hline 762 \\ +\ 4 \\ \hline 766 \end{array}
$$

Divide and check.

1. 4)868

2. 2)657

3. 7)8,473

1. Students made large soap bubbles at a party. They used 224 ounces of dish soap to make the bubble mixture. The dish soap came in 4 containers of the same size. How many ounces of dish soap were in each container?

(A) 51 ounces

(B) 55 ounces

(C) 56 ounces

(D) 66 ounces

2. A toy manufacturer has 627 yo-yos to divide equally among 3 stores. How many yo-yos will each store receive?

(A) 29

(B) 209

(C) 219

(D) 309

3. Students are making pizza. They put a total of 108 ounces of cheese on 9 pizzas. Each pizza has the same amount of cheese. How many ounces of cheese are on each pizza?

(A) 15 ounces

(B) 14 ounces

(C) 13 ounces

(D) 12 ounces

4. A store gave away 1,932 calendars in 7 days. They gave away the same number of calendars each day. How many calendars did the store give away each day?

(A) 276

(B) 281

(C) 286

(D) 776

5. An office supply store packed 416 notepads with the same number in each of 4 boxes. Milo said there are exactly 100 notepads in each box. Do you agree? Explain.

_____

_____

_____

_____

Equivalent Fractions

Write two fractions that are equivalent to $\frac{2}{6}$.

Step 1 Make a model to represent $\frac{2}{6}$.

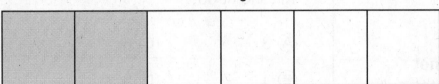

The rectangle is divided into 6 equal parts, with 2 parts shaded.

Step 2 Divide the rectangle from Step 1 in half.

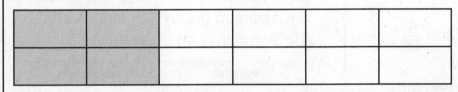

The rectangle is now divided into 12 equal parts, with 4 parts shaded.

The model shows the fraction $\frac{4}{12}$. So, $\frac{2}{6}$ and $\frac{4}{12}$ are equivalent.

Step 3 Draw the same rectangle as in Step 1, but with only 3 equal parts. Keep the same amount of the rectangle shaded.

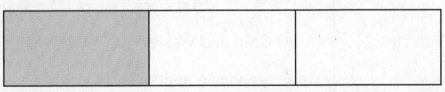

The rectangle is now divided into 3 equal parts, with 1 part shaded.

The model shows the fraction $\frac{1}{3}$. So, $\frac{2}{6}$ and $\frac{1}{3}$ are equivalent.

Use models to write two equivalent fractions.

1. $\frac{2}{4}$

_____

2. $\frac{4}{6}$

_____

1. Julie sewed squares together to make a quilt. The shaded squares show where she used a blue square.

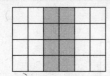

   What pair of fractions is **not** equivalent to the part of the quilt with blue squares?

   (A) $\frac{1}{3}$ and $\frac{8}{24}$ (C) $\frac{1}{3}$ and $\frac{2}{6}$

   (B) $\frac{2}{6}$ and $\frac{4}{12}$ (D) $\frac{1}{2}$ and $\frac{6}{18}$

2. Joey divides a small garden into 20 equal sections. He plants tulips in 16 of the sections. Which fraction is equivalent to the part of the garden planted with tulips?

   (A) $\frac{4}{5}$ (C) $\frac{1}{2}$

   (B) $\frac{3}{4}$ (D) $\frac{2}{5}$

3. Ann uses three $\frac{1}{4}$ size strips to model $\frac{3}{4}$. She wants to use $\frac{1}{8}$ size strips to model an equivalent fraction. How many $\frac{1}{8}$ size strips will she need?

   (A) 3   (C) 6

   (B) 4   (D) 8

4. Four friends shared a pizza. The table shows how much of the pizza each person ate. Which friends ate the same amount of pizza?

Name	Pizza Eaten
Colin	$\frac{3}{9}$
Stephanie	$\frac{2}{8}$
Vicki	$\frac{3}{12}$
Wesley	$\frac{1}{6}$

   (A) Colin and Wesley

   (B) Stephanie and Vicki

   (C) Stephanie and Wesley

   (D) Colin and Vicki

5. Lizzie walked $\frac{8}{10}$ mile and Billy walked $\frac{12}{15}$ mile. Lizzie says they walked the same distance. Do you agree with Lizzie? Explain your answer.

_____

_____

_____

Generate Equivalent Fractions

Write an equivalent fraction for $\frac{4}{5}$.

Step 1 Choose a whole number, like 2.
Step 2 Create a fraction using 2 as the numerator and denominator: $\frac{2}{2}$. This fraction is equal to 1. You can multiply a number by 1 without changing the value of the number.
Step 3 Multiply $\frac{4}{5}$ by $\frac{2}{2}$: $\frac{4 \times 2}{5 \times 2} = \frac{8}{10}$.
So, $\frac{4}{5}$ and $\frac{8}{10}$ are equivalent.

Write another equivalent fraction for $\frac{4}{5}$.

Step 1 Choose a different whole number, like 20.
Step 2 Create a fraction using 20 as the numerator and denominator: $\frac{20}{20}$.
Step 3 Multiply $\frac{4}{5}$ by $\frac{20}{20}$: $\frac{4 \times 20}{5 \times 20} = \frac{80}{100}$.
So, $\frac{4}{5}$ and $\frac{80}{100}$ are equivalent.

Write two equivalent fractions.

1. $\frac{2}{6}$

2. $\frac{4}{10}$

3. $\frac{3}{8}$

4. $\frac{3}{5}$

1. Kyle drank $\frac{2}{3}$ cup of apple juice. Which fraction is equivalent to $\frac{2}{3}$?

   Ⓐ $\frac{2}{9}$

   Ⓑ $\frac{2}{6}$

   Ⓒ $\frac{6}{9}$

   Ⓓ $\frac{9}{6}$

2. Nicolette needs $\frac{1}{3}$ yard of fabric. Which fraction is equivalent to $\frac{1}{3}$?

   Ⓐ $\frac{1}{9}$

   Ⓑ $\frac{5}{15}$

   Ⓒ $\frac{2}{3}$

   Ⓓ $\frac{15}{5}$

3. There are 5 marbles in each bag. One of the marbles in each bag is striped. Which two fractions are equivalent to $\frac{1}{5}$?

   Ⓐ $\frac{2}{10}, \frac{3}{15}$

   Ⓑ $\frac{2}{8}, \frac{3}{12}$

   Ⓒ $\frac{2}{10}, \frac{4}{16}$

   Ⓓ $\frac{2}{8}, \frac{4}{15}$

4. Amy's banana bread recipe calls for $\frac{3}{4}$ cup of brown sugar. She only has a $\frac{1}{8}$-cup measure. Which equivalent fraction shows the amount of brown sugar she needs for the recipe?

   Ⓐ $\frac{2}{8}$ cup

   Ⓑ $\frac{3}{8}$ cup

   Ⓒ $\frac{4}{8}$ cup

   Ⓓ $\frac{6}{8}$ cup

Problem Solving  REAL WORLD

5. Jan has a 12-ounce milkshake. Four ounces in the milkshake are vanilla, and the rest is chocolate. What are two equivalent fractions that represent the fraction of the milkshake that is vanilla?

6. Kareem lives $\frac{4}{10}$ of a mile from the mall. Write two equivalent fractions that show what fraction of a mile Kareem lives from the mall.

Name _____

Lesson 49

COMMON CORE STANDARD CC.4.NF.1

Lesson Objective: Write and identify
equivalent fractions in simplest form.

Simplest Form

A fraction is in **simplest form** when 1 is the only factor that the
numerator and denominator have in common.

Tell whether the fraction $\frac{7}{8}$ is in simplest form.

Look for common factors in the numerator and the denominator.

Step 1 The numerator of $\frac{7}{8}$ is 7. List all the factors of 7.	$1 \times 7 = 7$ The factors of 7 are 1 and 7.
Step 2 The denominator of $\frac{7}{8}$ is 8. List all the factors of 8.	$1 \times 8 = 8$ $2 \times 4 = 8$ The factors of 8 are 1, 2, 4, and 8.
Step 3 Check if the numerator and denominator of $\frac{7}{8}$ have any common factors greater than 1.	The only common factor of 7 and 8 is 1.
So, $\frac{7}{8}$ is in simplest form.	

Tell whether the fraction is in simplest form. Write *yes* or *no*.

1. $\frac{4}{10}$

2. $\frac{2}{8}$

3. $\frac{3}{5}$

_____   _____   _____

Write the fraction in simplest form.

4. $\frac{4}{12}$

5. $\frac{6}{10}$

6. $\frac{3}{6}$

_____   _____   _____

Name _____

1. Jamal made a list of fractions and asked Will to find the fraction written in simplest form. Which fraction should Will choose?

   (A) $\frac{1}{8}$

   (B) $\frac{3}{9}$

   (C) $\frac{9}{18}$

   (D) $\frac{6}{10}$

3. In the school chorus, $\frac{2}{12}$ of the students are fourth graders. In simplest form, what fraction of the students in the school chorus are fourth graders?

   (A) $\frac{4}{12}$

   (B) $\frac{2}{12}$

   (C) $\frac{2}{6}$

   (D) $\frac{1}{6}$

2. In the Jones School Library, $\frac{5}{10}$ of the computers have scanners. In simplest form, what fraction of the computers have scanners?

   (A) $\frac{5}{10}$

   (B) $\frac{1}{4}$

   (C) $\frac{1}{2}$

   (D) $\frac{6}{12}$

4. Ten of 12 balloons at Jean's party are filled with helium. In simplest form, what fraction of the balloons are filled with helium?

   (A) $\frac{4}{6}$

   (B) $\frac{5}{6}$

   (C) $\frac{10}{12}$

   (D) $\frac{12}{10}$

Problem Solving REAL WORLD

5. At Memorial Hospital, 9 of the 12 babies born on Tuesday were boys. In simplest form, what fraction of the babies born on Tuesday were boys?

6. Cristina uses a ruler to measure the length of her math textbook. She says that the book is $\frac{4}{10}$ meter long. Is her measurement in simplest form? If not, what is the length of the book in simplest form?

Name _____

Lesson 50
COMMON CORE STANDARD CC.4.NF.1

Lesson Objective: Use equivalent fractions to represent a pair of fractions with a common denominator.

Common Denominators

A **common denominator** is a common multiple of the denominators of two or more fractions.

Write $\frac{2}{3}$ and $\frac{3}{4}$ as a pair of fractions with common denominators.

Step 1 Identify the denominators of $\frac{2}{3}$ and $\frac{3}{4}$.	$\frac{2}{3}$ and $\frac{3}{4}$ The denominators are 3 and 4.
Step 2 List multiples of 3 and 4. Circle common multiples.	**3:** 3, 6, 9, ⓬, 15, 18 **4:** 4, 8, ⓬, 16, 20 12 is a common multiple of 3 and 4.
Step 3 Rewrite $\frac{2}{3}$ as a fraction with a denominator of 12.	$\frac{2}{3} = \frac{2 \times 4}{3 \times 4} = \frac{8}{12}$
Step 4 Rewrite $\frac{3}{4}$ as a fraction with a denominator of 12.	$\frac{3}{4} = \frac{3 \times 3}{4 \times 3} = \frac{9}{12}$
So, you can rewrite $\frac{2}{3}$ and $\frac{3}{4}$ as $\frac{8}{12}$ and $\frac{9}{12}$.	

Write the pair of fractions as a pair of fractions with a common denominator.

1. $\frac{1}{2}$ and $\frac{1}{3}$

   _____

2. $\frac{2}{4}$ and $\frac{5}{8}$

   _____

3. $\frac{1}{2}$ and $\frac{3}{5}$

   _____

4. $\frac{1}{4}$ and $\frac{5}{6}$

   _____

5. $\frac{2}{5}$ and $\frac{2}{3}$

   _____

6. $\frac{4}{5}$ and $\frac{7}{10}$

   _____

1. Elise is doing her homework. She plans to spend $\frac{1}{2}$ hour on math and $\frac{1}{6}$ hour on spelling words. Which of the following is a common denominator for $\frac{1}{2}$ and $\frac{1}{6}$?

   (A) 4

   (B) 12

   (C) 20

   (D) 26

3. Allie jogged for $\frac{1}{2}$ hour on Saturday and for $\frac{3}{4}$ hour on Sunday. Which of the following is a common denominator for $\frac{1}{2}$ and $\frac{3}{4}$?

   (A) 1

   (B) 4

   (C) 6

   (D) 10

2. Miguel walked $\frac{1}{2}$ mile to the library and then $\frac{3}{5}$ mile to the post office. How can he write $\frac{1}{2}$ and $\frac{3}{5}$ as a pair of fractions with a common denominator?

   (A) $\frac{1}{10}$ and $\frac{3}{10}$

   (B) $\frac{3}{6}$ and $\frac{3}{5}$

   (C) $\frac{2}{4}$ and $\frac{15}{25}$

   (D) $\frac{5}{10}$ and $\frac{6}{10}$

4. Jamal helps in the library. He put away $\frac{1}{3}$ of the returned books on Monday and $\frac{5}{6}$ of the returned books on Tuesday. Which of the following is a common denominator for $\frac{1}{3}$ and $\frac{5}{6}$?

   (A) 2

   (B) 3

   (C) 6

   (D) 9

Problem Solving REAL WORLD

5. Adam drew two same size rectangles and divided them into the same number of equal parts. He shaded $\frac{1}{3}$ of one rectangle and $\frac{1}{4}$ of other rectangle. What is the least number of parts into which both rectangles could be divided?

6. Mera painted equal sections of her bedroom wall to make a pattern. She painted $\frac{2}{5}$ of the wall white and $\frac{1}{2}$ of the wall lavender. Write an equivalent fraction for each using a common denominator.

_____

Lesson 51

COMMON CORE STANDARD CC.4.NF.1

Lesson Objective: Use the strategy *make a table* to solve problems using equivalent fractions.

Problem Solving • Find Equivalent Fractions

Kyle's mom bought bunches of balloons for a family party.
Each bunch has 4 balloons, and $\frac{1}{4}$ of the balloons are blue.
If Kyle's mom bought 5 bunches of balloons, how many
balloons did she buy? How many of the balloons are blue?

Read the Problem		
What do I need to find?	**What information do I need to use?**	**How will I use the information?**
I need to find how many balloons Kyle's mom bought and how many of the balloons are blue.	Each bunch has 1 out of 4 balloons that are blue, and there are 5 bunches.	I will make a table to find the total number balloons Kyle's mom bought and the fraction of balloons that are blue.

Solve the Problem					

I can make a table.

Number of Bunches	1	2	3	4	5
Total Number of Blue Balloons	$\frac{1}{4}$	$\frac{2}{8}$	$\frac{3}{12}$	$\frac{4}{16}$	$\frac{5}{20}$
Total Number of Balloons					

Kyle's mom bought 20 balloons. 5 of the balloons are blue.

Make a table to solve.

1. Jackie is making a beaded bracelet. The bracelet will have no more than 12 beads. $\frac{1}{3}$ of the beads on the bracelet will be green. What other fractions could represent the part of the beads on the bracelet that will be green?

2. Ben works in his dad's bakery packing bagels. Each package can have no more than 16 bagels. $\frac{3}{4}$ of the bagels in each package are plain. What other fractions could represent the part of the bagels in each package that will be plain?

_____   _____

1. Malia is making a bracelet with beads. She wants $\frac{1}{4}$ of the beads to be blue. If the greatest number of beads that will fit on the bracelet is 20, what fraction does **not** represent the part of the beads on the bracelet that are blue?

Ⓐ $\frac{4}{8}$

Ⓑ $\frac{5}{20}$

Ⓒ $\frac{4}{16}$

Ⓓ $\frac{3}{12}$

2. Liam works in a toy store that sells bags of marbles. He puts 10 marbles in each bag, and $\frac{2}{10}$ of the marbles are striped. If Liam makes 3 bags of marbles, how many striped marbles does he use?

Ⓐ 2

Ⓑ 6

Ⓒ 20

Ⓓ 30

3. Suzanne arranges flowers at her restaurant. She puts 8 flowers in each vase. Three flowers in each vase are yellow. If Suzanne uses 32 flowers, how many are yellow?

Ⓐ 6

Ⓑ 9

Ⓒ 12

Ⓓ 24

4. Every $\frac{1}{2}$ mile along a hiking path there is a water fountain, every $\frac{1}{4}$ mile there is a bench, and every $\frac{1}{8}$ mile there is a marker. Which of the following will be at $\frac{3}{4}$ mile along the path?

Ⓐ water fountain, bench, and marker

Ⓑ water fountain and marker

Ⓒ water fountain and bench

Ⓓ bench and marker

5. Sandra is making fruit baskets. She wants $\frac{1}{6}$ of the fruit in each basket to be bananas. If the greatest number of pieces of fruit that will fit in each basket is 24, what fractions represent the possible ways Sandra can have bananas in the fruit basket? Explain how you found your answer.

_____

_____

Name _____

Lesson 52
COMMON CORE STANDARD CC.4.NF.2
Lesson Objective: Compare fractions using benchmarks.

Compare Fractions Using Benchmarks

A **benchmark** is a known size or amount that helps you understand a different size or amount. You can use $\frac{1}{2}$ as a benchmark.

Sara reads for $\frac{3}{6}$ hour every day after school. Connor reads for $\frac{2}{3}$ hour. Who reads for a longer amount of time?

Compare the fractions. $\frac{3}{6}$ $\frac{2}{3}$

Step 1 Divide one circle into 6 equal parts. Divide another circle into 3 equal parts.

Step 2 Shade $\frac{3}{6}$ of the first circle. How many parts will you shade? **3 parts**

Step 3 Shade $\frac{2}{3}$ of the second circle. How many parts will you shade? **2 parts**

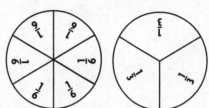

Step 4 Compare the shaded parts of each circle. Half of Sara's circle is shaded. More than half of Connor's circle is shaded.

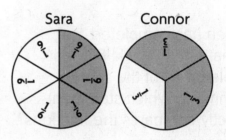

Sara   Connor

$\frac{3}{6}$ is less than $\frac{2}{3}$. $\frac{3}{6}$ $<$ $\frac{2}{3}$

So, **Connor** reads for a longer amount of time.

---

1. Compare $\frac{2}{8}$ and $\frac{3}{4}$. Write $<$ or $>$.

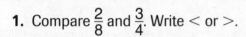

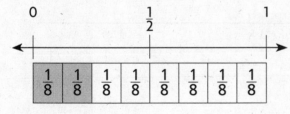

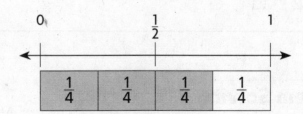

$\frac{2}{8}$ $\frac{3}{4}$

Compare. Write $<$ or $>$.

2. $\frac{1}{4}$ ◯ $\frac{8}{10}$

3. $\frac{7}{8}$ ◯ $\frac{1}{3}$

4. $\frac{5}{12}$ ◯ $\frac{1}{2}$

5. $\frac{2}{8}$ ◯ $\frac{8}{12}$

6. $\frac{4}{6}$ ◯ $\frac{4}{8}$

7. $\frac{7}{12}$ ◯ $\frac{2}{4}$

1. Asa runs $\frac{2}{5}$ mile. Kim runs $\frac{1}{2}$ mile. Which statement is **true**?

   (A) $\frac{2}{5} > \frac{1}{2}$

   (B) $\frac{1}{2} > \frac{2}{5}$

   (C) $\frac{1}{2} = \frac{2}{5}$

   (D) $\frac{1}{2} < \frac{2}{5}$

3. James and Ella biked around Eagle Lake. James biked $\frac{3}{10}$ of the distance in an hour. Ella biked $\frac{4}{8}$ of the distance in an hour. Which statement correctly compares the fractions?

   (A) $\frac{3}{10} > \frac{4}{8}$

   (B) $\frac{4}{8} = \frac{3}{10}$

   (C) $\frac{3}{10} < \frac{4}{8}$

   (D) $\frac{4}{8} < \frac{3}{10}$

2. Carmen has completed $\frac{1}{2}$ of her math homework. Billy has completed $\frac{7}{12}$ of the same assignment. Which statement correctly compares the fractions?

   (A) $\frac{1}{2} > \frac{7}{12}$

   (B) $\frac{7}{12} < \frac{1}{2}$

   (C) $\frac{7}{12} = \frac{1}{2}$

   (D) $\frac{1}{2} < \frac{7}{12}$

4. Suki rode her bike $\frac{4}{5}$ mile. Claire rode her bike $\frac{1}{3}$ mile. Which statement is **true**?

   (A) $\frac{4}{5} > \frac{1}{3}$

   (B) $\frac{1}{3} > \frac{4}{5}$

   (C) $\frac{1}{3} = \frac{4}{5}$

   (D) $\frac{4}{5} < \frac{1}{3}$

Problem Solving REAL WORLD

5. Erika ran $\frac{3}{8}$ mile. Maria ran $\frac{3}{4}$ mile. Who ran farther?

6. Carlos finished $\frac{1}{3}$ of his art project on Monday. Tyler finished $\frac{1}{2}$ of his art project on Monday. Who finished more of his art project on Monday?

Name _____

Lesson 53

COMMON CORE STANDARD CC.4.NF.2
Lesson Objective: Compare fractions by
first writing them as fractions with a common
numerator or a common denominator.

Compare Fractions

Theo filled a beaker $\frac{2}{4}$ full with water. Angelica filled a
beaker $\frac{3}{8}$ full with water. Whose beaker has more water?

Compare $\frac{2}{4}$ and $\frac{3}{8}$.

Step 1 Divide one beaker into 4 equal parts.
Divide another beaker into 8 equal parts.

Step 2 Shade $\frac{2}{4}$ of the first beaker.

Step 3 Shade $\frac{3}{8}$ of the second beaker.

Step 4 Compare the shaded parts of each beaker.
Half of Theo's beaker is shaded. Less than half of
Angelica's beaker is shaded.

$\frac{2}{4}$ is greater than $\frac{3}{8}$.

$\frac{2}{4}$ $\bigcirc\!>$ $\frac{3}{8}$

So, Theo's beaker has more water.

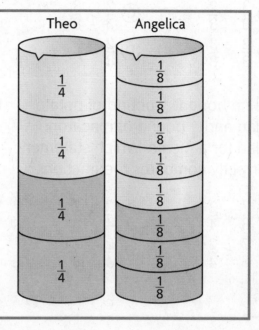

---

1. Compare $\frac{1}{2}$ and $\frac{1}{4}$.

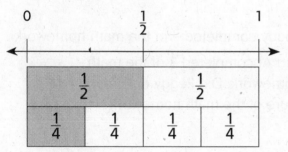

Which is greater? _____

2. Compare $\frac{2}{3}$ and $\frac{3}{6}$.

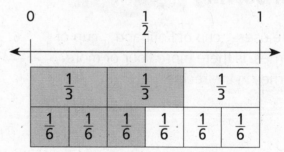

Which is less? _____

Compare. Write <, >, or =.

3. $\frac{1}{2}$ $\bigcirc$ $\frac{3}{4}$

4. $\frac{6}{12}$ $\bigcirc$ $\frac{5}{8}$

5. $\frac{2}{3}$ $\bigcirc$ $\frac{4}{6}$

6. $\frac{3}{8}$ $\bigcirc$ $\frac{1}{4}$

1. Bill used $\frac{3}{8}$ cup of raisins and $\frac{2}{3}$ cup of banana chips to make a snack. Which statement correctly compares the fractions?

   (A) $\frac{3}{8} > \frac{2}{3}$ (C) $\frac{2}{3} > \frac{3}{8}$

   (B) $\frac{2}{3} < \frac{3}{8}$ (D) $\frac{2}{3} = \frac{3}{8}$

2. Elaine bought $\frac{7}{8}$ pound of potato salad and $\frac{2}{4}$ pound of macaroni salad for a picnic. Which statement correctly compares the fractions?

   (A) $\frac{7}{8} > \frac{2}{4}$ (C) $\frac{2}{4} = \frac{7}{8}$

   (B) $\frac{7}{8} < \frac{2}{4}$ (D) $\frac{2}{4} > \frac{7}{8}$

3. Brad uses $\frac{3}{4}$ cup of milk and $\frac{1}{8}$ cup of yogurt in a recipe. Which statement correctly compares the fractions?

   (A) $\frac{3}{4} < \frac{1}{8}$ (C) $\frac{3}{4} = \frac{1}{8}$

   (B) $\frac{3}{4} > \frac{1}{8}$ (D) $\frac{1}{8} > \frac{3}{4}$

4. In a parade, $\frac{2}{6}$ of the floats have musicians on them. In the same parade, $\frac{4}{12}$ of the floats have animals on them. Which statement correctly compares the fractions?

   (A) $\frac{2}{6} > \frac{4}{12}$ (C) $\frac{4}{12} > \frac{2}{6}$

   (B) $\frac{2}{6} < \frac{4}{12}$ (D) $\frac{4}{12} = \frac{2}{6}$

Problem Solving REAL WORLD

5. A recipe uses $\frac{2}{3}$ cup of flour and $\frac{5}{8}$ cup of blueberries. Is there more flour or more blueberries in the recipe?

6. Peggy completed $\frac{5}{6}$ of the math homework and Al completed $\frac{4}{5}$ of the math homework. Did Peggy or Al complete more of the math homework?

Compare and Order Fractions

Write $\frac{3}{8}$, $\frac{1}{4}$, and $\frac{1}{2}$ in order from least to greatest.

Step 1 Identify a common denominator.	Multiples of 8: ⑧, 16, 24
	Multiples of 4: 4, ⑧, 16,
	Multiples of 2: 2, 4, 6, ⑧
	Use 8 as a common denominator.
Step 2 Use the common denominator to write equivalent fractions.	$\frac{3}{8}$
	$\frac{1}{4} = \frac{1 \times 2}{4 \times 2} = \frac{2}{8}$
	$\frac{1}{2} = \frac{1 \times 4}{2 \times 4} = \frac{4}{8}$
Step 3 Compare the numerators.	$2 < 3 < 4$
Step 4 Order the fractions from least to greatest, using $<$ or $>$ symbols. So, $\frac{1}{4} < \frac{3}{8} < \frac{1}{2}$.	$\frac{2}{8} < \frac{3}{8} < \frac{4}{8}$

Write the fraction with the greatest value.

1. $\frac{2}{3}$, $\frac{1}{4}$, $\frac{1}{6}$

2. $\frac{3}{10}$, $\frac{1}{2}$, $\frac{2}{5}$

3. $\frac{1}{8}$, $\frac{5}{12}$, $\frac{9}{10}$

_____   _____   _____

Write the fractions in order from least to greatest.

4. $\frac{9}{10}$, $\frac{1}{2}$, $\frac{4}{5}$

5. $\frac{3}{4}$, $\frac{7}{8}$, $\frac{1}{2}$

6. $\frac{2}{3}$, $\frac{3}{4}$, $\frac{5}{6}$

_____   _____   _____

1. Jeff is making muffins. He combines $\frac{1}{6}$ cup milk, $\frac{1}{8}$ cup raisins, and $\frac{1}{3}$ cup butter. Which list shows the amounts of ingredients in order from **least** to **greatest**?

   Ⓐ $\frac{1}{8}, \frac{1}{6}, \frac{1}{3}$

   Ⓑ $\frac{1}{8}, \frac{1}{3}, \frac{1}{6}$

   Ⓒ $\frac{1}{3}, \frac{1}{6}, \frac{1}{8}$

   Ⓓ $\frac{1}{3}, \frac{1}{8}, \frac{1}{6}$

2. Shing is wrapping gifts. He has $\frac{5}{6}$ yard of blue ribbon, $\frac{2}{4}$ yard of gold ribbon, and $\frac{5}{12}$ yard of pink ribbon. Which list shows the lengths of the ribbons in order from **least** to **greatest**?

   Ⓐ $\frac{2}{4}, \frac{5}{12}, \frac{5}{6}$

   Ⓑ $\frac{5}{12}, \frac{2}{4}, \frac{5}{6}$

   Ⓒ $\frac{2}{4}, \frac{5}{6}, \frac{5}{12}$

   Ⓓ $\frac{5}{6}, \frac{2}{4}, \frac{5}{12}$

3. Mr. Adams is driving Betsy, Ed, and Beth home from the mall. Betsy lives $\frac{1}{4}$ mile from the mall. Ed lives $\frac{2}{3}$ mile from the mall, and Beth lives $\frac{1}{2}$ mile from the mall. Which list shows the distances in order from **closest** to **farthest**?

   Ⓐ $\frac{1}{4}, \frac{2}{3}, \frac{1}{2}$

   Ⓑ $\frac{1}{4}, \frac{1}{2}, \frac{2}{3}$

   Ⓒ $\frac{1}{2}, \frac{1}{4}, \frac{2}{3}$

   Ⓓ $\frac{2}{3}, \frac{1}{2}, \frac{1}{4}$

4. Katie is making necklaces. She has $\frac{1}{3}$ yard of blue ribbon, $\frac{3}{4}$ yard of pink ribbon, and $\frac{7}{8}$ yard of green ribbon. Which list shows the lengths of the ribbons in order from **least** to **greatest**?

   Ⓐ $\frac{7}{8}, \frac{1}{3}, \frac{3}{4}$

   Ⓑ $\frac{7}{8}, \frac{3}{4}, \frac{1}{3}$

   Ⓒ $\frac{1}{3}, \frac{3}{4}, \frac{7}{8}$

   Ⓓ $\frac{3}{4}, \frac{7}{8}, \frac{1}{3}$

5. Three friends shared a loaf of garlic bread. Ray ate $\frac{2}{6}$ of the loaf, Jay ate $\frac{5}{12}$ of the loaf, and Kay ate $\frac{1}{4}$ of the loaf. List the names in order of **least** to **greatest** amount of the loaf eaten. Explain how you know.

   _____

   _____

   _____

   _____

Name _____

Lesson 55

COMMON CORE STANDARD CC.4.NF.3a

Lesson Objective: Understand that to add or subtract fractions, they must refer to parts of the same wholes.

Add and Subtract Parts of a Whole

Justin has $\frac{3}{8}$ pound of cheddar cheese and $\frac{2}{8}$ pound of brick cheese. How much cheese does he have in all?

Step 1 Use fraction strips to model the problem. Use three $\frac{1}{8}$-strips to represent $\frac{3}{8}$ pound of cheddar cheese.

Step 2 Join two more $\frac{1}{8}$-strips to represent the amount of brick cheese.

Step 3 Count the number of $\frac{1}{8}$-strips. There are

_____five_____ $\frac{1}{8}$-strips. Write the amount as a

fraction. Justin has ___$\frac{5}{8}$___ pound of cheese.

Step 4 Use the model to write an equation.

$$\frac{3}{8} + \frac{2}{8} = \frac{5}{8}$$

Suppose Justin eats $\frac{1}{8}$ pound of cheese. How much cheese is left?

Step 1 Use five $\frac{1}{8}$-strips to represent the $\frac{5}{8}$ pound of cheese.

Step 2 Remove one $\frac{1}{8}$-strip to show the amount eaten.

Step 3 Count the number of $\frac{1}{8}$-strips left. There are

_____four_____ $\frac{1}{8}$ fraction strips. There is ___$\frac{4}{8}$___ pound left.

Step 4 Write an equation for the model.

$$\frac{5}{8} - \frac{1}{8} = \frac{4}{8}$$

Use the model to write an equation.

1.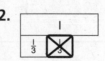

_____

2.

_____

3.

_____

4.

_____

Use the fraction model for 1–2.

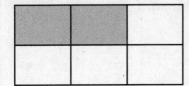

Use the fraction model for 3–4.

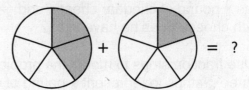

1. Ed cuts a pan of lasagna into 6 equal pieces. He serves 2 of the pieces for dinner. What fraction describes the part of the lasagna Ed serves?

   (A) $\frac{4}{6}$ (C) $\frac{2}{4}$

   (B) $\frac{1}{4}$ (D) $\frac{2}{6}$

3. Which equation represents the shaded parts of the model?

   (A) $\frac{5}{5} + \frac{5}{5} = \frac{10}{5}$

   (B) $\frac{3}{5} + \frac{4}{5} = \frac{5}{5}$

   (C) $\frac{2}{5} + \frac{1}{5} = \frac{3}{5}$

   (D) $\frac{1}{5} + \frac{1}{5} = \frac{2}{5}$

2. The next day, Ed serves 3 leftover pieces of lasagna. What fraction describes the part of the lasagna that still remains?

   (A) $\frac{1}{6}$ (C) $\frac{1}{2}$

   (B) $\frac{4}{6}$ (D) $\frac{5}{6}$

4. For the circle on the left, which equation shows the part of the circle that remains if the gray parts are removed?

   (A) $\frac{5}{5} - \frac{1}{5} = \frac{4}{5}$

   (B) $\frac{5}{5} - \frac{2}{5} = \frac{3}{5}$

   (C) $\frac{5}{5} - \frac{3}{5} = \frac{2}{5}$

   (D) $\frac{10}{5} - \frac{2}{5} = \frac{8}{5}$

5. Look at the fraction models. Write one statement about how the shaded parts are **alike**. Write one statement about how they are **different**.

_____

_____

_____

_____

Lesson 56

COMMON CORE STANDARD CC.4.NF.3b

Lesson Objective: Decompose a fraction by writing it as a sum of fractions with the same denominators.

Write Fractions as Sums

A **unit fraction** tells the part of the whole that 1 piece represents.
A unit fraction always has a numerator of 1.

Bryan has $\frac{4}{10}$ pound of clay for making clay figures. He wants
to use $\frac{1}{10}$ pound of clay for each figure. How many clay figures can he make?

Use fraction strips to write $\frac{4}{10}$ as a sum of unit fractions.

Step 1 Represent $\frac{4}{10}$ with fraction strips.

Step 2 Each $\frac{1}{10}$ is a unit fraction. Write a $\frac{1}{10}$ addend
for each $\frac{1}{10}$-strip you used to show $\frac{4}{10}$.

Step 3 Count the number of addends. The number
of addends represents the number of clay
figures Bryan can make.

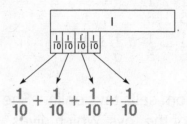

$$\frac{1}{10} + \frac{1}{10} + \frac{1}{10} + \frac{1}{10}$$

So, Bryan can make ____4____ clay figures.

Write the fraction as the sum of unit fractions.

1.

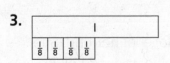

$\frac{3}{6} = $ ____ + ____ + ____

2.

$\frac{2}{4} = $ ____ + ____

3.

$\frac{4}{8} = $ ____ + ____ + ____ + ____

4.

$\frac{5}{5} = $ ____ + ____ + ____ + ____ + ____

1. Dillon's dad sells golf balls online. He sells $\frac{4}{5}$ of the golf balls. Which gives the sum of $\frac{4}{5}$?

   Ⓐ $\frac{1}{5} + \frac{1}{5} + \frac{1}{5}$

   Ⓑ $\frac{1}{5} + \frac{1}{5} + \frac{2}{5}$

   Ⓒ $\frac{2}{5} + \frac{2}{5} + \frac{1}{5}$

   Ⓓ $\frac{1}{5} + \frac{1}{5} + \frac{1}{5} + \frac{1}{5} + \frac{1}{5}$

2. Ellie's mom sells toys online. She sells $\frac{7}{10}$ of the toys. Which gives the sum of $\frac{7}{10}$?

   Ⓐ $\frac{1}{10} + \frac{1}{10} + \frac{1}{10} + \frac{1}{10} + \frac{2}{10}$

   Ⓑ $\frac{1}{10} + \frac{2}{10} + \frac{3}{10} + \frac{1}{10}$

   Ⓒ $\frac{2}{10} + \frac{2}{10} + \frac{2}{10} + \frac{2}{10}$

   Ⓓ $\frac{4}{10} + \frac{1}{10} + \frac{1}{10} + \frac{1}{10} + \frac{1}{10}$

3. Santos used a unit fraction to describe how much of his book he has read. Which fraction could Santos have used?

   Ⓐ $\frac{9}{10}$

   Ⓑ $\frac{4}{5}$

   Ⓒ $\frac{5}{8}$

   Ⓓ $\frac{1}{3}$

4. Dawn used a unit fraction to describe how much of her chores she has done. Which fraction could Dawn have used?

   Ⓐ $\frac{7}{8}$

   Ⓑ $\frac{3}{10}$

   Ⓒ $\frac{1}{6}$

   Ⓓ $\frac{3}{24}$

Problem Solving REAL WORLD

5. Miguel's teacher asks him to color $\frac{4}{8}$ of his grid. He must use 3 colors: red, blue, and green. There must be more green sections than red sections. How can Miguel color the sections of his grid to follow all the rules?

   _____

   _____

   _____

6. Petra is asked to color $\frac{6}{6}$ of her grid. She must use 3 colors: blue, red, and pink. There must be more blue sections than red sections or pink sections. What are the different ways Petra can color the sections of her grid and follow all the rules?

   _____

   _____

   _____

Name _____

Lesson 57
COMMON CORE STANDARD CC.4.NF.3b
Lesson Objective: Write fractions greater than 1 as mixed numbers and write mixed numbers as fractions greater than 1.

Rename Fractions and Mixed Numbers

A **mixed number** is made up of a whole number and a fraction. You can use multiplication and addition to rename a mixed number as a fraction greater than 1.

Rename $2\frac{5}{6}$ as a fraction.

First, multiply the denominator, or the number of parts in the whole, by the whole number.

$6 \times 2 = 12$

Then, add the numerator to your product.

$12 + 5 = 17$

So, $2\frac{5}{6} = \frac{17}{6}$.

$$2\frac{5}{6} = \frac{\boxed{17}}{6}$$

total number of parts
number of parts in the whole

You can use division to write a fraction greater than 1 as a mixed number.

Rename $\frac{16}{3}$ as a mixed number.

To rename $\frac{16}{3}$ as a mixed number, divide the numerator by the denominator.

Use the quotient and remainder to write a mixed number.

$$\begin{array}{r} 5 \\ 3\overline{)16} \\ -15 \\ \hline 1 \end{array}$$

So, $\frac{16}{3} = 5\frac{1}{3}$.

Write the mixed number as a fraction.

1. $3\frac{2}{3} =$ _____

2. $4\frac{3}{5} =$ _____

3. $4\frac{3}{8} =$ _____

4. $2\frac{1}{6} =$ _____

Write the fraction as a mixed number.

5. $\frac{32}{5} =$ _____

6. $\frac{19}{3} =$ _____

7. $\frac{15}{4} =$ _____

8. $\frac{51}{10} =$ _____

1. Wanda rode her bike $\frac{21}{10}$ miles. Which mixed number shows how far Wanda rode her bike?

   (A) $1\frac{1}{10}$ miles

   (B) $1\frac{2}{10}$ miles

   (C) $2\frac{1}{10}$ miles

   (D) $2\frac{10}{10}$ miles

2. Ilene is making smoothies. The recipe calls for $1\frac{1}{4}$ cups of strawberries. What is this amount written as a fraction greater than one?

   (A) $\frac{4}{5}$ cup

   (B) $\frac{5}{4}$ cups

   (C) $\frac{6}{4}$ cups

   (D) $\frac{11}{4}$ cups

3. Lee's vacation is in $3\frac{4}{7}$ weeks. Which shows the number of weeks until Lee's vacation written as a fraction greater than one?

   (A) $\frac{34}{7}$

   (B) $\frac{25}{7}$

   (C) $\frac{24}{7}$

   (D) $\frac{14}{7}$

4. Derek and his friend shared two small pizzas. Derek ate $\frac{7}{6}$ of the pizzas. Which mixed number shows how much pizza Derek ate?

   (A) $1\frac{1}{6}$

   (B) $1\frac{3}{6}$

   (C) $1\frac{4}{6}$

   (D) $2\frac{1}{6}$

Problem Solving REAL WORLD

5. A recipe calls for $2\frac{2}{4}$ cups of raisins, but Julie only has a $\frac{1}{4}$-cup measuring cup. How many $\frac{1}{4}$ cups does Julie need to measure out $2\frac{2}{4}$ cups of raisins?

6. If Julie needs $3\frac{1}{4}$ cups of oatmeal, how many $\frac{1}{4}$ cups of oatmeal will she use?

Add and Subtract Mixed Numbers

Find the sum. $3\frac{1}{4} + 2\frac{1}{4}$

Add the whole number and fraction parts.

• Add the whole numbers: $3 + 2 = 5$
• Add the fractions: $\frac{1}{4} + \frac{1}{4} = \frac{2}{4}$

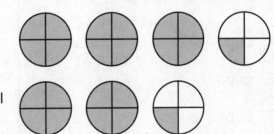

Write the sum as a mixed number, so the fractional

part is less than 1. $3\frac{1}{4} + 2\frac{1}{4} = 5\frac{2}{4}$

Find the difference. $4\frac{5}{8} - 3\frac{1}{8}$

Subtract the fraction and the
whole number parts.

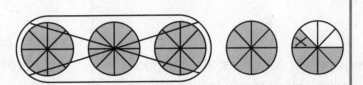

• Subtract the fractions: $\frac{5}{8} - \frac{1}{8} = \frac{4}{8}$
• Subtract the whole numbers:
  $4 - 3 = 1$

$4\frac{5}{8} - 3\frac{1}{8} = 1\frac{4}{8}$

Find the sum or difference.

1. $3\frac{4}{5}$
   $+ 4\frac{3}{5}$
   _____

2. $7\frac{2}{3}$
   $- 3\frac{1}{3}$
   _____

3. $4\frac{7}{12}$
   $+ 6\frac{5}{12}$
   _____

4. $12\frac{3}{4}$
   $- 6\frac{1}{4}$
   _____

5. $2\frac{3}{8}$
   $+ 8\frac{1}{8}$
   _____

6. $11\frac{9}{10}$
   $- 3\frac{7}{10}$
   _____

7. $7\frac{3}{5}$
   $+ 4\frac{3}{5}$
   _____

8. $8\frac{3}{6}$
   $- 3\frac{1}{6}$
   _____

1. Sue used $2\frac{3}{8}$ cups of walnuts and $1\frac{2}{8}$ cups of almonds to make a nut mix. How many more cups of walnuts than almonds did Sue use?

   (A) $\frac{1}{8}$ cup

   (B) $1\frac{1}{8}$ cups

   (C) $3\frac{1}{8}$ cups

   (D) $3\frac{5}{8}$ cups

2. Paige hiked $5\frac{5}{6}$ miles. Xavier hiked $2\frac{1}{6}$ miles. How many fewer miles did Xavier hike than Paige?

   (A) $2\frac{1}{6}$ miles

   (B) $3\frac{2}{6}$ miles

   (C) $3\frac{4}{6}$ miles

   (D) 8 miles

3. Kate has two lengths of ribbon. The pink ribbon is $4\frac{6}{12}$ feet long, and the purple ribbon is $2\frac{4}{12}$ feet long. How much ribbon does Kate have in all?

   (A) $\frac{10}{12}$ foot

   (B) $2\frac{2}{12}$ feet

   (C) $6\frac{10}{12}$ feet

   (D) $6\frac{11}{12}$ feet

4. Max used $3\frac{7}{8}$ pounds of yellow potatoes and $2\frac{5}{8}$ pounds of sweet potatoes to make a potato salad. How many more pounds of yellow potatoes than sweet potatoes did Max use?

   (A) $6\frac{4}{8}$ pounds

   (B) $5\frac{2}{8}$ pounds

   (C) $1\frac{2}{4}$ pounds

   (D) $1\frac{2}{8}$ pounds

Problem Solving REAL WORLD

5. James wants to send two gifts by mail. The first package weighs $2\frac{3}{4}$ pounds. The other package weighs $1\frac{3}{4}$ pounds. What is the total weight of the packages?

6. Tierra bought $4\frac{3}{8}$ yards blue ribbon and $2\frac{1}{8}$ yards yellow ribbon for a craft project. How much more blue ribbon than yellow ribbon did Tierra buy?

Name _____

Lesson 59
COMMON CORE STANDARD CC.4.NF.3c
Lesson Objective: Rename mixed numbers to subtract.

Subtraction with Renaming

Fraction strips can help you subtract mixed numbers or subtract a mixed number from a whole number.

Find the difference. $3\frac{1}{3} - 2\frac{2}{3}$

Step 1 Model the number you are subtracting from, $3\frac{1}{3}$.

Step 2 Because you cannot subtract $\frac{2}{3}$ from $\frac{1}{3}$ without renaming, change one of the 1 strips to three $\frac{1}{3}$ strips. Then subtract by crossing out two wholes and two $\frac{1}{3}$ strips.

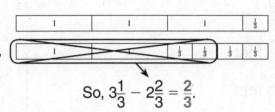

So, $3\frac{1}{3} - 2\frac{2}{3} = \frac{2}{3}$.

Find the difference. $2 - 1\frac{1}{4}$

Step 1 Model the number you are subtracting from, 2.

Step 2 Because you cannot subtract $\frac{1}{4}$ from 1 without renaming, change one of the 1 strips to four $\frac{1}{4}$ strips. Then subtract by crossing out one whole and one $\frac{1}{4}$ strip.

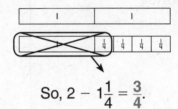

So, $2 - 1\frac{1}{4} = \frac{3}{4}$.

Find the difference.

1. $3 - 2\frac{2}{5} =$ _____

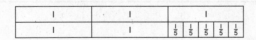

2. $2\frac{1}{4} - 1\frac{3}{4} =$ _____

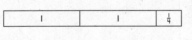

3. $3\frac{3}{5}$
  $-2\frac{4}{5}$
  _____

4. $3\frac{1}{12}$
  $-2\frac{11}{12}$
  _____

5. $4\frac{5}{8}$
  $-2\frac{7}{8}$
  _____

1. Thomas got $9\frac{1}{3}$ feet of wood to fix his fence. When he finished, he had $3\frac{2}{3}$ feet of wood left. How much wood did Thomas use to fix his fence?

   Ⓐ $5\frac{1}{3}$ feet

   Ⓑ $5\frac{2}{3}$ feet

   Ⓒ $6\frac{1}{3}$ feet

   Ⓓ $6\frac{2}{3}$ feet

2. SuLee has $8\frac{1}{4}$ yards of blue fabric and $4\frac{2}{4}$ yards of green fabric. How much more blue fabric does SuLee have than green fabric?

   Ⓐ $3\frac{1}{4}$ yards

   Ⓑ $3\frac{3}{4}$ yards

   Ⓒ $4\frac{1}{4}$ yards

   Ⓓ $4\frac{3}{4}$ yards

3. Alicia had $3\frac{1}{6}$ yards of fabric to make a tablecloth. When she finished the tablecloth, she had $1\frac{4}{6}$ yards of fabric left. How many yards of fabric did Alicia use to make the tablecloth?

   Ⓐ $1\frac{3}{6}$ yards

   Ⓑ $2\frac{3}{6}$ yards

   Ⓒ $2\frac{5}{6}$ yards

   Ⓓ $4\frac{5}{6}$ yards

4. Gina has $5\frac{2}{6}$ feet of silver ribbon and $2\frac{4}{6}$ feet of gold ribbon. How much more silver ribbon does Gina have than gold ribbon?

   Ⓐ 8

   Ⓑ $3\frac{4}{6}$

   Ⓒ $3\frac{2}{6}$

   Ⓓ $2\frac{4}{6}$

Problem Solving REAL WORLD

5. Alicia buys a 5-pound bag of rocks for a fish tank. She uses $1\frac{1}{8}$ pounds for a small fish bowl. How much is left?

6. Xavier made 25 pounds of roasted almonds for a fair. He has $3\frac{1}{2}$ pounds left at the end of the fair. How many pounds of roasted almonds did he sell at the fair?

Lesson 60

COMMON CORE STANDARD CC.4.NF.3c

Lesson Objective: Use the properties of addition to add fractions.

Algebra • Fractions and Properties of Addition

Properties of addition can help you group and order addends so you can use mental math to find sums.

The **Commutative Property of Addition** states that when the order of two addends is changed, the sum is the same. $6 + 3 = 3 + 6$

The **Associative Property of Addition** states that when the grouping of addends is changed, the sum is the same. $(3 + 6) + 4 = 3 + (6 + 4)$

Use the properties and mental math to add $10\frac{3}{8} + 4\frac{7}{8} + 6\frac{5}{8}$.

Step 1 Look for fractions that combine to make 1. $10\frac{3}{8} + 4\frac{7}{8} + 6\frac{5}{8}$

Step 2 Use the Commutative Property to order the addends so that the fractions with a sum of 1 are together. $10\frac{3}{8} + 4\frac{7}{8} + 6\frac{5}{8} = 10\frac{3}{8} + 6\frac{5}{8} + 4\frac{7}{8}$

Step 3 Use the Associative Property to group the addends that you can add mentally. $= \left(10\frac{3}{8} + 6\frac{5}{8}\right) + 4\frac{7}{8}$

Step 4 Add the grouped numbers and then add the other mixed number. $= (17) + 4\frac{7}{8}$

Step 5 Write the sum. $= 21\frac{7}{8}$

Use the properties and mental math to find the sum.

1. $\left(3\frac{1}{5} + 1\frac{2}{5}\right) + 4\frac{4}{5}$

2. $\left(5\frac{7}{10} + 1\frac{4}{10}\right) + 6\frac{3}{10}$

3. $7\frac{3}{4} + \left(5 + 3\frac{1}{4}\right)$

_____

_____

_____

4. $\left(2\frac{5}{12} + 3\frac{11}{12}\right) + 1\frac{7}{12}$

5. $4\frac{7}{8} + \left(6\frac{3}{8} + \frac{1}{8}\right)$

6. $9\frac{2}{6} + \left(4\frac{1}{6} + 7\frac{4}{6}\right)$

_____

_____

_____

1. To get the correct color, Johan mixed $3\frac{1}{4}$ quarts of white paint, $1\frac{2}{4}$ quarts of blue paint, and $2\frac{3}{4}$ quarts of green paint. How much paint did Johan mix?

   (A) $6\frac{2}{4}$ quarts   (C) 7 quarts

   (B) $6\frac{3}{4}$ quarts   (D) $7\frac{2}{4}$ quarts

2. Kinsey recorded the amount of time she spent swimming during 3 days.

   Times Spent Swimming

Day	Mon	Wed	Fri
Time (in hours)	$1\frac{5}{6}$	$2\frac{2}{6}$	$2\frac{1}{6}$

   What is the total number of hours Kinsey spent swimming?

   (A) $5\frac{2}{6}$ hours   (C) $6\frac{2}{6}$ hours

   (B) $5\frac{5}{6}$ hours   (D) $6\frac{8}{6}$ hours

3. Bobby biked $1\frac{2}{3}$ hours on Monday, $2\frac{1}{3}$ hours on Tuesday, and $2\frac{2}{3}$ hours on Wednesday. What is the total number of hours Bobby spent biking?

   (A) $5\frac{2}{3}$ hours   (C) $6\frac{1}{3}$ hours

   (B) 6 hours   (D) $6\frac{2}{3}$ hours

4. Hector recorded the amount of time he spent running during 3 days.

   Times Spent Running

Day	Tue	Wed	Thu
Time (in hours)	$1\frac{6}{12}$	$2\frac{1}{12}$	$1\frac{9}{12}$

   What is the total number of hours Hector spent running?

   (A) $4\frac{4}{12}$ hours   (C) $5\frac{5}{12}$ hours

   (B) $5\frac{4}{12}$ hours   (D) $5\frac{16}{12}$ hours

Problem Solving REAL WORLD

5. Nate's classroom has three tables of different lengths. One has a length of $4\frac{1}{2}$ feet, another has a length of 4 feet, and a third has a length of $2\frac{1}{2}$ feet. What is the length of all three tables when pushed end to end?

6. Mr. Warren uses $2\frac{1}{4}$ bags of mulch for his garden and another $4\frac{1}{4}$ bags for his front yard. He also uses $\frac{3}{4}$ bag around a fountain. How many total bags of mulch does Mr. Warren use?

Name _____

Lesson 61

COMMON CORE STANDARD CC.4.NF.3d

Lesson Objective: Use models to represent and find sums involving fractions.

Add Fractions Using Models

Fractions with like denominators have the same denominator. You can add fractions with like denominators using a number line.

Model $\frac{4}{6} + \frac{1}{6}$.

Step 1 Draw a number line labeled with sixths. Model the fraction $\frac{4}{6}$ by starting at 0 and shading 4 sixths.

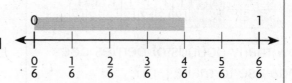

Step 2 Add the fraction $\frac{1}{6}$ by shading 1 more sixth.

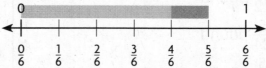

Step 3 How many sixths are there in all? **5** sixths

Write the number of sixths as a fraction.

$$5 \text{ sixths} = \frac{5}{6} \qquad \frac{4}{6} + \frac{1}{6} = \frac{5}{6}$$

1. Model $\frac{1}{5} + \frac{4}{5}$.

$$\frac{1}{5} + \frac{4}{5} = \underline{\hspace{3cm}}$$

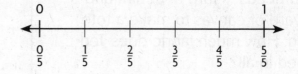

Find the sum. Use a model to help.

2. $\frac{2}{10} + \frac{4}{10}$

_____

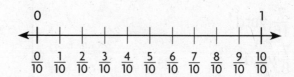

3. $\frac{1}{4} + \frac{1}{4}$

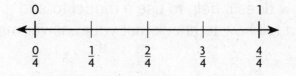

_____

1. Linda uses $\frac{3}{12}$ pound of strawberries and $\frac{2}{12}$ pound of blueberries to make jam.

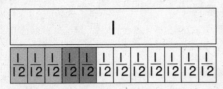

How many pounds of berries does Linda use to make jam?

Ⓐ $\frac{1}{12}$ pound

Ⓑ $\frac{5}{24}$ pound

Ⓒ $\frac{5}{12}$ pound

Ⓓ $\frac{1}{2}$ pound

2. Ted needs $\frac{5}{8}$ yard of denim and $\frac{2}{8}$ yard of canvas to make a tote bag. How much fabric does Ted need in all?

Ⓐ $\frac{1}{8}$ yard

Ⓑ $\frac{3}{8}$ yard

Ⓒ $\frac{7}{16}$ yard

Ⓓ $\frac{7}{8}$ yard

3. In a survey, $\frac{3}{6}$ of the students chose summer as their favorite season and $\frac{1}{6}$ chose winter. What fraction of the students surveyed chose summer or winter?

Ⓐ $\frac{1}{6}$

Ⓑ $\frac{2}{6}$

Ⓒ $\frac{4}{12}$

Ⓓ $\frac{4}{6}$

4. A painter mixed $\frac{1}{4}$ quart of red paint with $\frac{3}{4}$ quart of blue paint to make purple paint.

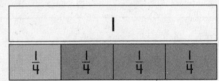

How much purple paint did the painter make?

Ⓐ $1\frac{3}{4}$ quarts

Ⓑ 1 quart

Ⓒ $\frac{2}{4}$ quart

Ⓓ $\frac{4}{8}$ quart

5. How does it help to use a model to add $\frac{3}{8}$ and $\frac{2}{8}$? Explain, and tell how to check that your answer makes sense.

_____

_____

_____

Name _____

Lesson 62

COMMON CORE STANDARD CC.4.NF.3d

Lesson Objective: Use models to represent and find differences involving fractions.

Subtract Fractions Using Models

You can subtract fractions with like denominators using fraction strips.

Model $\frac{5}{8} - \frac{2}{8}$.

Step 1 Shade the eighths you start with.
Shade 5 eighths.

1
$\frac{1}{8}$ $\frac{1}{8}$ $\frac{1}{8}$ $\frac{1}{8}$ $\frac{1}{8}$ $\frac{1}{8}$ $\frac{1}{8}$ $\frac{1}{8}$

Step 2 Subtract $\frac{2}{8}$.

Think: How many eighths are taken away?
Cross out 2 of the shaded eighths.

1
$\frac{1}{8}$ $\frac{1}{8}$ $\frac{1}{8}$ $\frac{1}{8}$ $\frac{1}{8}$ $\frac{1}{8}$ $\frac{1}{8}$ $\frac{1}{8}$

Step 3 Count the shaded eighths that remain.
There are 3 eighths remaining.

Step 4 Write the number of eighths that remain as a fraction.

3 eighths $= \frac{3}{8}$ $\frac{5}{8} - \frac{2}{8} = \frac{3}{8}$

1. Model $\frac{3}{3} - \frac{2}{3}$.

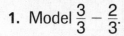

1		
$\frac{1}{3}$	$\frac{1}{3}$	$\frac{1}{3}$

$\frac{3}{3} - \frac{2}{3} =$ _____

Subtract. Use fraction strips to help.

2. $\frac{5}{6} - \frac{1}{6}$

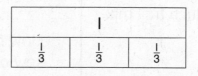

1					
$\frac{1}{6}$	$\frac{1}{6}$	$\frac{1}{6}$	$\frac{1}{6}$	$\frac{1}{6}$	$\frac{1}{6}$

3. $\frac{6}{10} - \frac{3}{10}$

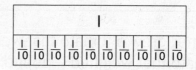

1									
$\frac{1}{10}$	$\frac{1}{10}$	$\frac{1}{10}$	$\frac{1}{10}$	$\frac{1}{10}$	$\frac{1}{10}$	$\frac{1}{10}$	$\frac{1}{10}$	$\frac{1}{10}$	$\frac{1}{10}$

$\frac{5}{6} - \frac{1}{6} =$ _____ $\frac{6}{10} - \frac{3}{10} =$ _____

Name _____

1. Ellen sewed $\frac{5}{8}$ yard of fringe on her scarf. Ling sewed $\frac{2}{8}$ yard of fringe on her scarf.

1							
$\frac{1}{8}$	$\frac{1}{8}$	$\frac{1}{8}$	$\frac{1}{8}$	$\frac{1}{8}$	$\frac{1}{8}$	$\frac{1}{8}$	$\frac{1}{8}$

How much more fringe did Ellen sew on her scarf than Ling?

Ⓐ $\frac{1}{8}$ yard

Ⓑ $\frac{2}{8}$ yard

Ⓒ $\frac{3}{8}$ yard

Ⓓ $\frac{7}{8}$ yard

2. Betsy brought $\frac{6}{12}$ pound of trail mix on a camping trip. She ate $\frac{4}{12}$ pound of the trail mix. How much trail mix was left?

Ⓐ $\frac{1}{12}$ pound   Ⓒ $\frac{3}{12}$ pound

Ⓑ $\frac{2}{12}$ pound   Ⓓ $\frac{10}{12}$ pound

3. Ryan has two pet hamsters. One hamster weighs $\frac{3}{10}$ pound. The other hamster weighs $\frac{4}{10}$ pound. What is the difference in the weights of Ryan's hamsters?

Ⓐ $\frac{1}{10}$ pound

Ⓑ $\frac{2}{10}$ pound

Ⓒ $\frac{7}{10}$ pound

Ⓓ $\frac{12}{10}$ pounds

4. Keiko sewed $\frac{3}{4}$ yard of lace on her backpack. Pam sewed $\frac{1}{4}$ yard of lace on her backpack.

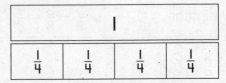

1			
$\frac{1}{4}$	$\frac{1}{4}$	$\frac{1}{4}$	$\frac{1}{4}$

How much more lace did Keiko sew on her backpack than Pam?

Ⓐ $\frac{4}{4}$ yard   Ⓒ $\frac{2}{4}$ yard

Ⓑ $\frac{3}{4}$ yard   Ⓓ $\frac{1}{4}$ yard

5. Homer grew a tomato that weighed $\frac{7}{8}$ pound. Ruth grew a tomato that weighed $\frac{4}{8}$ pound. Whose tomato weighed more? How many more pounds did it weigh? Explain how you know.

_____

_____

_____

_____

Name _____

Lesson 63
COMMON CORE STANDARD CC.4.NF.3d
Lesson Objective: Solve word problems involving addition and subtraction with fractions.

Add and Subtract Fractions

You can find and record the sums and the differences of fractions.

Add. $\dfrac{2}{6} + \dfrac{4}{6}$

Step 1 Model it.	**Step 2** Think: How many sixths are there in all?	**Step 3** Record it.
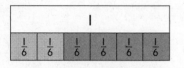	There are **6** sixths. 6 sixths $= \dfrac{6}{6}$	Write the sum as an addition equation. $\dfrac{2}{6} + \dfrac{4}{6} = \dfrac{6}{6}$

Subtract. $\dfrac{6}{10} - \dfrac{2}{10}$

Step 1 Model it.	**Step 2** Think: There are 6 tenths. I take away 2 tenths. How many tenths are left?	**Step 3** Record it.
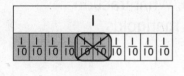	There are **4** tenths left. 4 tenths $= \dfrac{4}{10}$	Write the difference as a subtraction equation. $\dfrac{6}{10} - \dfrac{2}{10} = \dfrac{4}{10}$

Find the sum or difference.

1. 7 eighth-size parts − 4 eighth-size parts = _____

   $\dfrac{7}{8} - \dfrac{4}{8} =$ _____

2. $\dfrac{11}{12} - \dfrac{4}{12} =$ _____

3. $\dfrac{2}{10} + \dfrac{2}{10} =$ _____

4. $\dfrac{6}{8} - \dfrac{4}{8} =$ _____

5. $\dfrac{2}{4} + \dfrac{2}{4} =$ _____

6. $\dfrac{4}{5} - \dfrac{3}{5} =$ _____

7. $\dfrac{1}{3} + \dfrac{2}{3} =$ _____

1. Mindi planted beans in $\frac{4}{10}$ of her garden and peas in $\frac{5}{10}$ of her garden. What fraction of the garden has beans or peas?

   (A) $\frac{1}{10}$

   (B) $\frac{9}{20}$

   (C) $\frac{8}{10}$

   (D) $\frac{9}{10}$

2. Harrison ate $\frac{3}{12}$ of a pizza. Miles ate $\frac{5}{12}$ of the same pizza. How much more of the pizza did Miles eat than Harrison?

   (A) $\frac{1}{12}$

   (B) $\frac{2}{12}$

   (C) $\frac{4}{12}$

   (D) $\frac{8}{12}$

3. Miguel is going to sell pet treats at the school fair. He made $\frac{3}{8}$ of the treats for dogs and $\frac{2}{8}$ of the treats for cats. The rest of the treats are for other types of pets. What fraction of the pet treats is for cats or dogs?

   (A) $\frac{1}{8}$

   (B) $\frac{2}{8}$

   (C) $\frac{5}{8}$

   (D) $\frac{7}{8}$

4. Teresa planted marigolds in $\frac{1}{6}$ of her garden and petunias in $\frac{4}{6}$ of her garden. What fraction of the garden has marigolds or petunias?

   (A) $\frac{6}{6}$

   (B) $\frac{5}{6}$

   (C) $\frac{5}{12}$

   (D) $\frac{1}{6}$

5. Don writes $\frac{6}{10} - \frac{3}{10} = \frac{9}{10}$. Is his answer correct? Explain, and tell how you find the correct answer if Don is wrong.

_____

_____

_____

_____

_____

_____

Name _____

Lesson 64

COMMON CORE STANDARD CC.4.NF.3d

Lesson Objective: Use the strategy *act it out* to solve multistep fraction problems.

Problem Solving • Multistep Fraction Problems

Jeff runs $\frac{3}{5}$ mile each day. He wants to know how many days he has to run before he has run a whole number of miles.

Read the Problem	Solve the Problem
What do I need to find? I need to find <u>how many days Jeff</u> <u>needs to run $\frac{3}{5}$ mile</u> until he has run a whole number of miles.	**Describe how to act it out.** **Use a number line.** Day 1: $\frac{3}{5}$ mile Day 2: $\frac{6}{5}$ mile $\underline{\frac{3}{5}} + \underline{\frac{3}{5}} = \underline{\frac{6}{5}}$ $\quad$ 1 whole mile and $\frac{1}{5}$ mile more Day 3: $\frac{9}{5}$ mile $\underline{\frac{3}{5}} + \underline{\frac{3}{5}} + \underline{\frac{3}{5}} = \underline{\frac{9}{5}}$ $\quad$ 1 whole mile and $\frac{4}{5}$ mile more Day 4: $\frac{12}{5}$ mile $\underline{\frac{3}{5}} + \underline{\frac{3}{5}} + \underline{\frac{3}{5}} + \underline{\frac{3}{5}} = \underline{\frac{12}{5}}$ $\quad$ 2 whole miles and $\frac{2}{5}$ mile more Day 5: $\frac{15}{5}$ mile $\underline{\frac{3}{5}} + \underline{\frac{3}{5}} + \underline{\frac{3}{5}} + \underline{\frac{3}{5}} + \underline{\frac{3}{5}} = \underline{\frac{15}{5}}$ $\quad$ 3 whole miles
What information do I need to use? Jeff runs $\underline{\frac{3}{5}}$ mile a day. He wants the distance run to be a <u>whole number</u>.	
How will I use the information? I can use a number line and <u>patterns</u> to <u>act out</u> the problem.	So, Jeff will run a total of <u>3</u> miles in <u>5</u> days.

1. Lena runs $\frac{2}{3}$ mile each day. She wants to know how many days she has to run before she has run a whole number of miles.

2. Mack is repackaging $\frac{6}{8}$-pound bags of birdseed into 1-pound bags of birdseed. What is the least number of $\frac{6}{8}$-pound bags of birdseed he needs in order to fill 1-pound bags without leftovers?

1. Ryan's collection is $\frac{3}{6}$ football cards and $\frac{2}{6}$ basketball cards. What part of Ryan's card collection is **not** football or basketball cards?

   Ⓐ $\frac{1}{6}$

   Ⓑ $\frac{5}{12}$

   Ⓒ $\frac{5}{6}$

   Ⓓ 1

2. Royce walks $\frac{3}{4}$ mile to school and $\frac{3}{4}$ mile home each day. In how many days will he have walked 3 miles?

   Ⓐ 8 days

   Ⓑ 6 days

   Ⓒ 4 days

   Ⓓ 2 days

3. Carson's album is $\frac{8}{12}$ vacation photos and $\frac{3}{12}$ holiday photos. What part of Carson's album is **not** vacation or holiday photos?

   Ⓐ 1

   Ⓑ $\frac{11}{12}$

   Ⓒ $\frac{5}{12}$

   Ⓓ $\frac{1}{12}$

4. A quarter is $\frac{1}{4}$ of a dollar. Victor has 32 quarters. How much money does he have?

   Ⓐ $16

   Ⓑ $8

   Ⓒ $6

   Ⓓ $5

5. Each day, Mrs. Hewes knits $\frac{1}{3}$ of a scarf in the morning and $\frac{1}{3}$ of a scarf in the afternoon. How many days will it take Mrs. Hewes to knit 2 scarves? Explain how you find the answer.

   _____

   _____

   _____

   _____

Name _____

Multiples of Unit Fractions

A unit fraction is a fraction with a numerator of 1. You can write a fraction as the product of a whole number and a unit fraction.

Write $\frac{7}{10}$ as the product of a whole number and a unit fraction.

Write $\frac{7}{10}$ as the sum of unit fractions.

$$\frac{7}{10} = \frac{1}{10} + \frac{1}{10} + \frac{1}{10} + \frac{1}{10} + \frac{1}{10} + \frac{1}{10} + \frac{1}{10}$$

Use multiplication to show repeated addition.

$$\frac{7}{10} = \underline{} 7 \times \frac{1}{10}$$

So, $\frac{7}{10} = \underline{} 7 \times \frac{1}{10}$.

The product of a number and a counting number is a multiple of the number. You can find multiples of unit fractions.

List the next 4 multiples of $\frac{1}{8}$.

Make a table and use repeated addition.

$1 \times \frac{1}{8}$	$2 \times \frac{1}{8}$	$3 \times \frac{1}{8}$	$4 \times \frac{1}{8}$	$5 \times \frac{1}{8}$
$\frac{1}{8}$	$\frac{1}{8} + \frac{1}{8}$	$\frac{1}{8} + \frac{1}{8} + \frac{1}{8}$	$\frac{1}{8} + \frac{1}{8} + \frac{1}{8} + \frac{1}{8}$	$\frac{1}{8} + \frac{1}{8} + \frac{1}{8} + \frac{1}{8} + \frac{1}{8}$
$\frac{1}{8}$	$\frac{2}{8}$	$\frac{3}{8}$	$\frac{4}{8}$	$\frac{5}{8}$

The next 4 multiples of $\frac{1}{8}$ are $\frac{2}{8}$, $\frac{3}{8}$, $\frac{4}{8}$, and $\frac{5}{8}$.

Write the fraction as the product of a whole number and a unit fraction.

1. $\frac{2}{5} =$ _____

2. $\frac{5}{12} =$ _____

3. $\frac{7}{2} =$ _____

List the next four multiples of the unit fraction.

4. $\frac{1}{4}$, ____, ____, ____, ____

5. $\frac{1}{6}$, ____, ____, ____, ____

1. Aaron made a list of some multiples of $\frac{1}{8}$. Which could be Aaron's list?

   (A) $\frac{1}{8}, \frac{1}{16}, \frac{1}{24}, \frac{1}{32}, \frac{1}{40}$

   (B) $\frac{1}{8}, \frac{2}{9}, \frac{3}{10}, \frac{4}{11}, \frac{5}{12}$

   (C) $\frac{1}{8}, \frac{2}{8}, \frac{3}{8}, \frac{4}{8}, \frac{5}{8}$

   (D) 1, 2, 3, 4, 5

2. Look at the number line. What fraction goes directly below the whole number 2?

   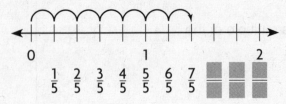

   (A) $\frac{3}{10}$

   (B) $\frac{3}{5}$

   (C) $\frac{8}{5}$

   (D) $\frac{10}{5}$

3. Sandi buys some fabric to make a quilt. She needs $\frac{1}{5}$ yard of each of 9 types of fabric. Sandi writes the following equation. What number goes in the box to make the statement true?

   $$\frac{9}{5} = \blacksquare \times \frac{1}{5}$$

   (A) 9   (C) 5

   (B) 8   (D) 4

4. A recipe for one dozen bran muffins needs $\frac{1}{3}$ cup of raisins.

Dozen	1	2	3	4	5	6	7	8
Cup(s) of Raisins	$\frac{1}{3}$	$\frac{2}{3}$	$\frac{3}{3}$					

   How many dozen bran muffins can be made with 2 cups of raisins?

   (A) 2   (C) 6

   (B) 4   (D) 8

Problem Solving REAL WORLD

5. So far, Monica has read $\frac{5}{6}$ of a book. She has read the same number of pages each day for 5 days. What fraction of the book does Monica read each day?

6. Nicholas buys $\frac{3}{8}$ pound of cheese. He puts the same amount of cheese on 3 sandwiches. How much cheese does Nicholas put on each sandwich?

Multiples of Fractions

Lesson Objective: Write a product of a whole number and a fraction as a product of a whole number and a unit fraction.

You have learned to write multiples of unit fractions. You can also write multiples of other fractions.

Write the next 4 multiples of $\frac{2}{5}$.

Make a table.

$1 \times \frac{2}{5}$	$2 \times \frac{2}{5}$	$3 \times \frac{2}{5}$	$4 \times \frac{2}{5}$	$5 \times \frac{2}{5}$
$\frac{2}{5}$	$\frac{2}{5} + \frac{2}{5}$	$\frac{2}{5} + \frac{2}{5} + \frac{2}{5}$	$\frac{2}{5} + \frac{2}{5} + \frac{2}{5} + \frac{2}{5}$	$\frac{2}{5} + \frac{2}{5} + \frac{2}{5} + \frac{2}{5} + \frac{2}{5}$
$\frac{2}{5}$	$\frac{4}{5}$	$\frac{6}{5}$	$\frac{8}{5}$	$\frac{10}{5}$

So, the next 4 multiples of $\frac{2}{5}$ are $\frac{4}{5}$, $\frac{6}{5}$, $\frac{8}{5}$, and $\frac{10}{5}$.

Write $3 \times \frac{2}{5}$ as the product of a whole number and a unit fraction.

Use a number line. Make three jumps of $\frac{2}{5}$.

$$3 \times \frac{2}{5} = \frac{6}{5}$$

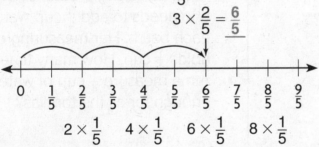

$2 \times \frac{1}{5} \qquad 4 \times \frac{1}{5} \qquad 6 \times \frac{1}{5} \qquad 8 \times \frac{1}{5}$

So, $3 \times \frac{2}{5} = \frac{6}{5}$, or $6 \times \frac{1}{5}$.

List the next four multiples of the fraction.

1. $\frac{3}{4}$, ____, ____, ____, ____

2. $\frac{5}{6}$, ____, ____, ____, ____

Write as the product of a whole number and a unit fraction.

3.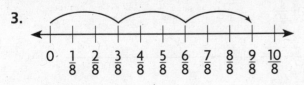

$3 \times \frac{3}{8} =$ _____

4.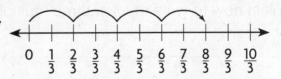

$4 \times \frac{2}{3} =$ _____

1. Phil drew a number line showing multiples of $\frac{3}{6}$.

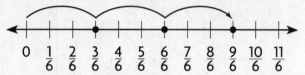

Which number on the number line shows the product $2 \times \frac{3}{6}$?

(A) $\frac{2}{6}$

(B) $\frac{3}{6}$

(C) $\frac{6}{6}$

(D) $\frac{9}{6}$

2. Gwen listed the multiples of $\frac{3}{10}$. Which is **not** a multiple of $\frac{3}{10}$?

(A) $\frac{8}{10}$

(B) $\frac{9}{10}$

(C) $\frac{15}{10}$

(D) $\frac{30}{10}$

3. Oleg drew a number line to help him multiply $4 \times \frac{2}{5}$.

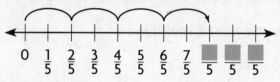

Which shows $4 \times \frac{2}{5}$ written as the product of a whole number and a unit fraction?

(A) $4 \times \frac{1}{5}$

(B) $4 \times \frac{2}{5}$

(C) $8 \times \frac{1}{5}$

(D) $8 \times \frac{1}{4}$

4. Alma is making 3 batches of tortillas. She needs to add $\frac{3}{4}$ cup water to each batch. Her measuring cup holds $\frac{1}{4}$ cup. How many times must Alma measure $\frac{1}{4}$ cup of water to have enough for all the tortillas?

(A) 4

(B) 6

(C) 8

(D) 9

5. Explain how to write the first three multiples of $\frac{4}{9}$.

_____

_____

_____

Name _____

Lesson 67

COMMON CORE STANDARD CC.4.NF.4b
Lesson Objective: Use a model to multiply
a fraction by a whole number.

Multiply a Fraction by a
Whole Number Using Models

You can use a model to multiply a fraction by a whole number.

Find the product of $4 \times \frac{3}{5}$.

Use fraction strips. Show 4 groups of $\frac{3}{5}$ each.

| $\frac{1}{5}$ | $\frac{1}{5}$ | $\frac{1}{5}$ | $\frac{1}{5}$ | $\frac{1}{5}$ |

1 group of $\frac{3}{5} = \frac{3}{5}$

| $\frac{1}{5}$ | $\frac{1}{5}$ | $\frac{1}{5}$ | $\frac{1}{5}$ | $\frac{1}{5}$ |

2 groups of $\frac{3}{5} = \frac{6}{5}$

| $\frac{1}{5}$ | $\frac{1}{5}$ | $\frac{1}{5}$ | $\frac{1}{5}$ | $\frac{1}{5}$ |

3 groups of $\frac{3}{5} = \frac{9}{5}$

| $\frac{1}{5}$ | $\frac{1}{5}$ | $\frac{1}{5}$ | $\frac{1}{5}$ | $\frac{1}{5}$ |

4 groups of $\frac{3}{5} = \frac{12}{5}$

So, $4 \times \frac{3}{5} = \frac{12}{5}$.

Multiply.

1.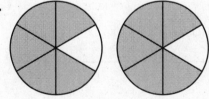

2.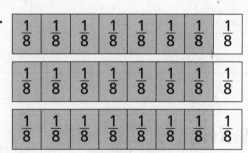

$2 \times \frac{5}{6} =$ _____

$3 \times \frac{7}{8} =$ _____

3. $6 \times \frac{2}{3} =$ _____

4. $2 \times \frac{9}{10} =$ _____

5. $5 \times \frac{3}{4} =$ _____

6. $4 \times \frac{5}{8} =$ _____

7. $7 \times \frac{2}{5} =$ _____

8. $8 \times \frac{4}{6} =$ _____

1. Alani uses $\frac{3}{4}$ cup pineapple juice to make one Hawaiian sweet bread. How much pineapple juice will she use to make 5 sweet breads?

  (A) $\frac{15}{4}$ cups

  (B) $\frac{11}{4}$ cups

  (C) $\frac{10}{4}$ cups

  (D) $\frac{8}{4}$ cups

2. Jason writes repeated addition to show $4 \times \frac{2}{3}$. Which shows an expression Jason could use?

  (A) $4 + \frac{1}{3} + \frac{1}{3} + \frac{1}{3}$

  (B) $\frac{2}{12} + \frac{2}{12} + \frac{2}{12} + \frac{2}{12}$

  (C) $\frac{2}{3} + \frac{2}{3} + \frac{2}{3} + \frac{2}{3}$

  (D) $\frac{1}{3} + \frac{1}{3} + \frac{1}{3} + \frac{1}{3}$

3. Mr. Tuyen uses $\frac{5}{8}$ of a tank of gas each week to drive to and from work. How many tanks of gas does Mr. Tuyen use in 5 weeks?

  (A) $\frac{40}{8}$

  (B) $\frac{25}{8}$

  (C) $\frac{10}{8}$

  (D) $\frac{5}{40}$

4. Mark bought 3 packages of grapes. Each package weighed $\frac{7}{8}$ pound. How many pounds of grapes did Mark buy?

  (A) $\frac{10}{8}$ pounds

  (B) $\frac{21}{8}$ pounds

  (C) 10 pounds

  (D) 21 pounds

Problem Solving REAL WORLD

5. Matthew walks $\frac{5}{8}$ mile to the bus stop each morning. How far will he walk in 5 days?

6. Emily uses $\frac{2}{3}$ cup of milk to make one batch of muffins. How many cups of milk will Emily use if she makes 3 batches of muffins?

Name _____

Lesson 68

COMMON CORE STANDARD CC.4.NF.4c
Lesson Objective: Multiply a fraction by a whole number to solve a problem.

Multiply a Fraction or Mixed Number by a Whole Number

To multiply a fraction by a whole number, multiply the numerators. Then multiply the denominators.

A recipe for one loaf of bread calls for $2\frac{1}{4}$ cups of flour. How many cups of flour will you need for 2 loaves of bread?

Step 1 Write and solve an equation.

$2 \times 2\frac{1}{4} = \frac{2}{1} \times \frac{9}{4}$ Write 2 as $\frac{2}{1}$. Write $2\frac{1}{4}$ as a fraction.

$= \frac{2 \times 9}{1 \times 4}$ Multiply the numerators.
Then multiply the denominators.

$= \frac{18}{4}$ Simplify.

Step 2 Write the product as a mixed number.

$\frac{18}{4} = \frac{1}{4} + \frac{1}{4} + \frac{1}{4} + \frac{1}{4} + \frac{1}{4} + \frac{1}{4} + \frac{1}{4} + \frac{1}{4} + \frac{1}{4} + \frac{1}{4} + \frac{1}{4} + \frac{1}{4} + \frac{1}{4} + \frac{1}{4} + \frac{1}{4} + \frac{1}{4} + \frac{1}{4} + \frac{1}{4}$

$\underbrace{}_{1} + \underbrace{}_{1} + \underbrace{}_{1} + \underbrace{}_{1} + \frac{1}{4} + \frac{1}{4}$

$= \frac{4}{} + \frac{\frac{1}{4}}{} + \frac{\frac{1}{4}}{}$ Combine the wholes. Then combine the remaining parts.

$= \frac{4\frac{2}{4}}{}$, or $\frac{4\frac{1}{2}}{}$ Add. Write the sum as a mixed number.

So, you will need $4\frac{1}{2}$ cups of flour.

Multiply. Write the product as a mixed number.

1. $3 \times \frac{2}{5} = $ _____

2. $4 \times \frac{3}{8} = $ _____

3. $5 \times \frac{1}{3} = $ _____

4. $2 \times 1\frac{3}{10} = $ _____

5. $4 \times 1\frac{2}{3} = $ _____

6. $7 \times 1\frac{1}{6} = $ _____

1. Malak solved a problem that had an answer of $\frac{33}{5}$. How can Malak write $\frac{33}{5}$ as a mixed number?

   (A) $6\frac{3}{5}$

   (B) $5\frac{3}{5}$

   (C) $4\frac{3}{5}$

   (D) $3\frac{3}{5}$

2. Bo recorded a basketball game that lasted $2\frac{1}{2}$ hours. Bo watched the game 3 times last week. How many hours did Bo spend watching the game?

   (A) $6\frac{1}{2}$ hours

   (B) $7\frac{1}{2}$ hours

   (C) 9 hours

   (D) 10 hours

3. Carrie spends $1\frac{1}{4}$ hours practicing the piano 3 times a week. How much time does Carrie spend practicing the piano in one week?

   (A) $4\frac{1}{4}$ hours

   (B) 4 hours

   (C) $3\frac{3}{4}$ hours

   (D) $3\frac{1}{4}$ hours

4. Yasuo always puts $1\frac{1}{2}$ teaspoons of honey in his tea. Yesterday Yasuo drank 5 cups of tea. How much honey did he use in all?

   (A) $6\frac{1}{2}$ teaspoons

   (B) $7\frac{1}{2}$ teaspoons

   (C) 8 teaspoons

   (D) $8\frac{1}{2}$ teaspoons

Problem Solving REAL WORLD

5. Brielle exercises for $\frac{3}{4}$ hour each day for 6 days in a row. Altogether, how many hours does she exercise during the 6 days?

6. A recipe for quinoa calls for $2\frac{2}{3}$ cups of milk. Conner wants to make 4 batches of quinoa. How much milk does he need?

Lesson 69

COMMON CORE STANDARD CC.4.NF.4c

Lesson Objective: Use the strategy *draw a diagram* to solve comparison problems with fractions.

Problem Solving • Comparison Problems with Fractions

The Great Salt Lake in Utah is about $\frac{4}{5}$ mile above sea level. Lake Titicaca in South America is about 3 times as high above sea level as the Great Salt Lake. About how high above sea level is Lake Titicaca?

Read the Problem	Solve the Problem
What do I need to find? I need to find <u>about how high above</u> <u>sea level Lake Titicaca is.</u>	Draw a comparison model. Compare the heights above sea level of the Great Salt Lake and Lake Titicaca, in miles. Great Salt Lake $\boxed{\dfrac{4}{5}}$ Lake Titicaca $\boxed{\dfrac{4}{5}}\ \boxed{\dfrac{4}{5}}\ \boxed{\dfrac{4}{5}}$ $\qquad\qquad\qquad\qquad t$
What information do I need to use? The Great Salt Lake is about $\underline{\dfrac{4}{5}}$ mile above sea level. Lake Titicaca is about $\underline{\quad 3 \quad}$ times as high above sea level.	Write an equation and solve. *t* is the height above sea level of <u>Lake Titicaca</u>, in miles.
How will I use the information? I can <u>draw a diagram</u> to compare the heights.	$t = \dfrac{3}{\ } \times \dfrac{4}{5}$ Write an equation. $t = \dfrac{12}{5}$ Multiply. $t = 2\dfrac{2}{5}$ Write the fraction as a mixed number.

So, Lake Titicaca is about $2\dfrac{2}{5}$ miles above sea level.

---

1. Amelia is training for a triathlon. She swims $\frac{3}{5}$ mile. Then she runs about 6 times farther than she swims. About how far does Amelia run?

_____

2. Last week, Meg bought $1\frac{3}{4}$ pounds of fruit at the market. This week, she buys 4 times as many pounds of fruit as last week. In pounds, how much fruit does Meg buy this week?

_____

1. Rudi is comparing shark lengths. He read that a sandbar shark is $4\frac{1}{2}$ feet long. A thresher shark is 3 times as long as that. How long is a thresher shark?

Sandbar Shark	$4\frac{1}{2}$		

Thresher Shark			

Ⓐ $13\frac{1}{2}$ feet

Ⓑ 12 feet

Ⓒ $7\frac{1}{2}$ feet

Ⓓ 7 feet

2. Cyndi made macaroni salad. She used $1\frac{1}{8}$ cups of mayonnaise. She used 9 times as much macaroni. How many cups of macaroni did Cyndi use?

Ⓐ $9\frac{2}{3}$ cups

Ⓑ $10\frac{1}{8}$ cups

Ⓒ 18 cups

Ⓓ 81 cups

3. A flight takes $1\frac{1}{4}$ hours to get from Dyson to Hardy. The flight takes 3 times as long to get from Dyson to Williams. How long is the flight from Dyson to Williams?

Ⓐ $3\frac{3}{4}$ hours

Ⓑ 4 hours

Ⓒ $4\frac{1}{4}$ hours

Ⓓ $4\frac{3}{4}$ hours

4. Paz weighed $5\frac{5}{8}$ pounds when she was born. By age 2, she weighed 4 times as much. If p stands for pounds, which equation could you use to find Paz's weight at age 2?

Ⓐ $p = 4 + 5\frac{5}{8}$

Ⓑ $p = (4 \times 5) + \frac{5}{8}$

Ⓒ $p = 4 \times 5\frac{5}{8}$

Ⓓ $p = \left(4 \times \frac{5}{8}\right) + 5$

5. A recipe for rice and beans uses $1\frac{1}{2}$ cups of beans and 4 times as much rice. Jess has plenty of beans but only 5 cups of rice. Does she have enough rice to make the recipe? Explain.

_____

_____

_____

Name _____

Lesson 70

COMMON CORE STANDARD CC.4.NF.5
Lesson Objective: Record tenths and
hundredths as fractions and decimals.

Equivalent Fractions and Decimals

Lori ran $\frac{20}{100}$ mile. How many tenths of a mile did she run?

Write $\frac{20}{100}$ as an equivalent fraction with a denominator of 10.

Step 1 **Think:** 10 is a common factor of the numerator and the denominator.

Step 2 Divide the numerator and denominator by 10.

$$\frac{20}{100} = \frac{20 \div 10}{100 \div 10} = \frac{2}{10}$$

So, Lori ran $\frac{2}{10}$ mile.

Use a place-value chart.

Step 1 Write $\frac{20}{100}$ as an equivalent decimal.

Ones	·	Tenths	Hundredths
0	·	2	0

Step 2 **Think:** 20 hundredths is ____2____ tenths ____0____ hundredths

Ones	·	Tenths
0	·	2

So, Lori ran 0.2 mile.

Write the number as hundredths in fraction form and decimal form.

1. $\frac{9}{10}$ 　　　　　　2. 0.6 　　　　　　3. $\frac{4}{10}$

_____　_____　_____

Write the number as tenths in fraction form and decimal form.

4. $\frac{70}{100}$ 　　　　　5. $\frac{80}{100}$ 　　　　　6. 0.50

_____　_____　_____

1. Greta lives 0.7 kilometer from the state capitol. Which fraction is equivalent to 0.7?

   (A) $\frac{0}{7}$

   (B) $\frac{1}{7}$

   (C) $\frac{7}{10}$

   (D) $\frac{7}{100}$

2. The U.S. Senate in Washington, D.C., has 100 elected members who make laws for the United States. Last year, 30 senators ran for reelection. Which decimal is equivalent to $\frac{30}{100}$?

   (A) 3.100

   (B) 0.3

   (C) 0.03

   (D) 0.003

3. Which of the following is **not** equivalent to seven tenths?

   (A) $\frac{7}{10}$

   (B) 0.7

   (C) 0.70

   (D) 0.07

4. Matthew walks $\frac{4}{10}$ mile to Zack's house. Which fraction is equivalent to $\frac{4}{10}$?

   (A) $\frac{4}{100}$

   (B) $\frac{40}{100}$

   (C) $\frac{44}{100}$

   (D) $\frac{40}{10}$

Problem Solving REAL WORLD

5. Billy walks $\frac{6}{10}$ mile to school each day. Write $\frac{6}{10}$ as hundredths in fraction form and in decimal form.

6. Four states have names that begin with the letter A. This represents 0.08 of all the states. Write 0.08 as a fraction.

Add Fractional Parts of 10 and 100

Sam uses 100 glass beads for a project. Of the beads, $\frac{35}{100}$ are gold and $\frac{4}{10}$ are silver. What fraction of the glass beads are gold or silver?

Add $\frac{35}{100}$ and $\frac{4}{10}$.

Step 1 Decide on a common denominator. Use __100__ .

Step 2 Write $\frac{4}{10}$ as an equivalent fraction with a denominator of 100.

$$\frac{4}{10} = \frac{4 \times 10}{10 \times 10} = \frac{40}{100}$$

Step 3 Add $\frac{35}{100}$ and $\frac{40}{100}$.

$$\frac{35}{100} + \frac{40}{100} = \frac{75}{100}$$ ←—Add the numerators.
←—Use 100 as the denominator.

So, $\frac{75}{100}$ of the glass beads are gold or silver.

Add $0.26 and $0.59.

Step 1 Write each amount as a fraction of a dollar.

$0.26 = \frac{26}{100}$ of a dollar $0.59 = \frac{59}{100}$ of a dollar

Step 2 Add $\frac{26}{100}$ and $\frac{59}{100}$.

$$\frac{26}{100} + \frac{59}{100} = \frac{85}{100}$$ ←—Add the numerators.
←—100 is the common denominator.

Step 3 Write the sum as a decimal.

$$\frac{85}{100} = 0.85$$

So, $0.26 + $0.59 = __$0.85__ .

Find the sum.

1. $\frac{75}{100} + \frac{2}{10} = $ _____

2. $0.73 + $0.25 = $ _____

$$\frac{73}{100} + \frac{25}{100} = $$

1. What is the sum of $\frac{4}{10}$ and $\frac{55}{100}$?

   (A) $\frac{15}{100}$

   (B) $\frac{59}{110}$

   (C) $\frac{59}{100}$

   (D) $\frac{95}{100}$

2. What is the sum of $\frac{4}{10}$ and $\frac{40}{100}$?

   (A) $\frac{8}{10}$

   (B) $\frac{44}{100}$

   (C) $\frac{44}{110}$

   (D) $\frac{8}{100}$

3. Suzi ran for $\frac{4}{10}$ mile. Then she walked for $\frac{16}{100}$ mile. How far did she go in all?

   (A) $\frac{20}{100}$ mile

   (B) $\frac{56}{100}$ mile

   (C) $\frac{20}{10}$ miles

   (D) $\frac{56}{10}$ miles

4. An artist is covering a tabletop with square tiles. So far, she has put blue tiles on $\frac{21}{100}$ of the tabletop and silver tiles on $\frac{3}{10}$ of it. How much of the tabletop has been tiled?

   (A) $\frac{51}{10}$

   (B) $\frac{24}{10}$

   (C) $\frac{51}{100}$

   (D) $\frac{24}{100}$

Problem Solving  REAL WORLD

5. Ned's frog jumped $\frac{38}{100}$ meter. Then his frog jumped $\frac{4}{10}$ meter. How far did Ned's frog jump in all?

6. Keiko walks $\frac{5}{10}$ kilometer from school to the park. Then she walks $\frac{19}{100}$ kilometer from the park to her home. How far does Keiko walk in all?

Relate Tenths and Decimals

Write the fraction and the decimal that are shown by the point on the number line.

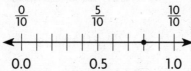

Step 1 Count the number of equal parts of the whole shown on the number line. There are ten equal parts.

This tells you that the number line shows tenths.

Step 2 Label the number line with the missing fractions. What fraction is shown by the point on the number line?

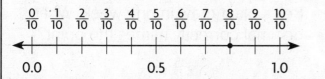

The fraction shown by the point on the number line is $\frac{8}{10}$.

Step 3 Label the number line with the missing decimals. What decimal is shown by the point on the number line?

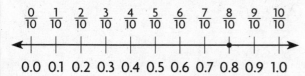

The decimal shown by the point on the number line is 0.8.

So, the fraction and decimal shown by the point on the number line are $\frac{8}{10}$ and 0.8.

Write the fraction or mixed number and the decimal shown by the model.

1.

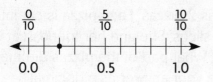

_____

2.

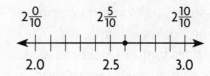

_____

1. Trisha walked $\frac{9}{10}$ of a mile to school. She shaded a model to show how far she had walked.

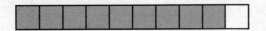

   Which decimal shows how far Trisha walked?

   Ⓐ 0.009 mile

   Ⓑ 0.09 mile

   Ⓒ 0.9 mile

   Ⓓ 9.0 miles

2. Denny ran $2\frac{1}{10}$ miles along a marathon route. What is this distance written as a decimal?

   Ⓐ 21.0 miles

   Ⓑ 2.1 miles

   Ⓒ 2.01 miles

   Ⓓ 0.21 mile

3. David hiked $3\frac{7}{10}$ miles along a trail in the state park. What is this distance written as a decimal?

   Ⓐ 37.10 miles

   Ⓑ 3.710 miles

   Ⓒ 3.7 miles

   Ⓓ 3.07 miles

4. The point shown on the number line represents the number of inches Bea's plant grew in one week. What decimal correctly names the point?

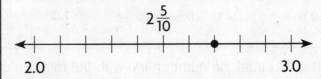

   Ⓐ 2.06

   Ⓑ 2.07

   Ⓒ 2.6

   Ⓓ 2.7

Problem Solving

5. There are 10 sports balls in the equipment closet. Three are kickballs. Write the portion of the balls that are kickballs as a fraction, as a decimal, and in word form.

6. Peyton has 2 pizzas. Each pizza is cut into 10 equal slices. She and her friends eat 14 slices. What part of the pizzas did they eat? Write your answer as a decimal.

Lesson 73

COMMON CORE STANDARD CC.4.NF.6
Lesson Objective: Record hundredths as fractions and as decimals.

Relate Hundredths and Decimals

Write the fraction or mixed number and the decimal shown by the model.

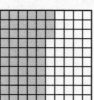

Step 1 Count the number of shaded squares in the model and the total number of squares in the whole model.	Number of shaded squares: 53 Total number of squares: 100
Step 2 Write a fraction to represent the part of the model that is shaded.	$\dfrac{\text{Number of Shaded Squares}}{\text{Total Number of Squares}} = \dfrac{53}{100}$ The fraction shown by the model is $\dfrac{53}{100}$.
Step 3 Write the fraction in decimal form.	**Think:** The fraction shown by the model is $\dfrac{53}{100}$. 0.53 names the same amount as $\dfrac{53}{100}$. The decimal shown by the model is 0.53.
The fraction and decimal shown by the model are $\dfrac{53}{100}$ and 0.53.	

Write the fraction or mixed number and the decimal shown by the model.

1.

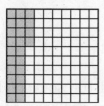

_____

2.

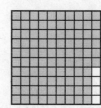

_____

1. Manuel read 75 out of 100 pages in his book. He shaded a model to show what part of the book he read.

Which decimal represents the part of the book Manuel read?

Ⓐ 0.25   Ⓒ 0.75

Ⓑ 0.70   Ⓓ 0.80

2. A shark tooth has a mass of $1\frac{6}{100}$ kilograms. Which decimal is equivalent to $1\frac{6}{100}$?

Ⓐ 0.006

Ⓑ 0.06

Ⓒ 1.06

Ⓓ 1.60

3. Kara made a model for some science data. Which decimal matches the model?

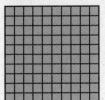 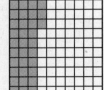

Ⓐ 0.33

Ⓑ 1.33

Ⓒ 1.43

Ⓓ 10.33

4. The weight of a diamond is measured in carats. Mrs. Wang has a diamond that weighs $1\frac{5}{100}$ carats. Which decimal is equivalent to $1\frac{5}{100}$?

Ⓐ 1.05

Ⓑ 1.15

Ⓒ 1.25

Ⓓ 1.5

Problem Solving REAL WORLD

5. There are 100 pennies in a dollar. What fraction of a dollar is 61 pennies? Write it as a fraction, as a decimal, and in word form.

_____

_____

6. Kylee has collected 100 souvenir thimbles from different places she has visited with her family. Twenty of the thimbles are carved from wood. Write the fraction of thimbles that are wooden as a decimal.

_____

Name _____

Lesson 74

COMMON CORE STANDARD CC.4.NF.6

Lesson Objective: Translate among representations of fractions, decimals, and money.

Relate Fractions, Decimals, and Money

Write the total money amount. Then write the amount as a fraction and as a decimal in terms of a dollar.

Step 1 Count the value of coins from greatest to least. Write the total money amount.

$0.25 ⟶ $0.35 ⟶ $0.40 ⟶ $0.45 ⟶ $0.50

Step 2 Write the total money amount as a fraction of a dollar.

The total money amount is $0.50, which is the same as 50 cents.

Think: There are 100 cents in a dollar.

So, the total amount written as a fraction of a dollar is:

$$\frac{50 \text{ cents}}{100 \text{ cents}} = \frac{50}{100}$$

Step 3 Write the total money amount as a decimal.

Think: I can write $0.50 as 0.50.

The total money amount is $\frac{50}{100}$ written as a fraction of a dollar, and 0.50 written as a decimal.

Write the total money amount. Then write the amount as a fraction or a mixed number and as a decimal in terms of a dollar.

1.

2.

1. Cora paid $\frac{65}{100}$ of a dollar to buy a postcard from Grand Canyon National Park in Arizona. What is $\frac{65}{100}$ written as a decimal in terms of dollars?

   Ⓐ 0.65   Ⓒ 6.5

   Ⓑ 6.05   Ⓓ 65

2. Maria has these coins.

   What is Maria's total amount as a fraction in terms of a dollar?

   Ⓐ $\frac{100}{59}$ Ⓒ $\frac{75}{100}$

   Ⓑ $\frac{134}{100}$ Ⓓ $\frac{59}{100}$

3. Ryan sold a jigsaw puzzle at a yard sale for three dollars and five cents. Which decimal names this money amount in terms of dollars?

   Ⓐ 3.50

   Ⓑ 3.05

   Ⓒ 0.55

   Ⓓ 0.05

4. Rick has one dollar and twenty-seven cents to buy a notebook. Which decimal names this money amount in terms of dollars?

   Ⓐ 0.27

   Ⓑ 1.027

   Ⓒ 1.27

   Ⓓ 12.7

Problem Solving

5. Kate has 1 dime, 4 nickels, and 8 pennies. Write Kate's total amount as a fraction in terms of a dollar.

   _____

6. Nolan says he has $\frac{75}{100}$ of a dollar. If he only has 3 coins, what are the coins?

   _____

Compare Decimals

Alfie found 0.2 of a dollar and Gemma found 0.23 of a dollar.
Which friend found more money?

To compare decimals, you can use a number line.

Step 1   Locate each decimal on a number line.

         0.0   0.10   0.20   0.30

Step 2   The number farther to the right is greater.

0.23 > 0.2, so __Gemma__ found more money.

To compare decimals, you can compare equal-size parts.

Step 1   Write 0.2 as a decimal in hundredths.

0.2 is 2 tenths, which is equivalent to __20__ hundredths.

0.2 = __0.20__

Step 2   Compare.

23 hundredths _is greater than_ 20 hundredths,
so 0.23 > 0.2.

So, __Gemma__ found more money.

Compare. Write <, >, or =.

1. 0.17 ◯ 0.13   **2.** 0.8 ◯ 0.08   **3.** 0.36 ◯ 0.63   **4.** 0.4 ◯ 0.40

5. 0.75 ◯ 0.69   **6.** 0.3 ◯ 0.7   **7.** 0.45 ◯ 0.37   **8.** 0.96 ◯ 0.78

1. Randy is comparing statistics from a baseball tournament. Which decimal is **less** than 0.4?

   Ⓐ 0.38

   Ⓑ 0.40

   Ⓒ 0.44

   Ⓓ 1.04

2. Haroun is comparing decimals. Which statement is **true**?

   Ⓐ 0.5 > 0.53

   Ⓑ 0.35 = 0.53

   Ⓒ 0.35 < 0.3

   Ⓓ 0.35 > 0.3

3. Mark needs more than 0.42 pound of cheese for a recipe. Which decimal is **greater** than 0.42?

   Ⓐ 0.24

   Ⓑ 0.39

   Ⓒ 0.41

   Ⓓ 0.5

4. Suria is comparing decimals. Which statement is **true**?

   Ⓐ 0.77 = 0.70

   Ⓑ 0.77 > 0.8

   Ⓒ 0.77 < 0.8

   Ⓓ 0.8 < 0.07

Problem Solving REAL WORLD

5. Kelly walks 0.7 mile to school. Mary walks 0.49 mile to school. Write an inequality using <, >, or = to compare the distances they walk to school.

6. Tyrone shades two decimal grids. He shades 0.03 of the squares on one grid blue. He shades 0.3 of another grid red. Which grid has the greater part shaded?

Lesson 76

COMMON CORE STANDARD CC.4.MD.1

Lesson Objective: Use benchmarks to understand the relative sizes of measurement units.

Measurement Benchmarks

You can use benchmarks to estimate measurements.

The chart shows benchmarks for customary units of measurement.

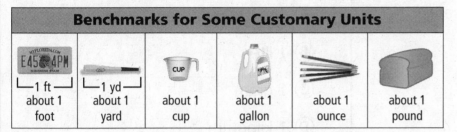

Benchmarks for Some Customary Units

| about 1 foot | about 1 yard | about 1 cup | about 1 gallon | about 1 ounce | about 1 pound |

Here are some more examples of estimating with customary units.

- The width of a professional football is about __1 foot__.
- A large fish bowl holds about __1 gallon__ of water.
- A box of cereal weighs about __1 pound__.

The chart shows benchmarks for metric units of measurement.

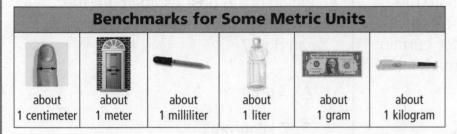

Benchmarks for Some Metric Units

| about 1 centimeter | about 1 meter | about 1 milliliter | about 1 liter | about 1 gram | about 1 kilogram |

Here are some more examples of estimating with metric units.

- The width of a large paper clip is about __1 centimeter__.
- A pitcher holds about __1 liter__ of juice.
- Three laps around a track is about __1 kilometer__.

Use benchmarks to choose the customary unit you would use to measure each.

1. length of a school bus

2. weight of a computer

_____   _____

Use benchmarks to choose the metric unit you would use to measure each.

3. the amount of liquid a bottle of detergent holds

4. distance between two cities

_____   _____

1. Mr. DeMarco is going to paint his porch. He wants to estimate the length of his porch so he knows how much paint to buy. Which is the best benchmark for him to use?

   (A) his fingertip

   (B) a license plate

   (C) a baseball bat

   (D) how far he could walk in 20 minutes

3. Which is the best estimate for the amount of liquid of a drop of food coloring?

   (A) 1 milliliter

   (B) 1 liter

   (C) 1 gram

   (D) 1 kilogram

2. Mrs. Miller wants to estimate the height of a window so she knows how much fabric to buy for curtains. Which is the best benchmark for her to use?

   (A) the thickness of a dime

   (B) her fingertip

   (C) a license plate

   (D) how far she could walk in 20 minutes

4. Which is the best estimate for the amount of lemonade a pitcher can hold?

   (A) 2 grams

   (B) 2 kilograms

   (C) 2 milliliters

   (D) 2 liters

Problem Solving REAL WORLD

5. What is the better estimate for the mass of a textbook, 1 gram or 1 kilogram?

   _____

6. What is the better estimate for the height of a desk, 1 meter or 1 kilometer?

   _____

Name _____

Lesson 77

COMMON CORE STANDARD CC.4.MD.1

Lesson Objective: Use models to compare customary units of length.

Customary Units of Length

A ruler is used to measure length. A ruler that is 1 foot long shows 12 inches in 1 foot. A ruler that is 3 feet long is called a yardstick. There are 3 feet in 1 yard.

How does the size of a foot compare to the size of an inch?

Step 1 A small paper clip is about 1 inch long. Below is a drawing of a chain of paper clips that is about 1 foot long. Number each paper clip, starting with 1.

Step 2 Complete this sentence.

In the chain of paper clips shown, there are __12__ paper clips.

Step 3 Compare the size of 1 inch to the size of 1 foot.

There are __12__ inches in __1__ foot.

So, 1 foot is __12__ times as long as 1 inch.

Complete.

1. 5 feet = _____ inches

2. 3 yards = _____ feet

3. 5 yards = _____ feet

4. 4 feet = _____ inches

5. 6 feet = _____ inches

6. 8 yards = _____ feet

1. Kirsten is 5 feet tall. How tall is she in inches?

   (A) 60 inches

   (B) 50 inches

   (C) 48 inches

   (D) 45 inches

2. Shirlee bought 2 yards of fabric. How many inches of fabric did Shirlee buy?

   (A) 24 inches

   (B) 36 inches

   (C) 48 inches

   (D) 72 inches

3. Hank bought 12 yards of computer cable. How many feet of cable is this?

   (A) 4 feet

   (B) 24 feet

   (C) 36 feet

   (D) 144 feet

4. Dwayne bought 5 yards of wrapping paper. How many inches of wrapping paper is this?

   (A) 180 inches

   (B) 60 inches

   (C) 50 inches

   (D) 15 inches

Problem Solving REAL WORLD

5. Carla has two lengths of ribbon. One ribbon is 2 feet long. The other ribbon is 30 inches long. Which length of ribbon is longer? **Explain.**

   _____

   _____

   _____

6. A football player gained 2 yards on one play. On the next play, he gained 5 feet. Was his gain greater on the first play or the second play? **Explain.**

   _____

   _____

   _____

Name _____

Lesson 78

COMMON CORE STANDARD CC.4.MD.1

Lesson Objective: Use models to compare customary units of weight.

Customary Units of Weight

Ounces and **pounds** are customary units of weight. A **ton** is a unit of weight that is equal to 2,000 pounds.

A slice of bread weighs about 1 ounce. Some loaves of bread weigh about 1 pound.

How does the size of 1 ounce compare to the size of 1 pound?

Step 1 You know a slice of bread weighs about 1 ounce. Below is a drawing of a loaf of bread that weighs about 1 pound. Number each slice of bread, starting with 1.

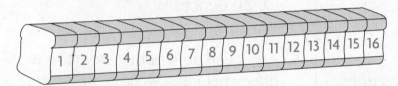

Step 2 Complete this sentence.

In the loaf of bread shown above, there are __16__ slices of bread.

Step 3 Compare the size of 1 ounce to the size of 1 pound.

There are __16__ ounces in __1__ pound.

So, 1 pound is __16__ times as heavy as 1 ounce.

Complete.

1. 2 pounds = _____ ounces

   Think: 2 × 16 = 32

2. 2 tons = _____ pounds

3. 7 pounds = _____ ounces

4. 4 pounds = _____ ounces

5. 3 tons = _____ pounds

6. 10 pounds = _____ ounces

1. An elephant living in a wildlife park weighs 4 tons. How many pounds does the elephant weigh?

   (A) 400 pounds

   (B) 800 pounds

   (C) 4,000 pounds

   (D) 8,000 pounds

2. Ayesha's backpack weighs 9 pounds. How many ounces does her backpack weigh?

   (A) 180 ounces

   (B) 144 ounces

   (C) 90 ounces

   (D) 72 ounces

3. Joan is making tomato sauce. She needs 2 pounds of tomatoes. How many ounces of tomatoes does she need?

   (A) 8 ounces

   (B) 16 ounces

   (C) 32 ounces

   (D) 36 ounces

4. An ocean aquarium is home to a gray whale that weighs 35 tons. How many pounds does this gray whale weigh?

   (A) 70,000 pounds

   (B) 35,000 pounds

   (C) 7,000 pounds

   (D) 3,500 pounds

Problem Solving REAL WORLD

5. A company that makes steel girders can produce 6 tons of girders in one day. How many pounds is this?

   _____

6. Larry's baby sister weighed 6 pounds at birth. How many ounces did the baby weigh?

   _____

Customary Units of Liquid Volume

Liquid volume is the measure of the space a liquid occupies. Some basic units for measuring liquid volume are **gallons, half gallons, quarts, pints, cups,** and **fluid ounces**. The table at the right shows the relationships among some units of liquid volume.

1 cup = 8 fluid ounces
1 pint = 2 cups
1 quart = 2 pints
1 half gallon = 2 quarts
1 gallon = 4 quarts

How does the size of a gallon compare to the size of a pint?

Step 1 Use the information in the table. Draw a bar to represent 1 gallon.

1 gallon

Step 2 The table shows that 1 gallon is equal to 4 quarts. Draw a bar to show 4 quarts.

1 quart	1 quart	1 quart	1 quart

Step 3 The table shows that 1 quart is equal to 2 pints. Draw a bar to show 2 pints for each of the 4 quarts.

1 pint	1 pint	1 pint	1 pint	1 pint	1 pint	1 pint	1 pint

Step 4 Compare the size of 1 gallon to the size of 1 pint.

There are ___8___ pints in ___1___ gallon.

So, 1 gallon is ___8___ times as much as 1 pint.

Complete. Draw a model to help.

1. 2 quarts = _____ pints

2. 1 gallon = _____ cups

3. 1 pint = _____ fluid ounces

4. 3 pints = _____ cups

5. 3 quarts = _____ cups

6. 1 half gallon = _____ pints

1. Randy is making a fruit punch for the class party. He mixes different types of fruit juices to make 1 gallon of punch. How many quarts of punch does Randy make?

   (A) 1 quart

   (B) 2 quarts

   (C) 3 quarts

   (D) 4 quarts

2. Celeste makes 6 quarts of lemonade. How many pints of lemonade does she make?

   (A) 3 pints

   (B) 8 pints

   (C) 12 pints

   (D) 24 pints

3. A carton of cider holds 2 quarts. What is the liquid volume of the carton in cups?

   (A) 4 cups

   (B) 6 cups

   (C) 8 cups

   (D) 12 cups

4. A pitcher can hold 6 cups. What is the liquid volume of the pitcher in fluid ounces?

   (A) 60 fluid ounces

   (B) 48 fluid ounces

   (C) 36 fluid ounces

   (D) 24 fluid ounces

Problem Solving REAL WORLD

5. A chef makes $1\frac{1}{2}$ gallons of soup in a large pot. How many 1-cup servings can the chef get from this large pot of soup?

6. Kendra's water bottle contains 2 quarts of water. She wants to add drink mix to it, but the directions for the drink mix give the amount of water in fluid ounces. How many fluid ounces are in her bottle?

Lesson 80

COMMON CORE STANDARD CC.4.MD.1

Lesson Objective: Use models to compare metric units of length.

Metric Units of Length

Meters (m), **decimeters** (dm), centimeters (cm), and **millimeters** (mm) are all metric units of length. You can use a ruler and a meterstick to find out how these units are related.

Materials: ruler, meterstick

Step 1 Look at a metric ruler. Most look like the one below.

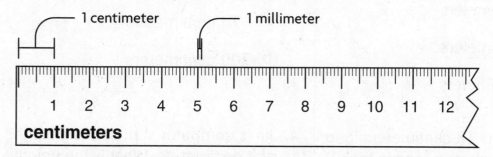

The short marks between each centimeter mark show millimeters.
1 centimeter has the same length as a group of 10 millimeters.

Step 2 Look at a meterstick. Most look like the one below.

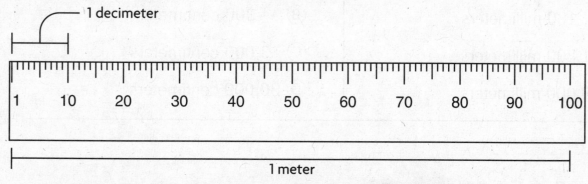

1 decimeter has the same length as a group of 10 centimeters.

Step 3 Use the ruler and the meterstick to compare metric units of length.

1 centimeter = __10__ millimeters   1 decimeter = __10__ centimeters

1 meter = __10__ decimeters   1 meter = __100__ centimeters

Complete.

1. 3 meters = _____ decimeters   **2.** 5 meters = _____ centimeters

3. 4 centimeters = _____ millimeters   **4.** 9 decimeters = _____ centimeters

1. Aruna walked 520 meters to her grandmother's house. How many decimeters did Aruna walk to her grandmother's house?

(A)   5.2 decimeters

(B)   52 decimeters

(C)   520 decimeters

(D) 5,200 decimeters

2. Carol's pencil is 18 centimeters long. How many millimeters long is the pencil?

(A)   80 millimeters

(B)   180 millimeters

(C) 1,800 millimeters

(D) 18,000 millimeters

3. Jakob plays the violin. His bow is 7 decimeters long. How many centimeters long is Jakob's bow?

(A)   0.07 centimeter

(B)   0.7 centimeter

(C) 70 centimeters

(D) 700 centimeters

4. Jim's computer screen has a height of 3 decimeters. What is the height of the screen in centimeters?

(A)   30 centimeters

(B)   300 centimeters

(C) 3,000 centimeters

(D) 30,000 centimeters

Problem Solving REAL WORLD

5. A flagpole is 4 meters tall. How many centimeters tall is the flagpole?

_____

6. A new building is 25 meters tall. How many decimeters tall is the building?

_____

Lesson 81

COMMON CORE STANDARD CC.4.MD.1

Lesson Objective: Use models to compare metric units of mass and liquid volume.

Metric Units of Mass and Liquid Volume

Mass is the amount of matter in an object. Metric units of mass include grams (g) and kilograms (kg). 1 kilogram represents the same mass as 1,000 grams.

One large loaf of bread has a mass of about 1 kilogram. Jacob has 3 large loaves of bread. About how many grams is the mass of the loaves?

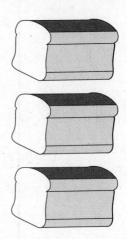

3 kilograms = 3 × __1,000__ grams

= __3,000__ grams

Liters (L) and **milliliters** (mL) are metric units of liquid volume. 1 liter represents the same liquid volume as 1,000 milliliters.

A large bowl holds about 2 liters of juice. Carmen needs to know the liquid volume in milliliters.

2 liters = 2 × __1,000__ milliliters

= __2,000__ milliliters

Complete.

1. 4 kilograms = _____ grams

2. 9 liters = _____ milliliters

3. 3 liters = _____ milliliters

4. 7 kilograms = _____ grams

5. 5 kilograms = _____ grams

6. 8 liters = _____ milliliters

1. Pam saw a koala at the zoo. It had a mass of 7 kilograms. How many grams is 7 kilograms?

   Ⓐ   70 grams

   Ⓑ   700 grams

   Ⓒ   7,000 grams

   Ⓓ 70,000 grams

2. Koji used 2 liters of water to water his plants. How many milliliters of water did he use?

   Ⓐ 2,000 milliliters

   Ⓑ   200 milliliters

   Ⓒ   20 milliliters

   Ⓓ   0.2 milliliter

3. June filled the birdbath in her yard with 4 liters of water. How many milliliters of water did she put in the birdbath?

   Ⓐ   4 milliliters

   Ⓑ   40 milliliters

   Ⓒ   400 milliliters

   Ⓓ 4,000 milliliters

4. A turkey has a mass of 6 kilograms. A bag of sweet potatoes has a mass of 2 kilograms. How many more grams does the turkey weigh than the sweet potatoes?

   Ⓐ   4 grams

   Ⓑ   40 grams

   Ⓒ   400 grams

   Ⓓ 4,000 grams

5. Harlan went fishing. The sunfish he caught had a mass of 865 grams. The perch he caught had a mass of 1 kilogram. Which fish had the greater mass? Explain your reasoning.

   _____

   _____

   _____

   _____

Units of Time

Some analog clocks have an hour hand, a minute hand, and a **second** hand.

There are 60 seconds in a minute. The second hand makes 1 full turn every minute. There are 60 minutes in an hour. The minute hand makes 1 full turn every hour. The hour hand makes 1 full turn every 12 hours.

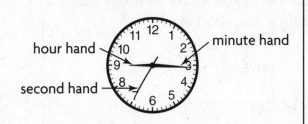

You can think of the clock as unrolling to become a number line.

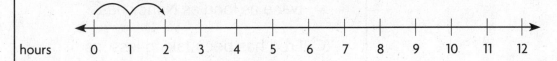

The hour hand moves from one number to the next in 1 hour.

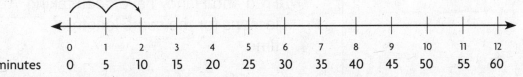

The minute hand moves from one number to the next in 5 minutes.

Use the table at the right to change between units of time.

Units of Time
1 minute = 60 seconds
1 hour = 60 minutes
1 day = 24 hours
1 week = 7 days
1 year = 12 months
1 year = 52 weeks

1 hour = 60 minutes, or 60 × 60 seconds, or
__3,600__ seconds.

So, 1 hour is __3,600__ times as long as 1 second.

1 day = 24 hours, so 3 days = 3 × 24 hours, or
__72__ hours.

1 year = 12 months, so 5 years = 5 × 12 months, or __60__ months.

Complete.

1. 3 hours = _____ minutes

2. 2 years = _____ weeks

3. 6 days = _____ hours

4. 5 weeks = _____ days

5. 8 minutes = _____ seconds

6. 7 years = _____ months

1. The Burke family is taking a 3-week vacation to Alaska. How many days will their vacation last?

   (A) 7 days

   (B) 14 days

   (C) 21 days

   (D) 30 days

2. Julio's little sister is 3 years old. How many months old is she?

   (A) 48 months old

   (B) 36 months old

   (C) 24 months old

   (D) 12 months old

3. Fred has been taking guitar lessons for 100 weeks. Nancy has been taking guitar lessons for 3 years. Which statement is true about Fred and Nancy?

   (A) Fred has been taking lessons a shorter time than Nancy has.

   (B) Fred has been taking lessons twice as long as Nancy has.

   (C) Fred has been taking lessons longer than Nancy has.

   (D) Fred and Nancy have been taking lessons for the same length of time.

4. A candle can burn for up to 600 minutes. Which amount of time is longer than 600 minutes?

   (A) 1 hour

   (B) 5 hours

   (C) 10 hours

   (D) 12 hours

5. Reese lay down for a nap. He set a timer to ring in 15 minutes to wake him up. Explain how to find the total number of seconds Reese could nap.

   _____

   _____

   _____

Lesson 83
OMMON CORE STANDARD CC.4.MD.1
Lesson Objective: Use patterns to write
number pairs for measurement units.

Algebra • Patterns in Measurement Units

Use the relationship between the number pairs to label the columns in the table.

?	?
1	8
2	16
3	24
4	32

Step 1 List the number pairs. __1 and 8; 2 and 16; 3 and 24; 4 and 32__

Step 2 Describe the relationship between the numbers in each pair.

__The second number is 8 times as great as the first number.__

Step 3 Look for a relationship involving 1 and 8 in the table below.

Length	Weight	Liquid Volume	Time
1 foot = 12 inches 1 yard = 3 feet 1 yard = 36 inches	1 pound = 16 ounces 1 ton = 2,000 pounds	1 cup = 8 fluid ounces 1 pint = 2 cups 1 quart = 2 pints 1 gallon = 4 quarts	1 minute = 60 seconds 1 hour = 60 minutes 1 day = 24 hours 1 week = 7 days 1 year = 12 months 1 year = 52 weeks

So, the label for the first column is ____Cups____ .
The label for the second column is ____Fluid Ounces____ .

Each table shows a pattern for two customary units. Label the columns of the table.

1.

1	12
2	24
3	36
4	48

2.

1	2,000
2	4,000
3	6,000
4	8,000

1. The table shows a pattern for units of time. Which are the best labels for this table?

1	52
2	104
3	156
4	208

Ⓐ Years, Months

Ⓑ Years, Weeks

Ⓒ Weeks, Days

Ⓓ Months, Days

3. The table shows a pattern for units of time. Which are the best labels for this table?

1	24
2	48
3	72
4	96

Ⓐ Years, Weeks

Ⓑ Minutes, Days

Ⓒ Minutes, Seconds

Ⓓ Days, Hours

2. The table shows a pattern for metric units. Which are the best labels for this table?

1	1,000
2	2,000
3	3,000
4	4,000

Ⓐ Centimeters, Meters

Ⓑ Centimeters, Kilometers

Ⓒ Kilograms, Grams

Ⓓ Milliliters, Liters

4. The table shows a pattern for metric units. Which are the best labels for this table?

1	1,000
2	2,000
3	3,000
4	4,000

Ⓐ Centimeters, Meters

Ⓑ Kilometers, Meters

Ⓒ Grams, Kilograms

Ⓓ Milliliters, Liters

5. Mac says the pattern in a table for feet and inches and a table for years and months would look the same without labels. Do you agree? Explain.

_____

_____

Lesson 84

COMMON CORE STANDARD CC.4.MD.2

Lesson Objective: Solve problems by using the strategy *act it out*.

Problem Solving • Money

Use the strategy *act it out* to solve the problem.

Jessica, Brian, and Grace earned $7.50. They want to share the money equally. How much will each person get?

Read the Problem	Solve the Problem
What do I need to find? I need to find the amount of money each person should get.	• Show the total amount, $7.50, using ___7___ one-dollar bills and ___2___ quarters.
What information do I need to use? I need to use the total amount, $7.50, and divide it by ___3___, the number of people sharing the money equally.	• Share the one-dollar bills equally. There is ___1___ one-dollar bill left.
How will I use the information? I will use dollar bills and coins to model the total amount and act out the problem.	• Change the dollar bill that is left for ___4___ quarters. Now there are ___6___ quarters. • Share the quarters equally. So, each person gets ___2___ one-dollar bills and ___2___ quarters, or $2.50.

1. Jacob, Dan, and Nathan were given $6.90 to share equally. How much money will each boy get?

2. Becky, Marlis, and Hallie each earned $2.15 raking leaves. How much did they earn together?

_____   _____

1. Chaz needs $4.77 for new batteries. He has $2.80. How much more money does he need?

   Ⓐ $1.97

   Ⓑ $2.10

   Ⓒ $2.17

   Ⓓ $7.57

2. Mrs. Golub wants to share $7.20 equally among her three grandchildren. How much money should each grandchild get?

   Ⓐ $1.40

   Ⓑ $2.07

   Ⓒ $2.40

   Ⓓ $4.20

3. Patty, Helene, and Mira share $0.96 that they found in an old wallet. How much money does each girl get?

   Ⓐ $0.48

   Ⓑ $0.38

   Ⓒ $0.36

   Ⓓ $0.32

4. Three boys share $1.92 equally. How much money does each boy get?

   Ⓐ $0.64

   Ⓑ $0.69

   Ⓒ $0.72

   Ⓓ $5.76

5. Bernie and his two brothers share $8.16 equally. How much money does each boy get? Explain the strategy you use to solve the problem.

   _____

   _____

   _____

   _____

   _____

   _____

   _____

Lesson 85

OMMON CORE STANDARD CC.4.MD.2

Lesson Objective: Use the strategy *draw a diagram* to solve elapsed time problems.

Problem Solving • Elapsed Time

Opal finished her art project at 2:25 P.M. She spent 50 minutes working on her project. What time did she start working on her project?

Read the Problem		
What do I need to find?	**What information do I need to use?**	**How will I use the information?**
I need to find Opal's start time.	End time: ____2:25 P.M.____ Elapsed time: ____50____ minutes	I can draw a diagram of a clock. I can then count back 5 minutes at a time until I reach 50 minutes.
Solve the Problem		

I start by showing 2:25 P.M. on the clock.
Then I count back 50 minutes by 5s.

Think: As I count back, I go past the 12.
The hour must be 1 hour less than the ending time.

The hour will be ____1 o'clock____.

So, Opal started on her project at ____1:35 P.M.____

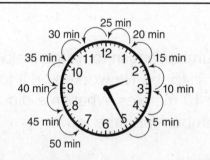

Draw hands on the clock to help you solve the problem.

1. Bill wants to be at school at 8:05 A.M. It takes him 20 minutes to walk to school. At what time should Bill leave his house?

   Bill should leave his house at _____.

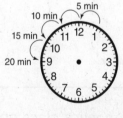

2. Mr. Gleason's math class lasts 40 minutes. Math class starts at 9:55 A.M. At what time does math class end?

   Math class ends at _____.

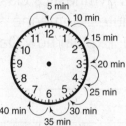

3. Hannah rode her bike for 1 hour and 15 minutes until she got a flat tire at 2:30 P.M. What time did Hannah start riding her bike?

   Hannah started riding her bike at _____.

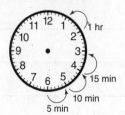

1. The tour of the art museum started at 9:35 A.M. It lasted for 1 hour 20 minutes. What time did the tour end?

   (A) 9:55 A.M.

   (B) 10:35 A.M.

   (C) 10:45 A.M.

   (D) 10:55 A.M.

2. The plumber began to fix the leaky sink at 1:45 P.M. He worked on it for 1 hour 45 minutes. What time did the plumber finish the job?

   (A) 2:45 P.M.

   (B) 3:00 P.M.

   (C) 3:20 P.M.

   (D) 3:30 P.M.

3. An author signed copies of her newest book for 57 minutes until the bookstore closed at 5:00 P.M. What time did the author begin signing books?

   (A) 4:03 P.M.

   (B) 4:57 P.M.

   (C) 5:03 P.M.

   (D) 5:57 P.M.

4. Aya was at the library for 48 minutes until it closed at 6:30 P.M. What time did Aya arrive at the library?

   (A) 5:32 P.M.

   (B) 5:42 P.M.

   (C) 5:52 P.M.

   (D) 7:18 P.M.

5. David's gymnastics class ended at 4:15 P.M. It lasted for 46 minutes. Someone asked David what time the class started. Explain how David could find the answer.

   _____

   _____

   _____

   _____

Mixed Measures

Gabrielle's puppy weighs 2 pounds 7 ounces. What is the weight of the puppy in ounces?

Step 1 Think of 2 pounds 7 ounces as 2 pounds + 7 ounces.

Step 2 Change the pounds to ounces.

Think: 1 pound = __16__ ounces

So, 2 pounds = 2 × 16 ounces, or __32__ ounces.

Step 3 Add like units to find the answer.

So, Gabrielle's puppy weighs __39__ ounces.

$$\begin{array}{r} 32 \text{ ounces} \\ + \ 7 \text{ ounces} \\ \hline 39 \text{ ounces} \end{array}$$

Gabrielle played with her puppy for 2 hours 10 minutes yesterday and 1 hour 25 minutes today. How much longer did she play with the puppy yesterday than today?

Step 1 Subtract the mixed measures. Write the subtraction with like units lined up.

Think: 25 minutes is greater than 10 minutes.

$$\begin{array}{r} 2 \text{ hr } 10 \text{ min} \\ - \ 1 \text{ hr } 25 \text{ min} \end{array}$$

Step 2 Rename 2 hours 10 minutes to subtract.

1 hour = 60 minutes

So, 2 hr 10 min = 1 hr + 60 min + 10 min, or __1__ hr __70__ min.

$$\begin{array}{r} 1 \quad 70 \\ \cancel{2} \text{ hr } \cancel{10} \text{ min} \\ - \ 1 \text{ hr } 25 \text{ min} \\ \hline 0 \text{ hr } 45 \text{ min} \end{array}$$

Step 3 Subtract like units.

1 hr − 1 hr = 0 hr; 70 min − 25 min = __45 min__

So, she played with the puppy __45__ minutes longer yesterday than today.

Complete.

1. 4 yd 2 ft = _____ ft

2. 1 hr 20 min = _____ min

3. 4 qt 1 pt = _____ pt

Add or subtract.

4. 2 gal 1 qt
    + 3 gal 2 qt

5. 3 lb 12 oz
    − 1 lb 8 oz

6. 4 yr 9 mo
    − 1 yr 10 mo

1. Mr. Wallis says he is 6 feet 3 inches tall. How tall is he in inches?

   Ⓐ 75 inches

   Ⓑ 72 inches

   Ⓒ 69 inches

   Ⓓ 33 inches

2. Erin ships a gift through the mail. The gift weighs 8 pounds 11 ounces. She packs the gift in a shipping box with bubble wrap. The package weighs 12 pounds 4 ounces. How much does the shipping box and bubble wrap weigh?

   Ⓐ 4 pounds 7 ounces

   Ⓑ 3 pounds 9 ounces

   Ⓒ 3 pounds 5 ounces

   Ⓓ 3 pounds 3 ounces

3. Adrianna mixed 4 quarts 2 pints of lemonade with 1 pint of grape juice to make party punch. How many pints of party punch does she have?

   Ⓐ 7 pints

   Ⓑ 9 pints

   Ⓒ 10 pints

   Ⓓ 11 pints

4. Mr. Leung told his students that his desk is 4 feet 6 inches long. What is this length in inches?

   Ⓐ 24 inches

   Ⓑ 48 inches

   Ⓒ 54 inches

   Ⓓ 60 inches

Problem Solving REAL WORLD

5. Michael's basketball team practiced for 2 hours 40 minutes yesterday and 3 hours 15 minutes today. How much longer did the team practice today than yesterday?

   _____

6. Rhonda had a piece of ribbon that was 5 feet 3 inches long. She removed a 5-inch piece to use in her art project. What is the length of the piece of ribbon now?

   _____

Lesson 87

COMMON CORE STANDARD CC.4.MD.3

Lesson Objective: Use a formula to find the perimeter of a rectangle.

Perimeter

Perimeter is the distance around a shape. You can use grid paper to count the number of units around the outside of a rectangle to find its perimeter.

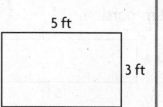

How many feet of ribbon are needed to go around the bulletin board?

Step 1 On grid paper, draw a rectangle that has a length of **5** units and a width of **3** units.

Step 2 Find the length of each side of the rectangle. Mark each unit of length as you count.

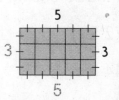

Step 3 Add the side lengths. 5 + 3 + 5 + 3 = 16

The perimeter is ___16___ feet.

So, _16 feet_ of ribbon are needed to go around the bulletin board.

---

1. What is the perimeter of this square?

___ + ___ + ___ + ___ = ___ centimeters

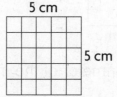

Find the perimeter of the rectangle or square.

2.

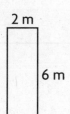

_____ meters

3.

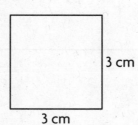

_____ centimeters

4.

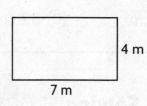

_____ meters

1. Jack plants a vegetable garden. The garden is in the shape of a rectangle. He wants to put fencing around the entire garden.

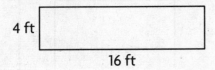

4 ft

16 ft

How much fencing does Jack need?

(A) 72 feet   (C) 40 feet

(B) 44 feet   (D) 22 feet

2. Ian hung a mirror on the wall.

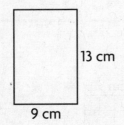

13 cm

9 cm

What is the perimeter of the mirror?

(A) 22 cm   (C) 44 cm

(B) 36 cm   (D) 52 cm

3. Mindy puts a rectangular poster of her favorite singer on a wall in her bedroom.

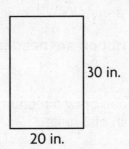

30 in.

20 in.

What is the perimeter of the poster?

(A) 100 inches   (C) 60 inches

(B) 70 inches   (D) 50 inches

4. Armando is tiling the top of his kitchen table. Each tile that he is using measures 9 inches along each side. What is the perimeter of a tile?

(A) 9 inches   (C) 36 inches

(B) 18 inches   (D) 81 inches

Problem Solving REAL WORLD

5. Troy is making a flag shaped like a square. Each side measures 12 inches. He wants to add ribbon along the edges. He has 36 inches of ribbon. Does he have enough ribbon? **Explain.**

6. The width of the Ochoa Community Pool is 20 feet. The length is twice as long as its width. What is the perimeter of the pool?

Name _____

Lesson 88

COMMON CORE STANDARD CC.4.MD.3

Lesson Objective: Use a formula to find the area of a rectangle.

Area

Area is the number of **square units** needed to cover a flat surface.

Find the area of the rectangle at the right.

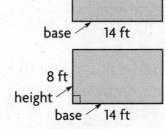

You can use the formula **Area = base × height**.

Step 1 Identify one side as the base.

The base is ___14___ feet.

Step 2 Identify a perpendicular side as the height.

The height is ___8___ feet.

Step 3 Use the formula to find the area.

$$Area = base \times height$$
$$= 14 \times 8$$
$$= 112$$

So, the area of the rectangle is 112 square feet.

Find the area of the rectangle or square.

1.
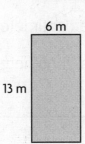

6 m

13 m

_____

2.
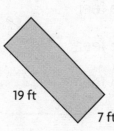

19 ft

7 ft

_____

3.
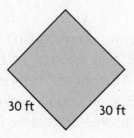

30 ft   30 ft

_____

4.
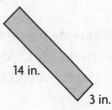

14 in.

3 in.

_____

1. Oscar is cutting a piece of glass that is 3 feet long on each side. What is the area of the glass?

   Ⓐ 12 square feet

   Ⓑ 9 square feet

   Ⓒ 6 square feet

   Ⓓ 3 square feet

2. Hiro painted a mural with the dimensions shown.

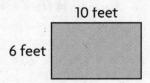

10 feet

6 feet

   What is the area of Hiro's mural?

   Ⓐ 4 square feet

   Ⓑ 16 square feet

   Ⓒ 32 square feet

   Ⓓ 60 square feet

3. Sherry made this arrangement of tiles as part of her art project.

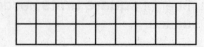

   Which of the following is true?

   Ⓐ area = 11 square units

   Ⓑ area = 14 square units

   Ⓒ area = 18 square units

   Ⓓ area = 22 square units

4. Laura bought a square canvas to paint a picture of her cat. One side measures 22 centimeters. What is the area of the canvas?

   Ⓐ 44 square centimeters

   Ⓑ 88 square centimeters

   Ⓒ 440 square centimeters

   Ⓓ 484 square centimeters

Problem Solving

5. Meghan is putting wallpaper on a wall that measures 8 feet by 12 feet. How much wallpaper does Meghan need to cover the wall?

6. Bryson is laying down sod in his yard to grow a new lawn. Each piece of sod is a 1-foot by 1-foot square. How many pieces of sod will Bryson need to cover his yard if his yard measures 30 feet by 14 feet?

_____ _____

Area of Combined Rectangles

Find the area of the combined rectangles.

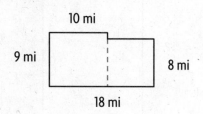

Step 1 First, find the area of each section of the shape.

LEFT   RIGHT

$A = b \times h$ $A = b \times h$

   $= 10 \times 9$ $= 8 \times 8$ **Think:** $18 - 10 = 8$

   $= 90$ $= 64$

Step 2 Add the two areas. $90 + 64 = 154$

So, the total area is ___154___ square miles.

Find the area of the combined rectangles.

1.

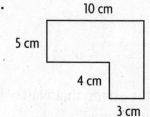

2.

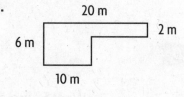

3.

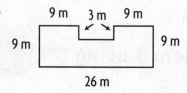

_____   _____   _____

4.

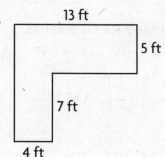

5.

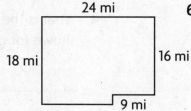

6.

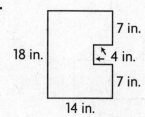

_____   _____   _____

1. Mr. Benson built a play area for his children and an office for himself.

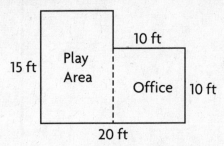

How much carpet does he need to cover the floor in both areas?

(A) 70 square feet

(B) 250 square feet

(C) 300 square feet

(D) 350 square feet

2. Mrs. Ericson is building a new balcony.

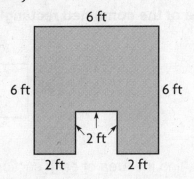

What is the area of Mrs. Ericson's new balcony?

(A) 44 square feet

(B) 36 square feet

(C) 32 square feet

(D) 28 square feet

Problem Solving REAL WORLD

Use the diagram for 3–4.

Nadia makes the diagram below to represent the counter space she wants to build in her craft room.

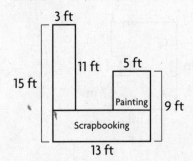

3. What is the area of the space that Nadia has shown for scrapbooking?

_____

4. What is the area of the space she has shown for painting?

_____

Lesson 90

COMMON CORE STANDARD CC.4.MD.3

Lesson Objective: Given perimeter or area, find the unknown measure of a side of a rectangle.

Find Unknown Measures

Fred has 30 yards of fencing to enclose a rectangular vegetable garden. He wants it to be 6 yards wide. How long will his vegetable garden be?

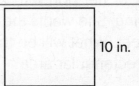

6 yd

Step 1 Decide whether this problem involves area or perimeter.

Think: The fencing goes *around the outside* of the garden. This is a measure of perimeter.

Step 2 Use a formula for perimeter. The width is 6. The perimeter is 30. The length is unknown.

$$P = (2 \times l) + (2 \times w)$$
$$30 = (2 \times l) + (2 \times 6)$$
$$30 = 2 \times l + 12$$

Step 3 Find the value of *l*.

$18 = 2 \times l$, so the value of *l* is 9.

The length of Fred's garden will be 9 yards.

Carol has 120 square inches of wood. The piece of wood is rectangular and has a height of 10 inches. How long is the base?

10 in.

?

Step 1 Decide whether this problem involves area or perimeter.

Think: *Square inches* is a measure of area.

Step 2 Use a formula for area. The height is 10. The area is 120. The length is unknown.

$$A = b \times h$$
$$120 = b \times 10$$

Step 3 Find the value of *b*.

Since $120 = 12 \times 10$, the value of *b* is 12.

The base of Carol's piece of wood is 12 inches.

Find the unknown measure.

1.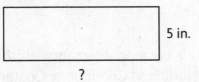

5 in.

?

Perimeter = 40 inches

width = _____

2.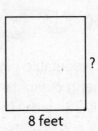

?

8 feet

Area = 72 square feet

height = _____

1. A rectangle has a perimeter of 50 centimeters. If the width of the rectangle is 10 centimeters, what is its length?

(A) 5 centimeters

(B) 15 centimeters

(C) 20 centimeters

(D) 40 centimeters

2. Kelly wants to enclose a rectangular area for her dog with 240 feet of fencing. She wants the width to be 20 feet. What will be the length of the rectangular area?

(A) 24 feet

(B) 100 feet

(C) 110 feet

(D) 200 feet

3. The Hernandez family built a backyard patio.

Area = 150 square feet

What could be the dimensions of the patio?

(A) 100 feet long by 50 feet wide

(B) 50 feet long by 25 feet wide

(C) 15 feet long by 10 feet wide

(D) 10 feet long by 5 feet wide

4. A rectangular window has an area of 144 square inches. The height of the window is 9 inches. What is the width of the window?

(A) 16 inches   (C) 135 inches

(B) 20 inches   (D) 153 inches

Problem Solving REAL WORLD

5. Susie is an organic vegetable grower. The perimeter of her rectangular vegetable garden is 72 yards. The width of the vegetable garden is 9 yards. How long is the vegetable garden?

6. An artist is creating a rectangular mural for the Northfield Community Center. The mural is 7 feet tall and has an area of 84 square feet. What is the length of the mural?

Problem Solving • Find the Area

Use the strategy *solve a simpler problem*.

Marilyn is going to paint a wall in her bedroom. The wall is 15 feet long and 8 feet tall. The window takes up an area 6 feet long and 4 feet high. How many square feet of the wall will Marilyn have to paint?

Read the Problem	Solve the Problem
What do I need to find? I need to find how many <u>square feet of the wall</u> Marilyn will paint.	First, find the area of the wall. $A = b \times h$ $\quad = 15 \times \underline{8}$ $\quad = \underline{120}$ square feet
What information do I need to use? The paint will cover the wall. The paint will not cover the <u>window</u>. The base of the wall is 15 feet and the height is <u>8 feet</u>. The base of the window is 6 feet and the height is <u>4 feet</u>.	Next, find the area of the window. $A = b \times h$ $\quad = \underline{6} \times \underline{4}$ $\quad = \underline{24}$ square feet Last, subtract the area of the window from the area of the wall.
How will I use the information? I can solve simpler problems. Find the area of the <u>wall</u>. Then, find the area of the window. Last, <u>subtract</u> the area of the <u>window</u> from the area of the wall.	$\begin{array}{r} 120 \\ -\ \ 24 \\ \hline \underline{96} \text{ square feet} \end{array}$ So, Marilyn will paint <u>96 square feet</u> of her bedroom wall.

1. Ned wants to wallpaper the wall of his bedroom that has the door. The wall is 14 feet wide and 9 feet high. The door is 3 feet wide and 7 feet high. How many square feet of wallpaper will Ned need for the wall?

2. Nicole has a rectangular canvas that is 12 inches long and 10 inches wide. She paints a blue square in the center of the canvas. The square is 3 inches on each side. How much of the canvas is NOT painted blue?

_____   _____

1. Melanie's blue notebook cover is 20 centimeters by 30 centimeters. She has a sticker for each letter in her name. Each sticker is a square that measures 2 centimeters on each side. If she puts all 7 stickers on her notebook, how much of the blue notebook cover will still be showing?

   (A) 596 square centimeters

   (B) 586 square centimeters

   (C) 572 square centimeters

   (D) 544 square centimeters

2. Aidan bought a frame for a photograph that he took.

   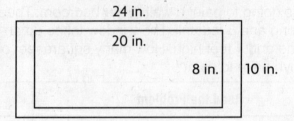

   What was the area of the frame that he bought?

   (A) 80 square inches

   (B) 120 square inches

   (C) 160 square inches

   (D) 240 square inches

3. Diane made a design using only squares. She shaded the inner square and the outer region.

   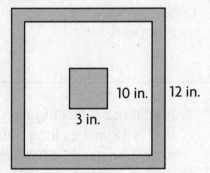

   Find the total area that is shaded. Explain how you found your answer.

   _____

   _____

   _____

   _____

Name _____

Lesson 92

COMMON CORE STANDARD CC.4.MD.4

Lesson Objective: Make and interpret line plots with fractional data.

Line Plots

Howard gave a piece of paper with several survey questions to his friends. Then he made a list to show how long it took for his friends to answer the survey. Howard wants to know how many surveys took longer than $\frac{2}{12}$ hour.

Time for Survey Answers (in hours)						
$\frac{1}{12}$	$\frac{3}{12}$	$\frac{1}{12}$	$\frac{2}{12}$	$\frac{6}{12}$	$\frac{3}{12}$	$\frac{5}{12}$

Make a line plot to show the data.

Step 1 Order the data from least to greatest.

$$\frac{1}{12}, \frac{1}{12}, \frac{2}{12}, \frac{3}{12}, \frac{3}{12}, \frac{5}{12}, \frac{6}{12}$$

Step 2 Make a tally table of the data.

Step 3 Label the fractions of an hour on the number line from least to greatest. Notice that $\frac{4}{12}$ is included even though it is not in the data.

Step 4 Plot an X above the number line for each piece of data. Write a title for the line plot.

Step 5 Count the number of Xs that represent data points greater than $\frac{2}{12}$ hour.

There are ___4___ data points greater than $\frac{2}{12}$ hour.

So, ___4___ surveys took more than $\frac{2}{12}$ hour.

Survey	
Time (in hours)	Tally
$\frac{1}{12}$	||
$\frac{2}{12}$	|
$\frac{3}{12}$	||
$\frac{5}{12}$	|
$\frac{6}{12}$	|

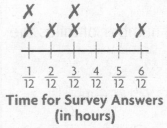

Time for Survey Answers
(in hours)

Use the line plot above for 1 and 2.

1. How many of the surveys that Howard

   gave to his friends were answered? _____

2. What is the difference in hours between the longest time and the shortest time that it took Howard's friends to answer the survey?

Use the line plot for 1 and 2.

The line plot shows the distance some students jogged.

Distance Students Jogged (in miles)

1. How many students jogged $\frac{3}{5}$ mile?

   Ⓐ 4   Ⓒ 2

   Ⓑ 3   Ⓓ 1

2. What is the total number of miles the group jogged?

   Ⓐ $\frac{4}{5}$ mile   Ⓒ 6 miles

   Ⓑ 3 miles   Ⓓ $6\frac{3}{5}$ miles

Use the line plot for 3 and 4.

The line plot shows the distance some students swam during a timed exercise.

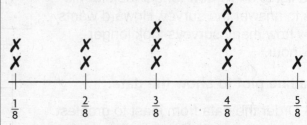

Distance Students Swam (in miles)

3. How many students swam $\frac{4}{8}$ mile?

   Ⓐ 1   Ⓒ 3

   Ⓑ 2   Ⓓ 4

4. What is the total number of miles the group swam?

   Ⓐ $4\frac{4}{8}$ miles   Ⓒ $1\frac{7}{8}$ miles

   Ⓑ 4 miles   Ⓓ $\frac{1}{2}$ mile

---

5. The tally table shows how much time students would spend walking home from school if they did not ride the bus. Use the tally table to complete the line plot.

Time Spent Walking Home

Time (in hours)	Tally
$\frac{1}{6}$	IIII
$\frac{2}{6}$	III
$\frac{3}{6}$	II
$\frac{4}{6}$	I

Angles and Fractional Parts of a Circle

Find how many $\frac{1}{6}$ turns make a complete circle.

Materials: fraction circles

Step 1 Place a $\frac{1}{6}$ piece so the tip of the fraction piece is on the center of the circle. Trace the fraction piece by drawing along the dashed lines in the circle.

Step 2 Shade and label the angle formed by the $\frac{1}{6}$ piece.

Step 3 Place the $\frac{1}{6}$ piece on the shaded angle. Turn it clockwise (in the direction that the hands on a clock move). Turn the fraction piece to line up directly beside the shaded section.

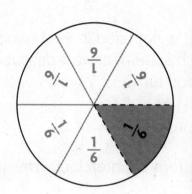

Step 4 Trace the fraction piece. Shade and label it. You have traced ___2___ sixths in all.

Step 5 Repeat until you have shaded the entire circle.

There are __six__ angles that come together in the center of the circle.

So, you need __six__ $\frac{1}{6}$ turns to make a circle.

Tell what fraction of the circle the shaded angle represents.

1.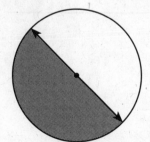

2.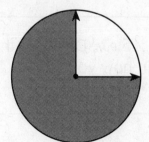

3.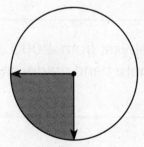

_____   _____   _____

Use the diagram for 1–2.

1. "Ray" is not used in the lesson. Which statement best describes the shaded turn?

   Ⓐ $\frac{1}{4}$ turn clockwise

   Ⓑ $\frac{1}{4}$ turn counterclockwise

   Ⓒ $\frac{3}{4}$ turn clockwise

   Ⓓ $\frac{3}{4}$ turn counterclockwise

2. What clockwise turn represents the white part of the circle?

   Ⓐ 1 full turn   Ⓒ $\frac{1}{2}$ turn

   Ⓑ $\frac{3}{4}$ turn   Ⓓ $\frac{1}{4}$ turn

3. Which shaded angle shows $\frac{1}{8}$ of the circle?

   Ⓐ 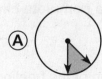   Ⓒ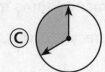

   Ⓑ 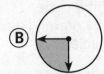   Ⓓ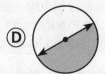

4. Which shaded angle shows $\frac{1}{3}$ of the circle?

   Ⓐ 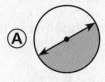   Ⓒ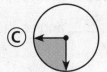

   Ⓑ   Ⓓ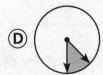

5. Jack babysat from 4:00 P.M. until 4:45 P.M. Describe the turn the minute hand made, and explain how you know.

   _____

   _____

   _____

   _____

Lesson 94

COMMON CORE STANDARD CC.4.MD.5b

Lesson Objective: Relate degrees to fractional parts of a circle by understanding that an angle that measures 1° turns through $\frac{n}{360}$ of a circle.

Name _____

Degrees

Angles are measured in units called **degrees.** The symbol for degrees is °. If a circle is divided into 360 equal parts, then an angle that turns through 1 part of the 360 measures 1°.

An angle that turns through $\frac{50}{360}$ of a circle measures 50°.

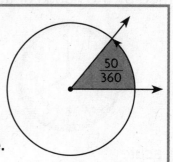

Find the measure of an angle that turns through $\frac{1}{6}$ of a circle.

Step 1 Find a fraction that is equivalent to $\frac{1}{6}$ with 360 in the denominator. **Think:** $6 \times 60 = 360$.

$$\frac{1}{6} = \frac{1 \times 60}{6 \times 60} = \frac{60}{360}$$

Step 2 Look at the numerator of $\frac{60}{360}$.

The numerator tells how many degrees are in $\frac{1}{6}$ of a circle.

So, an angle that turns through $\frac{1}{6}$ of a circle measures __**60°**__.

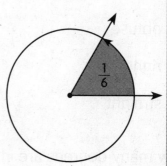

Tell the measure of the angle in degrees.

1.

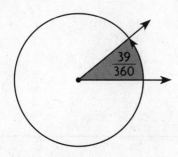

_____

2.

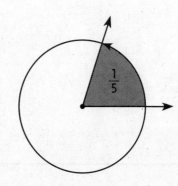

_____

3.

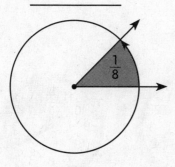

_____

4.

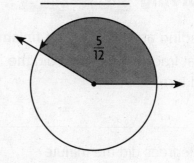

_____

1. What term best describes the angle formed by the hands of the clock?

Ⓐ acute

Ⓑ obtuse

Ⓒ right

Ⓓ straight

2. How many degrees are in an angle that turns through $\frac{3}{4}$ of a circle?

Ⓐ 90°

Ⓑ 180°

Ⓒ 270°

Ⓓ 360°

3. What name is given to an angle that measures 180°?

Ⓐ acute angle

Ⓑ obtuse angle

Ⓒ right angle

Ⓓ straight angle

4. In degrees, what is the angle measure of the shaded part?

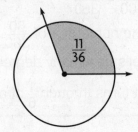

$\frac{11}{36}$

Ⓐ 250°

Ⓑ 110°

Ⓒ 36°

Ⓓ 11°

Problem Solving REAL WORLD

Ann started reading at 4:00 P.M. and finished at 4:20 P.M.

5. Through what fraction of a circle did the minute hand turn?

_____

6. How many degrees did the minute hand turn?

_____

Start

End

Name _____

Lesson 95

COMMON CORE STANDARD CC.4.MD.6
Lesson Objective: Use a protractor to measure an angle and to draw an angle with a given measure.

Measure and Draw Angles

A **protractor** is a tool for measuring the size of an angle.

Follow the steps below to measure ∠ABC.

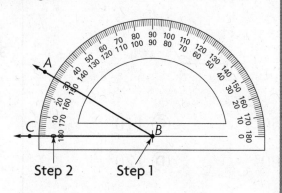

Step 1 Place the center point of the protractor on vertex *B* of the angle.

Step 2 Align the 0° mark on the protractor with ray *BC.* Note that the 0° mark is on the outer scale or top scale.

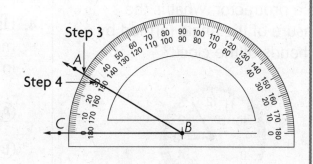

Step 3 Find where ray *BA* intersects the same scale.

Step 4 Read the angle measure on the scale.

The m∠*ABC* = __**30°**__.

Use a protractor to find the angle measure.

1.

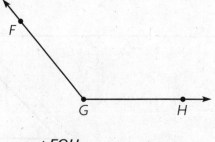

m∠*FGH* _____

2.

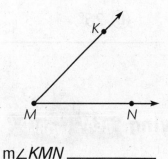

m∠*KMN* _____

Use a protractor to draw the angle.

3. 110°

4. 55°

1. Use a protractor. What is the measure of ∠JKL?

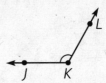

Ⓐ 50°   Ⓒ 110°

Ⓑ 60°   Ⓓ 120°

2. Use a protractor. What is the measure of the angle formed by the hands of the clock?

Ⓐ 115°   Ⓒ 50°

Ⓑ 62°   Ⓓ 25°

Use the diagram for 3–4.

3. Use a protractor. What is the measure of the **largest** angle in the triangle?

Ⓐ 175°   Ⓒ 110°

Ⓑ 130°   Ⓓ 95°

4. Use a protractor. What is the measure of the **smallest** angle in the triangle?

Ⓐ 40°

Ⓑ 30°

Ⓒ 20°

Ⓓ 10°

Problem Solving

The drawing shows the angles a stair tread makes with a support board along a wall. Use your protractor to measure the angles.

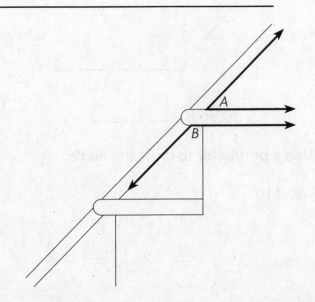

5. What is the measure of ∠A? _____

6. What is the measure of ∠B? _____

Name _____

Lesson 96
COMMON CORE STANDARD CC.4.MD.7
Lesson Objective: Determine the measure
of an angle separated into parts.

Join and Separate Angles

The measure of an angle equals the sum of the measures of its parts.

Use your protractor and the angles at the right.

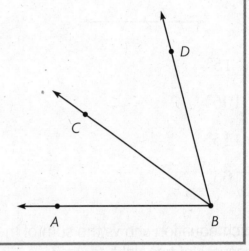

Step 1 Measure ∠ABC and ∠CBD. Record the measures.

m∠ABC = __35°__ ; m∠CBD = __40°__

Step 2 Find the sum of the measures.

__35°__ + __40°__ = __75°__

Step 3 Measure ∠ABD. Record the measure.

m∠ABD = __75°__

So, m∠ABC + m∠CBD = m∠ABD.

Add to find the measure of the angle. Write an equation to record your work.

1.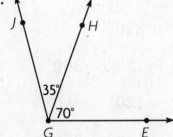

m∠EGJ = _____

2.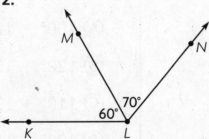

m∠KLN = _____

3.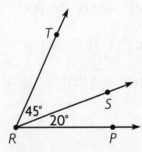

m∠PRT = _____

Use a protractor and the art at the right.

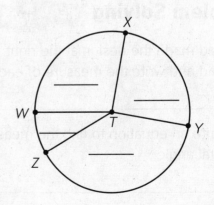

4. Find the measure of each angle. Label each angle with its measure.

5. Write the sum of the angle measures as an equation.

_____

1. What is the measure of the unknown angle in the figure?

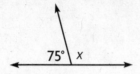

Ⓐ 15°

Ⓑ 105°

Ⓒ 115°

Ⓓ 165°

2. Which equation shows the sum of the measures of two right angles?

Ⓐ 45° + 45° = 90°

Ⓑ 50° + 50° = 100°

Ⓒ 90° + 90° = 180°

Ⓓ 180° + 180° = 360°

3. What is the measure of the unknown angle in the figure?

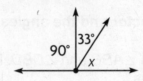

Ⓐ 47°   Ⓒ 90°

Ⓑ 57°   Ⓓ 123°

4. Use a protractor. Which equation shows the correct sum of the angle measures in the figure?

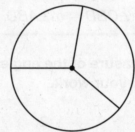

Ⓐ 100° + 120° = 220°

Ⓑ 120° + 120° + 120° = 360°

Ⓒ 110° + 120° + 130° = 360°

Ⓓ 100° + 120° + 140° = 360°

Problem Solving REAL WORLD

5. Ned made the design at the right. Use a protractor. Find and write the measure of each of the 3 angles.

_____

6. Write an equation to find the measure of the total angle.

_____

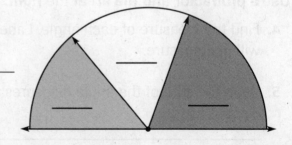

Lesson 97

COMMON CORE STANDARD CC.4.MD.7

Lesson Objective: Use the strategy *draw a diagram* to solve angle measurement problems.

Name _____

Problem Solving • Unknown Angle Measures

Use the strategy *draw a diagram*.

Mrs. Allen is cutting a piece of wood for a set for the school play. She needs a piece of wood with a 60° angle. After the cut, what is the angle measure of the part left over?

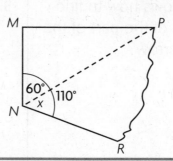

Read the Problem		
What do I need to find?	**What information do I need to use?**	**How will I use the information?**
I need to find <u>the angle</u> <u>measure of the part left</u> <u>over, or m∠PNR</u>.	I can use <u>the angle</u> measures I know: <u>m∠MNP = 60° and</u> <u>m∠MNR = 110°</u>	I can <u>draw a bar model to</u> <u>find the unknown angle</u> <u>measure, or m∠PNR</u>

Solve the Problem

I can <u>draw a bar model to represent the problem</u>.

Then I can <u>write an equation to solve the problem</u>.

m∠MNP + m∠PNR = m∠MNR

$\underline{\quad 60° \quad}$ + x = $\underline{\quad 110° \quad}$

x = $\underline{\quad 110° \quad}$ − $\underline{\quad 60° \quad}$, or $\underline{\quad 50° \quad}$

So, m∠PNR = $\underline{\quad 50° \quad}$

The angle measure of the part left over is $\underline{\quad 50° \quad}$.

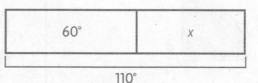

1. Cal is cutting a rectangular board as shown. What is the angle measure of the part left over? _____

2. What equation did you use to solve?

_____

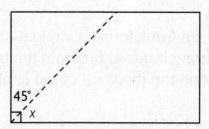

Core Standards for Math, Grade 4

1. Which equation shows how to find the angle measure of the part of the circle without the arrow?

Ⓐ 180° − 90° = ▩

Ⓑ 360° − 90° = ▩

Ⓒ 360° − 180° = ▩

Ⓓ 360° − 270° = ▩

2. Moises has a piece of paper that is $\frac{1}{4}$ of a large circle. He cuts the paper into three equal parts from the center point of the circle. What is the angle measure of each part?

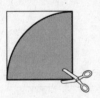

Ⓐ 90°   Ⓒ 45°

Ⓑ 60°   Ⓓ 30°

3. Ian is making a design using wedge-shaped tiles. The wedge of each tile has an angle measure of 30°. How many tiles would he need to put together to form a 180° angle?

Ⓐ 12   Ⓒ 3

Ⓑ 6   Ⓓ 2

4. Marla has a piece of felt that is $\frac{1}{3}$ of a large circle. She cuts her piece of felt in half from the point that would be at the center of the circle. What is the angle measure of each part?

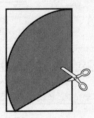

Ⓐ 120°

Ⓑ 90°

Ⓒ 60°

Ⓓ 45°

5. A tree trunk forms a straight angle that measures 180°. A branch grows out from the trunk at a 125° angle. Explain how to find the measure of the angle **above** the branch.

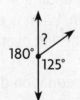

_____

_____

_____

Name _____

Lesson 98
COMMON CORE STANDARD CC.4.G.1
Lesson Objective: Identify and draw points, lines, line segments, rays, and angles.

Lines, Rays, and Angles

Name	What it looks like	Think
point D	$D.$	A **point** names a location in space.
line AB; $\overleftrightarrow{AB}$ line BA; $\overleftrightarrow{BA}$	$A \quad B$	A **line** extends without end in opposite directions.
line segment AB; $\overline{AB}$ line segment BA; $\overline{BA}$	$A \quad B$	"Segment" means part. A **line segment** is part of a line. It is named by its two endpoints.
ray MN; $\overrightarrow{MN}$ ray NM; $\overrightarrow{NM}$	$M \quad N$ $M \quad N$	A **ray** has one endpoint and extends without end in one direction. A ray is named using two points. The endpoint is always named first.
angle XYZ; $\angle XYZ$ angle ZYX; $\angle ZYX$ angle Y; $\angle Y$	X Y Z	Two rays or line segments that share an endpoint form an angle. The shared point is the vertex of the angle.

A **right angle** forms a square corner.	An **acute angle** opens less than a right angle.	An **obtuse angle** opens more than a right angle and less than a straight angle.	A **straight angle** forms a line.

Draw and label an example of the figure.

1. $\overline{PQ}$

2. $\overrightarrow{KJ}$

3. obtuse $\angle FGH$

1. Tenley makes stained glass windows. She used this piece of stained glass in one of the windows. How many right angles does this piece have?

(A) 3   (C) 1

(B) 2   (D) 0

2. Which of the following terms best describes this figure?

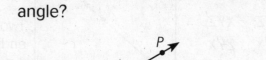

(A) line segment

(B) line

(C) ray

(D) angle

3. Vinny draws an angle like the one below for the first letter of his name.

What kind of angle does Vinny draw?

(A) right angle   (C) acute angle

(B) straight angle   (D) obtuse angle

4. Which is a correct way to name this angle?

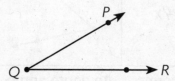

(A) ∠PRQ   (C) ∠RPQ

(B) ∠PQR   (D) ∠PR

Problem Solving REAL WORLD

Use the figure at the right for 5–7.

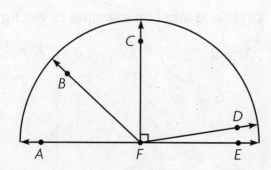

5. Classify ∠AFD. _____

6. Classify ∠CFE. _____

7. Name two acute angles.

Name _____

Lesson 99
COMMON CORE STANDARD CC.4.G.1
Lesson Objective: Identify and draw
parallel lines and perpendicular lines.

Parallel Lines and Perpendicular Lines

Parallel lines are lines in a plane that are always the same distance apart. Parallel lines or line segments never meet.

In the figure, lines AB and CD, even if extended, will never meet. The lines are parallel. Write $\overleftrightarrow{AB} \parallel \overleftrightarrow{CD}$.

Lines ___AD___ and ___BC___ are also parallel. So, $\overleftrightarrow{AD} \parallel \overleftrightarrow{BC}$.

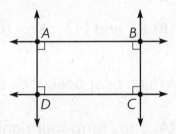

Intersecting lines cross at exactly one point. Intersecting lines that form right angles are **perpendicular.**

In the figure, lines ___AD___ and ___AB___ are perpendicular because they form right angles at vertex A. Write $\overleftrightarrow{AD} \perp \overleftrightarrow{AB}$.

Lines ___BC___ and ___CD___ are also perpendicular. So, $\overleftrightarrow{BC} \perp \overleftrightarrow{CD}$.

Use the figure for 1–3.

1. Name two sides that appear to be parallel.

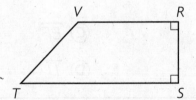

   _____

2. Name two sides that appear to be perpendicular.

   _____

3. Name two sides that appear to be intersecting, but not perpendicular.

   _____

1. Virginia and Susan are discussing properties of lines during math class. Which best describes intersecting lines?

   Ⓐ They cross each other at one point.

   Ⓑ They always form obtuse angles.

   Ⓒ They only form right angles.

   Ⓓ They never cross each other.

2. Logan draws a map of his neighborhood.

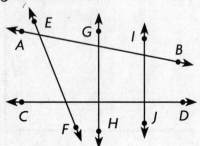

   Which line appears to be parallel to $\overleftrightarrow{GH}$?

   Ⓐ $\overleftrightarrow{AB}$ Ⓒ $\overleftrightarrow{EF}$

   Ⓑ $\overleftrightarrow{CD}$ Ⓓ $\overleftrightarrow{IJ}$

3. Joe drew a figure. Which two sides of the figure are perpendicular?

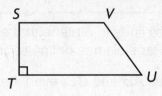

   Ⓐ $\overline{TU}$ and $\overline{UV}$ Ⓒ $\overline{SV}$ and $\overline{TU}$

   Ⓑ $\overline{ST}$ and $\overline{VU}$ Ⓓ $\overline{TU}$ and $\overline{ST}$

4. Which best describes parallel lines?

   Ⓐ They form four right angles.

   Ⓑ They never cross each other.

   Ⓒ They form four acute angles.

   Ⓓ They form two acute angles and two obtuse angles.

5. Which lines appear to be perpendicular in this figure? Explain your answer.

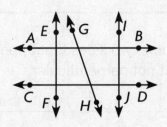

_____

_____

_____

_____

Classify Triangles

A **triangle** is a polygon with __3__ sides
and __3__ angles.
Each pair of sides joins at a vertex.

You can name a triangle by its vertices.

ΔPQR ΔQRP ΔRPQ
ΔPRQ ΔQPR ΔRQP

There are __3__ types of triangles. All triangles have
at least __2__ acute angles.

Obtuse triangle
one obtuse angle

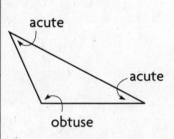

Right triangle
one right angle

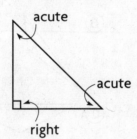

Acute triangle
three acute angles

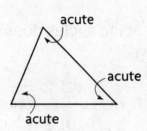

---

1. Name the triangle. Tell whether each angle is
   acute, *right*, or *obtuse*. A name for the triangle

   is _____.

   ∠X is _____.

   ∠Y is _____.

   ∠Z is _____.

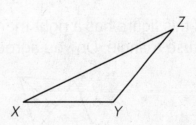

Classify each triangle. Write *acute*, *right*, or *obtuse*.

2.

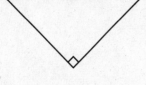

_____

3.

_____

4.

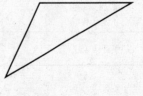

_____

1. A sign is in the shape of an acute triangle. Which of the following could be the shape of the sign?

   Ⓐ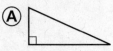

   Ⓑ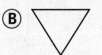

   Ⓒ

   Ⓓ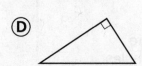

2. How many acute angles does a right triangle have?

   Ⓐ 0   Ⓒ 2

   Ⓑ 1   Ⓓ 3

3. How many acute angles does an obtuse triangle have?

   Ⓐ 0   Ⓒ 2

   Ⓑ 1   Ⓓ 3

4. Janelle made a flag in the shape of a right triangle. Which of the triangles could be Janelle's flag?

   Ⓐ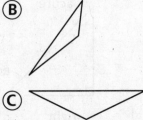

   Ⓑ

   Ⓒ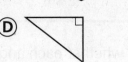

   Ⓓ

5. Marla says this figure has a right triangle, an acute triangle, and an obtuse triangle. Do you agree? Explain your answer.

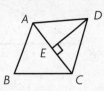

_____

_____

_____

_____

Classify Quadrilaterals

A **quadrilateral** is a polygon with __4__ sides and __4__ angles.
Some quadrilaterals have special names:

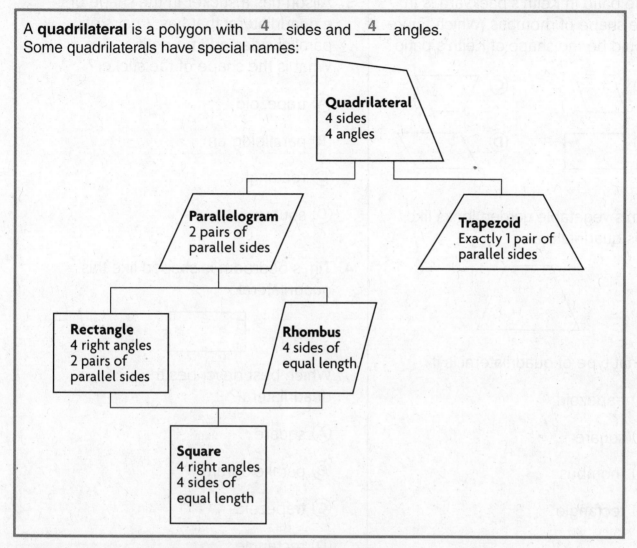

Quadrilateral
4 sides
4 angles

Parallelogram
2 pairs of
parallel sides

Trapezoid
Exactly 1 pair of
parallel sides

Rectangle
4 right angles
2 pairs of
parallel sides

Rhombus
4 sides of
equal length

Square
4 right angles
4 sides of
equal length

Classify each figure as many ways as possible. Write
quadrilateral, trapezoid, parallelogram, rhombus, rectangle, or *square.*

1.

_____

_____

_____

_____

2.

_____

_____

_____

_____

3.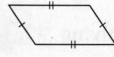

_____

_____

_____

_____

1. The patio in Keith's backyard is in the shape of rhombus. Which figure could be the shape of Keith's patio?

Ⓐ   Ⓒ

Ⓑ   Ⓓ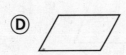

2. Jim's vegetable garden looks like this quadrilateral.

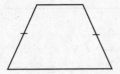

What type of quadrilateral is it?

Ⓐ trapezoid

Ⓑ square

Ⓒ rhombus

Ⓓ rectangle

3. Alison has a sticker in the shape of a quadrilateral that has 2 pairs of parallel sides and no right angles. What is the shape of the sticker?

Ⓐ trapezoid

Ⓑ parallelogram

Ⓒ rectangle

Ⓓ square

4. Tim's bedroom is shaped like this quadrilateral.

Which best describes the quadrilateral?

Ⓐ square

Ⓑ parallelogram

Ⓒ trapezoid

Ⓓ rectangle

Problem Solving REAL WORLD

5. Alan drew a polygon with four sides and four angles. All four sides are equal. None of the angles are right angles. What figure did Alan draw?

_____

6. Teresa drew a quadrilateral with 2 pairs of parallel sides and 4 right angles. What quadrilateral could she have drawn?

_____

Name _____

Lesson 102
COMMON CORE STANDARD CC.4.G.3
Lesson Objective: Determine whether a figure has a line of symmetry.

Line Symmetry

**Tell whether the parts on each side of the line match.
Is the line a line of symmetry?**

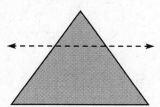

Step 1 Trace and cut out the shape.

Fold the shape along the dashed line.

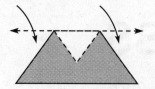

Step 2 Tell whether the parts on each side match.

Compare the parts on each side.

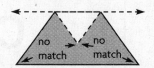

The parts do not match.

Step 3 Decide if the line is a line of symmetry.

The parts on each side of the line do not match.

So, the line __is not__ a line of symmetry.

Tell if the line appears to be a line of symmetry. Write _yes_ or _no_.

1.

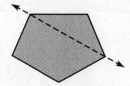

_____

2.

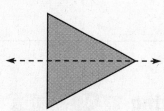

_____

3.

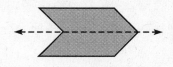

_____

4.

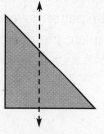

_____

1. Which shape can be folded on the line to show symmetry?

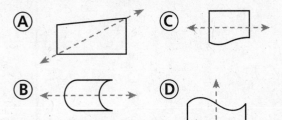

2. Rosie drew a triangle and its line of symmetry. Which could be the figure that Rosie drew?

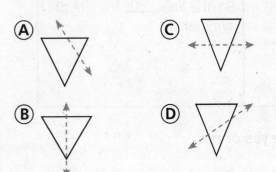

3. Which line does **not** show a line of symmetry?

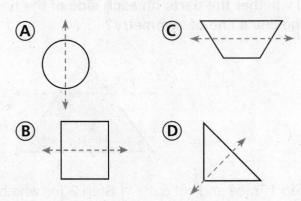

4. Which of the letters does **not** have line symmetry?

CABS

Ⓐ C   Ⓒ B

Ⓑ A   Ⓓ S

Problem Solving REAL WORLD

5. Kara uses the pattern at the right to make paper dolls. The dashed line represents a line of symmetry. A complete doll includes the reflection of the pattern over the line of symmetry. Complete the design to show what one of Kara's paper dolls looks like.

Lesson 103
COMMON CORE STANDARD CC.4.G.3

Lesson Objective: Identify and draw lines of symmetry in two-dimensional figures.

Find and Draw Lines of Symmetry

Tell whether the shape appears to have zero lines, 1 line, or more than 1 line of symmetry. Write *zero, 1,* or *more than 1.*

Step 1 Decide if the shape has a line of symmetry.

Trace and cut out the shape. Fold the shape along a vertical line.

Do the two parts match exactly? ___yes___

Step 2 Decide if the shape has another line of symmetry.

Open the shape and fold it along a horizontal line.

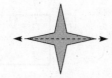

Do the two parts match exactly? ___yes___

Step 3 Find any other lines of symmetry.

Think: Can I fold the shape in other ways so that the two parts match exactly?

I can fold the paper diagonally two different ways, and the parts match exactly.

So, the shape appears to have ___more than 1___ line of symmetry.

Tell whether the shape appears to have zero lines, 1 line, or more than 1 line of symmetry. Write *zero, 1,* or *more than 1.*

1.

_____

2.

_____

3.

_____

1. Claire painted the following figures. Which figure has more than one line of symmetry?

 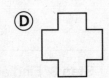

2. Hailey wrote the first letter of her name on a piece of paper.

How many lines of symmetry does the letter *H* appear to have?

Ⓐ 0   Ⓒ 2

Ⓑ 1   Ⓓ 3

3. The figure shown has 8 sides of equal length.

How many lines of symmetry does the figure appear to have?

Ⓐ 2   Ⓒ 8

Ⓑ 4   Ⓓ 10

4. Jared drew a figure with two lines of symmetry. Which figure could be what Jared drew?

Ⓐ    Ⓒ

Ⓑ   Ⓓ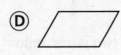

Problem Solving

Use the chart for 5–6.

5. Which number or numbers appear to have only 1 line of symmetry?

_____

6. Which number or numbers appear to have 2 lines of symmetry?

_____

Answer Key

Name _____

Lesson 1
COMMON CORE STANDARD CC.4.OA.1
Lesson Objective: Relate multiplication equations and comparison statements.

Algebra • Multiplication Comparisons

Tara has 3 times as many soccer medals as Greg. Greg has 4 soccer medals. How many soccer medals does Tara have?

Step 1 Draw a model.

Greg ○○○○

Tara ○○○○ ○○○○ ○○○○

Step 2 Use the model to write an equation.

$n = \underline{3} \times \underline{4}$ **Think:** n is how many soccer medals Tara has.

Step 3 Solve the equation.

$n = \underline{12}$

So, Tara has $\underline{12}$ soccer medals.

Draw a model and write an equation.   *Check student's models.*

1. 4 times as many as 7 is 28.   2. 16 is 8 times as many as 2.

$$4 \times 7 = 28 \qquad 16 = 8 \times 2$$

3. 3 times as many as 6 is 18.   4. 10 is 2 times as many as 5.

$$3 \times 6 = 18 \qquad 10 = 2 \times 5$$

www.harcourtschoolsupply.com
© Houghton Mifflin Harcourt Publishing Company   1   Core Standards for Math, Grade 4

Name _____

Lesson 1
CC.4.OA.1

1. Mei has 32 shells. This is 4 times as many shells as Rob has. Mei made a model to compare the numbers of shells.

Which equation represents how to find the value of n?

Ⓐ $32 = n + 4$ Ⓒ $32 + 4 = n$
Ⓑ $32 = 4 \times n$ Ⓓ $32 \times 4 = n$

2. Julia has 24 baseball cards. This is 4 times as many as Chad has. How many baseball cards does Chad have?

Ⓐ 4   Ⓒ 20
Ⓑ 6   Ⓓ 96

3. Kirin has 28 books. This is 7 times as many books as Gail has. Kirin made a model to compare the numbers.

Which equation represents how to find the value of n?

Ⓐ $28 = n + 7$ Ⓒ $28 + 7 = n$
Ⓑ $28 \times 7 = n$ **Ⓓ** $28 = 7 \times n$

4. Robin bought 40 flowers. This is 8 times as many as the number of vases that she has. How many vases does Robin have?

Ⓐ 3   **Ⓒ** 5
Ⓑ 4   Ⓓ 8

Problem Solving REAL WORLD

5. Alan is 14 years old. This is twice as old as his brother James is. How old is James?

7 years old

6. There are 27 campers. This is nine times as many as the number of counselors. How many counselors are there?

3 counselors

www.harcourtschoolsupply.com
© Houghton Mifflin Harcourt Publishing Company   2   Core Standards for Math, Grade 4

Name _____

Lesson 2
COMMON CORE STANDARD CC.4.OA.2
Lesson Objective: Solve problems involving multiplicative comparison and additive comparison.

Algebra • Comparison Problems

Jamie has 3 times as many baseball cards as Rick. Together, they have 20 baseball cards. How many cards does Jamie have?

Step 1 Draw a box with the letter n in it to show that Rick has an unknown number of cards. Jamie has 3 times as many cards as Rick, so draw three identical boxes to represent Jamie's cards.

Jamie | n | n | n |
Rick | n | } 20

Step 2 Use the model to write an equation.
Think: There are 4 equal bars. The number in each bar is represented by n.

There are a total of 20 cards. So, $\underline{4} \times n = \underline{20}$

Step 3 Solve the equation to find the value of n.
Think: 4 times what number is 20?

Since $4 \times \underline{5} = 20$, the value of n is $\underline{5}$.

Rick has $\underline{5}$ cards.

Step 4 Find how many cards Jamie has.
Think: Jamie has 3 times as many cards as Rick.

So, Jamie has $3 \times \underline{5} = \underline{15}$ baseball cards.

Draw a model. Write an equation and solve.

1. Maddie has 2 times as many stickers on her notebook as Meg. Together, they have 15 stickers. How many stickers are on Maddie's notebook?

Maddie | n | n |
Meg | n | } 15

10 stickers

2. How many more stickers are on Maddie's notebook than on Meg's notebook?

Maddie | 10 |
Meg | 5 |

5 more stickers

www.harcourtschoolsupply.com
© Houghton Mifflin Harcourt Publishing Company   3   Core Standards for Math, Grade 4

Name _____

Lesson 2
CC.4.OA.2

1. Maria has 4 times as many necklaces as Sheila. Together, they have 25 necklaces. How many necklaces does Maria have?

Ⓐ 4   Ⓒ 15
Ⓑ 5   **Ⓓ** 20

2. Fernando ran 3 times as far as Aaron. They ran a total of 12 miles. How many miles did Fernando run?

Ⓐ 9 miles
Ⓑ 6 miles
Ⓒ 3 miles
Ⓓ 2 miles

3. Mr. Anson made a walkway using 4 times as many red bricks as gray bricks. He used a total of 80 bricks. How many red bricks did Mr. Anson use?

Ⓐ 5   Ⓒ 16
Ⓑ 8   **Ⓓ** 64

4. Sam worked a total of 36 hours over two weeks. He worked twice as many hours in the second week as the first. How many hours did he work in the first week?

Ⓐ 6   Ⓒ 24
Ⓑ 12   Ⓓ 36

Problem Solving REAL WORLD

5. Rafael counted a total of 40 white cars and yellow cars. There were 9 times as many white cars as yellow cars. How many white cars did Rafael count?

36 white cars

6. Sue scored a total of 35 points in two games. She scored 6 times as many points in the second game as in the first. How many more points did she score in the second game?

25 more points

www.harcourtschoolsupply.com
© Houghton Mifflin Harcourt Publishing Company   4   Core Standards for Math, Grade 4

---

www.harcourtschoolsupply.com
© Houghton Mifflin Harcourt Publishing Company   **207**   Core Standards for Math, Grade 4

Answer Key

Name _____

Lesson **3**
COMMON CORE STANDARD CC.4.OA.3
Lesson Objective: Use the draw a diagram strategy to solve multistep problems.

Problem Solving • Multistep Multiplication Problems

Use the strategy *draw a diagram* to solve a multistep multiplication problem.

Amy planted 8 rows with 18 tulips in each row. In each of the 4 middle rows, there are 4 red tulips. All of the other tulips are yellow. How many of the tulips are yellow tulips?

Read the Problem	Solve the Problem
What do I need to find?	I drew a diagram for each color of tulip.
I need to find the total number of _yellow_ tulips.	18 tulips
What information do I need to use?	8 rows
There are _8_ rows of tulips with _18_ tulips in each row.	4 tulips
There are _4_ rows of tulips with _4_ red tulips in each row.	Next, I found the number in each section.
How will I use the information?	**All Tulips** **Red Tulips**
I can _multiply_ to find the total number of tulips and the number of red tulips.	$8 \times 18 = 144$ $4 \times 4 = 16$
Then I can _subtract_ to find the number of yellow tulips.	Last, I subtracted the number of red tulips from the total number of tulips.
	_144_ – _16_ = _128_
	So, there are _128_ yellow tulips.

1. A car dealer has 8 rows of cars with 16 cars in each row. In each of the first 3 rows, 6 are used cars. The rest of the cars are new cars. How many new cars does the dealer have?

   110 new cars

2. An orchard has 4 rows of apple trees with 12 trees in each row. There are also 6 rows of pear trees with 15 trees in each row. How many apple and pear trees are in the orchard?

   138 apple and pear trees

---

1. All the seats in two sections of a movie theater are occupied. In one section, there are 8 rows with 18 seats in each row. In the other section, there are 12 rows with 6 seats in each row. How many people are seated in these two sections of the theater?

   (A) 44   (C) 144
   (B) 72   **(D) 216**

2. Savannah makes 18 gift baskets to sell in her store. She puts 4 peaches in 10 of the baskets and 2 peaches in the remaining 8 baskets. How many peaches does Savannah place in the gift baskets?

   (A) 24   **(C) 56**
   (B) 40   (D) 108

3. All the seats in two sections of a concert hall are occupied. In one section, there are 18 rows with 9 seats in each row. In the other section, there are 14 rows with 8 seats in each row. How many people are seated in these two sections of the concert hall?

   (A) 274   (C) 112
   (B) 162   (D) 49

4. Mrs. Klein delivered 3 books to 11 classrooms and 4 books to 6 classrooms. How many books did Mrs. Klein deliver to all the classrooms?

   (A) 24   **(C) 57**
   (B) 33   (D) 119

5. Peter baked 5 pies for a bake sale. He cut each pie into 12 slices. He sold 9 slices from each of the 5 pies. How many slices of pie did Peter get to take home? Explain how you found your answer.

   First, I modeled the pies by drawing 5 circles with 12 sections each. I found the total number of slices of pie: $5 \times 12 = 60$, and I found the total number of slices that were sold: $5 \times 9 = 45$. I subtracted the slices that were sold from the total number of slices to find how many slices Peter took home: $60 - 45 = 15$.

Name _____

Lesson **4**
COMMON CORE STANDARD CC.4.OA.3
Lesson Objective: Represent and solve multistep problems using equations.

Algebra • Solve Multistep Problems Using Equations

The **Order of Operations** is a special set of rules which gives the order in which calculations are done in an expression. First, multiply and divide from left to right. Then, add and subtract from left to right.

Use the order of operations to find the value of n.

$6 \times 26 + 3 \times 45 - 11 = n$

Step 1 Circle the first multiplication expression in the equation.

$(6 \times 26) + 3 \times 45 - 11 = n$

Step 2 Multiply 6×26.

$156 + 3 \times 45 - 11 = n$

Step 3 Circle the next multiplication expression in the equation.

$156 + (3 \times 45) - 11 = n$

Step 4 Multiply 3×45.

$156 + 135 - 11 = n$

Step 5 There are no more multiplication or division expressions. Circle the first addition expression in the equation.

$(156 + 135) - 11 = n$

Step 6 Add $156 + 135$.

$291 - 11 = n$

Step 7 Subtract $291 - 11$.

$280 = n$

Find the value of n.

1. $5 \times 43 + 9 \times 24 + 25 = n$

   _456_ = n

2. $7 \times 29 + 4 \times 46 - 56 = n$

   _331_ = n

---

1. In his stamp book, Dane has 6 pages with 15 stamps on each and 9 pages with 20 stamps on each. He gives 25 stamps away. Which equation can Dane use to find how many stamps he has left?

   (A) $6 \times 15 \times 9 \times 20 - 25 = n$
   (B) $6 \times 15 + 9 \times 20 - 25 = n$
   (C) $6 + 15 \times 9 + 20 - 25 = n$
   (D) $6 + 15 \times 9 \times 20 + 25 = n$

2. Tim has 5 boxes with 18 sports cards in each. He buys 7 packs of sports cards with 13 cards in each. If Tim buys another 10 sports cards, how many sports cards will he have?

   (A) 53   (C) 191
   (B) 181   (D) 1,271

3. Latisha has 7 boxes with 21 shells in each. She has 6 bags with 17 shells in each. She gives away 18 shells. Which equation can Latisha use to find how many shells she has left?

   (A) $7 + 21 \times 6 \times 17 - 18 = n$
   (B) $7 \times 21 + 6 \times 17 + 18 = n$
   (C) $7 + 21 + 6 + 17 - 18 = n$
   (D) $7 \times 21 + 6 \times 17 - 18 = n$

4. Sara has 6 albums with 15 photos in each. Maya has 8 albums with 13 photos in each. If Sara adds 12 more photos, how many photos will Sara and Maya have in all?

   (A) 54   (C) 206
   (B) 182   (D) 404

Problem Solving REAL WORLD

5. A bakery has 4 trays with 16 muffins on each tray. The bakery has 3 trays of cupcakes with 24 cupcakes on each tray. If 15 cupcakes are sold, how many muffins and cupcakes are left?

   121 muffins and cupcakes

6. Katy bought 5 packages of stickers with 25 stickers in each package. She also bought 3 boxes of markers with 12 markers in each box. If she receives 8 stickers from a friend, how many stickers and markers does Katy have now?

   169 stickers and markers

Lesson 5
COMMON CORE STANDARD CC.4.OA.3
Lesson Objective: Use the strategy draw a diagram to solve multistep multiplication problems.

Problem Solving • Multiply 2-Digit Numbers

A library ordered 17 cases with 24 books in each case. In 12 of the cases, 18 books were fiction books. The rest of the books were nonfiction. How many nonfiction books did the library order?

Read the Problem	Solve the Problem
What do I need to find? I need to find _how many nonfiction books_ were ordered.	• First, find the total number of books ordered. $\underline{17} \times \underline{24} = \underline{408}$ books ordered • Next, find the number of fiction books. $\underline{12} \times \underline{18} = \underline{216}$ fiction books
What information do I need to use? $\underline{17}$ cases of $\underline{24}$ books each were ordered. In $\underline{12}$ cases, $\underline{18}$ books were fiction books.	• Last, draw a bar model. I need to subtract. [408 books ordered] [216 fiction books] [?]
How will I use the information? I can find the _total number of books ordered_ and the _number of fiction books ordered_. Then I can draw a bar model to compare the _total number of books_ to the _number of fiction books_.	$408 - 216 = \underline{192}$ So, the library ordered $\underline{192}$ nonfiction books.

1. A grocer ordered 32 cases with 28 small cans of fruit in each case. The grocer also ordered 24 cases with 18 large cans of fruit in each case. How many more small cans of fruit did the grocer order?

464 more small cans of fruit

2. Rebecca rode her bike 16 miles each day for 30 days. Michael rode his bike 25 miles for 28 days. Who rode farther? How much farther?

Michael rode 220 miles farther.

Lesson 5
CC.4.OA.3

1. In July, traffic officers wrote an average of 34 tickets each day. In August, they wrote an average of 47 tickets each day. How many more tickets did traffic officers write in August than in July? (Hint: July and August have 31 days each.)

- (A) 403
- (B) 1,045
- (C) 1,457
- (D) 2,511

2. An arena's lower-level section has 32 rows with 50 seats in each row. The upper-level section has 28 rows with 42 seats in each row. How many more seats are in the lower-level section than in the upper-level section?

- (A) 400
- (B) 424
- (C) 1,176
- (D) 1,600

3. A concert hall has seats on a main floor and in a balcony. The main floor has 24 rows of 28 seats in each row. The balcony has 9 rows of 22 seats in each row. How many more seats are on the main floor than in the balcony?

- (A) 870
- (B) 672
- (C) 474
- (D) 198

4. Jevonne lives in a large apartment complex. Building A has 17 floors with 8 apartments on each floor. Building B has 12 floors with 8 apartments on each floor. How many more apartments are in Building A than in Building B?

- (A) 40
- (B) 96
- (C) 136
- (D) 204

5. A chess club orders a T-shirt and a notebook for each of its 24 members. Each T-shirt costs $13, and each notebook costs $2 each. How much more do the T-shirts cost in all than the notebooks? Explain how you found your answer.

$264 more; Possible explanation:
I found 24 × 13 and 24 × 2, and then subtracted to find
the difference in cost. 312 − 48 = 264. The T-shirts cost
$264 more than the notebooks.

Lesson 6
COMMON CORE STANDARD CC.4.OA.3
Lesson Objective: Use remainders to solve division problems.

Interpret the Remainder

When you solve a division problem with a remainder, the way you interpret the remainder depends on the situation and the question.

Way 1: Write the remainder as a fraction.
Callie has a board that is 60 inches long. She wants to cut 8 shelves of equal length from the board and use the entire board. How long will each shelf be?

Divide. $60 \div 8$ _____ 7 r4

The remainder, 4 inches, can be divided into 8 equal parts.

$\begin{array}{c} 4 \leftarrow \text{remainder} \\ 8 \leftarrow \text{divisor} \end{array}$

Write the remainder as a fraction.

Each shelf will be $7\frac{4}{8}$ inches long.

Way 3: Add 1 to the quotient.
Callie has 60 beads. She wants to put 8 beads in each container. How many containers will she need?

Divide. $60 \div 8$ _____ 7 r4

The answer shows that Callie can fill 7 containers but will have 4 beads left over. She will need 1 more container for the 4 leftover beads. Add 1 to the quotient.

Callie will need $\underline{8}$ containers.

Way 2: Drop the remainder.
Callie has 60 beads. She wants to make 8 identical bracelets and use as many beads as possible on each bracelet. How many beads will be on each bracelet?

Divide. $60 \div 8$ _____ 7 r4

The remainder is the number of beads left over. Those beads will not be used. Drop the remainder.

Callie will use $\underline{7}$ beads on each bracelet.

Way 4: Use only the remainder.
Callie has 60 stickers. She wants to give an equal number of stickers to 8 friends. She will give the leftover stickers to her sister. How many stickers will Callie give to her sister?

Divide. $60 \div 8$ _____ 7 r4

The remainder is the number of stickers left over. Use the remainder as the answer.

Callie will give her sister $\underline{4}$ stickers.

1. There are 35 students going to the zoo. Each van can hold 6 students. How many vans are needed?

6 vans

2. Sue has 55 inches of ribbon. She wants to cut the ribbon into 6 equal pieces. How long will each piece be?

$9\frac{1}{6}$ inches

Lesson 6
CC.4.OA.3

1. A group of 40 people takes the swan boat ride. Each boat can carry 6 people. If the guide fills as many boats as possible, how many people will ride in the last boat?

- (A) 34
- (B) 7
- (C) 6
- (D) 4

2. Vanna uses thank-you notes that come in packs of 8. She has to write 29 thank-you notes. How many packs of thank-you notes should she buy?

- (A) 3
- (B) $3\frac{5}{8}$
- (C) 4
- (D) 5

3. Nolan divides his 88 toy cars into boxes. Each box can hold 9 cars. How many boxes can Nolan fill?

- (A) 7
- (B) 9
- (C) 10
- (D) 12

4. Selim puts 30 ounces of trail mix equally into 9 bags. How many ounces will be in each bag?

- (A) 4 ounces
- (B) $3\frac{1}{3}$ ounces
- (C) 3 ounces
- (D) $2\frac{1}{2}$ ounces

Problem Solving REAL WORLD

5. Joanna has 70 beads. She uses 8 beads for each bracelet. She makes as many bracelets as possible. How many beads will Joanna have left over?

6 beads left over

6. A teacher wants to give 3 markers to each of her 25 students. Markers come in packages of 8. How many packages of markers will the teacher need?

10 packages

Answer Key

Name _____

Lesson 7
COMMON CORE STANDARD CC.4.OA.3
Lesson Objective: Solve problems by using the strategy draw a diagram.

Problem Solving • Multistep Division Problems

There are 72 third graders and 84 fourth graders going on a field trip. An equal number of students will ride on each of 4 buses. How many students will ride on each bus?

Read the Problem	Solve the Problem
What do I need to find? I need to find the number of _students_ who will ride on each bus.	I can model the number of students in all using a bar diagram.
What information do I need to use? There are _72_ third graders and _84_ fourth graders. There will be _4_ buses.	<table><tr><td>72</td><td>84</td></tr></table> 156
How will I use the information? I will make a bar diagram for each step. I will add _72 and 84_ to find the total number of students. I will divide by _4_ to find how many students will ride on each bus.	I can model the number of buses and divide to find the number of students on each bus. <table><tr><td>39</td><td>39</td><td>39</td><td>39</td></tr></table> 156
	So, _39_ students will ride on each bus.

1. Miranda has 180 beads for making jewelry. She buys 240 more beads. She wants to store the beads in a case with 6 sections. She wants to put the same number of beads in each section. How many beads should Miranda put in each section?

70 beads

2. All 203 students at Polk School eat lunch at the same time. One day 19 students were absent. If 8 students sit at each table in the lunchroom, how many tables were used that day at lunch?

23 tables

Name _____

Lesson 7
CC.4.OA.3

1. There are 112 seats in a school auditorium. There are 7 seats in each row. There are 70 people seated. They filled all the seats in a row before starting to sit in a new row. How many rows are empty?

- Ⓐ 6
- Ⓑ 10
- Ⓒ 16
- Ⓓ 28

2. Ursula bought 9 dozen gauze pads for the health office. The gauze pads were divided equally into 4 boxes. How many gauze pads are in each box?

- Ⓐ 108
- Ⓑ 36
- Ⓒ 27
- Ⓓ 24

3. The school choir has 48 singers with high voices, 53 singers with middle voices, and 39 singers with low voices. The singers stand in 4 equal rows at concerts. How many singers are in each row?

- Ⓐ 140
- Ⓑ 45
- Ⓒ 35
- Ⓓ 34

4. The are 126 seats in a meeting room. There are 9 seats in each row. There are 90 people seated. They filled all the seats in a row before starting to sit in a new row. How many rows are empty?

- Ⓐ 36
- Ⓒ 9
- Ⓑ 10
- Ⓓ 4

5. An orchestra has 18 string players, 9 percussion players, 15 brass players, and 12 woodwind players. If all the players sit in rows of 9 chairs each, how many rows of chairs are needed? Explain your answer.

6 rows; Possible explanation: I added 18 + 9 + 15 + 12 = 54 to find the total number of people. Then I divided 54 by 9 to find the number of rows of chairs needed, 6.

Name _____

Lesson 8
COMMON CORE STANDARD CC.4.OA.4
Lesson Objective: Find all the factors of a number by using models.

Model Factors

Use tiles to find all the factors of 25. Record the arrays and write the factors shown.

Step 1 Record the array and list the factors. **Think:** Every whole number greater than 1 has at least two factors, that number and 1.	$1 \times 25 = 25$ Factors: _1_ , _25_
Step 2 Make an array to see if 2 is a factor of 25. **Think:** An array has the same number of tiles in every row and the same number of tiles in every column.	You cannot use all 25 tiles to make an array that has 2 rows. There is 1 tile left. So, _2_ is not a factor of 25.

Step 3 Continue making arrays, counting by 1, to find all the other factors of 25.

Is 3 a factor? ▦ 3 rows, 1 tile left No, 3 is not a factor of 25.

Is 4 a factor? ▦ 4 rows, 1 tile left No, 4 is not a factor of 25.

Is 5 a factor? ▦ _5_ rows, all tiles used. $5 \times 5 = 25$ There are the same number of tiles in each row and column. Yes, 5 is a factor of 25.

If you continue to make arrays up to 24, you will find there are no additional factors of 25.

So, the factors of 25 are _1, 5, and 25_.

Two factors that make a product are sometimes called a factor pair. What are the factor pairs for 25? _1 and 25, 5 and 5_

Use tiles to find all the factors of the product. Record the arrays and write the factors shown.

Check students' work.

1. 35
1, 5, 7, 35

2. 36
1, 2, 3, 4, 6, 9, 12, 18, 36

Name _____

Lesson 8
CC.4.OA.4

1. Sean helps his coach at the end of the game. He needs to put away 24 baseballs. He puts the same number of baseballs into each box. Which list shows how many baseballs could be in each box?

- Ⓐ 2, 3, 4, or 7
- Ⓑ 2, 4, 6, or 7
- Ⓒ 2, 6, 8, or 10
- Ⓓ 3, 4, 6, or 8

2. Jenn will use 18 connecting cubes to make a model of a park. The model will be in the shape of a rectangle and will have a height of one cube. In how many different ways can Jenn make the model of the park?

- Ⓐ 1
- Ⓑ 2
- Ⓒ 3
- Ⓓ 17

3. Elaine uses 19 connecting cubes to make a model of a house. The house model is in the shape of a rectangle and is one cube high. How many different ways could Elaine make the model of the house?

- Ⓐ 1
- Ⓑ 2
- Ⓒ 4
- Ⓓ 19

4. Which list shows the factors of 16?

- Ⓐ 1, 2, 3, 8, 16
- Ⓑ 1, 3, 4, 8, 16
- Ⓒ 1, 2, 4, 8, 16
- Ⓓ 1, 2, 4, 6, 16

Problem Solving REAL WORLD

5. Brooke has to set up 70 chairs in equal rows for the class talent show. But, there is not room for more than 20 rows. What are the possible number of rows that Brooke could set up?

1, 2, 5, 7, 10, or 14 rows

6. Eduardo thinks of a number between 1 and 20 that has exactly 5 factors. What number is he thinking of?

16

Answer Key

Name _____

Lesson 9
COMMON CORE STANDARD CC.4.OA.4
Lesson Objective: Determine whether a number is a factor of a given number.

Factors and Divisibility

A number is divisible by another number if the quotient is a counting number and the remainder is 0.
You can decide if a number is divisible by 2, 3, 5, 6, or 9 by using divisibility rules instead of dividing. Divisibility rules help you decide if one number is a factor of another.

Is 39 divisible by 2, 3, 5, 6, or 9?

	Result	Conclusion	Divisibility Rules
39 ÷ 2	19 r1	39 is not divisible by 2.	The last digit, 9, is not even, so 39 is not divisible by 2.
39 ÷ 3	13 r0	39 is divisible by 3.	The sum of the digits, 3 + 9 = 12, is divisible by 3, so 39 is divisible by 3.
39 ÷ 5	7 r4	39 is not divisible by 5.	The last digit, 9, is not a 0 or 5, so 39 is not divisible by 5.
39 ÷ 6	6 r3	39 is not divisible by 6.	39 is not divisible by both 2 and 3, so it is not divisible by 6.
39 ÷ 9	4 r3	39 is not divisible by 9.	The sum of the digits, 3 + 9 = 12, is not divisible by 9, so 39 is not divisible by 9.

39 is divisible by 3.
So, 3 is a factor of 39.

Use the chart to tell whether 30 is divisible by each divisor. Explain.

		Result	Conclusion (yes/no)	Explanation
1.	30 ÷ 2	15	yes	30 is even.
2.	30 ÷ 3	10	yes	3 + 0 = 3; 3 is divisible by 3.
3.	30 ÷ 5	6	yes	The last digit is a 0.
4.	30 ÷ 6	5	yes	30 is divisible by both 2 and 3.
5.	30 ÷ 9	3 r3	no	3 + 0 = 3; 3 is not divisible by 9.

Is 4 a factor of the number? Write yes or no.

6. 81   no   7. 24   yes   8. 56   yes

Name _____

Lesson 9
CC.4.OA.4

1. Mariska was decorating her room. She arranged 63 picture tiles on a wall in the shape of a rectangle. How many rows of tiles could be on the wall?
   - (A) 2
   - (B) 5
   - (C) 6
   - **(D) 9**

2. Janice spent $54 to buy some pairs of pants. Each pair of pants cost the same whole-dollar amount. How many pairs of pants could she have bought?
   - **(A) 3**
   - (B) 4
   - (C) 5
   - (D) 7

3. Jorge gives an equal number of marbles to 6 friends. Which could be the total number of marbles he gave to his friends?
   - (A) 15
   - (B) 33
   - (C) 56
   - **(D) 60**

4. Lee and 4 friends want to play marbles. Lee has 40 marbles to share among them. All players must have the same number of marbles to start the game. How many marbles should each player get?
   - (A) 5
   - **(B) 8**
   - (C) 10
   - (D) 20

Problem Solving REAL WORLD

5. Bryson buys a bag of 64 plastic miniature dinosaurs. Could he distribute them equally into six storage containers and not have any left over? **Explain.**

   No, 64 is not divisible by 6.

6. Lori wants to distribute 35 peaches equally into baskets. She will use more than 1 but fewer than 10 baskets. How many baskets does Lori need?

   Lori needs 5 baskets or 7 baskets.

Name _____

Lesson 10
COMMON CORE STANDARD CC.4.OA.4
Lesson Objective: Solve problems by using the strategy make a list.

Problem Solving • Common Factors

Susan sorts a collection of beads. There are 35 blue, 49 red, and 21 pink beads. She arranges all the beads into rows. Each row will have the same number of beads, and all the beads in a row will be the same color. How many beads can she put in each row?

Read the Problem		Solve the Problem		
What do I need to find?				
I need to find the number of beads in each row, if each row is equal and has only one color		Factors of 35	Factors of 49	Factors of 21
		1	1	1
		5	7	3
		7	49	7
		35		21
What information do I need to use?				
Susan has 35 blue, 49 red, and 21 pink beads		The common factors are 7 and 1		
How will I use the information?				
I can make a list to find all of the factors of 35, 49, and 21		So, Susan can put 1 or 7 beads in each row.		
Then I can use the list to find the common factors				

1. Allyson has 60 purple buttons, 36 black buttons, and 24 green buttons. She wants to put all of the buttons in bins. She wants each bin to have only one color and all bins to have the same number of buttons. How many buttons can Allyson put in one bin?

   1, 2, 3, 4, 6, or 12 buttons

2. Ricardo has a marble collection with 54 blue marbles, 24 red marbles, and 18 yellow marbles. He arranges the marbles into equal rows. The marbles in each row will be the same color. How many marbles can he put in one row?

   1, 2, 3, or 6 marbles

Name _____

Lesson 10
CC.4.OA.4

1. Miles has 36 engines, 54 boxcars, and 18 cabooses. He wants to arrange the train cars in equal rows, with just one type of car in each row. How many train cars can he put in each row?
   - (A) 1 or 18
   - (B) 1, 2, 9, or 18
   - **(C) 1, 2, 3, 6, 9, or 18**
   - (D) 1, 2, 3, 4, 6, 8, 9, 12, 18, 24, 36, or 72

2. Gina made a list of all the common factors of 24 and 36. Which list shows the common factors of 24 and 36?
   - (A) 1, 2, 3, 4, 6, 8, 12, 24
   - (B) 1, 2, 4, 6, 8, 9, 12, 24
   - **(C) 1, 2, 3, 4, 6, 12**
   - (D) 1, 6, 8, 12, 18

3. Kendall has 45 dolphin stickers, 15 shark stickers, and 20 whale stickers. She wants to put an equal number of stickers into bags, with only one type of sticker in each bag. How many stickers can Kendall put in each bag?
   - (A) 1
   - (B) 1 or 5
   - **(C) 1, 3, 4 or 5**
   - (D) 1, 2, 3, 4, 5, 9, 10, 15, 20 or 45

4. Which of the following is **not** a common factor of 24, 32, and 64?
   - **(A) 12**
   - (B) 8
   - (C) 4
   - (D) 2

5. Karen is making two displays. One display has 57 red mugs. The other display has 76 sports mugs. The rows of each display must have the same number of mugs. What would be the greatest number of mugs possible to have in a row? Explain your answer.

   Possible answer: the number of mugs in a row must be a factor of 76 and 57. The factors of 57 are 1, 3, 19, and 57. The factors of 76 are 1, 2, 4, 19, 38, and 76. The greatest is 19.

Answer Key

Factors and Multiples

You know that $1 \times 10 = \underline{10}$ and $2 \times 5 = \underline{10}$.

So, 1, 2, 5, and 10 are all **factors** of 10.

You can skip count to find **multiples** of a number:

Count by 1s: 1, 2, 3, 4, 5, 6, 7, 8, 9, **10**, . . .

Count by 2s: 2, 4, 6, 8, **10**, 12, . . .

Count by 5s: 5, **10**, 15, 20, 25, . . .

Count by 10s: **10**, 20, 30, 40, . . .

Note that 10 is a multiple of 1, 2, 5, and 10. A number is a multiple of all of its factors.

A **common multiple** is a multiple of two or more numbers. So, 10 is a common multiple of 1, 2, 5, and 10.

1. Multiply to list the next five multiples of 3.

3   6   9   12   15   18

2. Multiply to list the next five multiples of 7.

7   14   21   28   35   42

Is the number a factor of 8? Write *yes* or *no*.

3. 2   **4.** 8   **5.** 15   **6.** 20

yes   yes   no   no

Is the number a multiple of 4? Write *yes* or *no*.

7. 2   **8.** 12   **9.** 16   **10.** 18

no   yes   yes   no

---

1. Paula is counting by 9s. Peter is counting by 4s. They pace the counting so that they will say the first common number together. What is the first number they both will say?

Ⓐ 16   Ⓒ 45
Ⓑ 36   Ⓓ 64

2. Ms. Ayers wrote a bonus problem on the board. If Jason correctly answers, he will get extra computer time. Jason must write a statement that correctly relates the numbers 5 and 10. Which statement should Jason write?

Ⓐ 5 is a multiple of 10.

Ⓑ 10 is a factor of 5.

Ⓒ 10 is a common multiple of 5 and 10.

Ⓓ 15 is a common multiple of 5 and 10.

3. Roger bought some boxes of pencils. There were 3 pencils in each box. Which could be the number of pencils he bought?

Ⓐ 16   Ⓒ 25
Ⓑ 21   Ⓓ 32

4. Manny makes dinner using 1 box of pasta and 1 jar of sauce. If pasta is sold in packages of 6 boxes and sauce is sold in packages of 3 jars, what is the least number of dinners that Manny can make without any supplies left over?

Ⓐ 3
Ⓑ 6
Ⓒ 9
Ⓓ 18

Problem Solving REAL WORLD

5. Ken paid $12 for two magazines. The cost of each magazine was a multiple of $3. What are the possible prices of the magazines?

$3 and $9; $6 and $6

6. Jodie bought some shirts for $6 each. Marge bought some shirts for $8 each. The girls spent the same amount of money on shirts. What is the least amount they could have spent?

$24

Prime and Composite Numbers

A **prime number** is a whole number greater than 1 that has exactly two factors, 1 and the number itself.

A **composite number** is a whole number greater than 1 that has more than two factors.

You can use division to find the factors of a number and tell whether the number is prime or composite.

Tell whether 55 is *prime* or *composite*.

Use division to find all the numbers that divide into 55 without a remainder. Those numbers are the factors of 55.

$55 \div 1 = 55$, so $\underline{1}$ and $\underline{55}$ are factors.

$55 \div 5 = 11$, so $\underline{5}$ and $\underline{11}$ are factors.

The factors of 55 are $\underline{1}$, $\underline{5}$, $\underline{11}$, and $\underline{55}$.

Because 55 has more than two factors, 55 is a composite number.

Tell whether 61 is *prime* or *composite*.

Use division to find all the numbers that divide into 61 without a remainder. Those numbers are the factors of 61.

$61 \div 1 = 61$, so $\underline{1}$ and $\underline{61}$ are factors.

There are no other numbers that divide into 61 evenly without a remainder.

The factors of 61 are $\underline{1}$ and $\underline{61}$.

Because 61 has exactly two factors, 61 is a prime number.

Tell whether the number is *prime* or *composite*.

1. 44   Think: Is 44 divisible by any number other than 1 and 44?

composite

2. 53   Think: Does 53 have other factors besides 1 and itself?

prime

3. 12   **4.** 50   **5.** 24   **6.** 67

composite   composite   composite   prime

7. 83   **8.** 27   **9.** 34   **10.** 78

prime   composite   composite   composite

---

1. Ms. Chan asked Dwight if 6 is a prime number or a composite number. How should he answer?

Ⓐ 6 is composite.

Ⓑ 6 is prime.

Ⓒ 6 is neither prime nor composite.

Ⓓ 6 is both prime and composite.

2. In a math game, Rob reads four statements about the number 51. He has to pick the true statement to win the game. Which statement should Rob choose?

Ⓐ 51 is divisible by 2.

Ⓑ 51 is divisible by 3.

Ⓒ 51 is divisible by 5.

Ⓓ 51 is a prime number.

3. Elina used 10 tiles in the shape of a rectangle to make a design. She drew a model of the design.

What can Elina conclude about the number 10 from her model?

Ⓐ 10 is a prime number.

Ⓑ 10 is a composite number.

Ⓒ 10 is neither prime nor composite.

Ⓓ 10 is both prime and composite.

4. Maria's friend wrote 4 numbers and asked Maria to identify the prime number. Which is the prime number?

Ⓐ 21   Ⓒ 23
Ⓑ 22   Ⓓ 27

5. Ramon tells his friend that he is learning about prime numbers in math class. His friend asks him to name all the prime numbers between 20 and 30. What numbers should Ramon name? Explain how you know.

23 and 29; Possible answer: prime numbers have exactly two factors, 1 and the number itself. Only 23 and 29 fit this definition.

Name _____

Lesson 13
COMMON CORE STANDARD CC.4.OA.5
Lesson Objective: Generate a number pattern and describe features of the pattern.

Algebra • Number Patterns

A pattern is an ordered set of numbers or objects, called terms.
The numbers below form a pattern. The first term in the pattern is 2.

+3 +3 +3 +3 +3 +3
2,   5,   8,   11, 14, 17, 20, . . .

First term
A rule is used to describe a pattern. The rule for this pattern is *add 3*.
You can describe other patterns in the numbers. Notice that the terms in
the pattern shown alternate between even and odd numbers.

For some patterns, the rule may have two operations.

−2 ×2 −2 ×2 −2 ×2
8,   6,   12, 10, 20, 18, 36, . . .

The rule for this pattern is *subtract 2, multiply by 2*. The first term is 8.
Notice that all of the terms in this pattern are even numbers.

Use the rule to write the numbers in the pattern.

1. Rule: Add 7.   First term: 12
   12, __19__ __26__ __33__ __40__ . . .

2. Rule: Multiply by 3, subtract 1.   First term: 2
   2, __6__ __5__ __15__ __14__ . . .

Use the rule to write the numbers in the pattern.
Describe another pattern in the numbers.

3. Rule: Subtract 5.   First term: 50
   50, __45__ __40__ __35__ __30__ . . .

   **Possible answer: the ones digit alternates
   between 0 and 5.**

4. Rule: Multiply by 2, add 1.   First term: 4
   4, __8__ __9__ __18__ __19__ . . .

   **Possible answer: after the first term, the
   ones digit alternates between 8 and 9.**

---

1. Caitlin's teacher wrote a row of
   numbers following a pattern.

   75, 68, 70, 63, 65, 58, 60

   What should the next number be?

   Ⓐ 51   Ⓒ 55
   Ⓑ 53   Ⓓ 62

2. Roberto wrote the number 60. If the
   rule is *subtract 3*, what is the fifth
   number in Roberto's pattern?

   Ⓐ 75   Ⓒ 48
   Ⓑ 72   Ⓓ 45

3. Julie wrote numbers on chairs
   for field day. She wrote the
   number 4 on the first chair. Her
   rule is *add 5*. What number did she
   write on the sixth chair?

   Ⓐ 28   Ⓒ 25
   Ⓑ 29   Ⓓ 34

4. Ben and Irie made a secret code.
   They wrote some numbers of the
   code so they could remember
   the pattern.

   7, 12, 10, 15, 13, 18, 16, 21

   What should the next number be?

   Ⓐ 18   Ⓒ 23
   Ⓑ 19   Ⓓ 26

Problem Solving REAL WORLD

5. Barb is making a bead necklace. She
   strings 1 white bead, then 3 blue beads,
   then 1 white bead, and so on. Write the
   numbers for the first eight beads that are
   white. What is a rule for the pattern?

   **1, 5, 9, 13, 17, 21, 25, 29;
   possible answer: add 4**

6. An artist is arranging tiles in rows to
   decorate a wall. Each new row has 2 fewer
   tiles than the row below it. If the first row
   has 23 tiles, how many tiles will be in the
   seventh row?

   __11 tiles__

Name _____

Lesson 14
COMMON CORE STANDARD CC.4.OA.5
Lesson Objective: Use the strategy *act it out* to solve problems.

Problem Solving • Shape Patterns

Use the strategy *act it out* to solve pattern problems.

What might be the next three figures in the pattern below?

△ ■ △ ■ △ ■ △ ■ △ ■ △ ■ △ ■ △

Read the Problem

What do I need to find?	What information do I need to use?	How will I use the information?
I need to find the next three __figures__ in the pattern.	I need to look for __a group of figures__ that repeat.	I will use pattern blocks to model the __pattern__ and act out the problem.

Solve the Problem

Look for a group of figures that repeat and circle that group.

The repeating group is __triangle__ __triangle__ __square__ __triangle__ __square__

I used __triangles__ and __squares__ to model and continue the pattern
by repeating the figures in the group.

These are the next three figures in the pattern: ■ △ ■

1. Describe the pattern shown at right. Draw
   what might be the next figure in the pattern.

   **Possible description:
   there is 1 more circle in
   the bottom layer and 1
   more layer in each new figure.**

2. Use the pattern. How many circles will be in
   the sixth figure?

   __21 dots__

---

1. Gloria painted this pattern on the
   wall of her bedroom.

   ♡ ◁ △ ▷ ♡ ◁ △

   Which could be the next three
   figures in this pattern?

   Ⓐ ◁ △ ▷
   Ⓑ ♡ ♡ △
   Ⓒ ♡ ♡ △
   Ⓓ △ △ ♡

2. Martha used counters to make
   this pattern.

   How many counters should she use
   in the missing figure?

   Ⓐ 10   Ⓒ 14
   Ⓑ 12   Ⓓ 18

3. Addison made this pattern by
   shading squares.

   If Addison continues this pattern,
   how many squares should she shade
   in the next figure?

   Ⓐ 13   Ⓒ 25
   Ⓑ 20   Ⓓ 36

4. Ramona made this pattern with
   stickers.

   ⇨ ⇦ ⇨ ⇦ ⇨ ⇦ ⇨

   Which could be the next three
   figures in this pattern?

   Ⓐ ⇨ ⇨ ⇨
   Ⓑ ⇨ ⇨ ⇨
   Ⓒ ⇦ ⇦ ⇦
   Ⓓ ⇦ ⇦ ⇦

5. Barb used square tiles to make this pattern.

   Tell how many tiles Barb should use in the missing figure.
   Explain how you found the answer.

   **9 tiles; Possible answer: I found that the
   rule for the pattern is add two more tiles
   than in the previous figure. The previous
   figure had 7 tiles: 2 + 7 = 9.**

Answer Key

Model Place Value Relationships

A hundred grid can help you understand place-value relationships.

- One small square has been shaded to represent 1.
- Shade the rest of the first column. Count the number of small squares. There are _10_ small squares. The model for 10 has _10_ times as many squares as the model for _1_.
- Shade the remaining 9 columns. Count the number of small squares. There are _100_ small squares. The model for 100 has _10_ times as many squares as the model for _10_.
- If you shade ten hundred grids, you will have shaded 1,000 squares. So, the model for 1,000 has _10_ times as many squares as the model for _100_.

A place-value chart helps you find the value of each digit in a number.

THOUSANDS			ONES		
Hundreds	Tens	Ones	Hundreds	Tens	Ones
		8,	5	1	6

In the number 8,516:

The value of the digit 8 is 8 thousands, or _8,000_.
The value of the digit 5 is 5 hundreds, or _500_.
The value of the digit 1 is 1 ten, or _10_.
The value of the digit 6 is 6 ones, or _6_.

Find the value of the underlined digit.

1. 7̲56   **700**
2. 1,0̲25   **20**
3. 4̲,279   **4,000**
4. 3̲5,703   **30,000**

Compare the values of the underlined digits.

5. 7̲00 and 7̲0
The value of 7 in **700** is **10** times the value of 7 in **70**.

6. 5̲,000 and 5̲00
The value of 5 in **5,000** is **10** times the value of 5 in **500**.

1. Darla copies her uncle's address and phone number into her contact list. His area code is 775. His ZIP code is 89507. Which statement about the value of the 5 in 775 and 89,507 is true?

   (A) It is the same in both numbers.
   (B) It is 10 times as great in the ZIP code than it is in the area code.
   (C) It is 100 times as great in the ZIP code than it is in the area code.
   (D) It is 10 times as great in the area code than it is in the ZIP code.

2. On Monday, a music site sold 96,527 downloads of the new song by a popular band. What is the value of the digit 6 in 96,527?

   (A) 60,000
   (B) 6,000
   (C) 600
   (D) 60

3. Mario fills out an information card. His ZIP code is 83628. His area code is 208. Which statement about the value of the 2 in 83,628 and 208 is true?

   (A) It is 10 times as great in the area code than it is in the ZIP code.
   (B) It is 10 times as great in the ZIP code than it is in the area code.
   (C) It is 100 times as great in the area code than it is in the ZIP code.
   (D) It is the same in both numbers.

4. The attendance at a rock concert was 79,408 people. What is the value of the digit 4 in 79,408?

   (A) 40
   (B) 400
   (C) 4,000
   (D) 40,000

5. Compare the values of the underlined digits in 4,3̲12 and 1,4̲32. Explain how you know.

   Possible answer: the value of 3 in 4,312 is 10 times the value of 3 in 1,432. In 4,312 the 3 is worth 300, but in 1,432 it is worth 30. 300 is ten times the value of 30.

Name _____

Lesson 16
COMMON CORE STANDARD CC.4.NBT.1
Lesson Objective: Rename whole numbers by regrouping.

Rename Numbers

You can use place value to rename whole numbers. Here are different ways to name the number 1,400.

- **As thousands and hundreds**
  Think: 1,400 = _1_ thousand _4_ hundreds.
  You can draw a quick picture to help.

- **As hundreds**
  Think: 1,400 = _14_ hundreds.
  You can draw a quick picture to help.

- **As tens**
  Think: 1,400 = _140_ tens.

- **As ones**
  Think: 1,400 = _1,400_ ones.

Rename the number. Draw a quick picture to help.

1. 180 = _18_ tens
2. 1,600 = _16_ hundreds

Check students' drawings.

3. 6,000 = _6_ thousands
4. 2,700 = 27 **hundreds**
5. 2 hundreds 6 tens = _26_ tens
6. 71 thousands = _71,000_

1. What is a way to rename 1 thousand 2 hundreds?

   (A) 12 thousands
   (B) 23 hundreds
   (C) 12 hundreds
   (D) 12 tens

2. Which renaming matches the number shown in the model?

   (A) 123 thousands
   (B) 123 tens
   (C) 123 ones
   (D) 1,203 ones

3. The computer lab provides blank CDs for students to use. The CDs come on spindles of 100. The lab ordered 25 spindles. How many CDs were ordered in all?

   (A) 2,500
   (B) 250
   (C) 125
   (D) 25

4. Pencils come in boxes of 100. The Zoller School ordered 30,000 pencils to start the school year. How many boxes were ordered?

   (A) 30,000
   (B) 3,000
   (C) 300
   (D) 20

Problem Solving REAL WORLD

5. For the fair, the organizers ordered 32 rolls of tickets. Each roll of tickets has 100 tickets. How many tickets were ordered in all?

   3,200 tickets

6. An apple orchard sells apples in bags of 10. The orchard sold a total of 2,430 apples one day. How many bags of apples was this?

   243 bags

Name _____

Read and Write Numbers

Look at the digit 6 in the place-value chart below. It is in the hundred thousands place. So, its value is 6 hundred thousands .

In **word form**, the value of this digit is six hundred thousands.

In **standard form**, the value of the digit 6 is 600,000.

◄——— PERIOD ———►

THOUSANDS			ONES		
Hundreds	Tens	Ones	Hundreds	Tens	Ones
6	5	9,	0	5	8

Read the number shown in the place-value chart. In word form, this number is written as six hundred fifty-nine thousand, fifty-eight.

> Note that when writing a number in words, a comma separates periods.

You can also write the number in **expanded form**:
600,000 + 50,000 + 9,000 + 50 + 8

Read and write each number in two other forms.

1. 40,000 + 1,000 + 300 + 70 + 8

   41,378; forty-one thousand, three hundred seventy-eight

2. twenty-one thousand, four hundred

   21,400; 20,000 + 1,000 + 400

3. 391,032

   three hundred ninety-one thousand, thirty-two; 300,000 + 90,000 + 1,000 + 30 + 2

Name _____

1. Members of a stamp-collecting club have 213,094 stamps altogether. What is 213,094 written in word form?

   Ⓐ two hundred thirteen, ninety-four

   Ⓑ two hundred thirteen thousand, ninety-four

   Ⓒ two hundred thirteen thousand, nine hundred four

   Ⓓ two hundred thirteen thousand, four

2. Two hundred three thousand, one hundred ten people watched the fireworks display in town. What is that number written in standard form?

   Ⓐ 200,010

   Ⓑ 203,101

   Ⓒ 203,110

   Ⓓ 230,110

3. In 2010, an animal shelter found new homes for one hundred thirty thousand, six hundred nine dogs and cats. What is that number written in standard form?

   Ⓐ 136,309

   Ⓑ 130,690

   Ⓒ 130,609

   Ⓓ 130,069

4. The tollbooth records show that 105,076 cars passed through the toll plaza on Saturday. What is the expanded form of 105,076?

   Ⓐ 10,000 + 5,000 + 70 + 6

   Ⓑ 100,000 + 5,000 + 60 + 7

   Ⓒ 100,000 + 50,000 + 7 + 6

   Ⓓ 100,000 + 5,000 + 70 + 6

5. The expanded form of a number is 50,000 + 2,000 + 800 + 6. Write this number in standard form. Then explain how you know if any of the digits in standard form are zero.

   52,806; Possible answer: this number goes up to ten thousands. Even though there are no tens in this number, it must have a zero for the tens place.

Name _____

Compare and Order Numbers

Compare 31,072 and 34,318. Write <, >, or =.

Step 1 Align the numbers by place value using grid paper.

Step 2 Compare the digits in each place value. Start at the greatest place.

Are the digits in the ten thousands place the same?
Yes. Move to the thousands place.
Are the digits in the thousands place the same?
No. 1 thousand is less than 4 thousands.

start here

3	1	0	7	2
3	4	3	1	8
3 = 3

3	1	0	7	2
3	4	3	1	8
1 < 4

Step 3 Use the symbols <, >, or = to compare the numbers.

< means *is less than*.   > means *is greater than*.   = means *is equal to*.

There are two ways to write the comparison.

31,072 Ⓒ< 34,318   or   34,318 Ⓒ> 31,072

1. Use the grid paper to compare 21,409 and 20,891.
   Write <, >, or =.

2	1	4	0	9
2	0	8	9	1

   21,409 Ⓒ> 20,891

Compare. Write <, >, or =.

2. $53,621 Ⓒ< $53,760

3. 82,550 Ⓒ> 80,711

Order from greatest to least.

4. 16,451; 16,250; 17,014

   17,014; 16,451; 16,250

5. 561,028; 582,073; 549,006

   582,073; 561,028; 549,006

Name _____

1. A theme park had 674,989 visitors in June and 812,383 visitors in July. In August, the park had more visitors than in June, but fewer visitors than in July. Which of the following could be the number of visitors in August?

   Ⓐ 544,989   Ⓒ 765,124

   Ⓑ 646,844   Ⓓ 820,486

2. Brenda used number tiles to make the number 735,512. Frank used number tiles to make the number 734,512. Which statement about these numbers is correct?

   Ⓐ 735,512 < 734,512

   Ⓑ 735,512 > 734,512

   Ⓒ 735,512 = 734,512

   Ⓓ 734,512 > 735,512

3. During summer vacation, a state park had 248,368 visitors and a water park had 214,626 visitors. The zoo had more visitors than the water park, but fewer than the state park. Which of the following could be the number of visitors at the zoo?

   Ⓐ 201,369   **Ⓒ** 244,321

   Ⓑ 212,729   Ⓓ 263,023

4. The typical number of travelers who use the airport in a month is 250,000. There were 221,829 travelers in October, 283,459 in November, and 282,999 in December. Which number is **less** than the typical number of travelers?

   Ⓐ 283,459   **Ⓒ** 250,000

   Ⓑ 282,999   **Ⓓ** 221,829

5. Mr. Lee got 11,302 votes. Ms. Miller got 11,298 votes. Jana said that Ms. Miller won the election. Is Jana correct? Explain how you know.

   No; Possible explanation: Mr. Lee received more votes than Ms. Miller. 11,302 is greater than 11,298 because 3 hundreds are greater than 2 hundreds. 11,302 > 11,298.

Answer Key

Round Numbers

When you round a number, you replace it with a number that is easier to work with but not as exact. You can round numbers to different place values.

Round 478,456 to the place value of the underlined digit.

Step 1 Identify the underlined digit.
The underlined digit, 4, is in the <u>hundred thousands place</u>

Step 2 Look at the number to the right of the underlined digit.

If that number is 0–4, the underlined digit stays the same.

If that number is 5–9, the underlined digit is increased by 1.

The number to the right of the underlined digit is <u>7</u>, so the underlined digit, 4, will be increased by one; 4 + 1 = <u>5</u>.

Step 3 Change all the digits to the right of the hundred thousands place to zeros.

So, 478,456 rounded to the nearest hundred thousand is <u>500,000</u>.

1. In 2010, the population of North Dakota was 672,591 people. Use the number line to round this number to the nearest hundred thousand.

672,591

|←——————|————————|————●—|——————→|
600,000   650,000   700,000

672,591 is closer to <u>700,000</u> than <u>600,000</u>

so it rounds to <u>700,000</u>

Round to the place value of the underlined digit.

2. 3,452
<u>3,500</u>

3. 180
<u>200</u>

4. $72,471
<u>$70,000</u>

5. 572,000
<u>600,000</u>

6. 950
<u>1,000</u>

7. 6,495
<u>6,000</u>

8. 835,834
<u>840,000</u>

9. 96,625
<u>96,600</u>

1. The population of Miguel's hometown is 23,718. What is 23,718 rounded to the nearest ten thousand?

Ⓐ 20,000
Ⓑ 23,700
Ⓒ 24,000
Ⓓ 30,000

2. A DVD rental business has 12,468 different movies. What is 12,468 rounded to the nearest thousand?

Ⓐ 10,000
Ⓑ 12,000
Ⓒ 12,500
Ⓓ 13,000

3. Last week, about 456,900 viewers watched a television show on the Egyptian pyramids. What is the **greatest** whole number that rounds to 456,900?

Ⓐ 456,850
Ⓑ 456,949
Ⓒ 460,000
Ⓓ 466,000

4. An office mailroom sorted 182,617 pieces of mail last year. What is 182,617 rounded to the nearest hundred thousand?

Ⓐ 100,000
Ⓑ 180,000
Ⓒ 183,000
Ⓓ 200,000

5. Flora says that she can round 72,586 at least four different ways, and all of them will be correct. Felix says that Flora's idea is impossible. What do you think? Use examples to support your thinking.

<u>Possible answer: Flora is right, because she could round 72,586 to the nearest ten thousand, thousand, hundred, or ten. So, she could correctly round to 70,000, 73,000, 72,600, or 72,590.</u>

Add Whole Numbers

Find the sum. 63,821 + 34,765

Step 1 Round each addend to estimate.
60,000 + 30,000 = <u>90,000</u>

Step 2 Use a place-value chart to line up the digits by place value.

Step 3 Start with the ones place. Add from right to left. Regroup as needed.

Hundred Thousands	Ten Thousands	Thousands	Hundreds	Tens	Ones
		1			
	6	3,	8	2	1
+	3	4,	7	6	5
	9	8,	5	8	6

The sum is <u>98,586</u>. Since 98,586 is close to the estimate 90,000, the answer is reasonable.

Estimate. Then find the sum. Estimates may vary.

1. Find 238,503 + 341,978. Use the grid to help.

		1	1		1	
	2	3	8,	5	0	3
+	3	4	1,	9	7	8
	5	8	0,	4	8	1

Estimate: <u>500,000</u>

2. Estimate: <u>120,000</u>
52,851
+ 65,601
<u>118,452</u>

3. Estimate: <u>70,000</u>
54,980
+ 24,611
<u>79,591</u>

4. Estimate: <u>690,000</u>
604,542
+ 87,106
<u>691,648</u>

5. Estimate: <u>200,000</u>
147,026
+ 106,792
<u>253,818</u>

6. Estimate: <u>700,000</u>
278,309
+ 422,182
<u>700,491</u>

7. Estimate: <u>900,000</u>
540,721
+ 375,899
<u>916,620</u>

1. The surface area of Lake Superior is 31,700 square miles. The surface area of Lake Michigan is 22,278 square miles. What is the total surface area of both lakes?

Ⓐ 9,422 square miles
Ⓑ 22,595 square miles
Ⓒ 53,278 square miles
Ⓓ 53,978 square miles

2. Last season, 57,690 fans went to football games at Oneida High School. This season 54,083 fans went to the games. What is the total number of fans who went to Oneida High School football games in both seasons?

Ⓐ 59,852
Ⓑ 110,673
Ⓒ 111,773
Ⓓ 112,673

3. A car wash cleaned 97,612 cars last year and 121,048 cars this year. What is the total number of cars washed in the two years?

Ⓐ 218,660
Ⓑ 118,650
Ⓒ 109,760
Ⓓ 109,716

4. Mrs. Torres paid $139,000 for her house. Eight years later, she built an addition for $67,500. How much did Mrs. Torres pay for her house and the addition?

Ⓐ $296,500
Ⓑ $206,500
Ⓒ $196,500
Ⓓ $81,400

5. The table shows the number of visitors to a cave over four years. In which two years did the cave have a total of about 90,000 visitors? Explain how you found the solution.

Year	Visitors
1	52,753
2	55,168
3	37,047
4	61,590

<u>Year 1 and Year 3; Possible answer: I rounded all the numbers to the nearest ten thousand. 52,753 is about 50,000; 55,168 is about 60,000; 37,047 is about 40,000; and 61,590 is about 60,000. 50,000 + 40,000 = 90,000.</u>

Answer Key

Name _____

Lesson 21
COMMON CORE STANDARD CC.4.NBT.4
Lesson Objective: Subtract whole numbers and determine whether solutions to subtraction problems are reasonable.

Subtract Whole Numbers

Find the difference. 5,128 − 3,956

Estimate first.
Think: 5,128 is close to 5,000. 3,956 is close to 4,000.
So, an estimate is 5,000 − 4,000 = 1,000.

Write the problem vertically. Use grid paper to align digits by place value.

Step 1 Subtract the ones.

	5,	1	2	8
−	3,	9	5	6
				2

8 − 6 = 2

Step 2 Subtract the tens.

	5,	1	12	8
−	3,	9	5	6
			7	2

There are not enough tens to subtract. Regroup 1 hundred as 10 tens.
12 tens − 5 tens = 7 tens

Step 3 Subtract the hundreds.

	5,	1	12	8
−	3,	9	5	6
		1	7	2

There are not enough hundreds to subtract. Regroup 1 thousand as 10 hundreds.
10 hundreds − 9 hundreds = 1 hundred

Step 4 Subtract the thousands.

	5,	1	12	8
−	3,	9	5	6
	1	1	7	2

4 thousands − 3 thousands = 1 thousand

The difference is __1,172__. Since 1,172 is close to the estimate of 1,000, the answer is reasonable.

Estimate. Then find the difference.

1. Estimate: __2,000__

6,253
− 3,718
2,535

2. Estimate: __30,000__

74,529
− 38,453
36,076

3. Estimate: __100,000__

232,318
− 126,705
105,613

Name _____

Lesson 21
CC.4.NBT.4

1. A total of 3,718 tickets were sold for a skating show. Of that total, 1,279 were adult tickets. The remaining tickets were child tickets. How many child tickets were sold?

 (A) 2,439   (C) 3,439
 (B) 2,561   (D) 4,997

2. The number of people who took the subway to work in Sean's city one day was 31,426. The number of people who took the bus was 8,317. How many **more** people took the subway?

 (A) 39,743   (C) 23,119
 (B) 33,109   (D) 23,109

3. Michigan State and Wayne State are two large colleges in Michigan. Michigan State has 45,166 students enrolled. Wayne State has 32,160 students enrolled. How many **fewer** students are enrolled in Wayne State?

 (A) 3,006   (C) 13,006
 (B) 13,000   (D) 13,326

4. A desktop computer that Ryan likes costs $1,275. A laptop model of the same computer costs $1,648. How much **more** does the laptop cost?

 (A) $473   (C) $373
 (B) $433   (D) $333

Problem Solving REAL WORLD

Use the table for 5 and 6.

5. How many more people attended the Magic's games than attended the Pacers' games?

 133,606

6. How many fewer people attended the Pacers' games than attended the Clippers' games?

 87,768

Season Attendance for Three NBA Teams	
Team	Attendance
Indiana Pacers	582,295
Orlando Magic	715,901
Los Angeles Clippers	670,063

Name _____

Lesson 22
COMMON CORE STANDARD CC.4.NBT.4
Lesson Objective: Use the strategy draw a diagram to solve comparison problems with addition and subtraction.

Problem Solving • Comparison Problems with Addition and Subtraction

For a community recycling project, a school collects aluminum cans and plastic containers. This year the fourth grade collected 5,923 cans and 4,182 containers. This is 410 more cans and 24 more containers than the fourth grade collected last year. How many cans did the fourth grade collect last year?

Read the Problem

What do I need to find?	What information do I need to use?	How will I use the information?
I need to find the number of cans the fourth grade collected last year.	The fourth grade students collected __5,923__ cans this year. They collected __410__ more cans this year than the fourth grade collected last year.	I can draw a __bar model__ to find the number of cans the fourth grade collected last year.

Solve the Problem

I can draw a bar model and write an equation to represent the problem.

5,923

410	
	5,513

5,923 − 410 = __5,513__

So, the fourth grade collected __5,513__ aluminum cans last year.

Use the information above for 1 and 2.

1. Altogether, how many aluminum cans and plastic containers did the fourth grade collect this year?

 10,105 aluminum cans and plastic containers

2. This year the fifth grade collected 216 fewer plastic containers than the fourth grade. How many plastic containers did the fifth grade collect?

 3,966 plastic containers

Name _____

Lesson 22
CC.4.NBT.4

1. The number of inner tubes rented at the river this year increased by 1,009 over last year. The number of inner tubes rented last year was 4,286. How many inner tubes were rented this year?

1,009	4,286

 (A) 3,277   (C) 5,285
 (B) 4,395   (D) 5,295

2. Mr. Rey and Ms. Klein both took long car trips. Mr. Rey drove 2,178 miles. Ms. Klein drove 1,830 miles. How much farther did Mr. Rey drive on his trip?

2,178 miles

1,830 miles

 (A) 348 miles   (C) 1,348 miles
 (B) 748 miles   (D) 4,008 miles

3. A science museum has collected a total of 8,536 plant fossils. They have also collected 3,855 animal fossils. Use the bar model to find the total number of fossils the museum has.

8,536	3,855

 (A) 12,481   (C) 11,381
 (B) 12,391   (D) 4,681

4. Volunteers worked for a total of 10,479 hours at the science center this year. Last year, they worked 8,231 hours. How many hours did the volunteers work in both years combined?

10,479	8,231

 (A) 18,710 hours   (C) 2,648 hours
 (B) 18,600 hours   (D) 2,248 hours

5. Mr. Dimka drove his truck 9,438 miles last year. This year he drove his truck 3,479 fewer miles. How many miles did Mr. Dimka drive this year? Draw a bar model to solve. Show your work.

 5,959 miles; Check students' work.

9,438 miles last year	
	3,439

Answer Key

Multiply Tens, Hundreds, and Thousands

You can use a pattern to multiply with tens, hundreds, and thousands.

Count the number of zeros in the factors.

$4 \times 6 = 24$	← basic fact
$4 \times 60 = 240$	← When you multiply by tens, the last digit in the product is 0.
$4 \times 600 = 2,400$	← When you multiply by hundreds, the last <u>two</u> digits in the product are 0.
$4 \times 6,000 = 24,000$	← When you multiply by thousands, the last <u>three</u> digits in the product are 0.

When the basic fact has a zero in the product, there will be an extra zero in the final product:

$5 \times 4 = 20$, so $5 \times 4,000 = 20,000$

Complete the pattern.

1. $9 \times 2 = 18$
$9 \times 20 = $ <u>180</u>
$9 \times 200 = $ <u>1,800</u>
$9 \times 2,000 = $ <u>18,000</u>

2. $8 \times 4 = 32$
$8 \times 40 = $ <u>320</u>
$8 \times 400 = $ <u>3,200</u>
$8 \times 4,000 = $ <u>32,000</u>

3. $6 \times 6 = 36$
$6 \times 60 = $ <u>360</u>
$6 \times 600 = $ <u>3,600</u>
$6 \times 6,000 = $ <u>36,000</u>

4. $4 \times 7 = 28$
$4 \times 70 = $ <u>280</u>
$4 \times 700 = $ <u>2,800</u>
$4 \times 7,000 = $ <u>28,000</u>

Find the product.

5. $7 \times 300 = 7 \times$ <u>3</u> hundreds
$= $ <u>21</u> hundreds
$= $ <u>2,100</u>

6. $5 \times 8,000 = 5 \times$ <u>8</u> thousands
$= $ <u>40</u> thousands
$= $ <u>40,000</u>

---

1. Hideki is collecting pennies. Each month in May, June, and July, he put 200 pennies in a jar. How many pennies did Hideki put in the jar during these 3 months?
   - (A) 60
   - (B) 600
   - (C) 6,000
   - (D) 60,000

2. A factory produced 4,000 crayons every hour during an 8-hour shift. How many crayons were produced during the shift?
   - (A) 320
   - (B) 3,200
   - (C) 32,000
   - (D) 320,000

3. Maria wrote this pattern in her math notebook.

   $8 \times 5 = 40$
   $8 \times 50 = 400$
   $8 \times 500 = 4,000$
   $8 \times 5,000 = $ ▦

   What is the unknown number in Maria's pattern?
   - (A) 40,000
   - (B) 4,000
   - (C) 400
   - (D) 4

4. Ling wrote this problem on his paper.

   $9 \times 300 = $ ▦ hundreds

   What is the unknown number in Ling's problem?
   - (A) 27
   - (B) 270
   - (C) 2,700
   - (D) 27,000

Problem Solving REAL WORLD

5. A bank teller has 7 rolls of coins. Each roll has 40 coins. How many coins does the bank teller have?

   280 coins

6. Theo buys 5 packages of paper. There are 500 sheets of paper in each package. How many sheets of paper does Theo buy?

   2,500 sheets

Estimate Products

You can use rounding to estimate products.

Round the greater factor. Then use mental math to estimate the product.

6×95

Step 1 Round 95 to the nearest hundred.   95 rounds to 100.

Step 2 Use patterns and mental math.
$6 \times 1 = 6$
$6 \times 10 = 60$
$6 \times 100 = 600$

Find two numbers the exact answer is between.

7×759

Step 1 Estimate by rounding to the lesser hundred.

7×759
$7 \times 700 = 4,900$

Think: $7 \times 7 = 49$
$7 \times 70 = 490$
$7 \times 700 = 4,900$

Step 2 Estimate by rounding to the greater hundred.

7×759
$7 \times 800 = 5,600$

Think: $7 \times 8 = 56$
$7 \times 80 = 560$
$7 \times 800 = 5,600$

So, the product is between 4,900 and 5,600.

Estimate the product by rounding. Possible estimates are given.

1. 6×316
   <u>1,800</u>

2. 5×29
   <u>150</u>

3. 4×703
   <u>2,800</u>

Estimate the product by finding two numbers the exact answer is between. Possible estimates are given.

4. 3×558
   <u>1,500 and 1,800</u>

5. 7×252
   <u>1,400 and 2,100</u>

6. 8×361
   <u>2,400 and 3,200</u>

---

1. In one hour, 1,048 cars stopped at a traffic light. Which is the best estimate of how many cars will stop in 8 hours?
   - (A) 800
   - (B) 1,000
   - (C) 8,000
   - (D) 10,000

2. Beth travels 244 miles every week. Which expression shows the best estimate for the number of miles she would travel in 9 weeks?
   - (A) 200×9
   - (B) 200×10
   - (C) 300×9
   - (D) 300×10

3. A black bear has a mass of about 135 kilograms. Which is the best estimate of the mass of 3 black bears?
   - (A) less than 300 kilograms
   - (B) between 300 and 600 kilograms
   - (C) between 600 and 900 kilograms
   - (D) more than 900 kilograms

4. The youth center sold 62 raffle tickets for $8 each. Mrs. Sosa says they collected about $480. Which statement best describes why Mrs. Sosa's estimate is reasonable?
   - (A) 10×70 is 700.
   - (B) 8×60 is 480.
   - (C) 480 is not the product of 8×62.
   - (D) 8×500 is 4,000.

5. Every package of chicken nuggets contains 48 nuggets. Is it reasonable to estimate that 6 packages contain over 300 chicken nuggets? Explain your answer.

   No; Possible answer: I found 2 numbers the exact answer is between: $6 \times 40 = 240$ and $6 \times 50 = 300$. So, 6 packages contain fewer than 300 nuggets.

Lesson 25 (Page 49)

Name _____

Lesson 25
COMMON CORE STANDARD CC.4.NBT.5
Lesson Objective: Use the Distributive Property to multiply a 2-digit number by a 1-digit number.

Multiply Using the Distributive Property

You can use rectangular models to multiply 2-digit numbers by 1-digit numbers.

Find 9 × 14.

Step 1 Draw a 9 by 14 rectangle on grid paper.

Step 2 Use the Distributive Property and products you know to break apart the model into two smaller rectangles.
Think: 14 = 10 + 4.

Step 3 Find the product each smaller rectangle represents.
$9 \times 10 = 90$
$9 \times 4 = 36$

Step 4 Find the sum of the products. $90 + 36 = 126$
So, $9 \times 14 = 126$.

Model the product on the grid. Possible models are shown.
Record the product.

1. 3×13 10   3
   39   3

2. 6×16 6   10
   96   6

3. 5×17 10   7
   85   5

4. 4×14 4   10
   56   4

Lesson 25 (Page 50)

Name _____

Lesson 25
CC.4.NBT.5

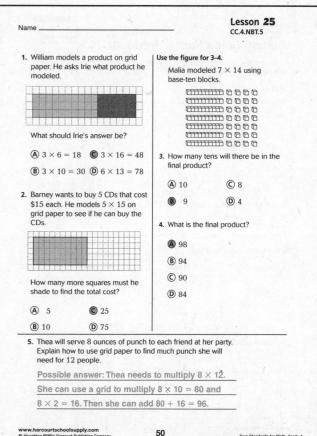

1. William models a product on grid paper. He asks Irie what product he modeled.

   What should Irie's answer be?
   Ⓐ $3 \times 6 = 18$ Ⓒ $3 \times 16 = 48$
   Ⓑ $3 \times 10 = 30$ Ⓓ $6 \times 13 = 78$

2. Barney wants to buy 5 CDs that cost $15 each. He models 5×15 on grid paper to see if he can buy the CDs.

   How many more squares must he shade to find the total cost?
   Ⓐ 5   Ⓒ 25
   Ⓑ 10   Ⓓ 75

Use the figure for 3–4.
Malia modeled 7×14 using base-ten blocks.

3. How many tens will there be in the final product?
   Ⓐ 10   Ⓒ 8
   Ⓑ 9   Ⓓ 4

4. What is the final product?
   Ⓐ 98
   Ⓑ 94
   Ⓒ 90
   Ⓓ 84

5. Thea will serve 8 ounces of punch to each friend at her party. Explain how to use grid paper to find much punch she will need for 12 people.

   Possible answer: Thea needs to multiply 8×12.
   She can use a grid to multiply $8 \times 10 = 80$ and
   $8 \times 2 = 16$. Then she can add $80 + 16 = 96$.

Lesson 26 (Page 51)

Name _____

Lesson 26
COMMON CORE STANDARD CC.4.NBT.5
Lesson Objective: Use expanded form to multiply a multidigit number by a 1-digit number.

Multiply Using Expanded Form

You can use expanded form or a model to find products.

Multiply. 3×26

Think and Write

Step 1 Write 26 in expanded form.
$26 = 20 + 6$
$3 \times 26 = 3 \times (20 + 6)$

Step 2 Use the Distributive Property.
$3 \times 26 = (3 \times 20) + (\underline{3} \times \underline{6})$

Step 3 Multiply the tens. Multiply the ones.
$3 \times 26 = (3 \times 20) + (3 \times 6)$
$= \underline{60} + \underline{18}$ 60 +18

Step 4 Add the partial products. 78

So, $3 \times 26 = \underline{78}$

Use a Model

Step 1 Show 3 groups of 26.

Step 2 Break the model into tens and ones.
$(3 \times 2 \text{ tens})$ $(3 \times 6 \text{ ones})$
(3×20) (3×6)
60   18

Step 3 Add to find the total product.
$\underline{60} + \underline{18} = \underline{78}$

Record the product. Use expanded form to help.

1. $6 \times 14 = \underline{84}$
   $6 \times (10 + 4)$
   $(6 \times 10) + (6 \times 4)$
   6 0 / +2 4 / 8 4

2. $4 \times 52 = \underline{208}$
   $4 \times (50 + 2)$
   $(4 \times 50) + (4 \times 2)$
   2 0 0 / + 8 / 2 0 8

3. $5 \times 162 = \underline{810}$
   $5 \times (100 + 60 + 2)$
   $(5 \times 100) + (5 \times 60) + (5 \times 2)$
   5 0 0 / 3 0 0 / + 1 0 / 8 1 0

4. $3 \times 279 = \underline{837}$
   $3 \times (200 + 70 + 9)$
   $(3 \times 200) + (3 \times 70) + (3 \times 9)$
   6 0 0 / 2 1 0 / + 2 7 / 8 3 7

Lesson 26 (Page 52)

Name _____

Lesson 26
CC.4.NBT.5

1. A factory produces 2,354 hammers every hour. Which expression can be used to find how many hammers the factory produces in 3 hours?
   Ⓐ $(3 \times 2,000) + 354$
   Ⓑ $(3 \times 2,000) + (3 \times 300) + 54$
   Ⓒ $(3 \times 2,000) + (3 \times 300) + (3 \times 50) + (3 \times 4)$
   Ⓓ $(3 \times 2,000) + (300 + 50 + 4)$

2. A large truck that can carry up to 168 boxes in a single trip will make 6 trips in one day. Which expression shows how to multiply 6×168 by using place value and expanded form?
   Ⓐ $(6 \times 100) + (6 \times 60) + (6 \times 8)$
   Ⓑ $(6 \times 800) + (6 \times 60) + (6 \times 1)$
   Ⓒ $(6 \times 100) + (6 \times 60)$
   Ⓓ $(6 \times 168) + (6 \times 16) + (6 \times 1)$

3. A grocery store has 367 cans of vegetables on each of 4 shelves. Which expression can be used to find how many cans of vegetables are on the four shelves?
   Ⓐ $(4 \times 300) + (6 \times 10) + (1 \times 7)$
   Ⓑ $(4 \times 300) + (4 \times 60) + 7$
   Ⓒ $(4 \times 300) + (4 \times 60) + (4 \times 7)$
   Ⓓ $(4 \times 300) + 60 + 7$

4. Suki uses place value and the expanded form $(7 \times 2,000) + (7 \times 800) + (7 \times 90)$ to help solve a multiplication problem. Which is Suki's multiplication problem?
   Ⓐ $7 \times 289 = 2,023$
   Ⓑ $7 \times 2,089 = 14,623$
   Ⓒ $7 \times 2,809 = 19,663$
   Ⓓ $7 \times 2,890 = 20,230$

Problem Solving REAL WORLD

5. The fourth-grade students at Riverside School are going on a field trip. There are 68 students on each of the 4 buses. How many students are going on the field trip?

   272 students

6. There are 5,280 feet in one mile. Hannah likes to walk 5 miles each week for exercise. How many feet does Hannah walk each week?

   26,400 feet

Answer Key

Name _____

Multiply Using Partial Products

Use partial products to multiply.

Multiply. 7 × $332

Step 1 Estimate the product.   332 rounds to 300; 7 × $300 = $2,100

Step 2 Multiply the 3 hundreds, $332 $300
or 300, by 7.   × 7   or × 7
                                                $2,100

Step 3 Multiply the 3 tens, or 30, by 7. $332 $30
                                               × 7   or × 7
                                                        $210

Step 4 Multiply the 2 ones, or 2, by 7. $332 $2
                                               × 7   or × 7
                                                        $14

Step 5 Add the partial products. $2,100 + $210 + $14 = $2,324

So, 7 × $332 = $2,324. Since $2,324 is close to the estimate of $2,100, it is reasonable.

Estimate. Then record the product.   *Possible estimates are given.*

1. Estimate: **400**   2. Estimate: **800**   3. Estimate: **$1,000**

   181   156 $210
  × 2   × 4   × 5
  362   **624**   **$1,050**

4. Estimate: **1,800**   5. Estimate: **$800**   6. Estimate: **$2,000**

  303        $427 $367
  × 6   × 2   × 5
  1,818   **$854**   **$1,835**

Name _____

1. Zac will make 3 payments of $135 to buy a mountain bike. He used partial products to find the total cost of the bike. Which shows the sum of the partial products?

Ⓐ $300 + $90 + $15 = $405
Ⓑ $300 + $90 + $5 = $395
Ⓒ $300 + $30 + $15 = $345
Ⓓ $3 + $9 + $15 = $27

2. A theater has 8 sections. There are 168 seats in each section. Which sum of partial products shows the total number of seats in the theater?

Ⓐ 800 + 60 + 8 = 868
Ⓑ 800 + 48 + 64 = 912
Ⓒ 800 + 480 + 8 = 1,288
Ⓓ 800 + 480 + 64 = 1,344

3. A parking garage has 5 levels. There are 256 parking spaces on each level. Which sum of partial products shows the total number of parking spaces?

Ⓐ 1,000 + 50 + 6 = 1,056
Ⓑ 1,000 + 25 + 30 = 1,055
Ⓒ 1,000 + 250 + 30 = 1,280
Ⓓ 1,000 + 250 + 300 = 1,550

4. A company received 329 orders for a DVD set that contains 3 movies. Which sum of partial products shows the total number of DVDs the company will ship?

Ⓐ 900 + 60 + 9 = 969
Ⓑ 900 + 60 + 27 = 987
Ⓒ 900 + 600 + 27 = 1,527
Ⓓ 900 + 600 + 270 = 1,770

Problem Solving REAL WORLD

5. A maze at a county fair is made from 275 bales of hay. The maze at the state fair is made from 4 times as many bales of hay. How many bales of hay are used for the maze at the state fair?

1,100 bales

6. Pedro gets 8 hours of sleep each night. How many hours does Pedro sleep in a year with 365 days?

2,920 hours

Name _____

Multiply Using Mental Math

Use addition to break apart the larger factor.	Use subtraction to break apart the larger factor.
Find 8 × 214.	**Find 6 × 298.**
Think: 214 = 200 + 14	**Think:** 298 = 300 − 2
8 × 214 = (8 × 200) + (8 × 14)	6 × 298 = (6 × 300) − (6 × 2)
= 1,600 + 112	= 1,800 − 12
= 1,712	= 1,788
Use halving and doubling.	When multiplying more than two numbers, use the Commutative Property to change the order of the factors.
Find 14 × 50.	**Find 2 × 9 × 50.**
Think: 14 can be evenly divided by 2.	**Think:** 2 × 50 = 100
14 ÷ 2 = 7	2 × 9 × 50 = 2 × 50 × 9
7 × 50 = 350	= 100 × 9
2 × 350 = 700	= 900

Find the product. Tell which strategy you used.   *Possible estimates are given.*

1. 5 × 7 × 20   2. 6 × 321

700; Commutative Property   **1,926; use addition**

3. 86 × 50   4. 9 × 399

4,300; halving and doubling   **3,591; use subtraction**

Name _____

1. An art store has 5 boxes of brushes. Each box contains 298 brushes. Which expression shows a strategy for finding the product of 5 × 298?

Ⓐ 5 × (300 + 2) = 1,150
Ⓑ 5 × (300 − 2) = 1,490
Ⓒ 5 × (300 × 3) = 4,500
Ⓓ 5 × (200 − 98) = 510

2. Carl plans to use a strategy to find 28 × 250. Which expression shows a strategy he could use?

Ⓐ 5 × 6 × 250 = 7,500
Ⓑ 4 × 7 × 25 = 700
Ⓒ 7 × 4 × 250 = 7,000
Ⓓ 28 × 2 × 50 = 2,800

3. Samantha has 4 boxes of action figures. Each box contains 198 figures. Which expression shows a strategy Samantha can use to find the product of 4 × 198?

Ⓐ 4 × (200 + 2) = 808
Ⓑ 4 × (200 − 2) = 792
Ⓒ 4 × (200 × 3) = 2,400
Ⓓ 4 × (200 + 98) = 1,192

4. Gino wants to multiply 4 × 125. Which is the best mental math strategy for him to use?

Ⓐ halving and doubling
Ⓑ use addition
Ⓒ Commutative Property
Ⓓ use subtraction

Problem Solving REAL WORLD

5. Section J in an arena has 20 rows. Each row has 15 seats. All tickets cost $18 each. If all the seats are sold, how much money will the arena collect for Section J?

$5,400

6. At a high-school gym, the bleachers are divided into 6 equal sections. Each section can seat 395 people. How many people can be seated in the gym?

2,370 people

Name _____

Multiply 2-Digit Numbers with Regrouping

Use place value to multiply with regrouping.

Multiply. 7×63

Step 1 Estimate the product. $7 \times 60 = 420$

Step 2 Multiply the ones. Regroup 21 ones as 2 tens 1 one. Record the 1 one below the ones column and the 2 tens above the tens column.

$$\begin{array}{r} \overset{2}{6}3 \\ \times\ 7 \\ \hline 1 \end{array}$$

7×3 ones = 21 ones

Step 3 Multiply the tens. Then, add the regrouped tens. Record the tens.

$$\begin{array}{r} \overset{2}{6}3 \\ \times\ 7 \\ \hline 441 \end{array}$$ 44 tens = 4 hundreds
4 tens

7×6 tens = 42 tens

Add the 2 regrouped tens.

42 tens + 2 tens = 44 tens

So, $7 \times 63 = 441$. Since 441 is close to the estimate of 420, it is reasonable.

Estimate. Then record the product.   Possible estimates are given.

1. Estimate: __240__
$$\begin{array}{r} 42 \\ \times\ 6 \\ \hline 252 \end{array}$$

2. Estimate: __$600__
$$\begin{array}{r} \$98 \\ \times\ 6 \\ \hline \$588 \end{array}$$

3. Estimate: __320__
$$\begin{array}{r} 37 \\ \times\ 8 \\ \hline 296 \end{array}$$

4. Estimate: __$450__
$$\begin{array}{r} \$54 \\ \times\ 9 \\ \hline \$486 \end{array}$$

5. Estimate: __200__
$$\begin{array}{r} 37 \\ \times\ 5 \\ \hline 185 \end{array}$$

6. Estimate: __360__
$$\begin{array}{r} 93 \\ \times\ 4 \\ \hline 372 \end{array}$$

7. Estimate: __810__
$$\begin{array}{r} 86 \\ \times\ 9 \\ \hline 774 \end{array}$$

8. Estimate: __420__
$$\begin{array}{r} 59 \\ \times\ 7 \\ \hline 413 \end{array}$$

Name _____

1. Ava can text 44 words each minute. How many words can she text in 8 minutes?
- Ⓐ 352
- Ⓑ 322
- Ⓒ 320
- Ⓓ 36

2. Sara's mom bought tickets to the Philadelphia Zoo. She bought 6 tickets. Each ticket cost $18. What was the total cost of the tickets?
- Ⓐ $32
- Ⓑ $68
- Ⓒ $108
- Ⓓ $114

3. Gordon's heart beats 72 times in one minute. If it continues beating at the same rate, how many times will it beat in 7 minutes?
- Ⓐ 79
- Ⓑ 494
- Ⓒ 504
- Ⓓ 604

4. Antonio and his friends bought tickets for a play. They bought 8 tickets in all. Each ticket cost $23. What was the total cost of the tickets?
- Ⓐ $31
- Ⓑ $164
- Ⓒ $171
- Ⓓ $184

Problem Solving REAL WORLD

5. Sharon is 54 inches tall. A tree in her backyard is 5 times as tall as she is. The floor of her treehouse is at a height that is twice as tall as she is. What is the difference, in inches, between the top of the tree and the floor of the treehouse?

162 inches

6. Mr. Diaz's class is taking a field trip to the science museum. There are 23 students in the class, and a student admission ticket is $8. How much will the student tickets cost?

$184

Name _____

Multiply 3-Digit and 4-Digit Numbers with Regrouping

When you multiply 3-digit and 4-digit numbers, you may need to regroup.

Estimate. Then find the product. $1,324
                                         $\times$ 7

Step 1 Estimate the product. $1,324 rounds to $1,000; $1,000 \times 7 = $7,000.

Step 2 Multiply the 4 ones by 7. Regroup the 28 ones as 2 tens 8 ones.
$$\begin{array}{r} \overset{2}{\$1,32}4 \\ \times\ 7 \\ \hline 8 \end{array}$$

Step 3 Multiply the 2 tens by 7. Add the regrouped tens. Regroup the 16 tens as 1 hundred 6 tens.
$$\begin{array}{r} \overset{1\ 2}{\$1,32}4 \\ \times\ 7 \\ \hline 68 \end{array}$$

Step 4 Multiply the 3 hundreds by 7. Add the regrouped hundred. Regroup the 22 hundreds as 2 thousands 2 hundreds.
$$\begin{array}{r} \overset{2\ 1\ 2}{\$1,32}4 \\ \times\ 7 \\ \hline 268 \end{array}$$

Step 5 Multiply the 1 thousand by 7. Add the regrouped thousands.
$$\begin{array}{r} \overset{2\ 1\ 2}{\$1,32}4 \\ \times\ 7 \\ \hline \$9,268 \end{array}$$

So, $7 \times \$1,324 = \$9,268$.
Since $9,268 is close to the estimate of $7,000, the answer is reasonable.

Estimate. Then find the product.   Possible estimates are given.

1. Estimate: __6,000__
$$\begin{array}{r} 3,184 \\ \times\ 2 \\ \hline 6,368 \end{array}$$

2. Estimate: __$3,200__
$$\begin{array}{r} \$828 \\ \times\ 4 \\ \hline \$3,312 \end{array}$$

3. Estimate: __15,000__
$$\begin{array}{r} 2,637 \\ \times\ 5 \\ \hline 13,185 \end{array}$$

4. Estimate: __$49,000__
$$\begin{array}{r} \$6,900 \\ \times\ 7 \\ \hline \$48,300 \end{array}$$

Name _____

1. Mr. Karros is buying 2 digital cameras for the yearbook club. The price of each camera is $259. What is the total price of the cameras?
- Ⓐ $408
- Ⓑ $418
- Ⓒ $508
- Ⓓ $518

2. Mr. Richards travels 163 miles each week for work. How far does he travel in 4 weeks for work?
- Ⓐ 442 miles
- Ⓑ 452 miles
- Ⓒ 642 miles
- Ⓓ 652 miles

3. Brandon has 4,350 digital photos saved on his computer. Linda has 3 times as many photos saved on her computer as Brandon has. How many digital photos does Linda have saved on her computer?
- Ⓐ 12,050
- Ⓑ 12,250
- Ⓒ 12,950
- Ⓓ 13,050

4. Jack has 2,613 songs saved on his MP3 player. Dexter has 4 times as many songs saved on his MP3 player as Jack has. How many songs does Dexter have saved on his MP3 player?
- Ⓐ 8,442   Ⓒ 10,452
- Ⓑ 10,442   Ⓓ 10,542

Problem Solving REAL WORLD

5. Lafayette County has a population of 7,022 people. Columbia County's population is 8 times as great as Lafayette County's population. What is the population of Columbia County?

56,176 people

6. A seafood company sold 9,125 pounds of fish last month. If 6 seafood companies sold the same amount of fish, how much fish did the 6 companies sell last month in all?

54,750 pounds

Answer Key

Name _____

Lesson 31
COMMON CORE STANDARD CC.4.NBT.5
Lesson Objective: Use place value and multiplication properties to multiply by tens.

Multiply by Tens

One section of seating at an arena has 40 rows. Each row has 30 seats. How many seats in all are in that section?

Multiply. 30 × 40

Step 1 Think of each factor as a multiple of 10 and as a repeated addition.

40 = _4_ × _10_ or _10_ + _10_ + _10_ + _10_

30 = _3_ × _10_ or _10_ + _10_ + _10_

Step 2 Draw a diagram to show the multiplication.

	10	10	10	10
10	100	100	100	100
10	100	100	100	100
10	100	100	100	100

40

30

Step 3 Each small square in the diagram shows 10 × 10, or _100_. Count the squares. There are _12_ squares of _100_.

Step 4 Use patterns and mental math to find 12 × 100.

12 × 1 = _12_

12 × 10 = _120_

12 × 100 = _1,200_

There are _1,200_ seats in that section.

Choose a method. Then find the product. Methods will vary.

1. 20 × 90 = _1,800_   2. 40 × 40 = _1,600_   3. 60 × 70 = _4,200_

4. 50 × 30 = _1,500_   5. 80 × 60 = _4,800_   6. 90 × 40 = _3,600_

Name _____

Lesson 31
CC.4.NBT.5

1. Mrs. Yang types 80 words in one minute. At that rate, how many words can she type in 15 minutes?
   - (A) 120
   - (B) 800
   - (C) 1,200
   - (D) 1,600

2. Teneka repeats a tongue twister 20 times in one minute. At that rate, how many times could she repeat the tongue twister in 12 minutes?
   - (A) 24
   - (B) 32
   - (C) 120
   - (D) 240

3. Ben swam laps in a pool nonstop for 11 minutes. There are 60 seconds in 1 minute. What is the total number of seconds Ben swam?
   - (A) 6,600 seconds
   - (B) 710 seconds
   - (C) 660 seconds
   - (D) 600 seconds

4. People can join a skating club by paying $40 a year. The club had 67 members this year. How much money in all did the skating club collect from members this year?
   - (A) $268
   - (B) $2,680
   - (C) $3,220
   - (D) $26,800

Problem Solving REAL WORLD

5. Kenny bought 20 packs of baseball cards. There are 12 cards in each pack. How many cards did Kenny buy?

   240 cards

6. The Hart family drove 10 hours to their vacation spot. They drove an average of 48 miles each hour. How many miles did they drive in all?

   480 miles

Name _____

Lesson 32
COMMON CORE STANDARD CC.4.NBT.5
Lesson Objective: Estimate products by rounding or by using compatible numbers.

Estimate Products

You can use rounding and compatible numbers to estimate products.

Use mental math and rounding to estimate the product.

Estimate. 62 × $23

Step 1 Round each factor to the nearest ten.

62 rounds to 60.
$23 rounds to $20.

Step 2 Rewrite the problem using the rounded numbers.

60 × $20

Step 3 Use mental math.

6 × $2 = $12
6 × $20 = $120
60 × $20 = $1,200

So, 62 × $23 is about _$1,200_.

Use mental math and compatible numbers to estimate the product.

Estimate. 24 × 78

Step 1 Use compatible numbers. 25 × 80

Step 2 Use 25 × 4 = 100 to help find 25 × 8.
25 × 8 = 200

Step 3 Since 80 has 1 zero, write 1 zero to the right of the product.

24 × 78
↓
25 × 80 = 2,000

So, 24 × 78 is about _2,000_. Possible estimates are given. Methods will vary.

Estimate the product. Choose a method.

1. 78 × 21   2. 59 × $46   3. 81 × 33   4. 67 × 21
   1,600 $3,000   2,400   1,400

5. 88 × $42   6. 51 × 36   7. 73 × 73   8. 99 × $44
   $3,600   2,000   4,900 $4,000

9. 92 × 19   10. 26 × 37   11. 89 × 18   12. 58 × 59
   1,800   1,000   1,800   3,600

Name _____

Lesson 32
CC.4.NBT.5

1. Doug rents a kayak for 12 days. The rental charge is $18 per day. Which is the **best** estimate for the total cost of the kayak rental?
   - (A) about $400
   - (B) about $200
   - (C) about $160
   - (D) about $120

2. Mr. Yu travels 44 miles for work every week. He worked 42 weeks last year. Which is the **best** estimate of the number of miles Mr. Yu traveled for work last year?
   - (A) about 2,000 miles
   - (B) about 3,000 miles
   - (C) about 8,000 miles
   - (D) about 10,000 miles

3. Cat cages cost $27 each. A cat hospital bought 12 new cages. Which is the **best** estimate of the total cost of the new cages?
   - (A) $600
   - (B) $300
   - (C) $270
   - (D) $200

4. On Friday, 17 buses left the bus station. Each bus carried a full load of 53 passengers. Which is the **best** way to estimate the total number of passengers who left the bus station that day?
   - (A) 7 × 50 = 350
   - (B) 10 × 50 = 500
   - (C) 10 × 60 = 600
   - (D) 20 × 50 = 1,000

Problem Solving REAL WORLD
Possible estimates are given.

5. A dime has a diameter of about 18 millimeters. About how many millimeters long would a row of 34 dimes be?

   about 600 millimeters

6. A half-dollar has a diameter of about 31 millimeters. About how many millimeters long would a row of 56 half-dollars be?

   about 1,800 millimeters

Name _____

Lesson 33
COMMON CORE STANDARD CC.4.NBT.5
Lesson Objective: Use area models and partial products to multiply 2-digit numbers.

Area Models and Partial Products

You can use area models to multiply 2-digit numbers by 2-digit numbers.

Use the model and partial products to solve.

Draw a rectangle to find 19 × 18.

The rectangle is 19 units long and 18 units wide.

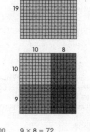

Step 1 Break apart the factors into tens and ones. Divide the area model into four smaller rectangles to show the factors.

Step 2 Find the products for each of the smaller rectangles.

10 × 10 = 100   10 × 8 = 80   9 × 10 = 90   9 × 8 = 72

Step 3 Find the sum of the products.   100 + 80 + 90 + 72 = 342

So, 19 × 18 = 342.

Models will vary.   Possible models are given.
Draw a model to represent the product. Then record the product.

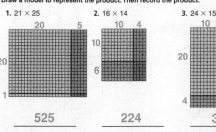

1. 21 × 25   **2.** 16 × 14   **3.** 24 × 15

525   224   360

Name _____

Lesson 33
CC.4.NBT.5

Use the model for 1–2.

Use the model for 3–4.

1. What partial product is missing from the model?

- (A) 60
- (B) 80
- (C) 600
- (D) 800

2. What is the product?

43 × 22

- (A) 172
- (B) 846
- (C) 946
- (D) 1,286

3. What partial product is missing from the model?

- (A) 36
- (B) 120
- (C) 180
- (D) 300

4. What is the product?

26 × 37

- (A) 962
- (B) 782
- (C) 780
- (D) 260

5. This model for 45 × 34 has two partial products shown. Explain how to find the other partial products, and how to use the partial products to find the final product.

Possible answer: the missing partial products are 40 × 4 = 160 on the top right, and 5 × 4 = 20 on the lower right. The final product is the sum of 1,200 + 160 + 150 + 20, which is 1,530.

Name _____

Lesson 34
COMMON CORE STANDARD CC.4.NBT.5
Lesson Objective: Use place value and partial products to multiply 2-digit numbers.

Multiply Using Partial Products

Multiply 25 × 43. Record the product.

tens ones

Think: I can use partial products to find 25 × 43.

```
      4 3
    × 2 5
```

Step 1 Multiply the tens by the tens.
20 × 4 tens = 80 tens, or 800.   →   8 0 0

Step 2 Multiply the ones by the tens.
20 × 3 ones = 60 ones, or 60.   →   6 0

Step 3 Multiply the tens by the ones.
5 × 4 tens = 20 tens, or 200.   →   2 0 0

Step 4 Multiply the ones by the ones.
5 × 3 ones = 15 ones, or 15.   →   + 1 5

Step 5 Add the partial products.
800 + 60 + 200 + 15 = 1,075.   →   1,0 7 5

So, 25 × 43 = __1,075__

Record the product.

1.
```
    25
  × 62
 1,200
   300
    40
 +  10
 1,550
```

2.
```
    59
  × 38
 1,500
   270
   400
 +  72
 2,242
```

3.
```
    85
  × 72
 5,600
   350
   160
 +  10
 6,120
```

4.
```
    46
  × 52
 2,000
   300
    80
 +  12
 2,392
```

5.
```
    76
  × 23
 1,400
   120
   210
 +  18
 1,748
```

6.
```
    38
  × 95
 2,700
   720
   150
 +  40
 3,610
```

Name _____

Lesson 34
CC.4.NBT.5

1. Lisa jumps rope at a rate of 86 jumps per minute. At this rate, what is the total number of times Lisa will jump in 15 minutes?

- (A) 1,200
- (B) 1,275
- (C) 1,290
- (D) 1,740

2. Students arranged 13 chairs in each of 32 rows for the school play. What is the total number of chairs the students arranged?

- (A) 300
- (B) 320
- (C) 384
- (D) 416

3. Rosa's vegetable garden has 15 rows of 32 corn plants each.

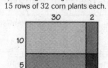

How many corn plants are in Rosa's vegetable garden?

- (A) 480   (C) 450
- (B) 465   (D) 300

4. Some students are reorganizing supplies in the art room. They put 25 crayons in each of 24 boxes. What is the total number of crayons the students put into boxes?

- (A) 760
- (B) 600
- (C) 582
- (D) 200

Problem Solving REAL WORLD

5. Evelyn drinks 8 glasses of water a day, which is 56 glasses of water a week. How many glasses of water does she drink in a year? (1 year = 52 weeks)

2,912 glasses

6. Joe wants to use the Hiking Club's funds to purchase new walking sticks for each of its 19 members. The sticks cost $26 each. The club has $480. Is this enough money to buy each member a new walking stick? If not, how much more money is needed?

No; $14 more is needed.

Answer Key

Name _____

Lesson 35
COMMON CORE STANDARD CC.4.NBT.5
Lesson Objective: Use regrouping to multiply 2-digit numbers.

Multiply with Regrouping

Estimate. Then use regrouping to find 28 × 43.

Step 1 Round to estimate the product.   30 × 40 = 1,200

Step 2 Think: 28 = 2 tens 8 ones.
Multiply 43 by 8 ones.
8 × 3 = 24. Record the 4. Write the
regrouped 2 above the tens place.
8 × 40 = 320. Add the regrouped
tens: 320 + 20 = 340.

$$\begin{array}{r} \overset{2}{4}3 \\ \times\ 28 \\ \hline 344 \end{array} \leftarrow 8 \times 43$$

Step 3 Multiply 43 by 2 tens.
20 × 3 = 60 and 20 × 40 = 800.
Record 860 below 344.

$$\begin{array}{r} \overset{2}{4}3 \\ \times\ 28 \\ \hline 344 \\ 860 \end{array} \leftarrow 20 \times 43$$

Step 4 Add the partial products.

$$1,204 \leftarrow 344 + 860$$

So, 28 × 43 = __1,204__. 1,204 is close to 1,200. The answer is reasonable.

Estimate. Then find the product. Possible estimates are given.

1. Estimate: __400__   2. Estimate: __1,200__   3. Estimate: __2,500__

$$\begin{array}{r} 36 \\ \times\ 12 \\ \hline 432 \end{array} \qquad \begin{array}{r} 43 \\ \times\ 29 \\ \hline 1,247 \end{array} \qquad \begin{array}{r} 51 \\ \times\ 47 \\ \hline 2,397 \end{array}$$

---

1. A farmer planted 29 rows of apple trees. There are 27 trees in each row. How many apple trees did the farmer plant altogether?

Ⓐ 261
Ⓑ 723
Ⓒ 783
Ⓓ 1,881

2. Maria packed 24 bags of dog treats for the animal shelter. She put 16 dog treats in each bag. What is the total number of dog treats Maria packed?

Ⓐ 168
Ⓑ 240
Ⓒ 384
Ⓓ 624

3. Keiko can text 55 words each minute. At this rate, how many words will Keiko text in 15 minutes?

Ⓐ 825
Ⓑ 805
Ⓒ 705
Ⓓ 330

4. There are 96 word search puzzles in a puzzle book. Each puzzle has 22 words. How many words in all does the puzzle book have?

Ⓐ 384
Ⓑ 2,002
Ⓒ 2,012
Ⓓ 2,112

Problem Solving REAL WORLD

5. Baseballs come in cartons of 84 baseballs. A team orders 18 cartons of baseballs. How many baseballs does the team order?

__1,512 baseballs__

6. There are 16 tables in the school lunch room. Each table can seat 22 students. How many students can be seated at lunch at one time?

__352 students__

Name _____

Lesson 36
COMMON CORE STANDARD CC.4.NBT.5
Lesson Objective: Choose a method to multiply 2-digit numbers.

Choose a Multiplication Method

Estimate. Then use regrouping to find 47 × 89.

$$\begin{array}{r} 89 \\ \times\ 47 \end{array}$$

Step 1 Estimate the product.   50 × 90 = 4,500

Step 2 Multiply the 9 ones by the 7 ones. Regroup the 63 ones as 6 tens 3 ones.

$$\begin{array}{r} \overset{6}{8}9 \\ \times\ 47 \\ \hline 3 \end{array}$$

Step 3 Multiply the 8 tens, or 80, by the 7 ones, or 7. Add the regrouped tens. Regroup the 62 tens as 6 hundreds 2 tens.

$$\begin{array}{r} \overset{6}{8}9 \\ \times\ 47 \\ \hline 623 \end{array}$$

Step 4 Multiply the 9 ones by the 4 tens, or 40. Regroup the 36 tens as 3 hundreds 6 tens.

$$\begin{array}{r} \overset{3}{8}9 \\ \times\ 47 \\ \hline 623 \\ 60 \end{array}$$

Step 5 Multiply the 8 tens, or 80, by the 4 tens, or 40. Add the regrouped tens. Regroup the 35 hundreds as 3 thousands 5 hundreds.

$$\begin{array}{r} \overset{3}{8}9 \\ \times\ 47 \\ \hline 623 \\ 3,560 \end{array}$$

Step 6 Add the partial products.

$$\begin{array}{r} \overset{3}{8}9 \\ \times\ 47 \\ \hline 623 \\ +\ 3,560 \\ \hline 4,183 \end{array}$$

So, 47 × 89 = 4,183. Since 4,183 is close to the estimate of 4,500, it is reasonable.

Estimate. Then choose a method to find the product. Possible estimates are given.

1. Estimate: __2,400__   2. Estimate: __800__   3. Estimate: __300__   4. Estimate: __3,600__

$$\begin{array}{r} 76 \\ \times\ 31 \\ \hline 2,356 \end{array} \quad \begin{array}{r} 24 \\ \times\ 35 \\ \hline 840 \end{array} \quad \begin{array}{r} 14 \\ \times\ 28 \\ \hline 392 \end{array} \quad \begin{array}{r} 64 \\ \times\ 56 \\ \hline 3,584 \end{array}$$

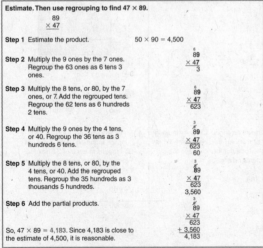

---

1. Gabe runs on a treadmill for 45 minutes every morning. His body uses about 12 calories per minute to keep him moving. How many calories does Gabe use during his run?

Ⓐ 135
Ⓑ 440
Ⓒ 540
Ⓓ 580

2. A youth center sold raffle tickets to raise money for supplies. They sold 62 books of raffle tickets for $18 each. How much money did the youth center raise?

Ⓐ $1,116
Ⓑ $1,016
Ⓒ $816
Ⓓ $558

3. A store sold 52 shirts on Saturday for $28 each. What is the total amount customers paid for the shirts?

Ⓐ $1,040
Ⓑ $1,046
Ⓒ $1,440
Ⓓ $1,456

4. There are 68 students in the book club. Each student reads 14 books during summer vacation. How many books do the students read in all during summer vacation?

Ⓐ 340
Ⓑ 922
Ⓒ 952
Ⓓ 1,020

Problem Solving REAL WORLD

5. A movie theatre has 26 rows of seats. There are 18 seats in each row. How many seats are there in all?

__468 seats__

6. Each class at Briarwood Elementary collected at least 54 cans of food during the food drive. If there are 29 classes in the school, what was the least number of cans collected?

__1,566 cans__

Name _____

Lesson **37**
COMMON CORE STANDARD CC.4.NBT.6
Lesson Objective: Use multiples to estimate quotients.

Estimate Quotients Using Multiples

Find two numbers the quotient of 142 ÷ 5 is between. Then estimate the quotient.

You can use multiples to estimate. A **multiple** of a number is the product of a number and a counting number.

Step 1 Think: What number multiplied by 5 is about 142? Since 142 is greater than 10 × 5, or 50, use counting numbers 10, 20, 30, and so on to find multiples of 5.

Step 2 Multiply 5 by multiples of 10 and make a table.

Counting Number	10	20	30	40
Multiple of 5	50	100	150	200

Step 3 Use the table to find multiples of 5 closest to 142.

20 × 5 = <u>100</u>
  ←— 142 is between <u>100</u> and <u>150</u>
30 × 5 = <u>150</u>

142 is closest to <u>150</u>, so 142 ÷ 5 is about <u>30</u>.

Find two numbers the quotient is between. Then estimate the quotient. **Possible answers are given.**

1. 136 ÷ 6
between <u>20</u> and <u>30</u>
about <u>20</u>

2. 95 ÷ 3
between <u>30</u> and <u>40</u>
about <u>30</u>

3. 124 ÷ 9
between <u>13</u> and <u>14</u>
about <u>14</u>

4. 238 ÷ 7
between <u>30</u> and <u>40</u>
about <u>30</u>

Name _____

Lesson **37**
CC.4.NBT.6

1. There are 9 showings of a film about endangered species at the science museum. A total of 458 people saw the film. About how many people were at each showing?

Ⓐ about 40
Ⓑ about 50
Ⓒ about 60
Ⓓ about 90

2. Kelli and her family went to the beach for a vacation. They drove 293 miles in 7 hours to get there. About how many miles did they drive each hour?

Ⓐ about 40 miles
Ⓑ about 30 miles
Ⓒ about 20 miles
Ⓓ about 10 miles

3. Between which two numbers is the quotient of 87 ÷ 5?

Ⓐ between 5 and 10
Ⓑ between 10 and 15
Ⓒ between 15 and 20
Ⓓ between 20 and 25

4. Between which two numbers is the quotient of 93 ÷ 5?

Ⓐ between 20 and 25
Ⓑ between 15 and 20
Ⓒ between 10 and 15
Ⓓ between 5 and 10

Problem Solving

5. Joy collected 287 aluminum cans in 6 hours. About how many cans did she collect per hour?

6. Paul sold 162 cups of lemonade in 5 hours. About how many cups of lemonade did he sell each hour?

about 50 cans per hour   **about 30 cups each**

Name _____

Lesson **38**
COMMON CORE STANDARD CC.4.NBT.6
Lesson Objective: Use models to divide whole numbers that do not divide evenly.

Remainders

Use counters to find the quotient and remainder.

9)26

• Use 26 counters to represent the dividend, 26.

• Since you are dividing 26 by 9, draw 9 circles. Divide the 26 counters into 9 equal-sized groups.

• There are 2 counters in each circle, so the quotient is 2. There are 8 counters left over, so the remainder is 8.

2 r8
9)26

Divide. Draw a quick picture to help.

7)66

• Use 66 counters to represent the dividend, 66.

• Since you are dividing 66 by 7, draw 7 circles. Divide 66 counters into 7 equal-sized groups.

• There are 9 counters in each circle, so the quotient is 9. There are 3 counters left over, so the remainder is 3.

9 r3
7)66

Use counters to find the quotient and remainder. **Check students' pictures.**

1. 6)19   3 r1

2. 3)14   4 r2

Divide. Draw a quick picture to help.

3. 39 ÷ 4   9 r3

4. 29 ÷ 3   9 r2

Name _____

Lesson **38**
CC.4.NBT.6

1. Look at the model. What division does it show?

Ⓐ 6 ÷ 3
Ⓑ 6 ÷ 4
Ⓒ 18 ÷ 3
Ⓓ 20 ÷ 3

2. Ed used counters to model 4)19. What quotient and remainder did he find?

Ⓐ quotient: 5 remainder: 1
Ⓑ quotient: 4 remainder: 3
Ⓒ quotient: 4 remainder: 2
Ⓓ quotient: 3 remainder: 7

3. Margie arranged 40 counters into 6 groups of 6. There were 4 counters left over. What quotient and remainder did she model?

Ⓐ quotient: 7 remainder: 2
Ⓑ quotient: 6 remainder: 5
Ⓒ quotient: 6 remainder: 4
Ⓓ quotient: 6 remainder: 2

4. Look at the model. What division does it show?

Ⓐ 4 ÷ 3
Ⓑ 12 ÷ 4
Ⓒ 12 ÷ 3
Ⓓ 13 ÷ 3

5. Stefan says this quick picture shows 31 ÷ 4. Is he correct? What other division does the picture model? Explain.

Yes, 31 ÷ 4 is 7 with a remainder of 3; Possible explanation: Stefan divided 31 circles into 4 equal groups, with 3 left over. The picture also shows 31 circles put into groups of 7. There are 3 left over showing 31 ÷ 7 is 4 with a remainder of 3.

Answer Key

Name

Lesson 39
COMMON CORE STANDARD CC.4.NBT.6
Lesson Objective: Divide tens, hundreds, and thousands by whole numbers through 10.

Divide Tens, Hundreds, and Thousands

You can use base-ten blocks, place value, and basic facts to divide.

Divide. $240 \div 3$

Use base-ten blocks.	Use place value.
Step 1 Draw a quick picture to show 240.	**Step 1** Identify the basic fact to use. Use $24 \div 3$
Step 2 You cannot divide 2 hundreds into 3 equal groups. Rename 2 hundreds as tens. $240 = \underline{24}$ tens	**Step 2** Use place value to rewrite 240 as tens. $240 = \underline{24}$ tens
Step 3 Separate the tens into 3 equal groups to divide. There are 3 groups of $\underline{8}$ tens. Write the answer. $240 \div 3 = \underline{80}$	**Step 3** Divide. 24 tens $\div 3 = \underline{8}$ tens $= \underline{80}$ Write the answer. $240 \div 3 = \underline{80}$

Use basic facts and place value to find the quotient.

1. $280 \div 4$

   What division fact can you use?
   $\underline{28 \div 4 = 7}$

   $280 = \underline{28}$ tens

   28 tens $\div 4 = \underline{7}$ tens

   $280 \div 4 = \underline{70}$

2. $1,800 \div 9$

   What division fact can you use?
   $\underline{18 \div 9 = 2}$

   $1,800 = \underline{18}$ hundreds

   18 hundreds $\div 9 = \underline{2}$ hundreds

   $1,800 \div 9 = \underline{200}$

3. $560 \div 7 = \underline{80}$

4. $180 \div 6 = \underline{30}$

5. $1,500 \div 5 = \underline{300}$

6. $3,200 \div 4 = \underline{800}$

Name

Lesson 39
CC.4.NBT.6

1. Taylor took 560 photographs while on summer vacation. She wants to place an equal number of photos in each of 7 albums. How many photos will Taylor place in each album?
   - (A) 7
   - (B) 8
   - **(C) 70**
   - (D) 80

2. Which number sentence is **not** true?
   - **(A)** $200 \div 5 = 50$
   - (B) $400 \div 8 = 50$
   - (C) $2,000 \div 4 = 500$
   - (D) $4,000 \div 4 = 1,000$

3. A crayon factory packs 5 crayons in a sample pack. The factory gives sample packs to visitors under 12. How many sample packs can be made with 2,500 crayons?
   - (A) 5
   - (B) 50
   - **(C) 500**
   - (D) 5,000

4. Bayshore Elementary students collected $3,200 for new library books. Each of the 8 classes collected the same amount. How much did each class collect?
   - (A) $4,000
   - **(B) $400**
   - (C) $40
   - (D) $4

5. A factory packs 6 bars of soap into each family pack. Explain how to use basic facts and place value to find how many family packs can be made with 5,400 bars of soap.

   Possible explanation: I think of 5,400 as 54 hundreds. I know 54 ÷ 6 = 9, so 54 hundreds divided by 6 is 9 hundreds, or 900. So, 900 family packs can be made with 5,400 bars of soap.

Name

Lesson 40
COMMON CORE STANDARD CC.4.NBT.6
Lesson Objective: Use compatible numbers to estimate quotients.

Estimate Quotients Using Compatible Numbers

Compatible numbers are numbers that are easy to compute mentally. In division, one compatible number divides evenly into the other. Think of the multiples of a number to help you find compatible numbers.

Estimate. $6\overline{)216}$

Step 1 Think of these multiples of 6:

6   12   18   24   30   36   42   48   54

Find multiples that are close to the first 2 digits of the dividend. $\underline{18}$ tens and $\underline{24}$ tens are both close to $\underline{21}$ tens. You can use either or both numbers to estimate the quotient.

Step 2 Estimate using compatible numbers.

$216 \div 6$ → $180 \div 6 = 30$

$216 \div 6$ → $240 \div 6 = 40$

So, $216 \div 6$ is between $\underline{30}$ and $\underline{40}$.

Step 3 Decide whether the estimate is closer to 30 or 40.

$216 - 180 = 36$ $240 - 216 = 24$

216 is closer to 240, so use $\underline{40}$ as the estimate.

Use compatible numbers to estimate the quotient.

Possible estimates are given.

1. $3\overline{)252}$ $\underline{80}$

2. $6\overline{)546}$ $\underline{90}$

3. $4\overline{)2,545}$ $\underline{600}$

4. $5\overline{)314}$ $\underline{60}$

5. $2\overline{)1,578}$ $\underline{800}$

6. $8\overline{)289}$ $\underline{40}$

Name

Lesson 40
CC.4.NBT.6

1. On Friday, 278 fourth graders went on a field trip to the Arizona State Museum. The staff divided them into 7 tour groups. Which is the **best** estimate of the number of students in each tour group?
   - (A) 50
   - **(B) 40**
   - (C) 20
   - (D) 7

2. Amanda and her four sisters divided 1,021 stickers equally. About how many stickers did each girl receive?
   - (A) about 300
   - (B) about 250
   - **(C) about 200**
   - (D) about 100

3. Use compatible numbers to estimate the quotient $531 \div 6$. Which is the **best** estimate?
   - (A) 9
   - **(B) 90**
   - (C) 900
   - (D) 9,000

4. For Earth Day, 264 students helped out at a tree farm. The staff divided the students into 9 teams. Which is the **best** estimate of the number of students on each team?
   - **(A) 30**
   - (B) 36
   - (C) 40
   - (D) 50

Problem Solving REAL WORLD

5. A CD store sold 3,467 CDs in 7 days. About the same number of CDs were sold each day. About how many CDs did the store sell each day?

   about 500 CDs

6. Marcus has 731 books. He puts about the same number of books on each of 9 shelves in his bookcase. About how many books are on each shelf?

   about 80 books

Lesson 41
COMMON CORE STANDARD CC.4.NBT.6
Lesson Objective: Use the Distributive Property to find quotients.

Division and the Distributive Property

Divide. 78 ÷ 6

Use the Distributive Property and quick pictures to break apart numbers to make them easier to divide.

Step 1 Draw a quick picture to show 78.

Step 2 Think about how to break apart 78. You know 6 tens ÷ 6 = 10, so use 78 = 60 + 18. Draw a quick picture to show 6 tens and 18 ones.

Step 3 Draw circles to show 6 tens ÷ 6 and 18 ones ÷ 6. Your drawing shows the use of the Distributive Property.
$78 ÷ 6 = \underline{(60 ÷ 6)} + \underline{(18 ÷ 6)}$

Step 4 Add the quotients to find 78 ÷ 6.
$78 ÷ 6 = (60 ÷ 6) + (18 ÷ 6)$
$= \underline{10} + \underline{3}$
$= \underline{13}$

Check students' pictures.

Use quick pictures to model the quotient.

1. $84 ÷ 4 = \underline{21}$ 2. $54 ÷ 3 = \underline{18}$ 3. $68 ÷ 2 = \underline{34}$

4. $65 ÷ 5 = \underline{13}$ 5. $96 ÷ 8 = \underline{12}$ 6. $90 ÷ 6 = \underline{15}$

Lesson 41
CC.4.NBT.6

1. Lakya is using the Distributive Property to divide 128 by 4. Which does **not** show a way she could break apart the dividend?

Ⓐ $128 ÷ 4 = (100 ÷ 4) + (28 ÷ 4)$
Ⓑ $128 ÷ 4 = (120 ÷ 4) + (8 ÷ 4)$
Ⓒ $128 ÷ 4 = (64 ÷ 4) + (64 ÷ 4)$
Ⓓ $128 ÷ 4 = (12 ÷ 4) + (28 ÷ 4)$

2. Dawn has 48 finger puppets in 3 baskets. Each basket has the same number of puppets. How many puppets are in each basket?

Ⓐ 14
Ⓑ 15
Ⓒ 16
Ⓓ 18

3. The Distributive Property can help you divide. Which is **not** a way to break apart the dividend to find the quotient of 132 ÷ 6?

Ⓐ $(120 ÷ 6) + (12 ÷ 6)$
Ⓑ $(100 ÷ 6) + (32 ÷ 6)$
Ⓒ $(90 ÷ 6) + (42 ÷ 6)$
Ⓓ $(72 ÷ 6) + (60 ÷ 6)$

4. Gordon took batting practice with a pitching machine. He hit 104 pitches in 8 minutes. If Gordon hit the same number of pitches, how many pitches did he hit each minute?

Ⓐ 12
Ⓑ 13
Ⓒ 14
Ⓓ 15

5. Steve has 68 tulips to divide into vases. There will be 4 tulips in each vase. Explain a way to use the Distributive Property to find the number of vases Steve will need.

Possible explanation: You need to divide 68 by 4. To divide 68 ÷ 4, you can rename 68 as 36 + 32. Then you can use 68 ÷ 4 = (36 ÷ 4) + (32 ÷ 4), which is 9 + 8. So, 68 ÷ 4 = 17.

Lesson 42
COMMON CORE STANDARD CC.4.NBT.6
Lesson Objective: Use repeated subtraction and multiples to find quotients.

Divide Using Repeated Subtraction

You can use repeated subtraction to divide. Use repeated subtraction to solve the problem.

Nestor has 27 shells to make bracelets. He needs 4 shells for each bracelet. How many bracelets can he make?

Divide. 27 ÷ 4

Write 4)27.

Step 1
Subtract the divisor until the remainder is less than the divisor. Record a 1 each time you subtract.

4)27	
−4	1
23	
−4	1
19	
−4	1
15	
−4	1
11	
−4	1
7	
−4	1
3	

Step 2
Count the number of times you subtracted the divisor, 4.

4 is subtracted six times with 3 left.

$27 ÷ 4$
$6 r3$

So, Nestor can make 6 bracelets. He will have 3 shells left.

Use repeated subtraction to divide.

1. $30 ÷ 4$
$7 r2$

2. $24 ÷ 5$
$4 r4$

3. $47 ÷ 7$
$6 r5$

Lesson 42
CC.4.NBT.6

1. There are 60 people waiting for a river raft ride. Each raft holds 15 people. Which number sentence can be used to find how many rafts will be needed?

Ⓐ $60 − 15 − 15 − 15 − 15 = 0$
Ⓑ $60 − 15 = 45$
Ⓒ $60 + 15 = 75$
Ⓓ $60 − 30 − 15 = 15$

2. There are 48 people waiting for a fishing tour. Each tour boat holds 12 people. Which number sentence can be used to find how many boats will be needed?

Ⓐ $12 + 48 = 60$
Ⓑ $48 − 12 = 36$
Ⓒ $48 − 24 = 24$
Ⓓ $48 − 12 − 12 − 12 − 12 = 0$

3. Jessie has 80 rubber bracelets. She arranges the bracelets in piles of 4. Which model shows 80 ÷ 4?

Ⓐ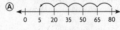
Ⓑ
Ⓒ
Ⓓ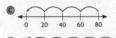

Problem Solving REAL WORLD

4. Gretchen has 48 small shells. She uses 2 shells to make one pair of earrings. How many pairs of earrings can she make?

24 pairs

5. James wants to purchase a telescope for $54. If he saves $3 per week, in how many weeks will he have saved enough to purchase the telescope?

18 weeks

Answer Key

Name _____

Lesson **43**

COMMON CORE STANDARD CC.4.NBT.6
Lesson Objective: Use partial quotients to divide.

Divide Using Partial Quotients

You can use partial quotients to divide.

Divide. 492 ÷ 4

Partial quotients

Step 1 Subtract greater multiples of the divisor. Repeat if needed.

Step 2 Subtract lesser multiples of the divisor. Repeat until the remaining number is less than the divisor.

Step 3 Add the partial quotients.

```
  4)492
   -400    100 × 4    100
    92
   - 80    20 × 4     20
    12
   - 12     3 × 4    + 3
     0               123
```

Use rectangular models to record partial quotients.

```
        100
  4 | 400 | 80 12 |    492
                      -400
                        92
```

```
        100     20
  4 | 400 | 80 12 |    92
                      - 80
                        12
```

```
        100    20  3
  4 | 400 | 80 12 |   12
                     -12
                       0
```

$$\underline{100} + \underline{20} + \underline{3} = \underline{123}$$

Divide. Use partial quotients.

1.
```
    219
  3)657
  -300    100 × 3    100
   357
  -300    100 × 3    100
    57
  - 30     10 × 3     10
    27
  - 27      9 × 3    + 9
     0               219
```

Divide. Use rectangular models to record the partial quotients.

2. 852 ÷ 6 = **142**

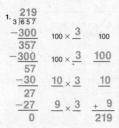

```
        100
  6 | 600 | 240 12 |   852
                      -600
                       252
```

```
        100    40
  6 | 600 | 240 12 |   252
                      -240
                        12
```

```
        100   40  2
  6 | 600 | 240 12 |   12
                      -12
                        0
```

$$\underline{100} + \underline{40} + \underline{2} = \underline{142}$$

---

1. Keith wants to fill 9 pages of his photo album with the same number of photographs on each page. If Keith has 117 photographs, how many photographs will he put on each page?

   (A) 8
   (B) 13
   (C) 17
   (D) 23

2. Diego bought 488 frozen yogurt bars in 4 different flavors for a party. If he bought the same number of each flavor, how many of each flavor did Diego buy?

   (A) 221
   (B) 211
   (C) 122
   (D) 62

3. Three popcorn stores donated a total of 636 bags of popcorn for the school fair. If each store donated the same number of bags, how many bags of popcorn did each store donate?

   (A) 112
   (B) 202
   (C) 210
   (D) 212

4. Sam filled 6 toy boxes with the same number of toys in each box. If he had 144 toys, how many toys did he put in each toy box?

   (A) 150
   (B) 24
   (C) 22
   (D) 14

Problem Solving

5. Allison took 112 photos on vacation. She wants to put them in a photo album that holds 4 photos on each page. How many pages can she fill?

   28 pages

6. Hector saved $726 in 6 months. He saved the same amount each month. How much did Hector save each month?

   $121

Name _____

Lesson **44**

COMMON CORE STANDARD CC.4.NBT.6
Lesson Objective: Use base-ten blocks to model division with regrouping.

Model Division with Regrouping

You can use base-ten blocks to model division with regrouping.

Use base-ten blocks to find the quotient 65 ÷ 4.

Step 1 Show 65 with base-ten blocks.

Step 2 Draw 4 circles to represent dividing 65 into 4 equal groups. Share the tens equally among the 4 groups.

Step 3 Regroup leftover tens as ones.

Step 4 Share the ones equally among the 4 groups.

There are $\underline{1}$ ten(s) and $\underline{6}$ one(s) in each group with $\underline{1}$ left over.

So, the quotient is $\underline{16\ r1}$.

Divide. Use base-ten blocks.

1. 37 ÷ 2

   18 r1

2. 74 ÷ 3

   24 r2

3. 66 ÷ 5

   13 r1

---

1. Zack needs to divide these base-ten blocks into 3 equal groups.

   Which model shows how many should be in each equal group?

   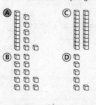

   (A) (C) (B) (D)

2. Emily earned $72 in 6 days walking dogs. She earned the same amount each day. How much did she earn each day?

   (A) $22   (C) $13
   (B) $14   (D) $12

3. Ethan needs to divide these base-ten blocks into 3 equal groups.

   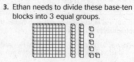

   Which model shows how many should be in each equal group?

   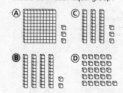

   (A) (C) (B) (D)

4. Zora blinked her eyes 96 times in 4 minutes. She blinked the same number of times each minute. How many times did Zora blink in one minute?

   (A) 22   (C) 24
   (B) 23   (D) 25

Problem Solving

5. Tamara sold 92 cold drinks during her 2-hour shift at a festival food stand. If she sold the same number of drinks each hour, how many cold drinks did she sell each hour?

   46 cold drinks

6. In 3 days Donald earned $42 running errands. He earned the same amount each day. How much did Donald earn from running errands each day?

   $14

Lesson 45

COMMON CORE STANDARD CC.4.NBT.6
Lesson Objective: Use place value to determine where to place the first digit of a quotient.

Name _____

Place the First Digit

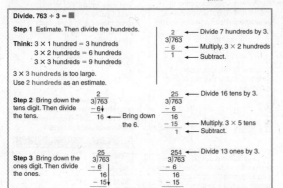

Divide. 763 ÷ 3 = ▦

Step 1 Estimate. Then divide the hundreds.

Think: 3 × 1 hundred = 3 hundreds
3 × 2 hundreds = 6 hundreds
3 × 3 hundreds = 9 hundreds

3 × 3 hundreds is too large.
Use 2 hundreds as an estimate.

$$\begin{array}{r} 2 \\ 3\overline{)763} \\ -6 \\ \hline 1 \end{array}$$ ← Divide 7 hundreds by 3.
← Multiply. 3 × 2 hundreds
← Subtract.

Step 2 Bring down the tens digit. Then divide the tens.

$$\begin{array}{r} 2 \\ 3\overline{)763} \\ -6\downarrow \\ \hline 16 \end{array}$$ ← Bring down the 6.

$$\begin{array}{r} 25 \\ 3\overline{)763} \\ -6 \\ \hline 16 \\ -15 \\ \hline 1 \end{array}$$ ← Divide 16 tens by 3.
← Multiply. 3 × 5 tens
← Subtract.

Step 3 Bring down the ones digit. Then divide the ones.

$$\begin{array}{r} 25 \\ 3\overline{)763} \\ -6 \\ \hline 16 \\ -15\downarrow \\ \hline 13 \end{array}$$ ← Bring down the 3.

$$\begin{array}{r} 254 \\ 3\overline{)763} \\ -6 \\ \hline 16 \\ -15 \\ \hline 13 \\ -12 \\ \hline 1 \end{array}$$ ← Divide 13 ones by 3.
← Multiply. 3 × 4 ones
← Subtract.

Step 4 Check to make sure that the remainder is less than the divisor. Write the answer.
$$\begin{array}{r} 254\,r1 \\ 3\overline{)763} \end{array}$$ 1 < 3

Divide.

1. 2)531 = **265 r1**
2. 4)628 = **157**
3. 9)349 = **38 r7**
4. 7)794 = **113 r3**

Lesson 45
CC.4.NBT.6

Name _____

1. Jake writes a division problem to find out how he can distribute 543 marbles among 7 of his friends. In what place is the first digit of the quotient?
   A thousands
   B hundreds
   C tens
   D ones

2. Sylvia plans to place 617 stamps in an album. Each page of the album holds 5 stamps. She uses division to find out how many full pages she will have. In what place is the first digit of the quotient?
   A hundreds   C tens
   B ones   D thousands

3. Jim will use division to find out how he can distribute 750 coupon books among 9 stores. In what place is the first digit of the quotient?
   A ones
   B tens
   C hundreds
   D thousands

4. Hilda wants to save 825 digital photographs in an online album. Each folder of the online album can save 6 photographs. She uses division to find out how many full folders she will have. In what place is the first digit of the quotient?
   A ones   **C hundreds**
   B tens   D thousands

Problem Solving REAL WORLD

5. There are 132 projects in the science fair. If 8 projects can fit in a row, how many full rows of projects can be made? How many projects are in the row that is not full?

   16 rows; 4 projects

6. There are 798 calories in six 10-ounce bottles of apple juice. How many calories are there in one 10-ounce bottle of apple juice?

   133 calories

Lesson 46

COMMON CORE STANDARD CC.4.NBT.6
Lesson Objective: Divide multidigit numbers by 1-digit divisors.

Name _____

Divide by 1-Digit Numbers

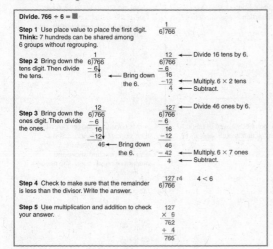

Divide. 766 ÷ 6 = ▦

Step 1 Use place value to place the first digit.
Think: 7 hundreds can be shared among 6 groups without regrouping.
$$\begin{array}{r} 1 \\ 6\overline{)766} \end{array}$$

Step 2 Bring down the tens digit. Then divide the tens.

$$\begin{array}{r} 1 \\ 6\overline{)766} \\ -6\downarrow \\ \hline 16 \end{array}$$ ← Bring down the 6.

$$\begin{array}{r} 12 \\ 6\overline{)766} \\ -6 \\ \hline 16 \\ -12 \\ \hline 4 \end{array}$$ ← Divide 16 tens by 6.
← Multiply. 6 × 2 tens
← Subtract.

Step 3 Bring down the ones digit. Then divide the ones.

$$\begin{array}{r} 12 \\ 6\overline{)766} \\ -6 \\ \hline 16 \\ -12\downarrow \\ \hline 46 \end{array}$$ ← Bring down the 6.

$$\begin{array}{r} 127 \\ 6\overline{)766} \\ -6 \\ \hline 16 \\ -12 \\ \hline 46 \\ -42 \\ \hline 4 \end{array}$$ ← Divide 46 ones by 6.
← Multiply. 6 × 7 ones
← Subtract.

Step 4 Check to make sure that the remainder is less than the divisor. Write the answer.
$$\begin{array}{r} 127\,r4 \\ 6\overline{)766} \end{array}$$ 4 < 6

Step 5 Use multiplication and addition to check your answer.
$$\begin{array}{r} 127 \\ \times\ 6 \\ \hline 762 \\ +\ 4 \\ \hline 766 \end{array}$$

Divide and check.

1. 4)868 = **217**
$$\begin{array}{r} 217 \\ \times\ 4 \\ \hline 868 \end{array}$$

2. 2)657 = **328 r1**
$$\begin{array}{r} 328 \\ \times\ 2 \\ \hline 656 \\ +\ 1 \\ \hline 657 \end{array}$$

3. 7)8,473 = **1,210 r3**
$$\begin{array}{r} 1,210 \\ \times\ 7 \\ \hline 8,470 \\ +\ 3 \\ \hline 8,473 \end{array}$$

Lesson 46
CC.4.NBT.6

Name _____

1. Students made large soap bubbles at a party. They used 224 ounces of dish soap to make the bubble mixture. The dish soap came in 4 containers of the same size. How many ounces of dish soap were in each container?
   A 51 ounces
   B 55 ounces
   C 56 ounces
   D 66 ounces

2. A toy manufacturer has 627 yo-yos to divide equally among 3 stores. How many yo-yos will each store receive?
   A 29
   B 209
   C 219
   D 309

3. Students are making pizza. They put a total of 108 ounces of cheese on 9 pizzas. Each pizza has the same amount of cheese. How many ounces of cheese are on each pizza?
   A 15 ounces
   B 14 ounces
   C 13 ounces
   D 12 ounces

4. A store gave away 1,932 calendars in 7 days. They gave away the same number of calendars each day. How many calendars did the store give away each day?
   A 276
   B 281
   C 286
   D 776

5. An office supply store packed 416 notepads with the same number in each of 4 boxes. Milo said there are exactly 100 notepads in each box. Do you agree? Explain.

   I disagree; Possible explanation: I can use multiplication to check division. 4 × 100 = 400. There are still 16 notepads that Milo's answer does not include.

   416 ÷ 100 = 104. Check: 4 × 104 = 416.

Answer Key

Equivalent Fractions

Write two fractions that are equivalent to $\frac{2}{6}$.

Step 1 Make a model to represent $\frac{2}{6}$.

The rectangle is divided into 6 equal parts, with 2 parts shaded.

Step 2 Divide the rectangle from Step 1 in half.

The rectangle is now divided into 12 equal parts, with 4 parts shaded.
The model shows the fraction $\frac{4}{12}$. So, $\frac{2}{6}$ and $\frac{4}{12}$ are equivalent.

Step 3 Draw the same rectangle as in Step 1, but with only 3 equal parts. Keep the same amount of the rectangle shaded.

The rectangle is now divided into 3 equal parts, with 1 part shaded.
The model shows the fraction $\frac{1}{3}$. So, $\frac{2}{6}$ and $\frac{1}{3}$ are equivalent.

Use models to write two equivalent fractions. Check students' models. Possible answers are given.

1. $\frac{2}{4}$ $\frac{1}{2}, \frac{4}{8}$

2. $\frac{4}{6}$ $\frac{2}{3}, \frac{8}{12}$

---

1. Julie sewed squares together to make a quilt. The shaded squares show where she used a blue square.

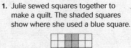

What pair of fractions is **not** equivalent to the part of the quilt with blue squares?

Ⓐ $\frac{1}{3}$ and $\frac{8}{24}$ Ⓒ $\frac{1}{3}$ and $\frac{2}{6}$

Ⓑ $\frac{2}{6}$ and $\frac{4}{12}$ Ⓓ $\frac{1}{2}$ and $\frac{6}{18}$

2. Joey divides a small garden into 20 equal sections. He plants tulips in 16 of the sections. Which fraction is equivalent to the part of the garden planted with tulips?

Ⓐ $\frac{4}{5}$ Ⓒ $\frac{1}{2}$

Ⓑ $\frac{3}{4}$ Ⓓ $\frac{2}{5}$

3. Ann uses three $\frac{1}{4}$ size strips to model $\frac{3}{4}$. She wants to use $\frac{1}{8}$ size strips to model an equivalent fraction. How many $\frac{1}{8}$ size strips will she need?

Ⓐ 3   Ⓒ 6

Ⓑ 4   Ⓓ 8

4. Four friends shared a pizza. The table shows how much of the pizza each person ate. Which friends ate the same amount of pizza?

Name	Pizza Eaten
Colin	$\frac{3}{9}$
Stephanie	$\frac{2}{8}$
Vicki	$\frac{3}{12}$
Wesley	$\frac{1}{6}$

Ⓐ Colin and Wesley

Ⓑ Stephanie and Vicki

Ⓒ Stephanie and Wesley

Ⓓ Colin and Vicki

5. Lizzie walked $\frac{8}{10}$ mile and Billy walked $\frac{12}{15}$ mile. Lizzie says they walked the same distance. Do you agree with Lizzie? Explain your answer.
I agree. Possible explanation: an equivalent fraction for $\frac{8}{10}$ is $\frac{4}{5}$ and an equivalent fraction for $\frac{12}{15}$ is $\frac{4}{5}$. So, they both walked the same distance.

Generate Equivalent Fractions

Write an equivalent fraction for $\frac{4}{5}$.

Step 1 Choose a whole number, like 2.

Step 2 Create a fraction using 2 as the numerator and denominator: $\frac{2}{2}$. This fraction is equal to 1. You can multiply a number by 1 without changing the value of the number.

Step 3 Multiply $\frac{4}{5}$ by $\frac{2}{2}$: $\frac{4 \times 2}{5 \times 2} = \frac{8}{10}$.

So, $\frac{4}{5}$ and $\frac{8}{10}$ are equivalent.

Write another equivalent fraction for $\frac{4}{5}$.

Step 1 Choose a different whole number, like 20.

Step 2 Create a fraction using 20 as the numerator and denominator: $\frac{20}{20}$.

Step 3 Multiply $\frac{4}{5}$ by $\frac{20}{20}$: $\frac{4 \times 20}{5 \times 20} = \frac{80}{100}$.

So, $\frac{4}{5}$ and $\frac{80}{100}$ are equivalent.

Write two equivalent fractions. Possible answers are given.

1. $\frac{2}{6}$ $\frac{6}{18}, \frac{8}{24}$

2. $\frac{4}{10}$ $\frac{8}{20}, \frac{12}{30}$

3. $\frac{3}{8}$ $\frac{9}{24}, \frac{18}{48}$

4. $\frac{3}{5}$ $\frac{12}{20}, \frac{21}{35}$

---

1. Kyle drank $\frac{2}{3}$ cup of apple juice. Which fraction is equivalent to $\frac{2}{3}$?

Ⓐ $\frac{2}{9}$

Ⓑ $\frac{2}{6}$

Ⓒ $\frac{6}{9}$

Ⓓ $\frac{9}{6}$

2. Nicolette needs $\frac{1}{3}$ yard of fabric. Which fraction is equivalent to $\frac{1}{3}$?

Ⓐ $\frac{1}{9}$

Ⓑ $\frac{5}{15}$

Ⓒ $\frac{2}{3}$

Ⓓ $\frac{15}{3}$

3. There are 5 marbles in each bag. One of the marbles in each bag is striped. Which two fractions are equivalent to $\frac{1}{5}$?

Ⓐ $\frac{2}{10}, \frac{3}{15}$

Ⓑ $\frac{2}{8}, \frac{3}{12}$

Ⓒ $\frac{2}{10}, \frac{4}{16}$

Ⓓ $\frac{2}{8}, \frac{4}{15}$

4. Amy's banana bread recipe calls for $\frac{3}{4}$ cup of brown sugar. She only has a $\frac{1}{8}$-cup measure. Which equivalent fraction shows the amount of brown sugar she needs for the recipe?

Ⓐ $\frac{2}{8}$ cup

Ⓑ $\frac{3}{8}$ cup

Ⓒ $\frac{4}{8}$ cup

Ⓓ $\frac{6}{8}$ cup

Problem Solving Possible answers are given.

5. Jan has a 12-ounce milkshake. Four ounces in the milkshake are vanilla, and the rest is chocolate. What are two equivalent fractions that represent the fraction of the milkshake that is vanilla?
$\frac{1}{3}$ and $\frac{2}{6}$

6. Kareem lives $\frac{4}{10}$ of a mile from the mall. Write two equivalent fractions that show what fraction of a mile Kareem lives from the mall.
$\frac{2}{5}$ and $\frac{4}{10}$

Lesson 49
COMMON CORE STANDARD CC.4.NF.1
Lesson Objective: Write and identify equivalent fractions in simplest form.

Simplest Form

A fraction is in **simplest form** when 1 is the only factor that the numerator and denominator have in common.

Tell whether the fraction $\frac{7}{8}$ is in simplest form.

Look for common factors in the numerator and the denominator.

Step 1 The numerator of $\frac{7}{8}$ is 7. List all the factors of 7.	$1 \times 7 = 7$
	The factors of 7 are 1 and 7.
Step 2 The denominator of $\frac{7}{8}$ is 8. List all the factors of 8.	$1 \times 8 = 8$ $2 \times 4 = 8$
	The factors of 8 are 1, 2, 4, and 8.
Step 3 Check if the numerator and denominator of $\frac{7}{8}$ have any common factors greater than 1.	The only common factor of 7 and 8 is 1.
So, $\frac{7}{8}$ is in simplest form.	

Tell whether the fraction is in simplest form. Write yes or no.

1. $\frac{4}{10}$ no
2. $\frac{2}{8}$ no
3. $\frac{3}{5}$ yes

Write the fraction in simplest form.

4. $\frac{4}{12}$ $\frac{1}{3}$
5. $\frac{6}{10}$ $\frac{3}{5}$
6. $\frac{3}{6}$ $\frac{1}{2}$

Lesson 49
CC.4.NF.1

1. Jamal made a list of fractions and asked Will to find the fraction written in simplest form. Which fraction should Will choose?
   - (A) $\frac{1}{8}$
   - (B) $\frac{3}{9}$
   - (C) $\frac{9}{12}$
   - (D) $\frac{6}{10}$

2. In the Jones School Library, $\frac{5}{10}$ of the computers have scanners. In simplest form, what fraction of the computers have scanners?
   - (A) $\frac{5}{10}$
   - (B) $\frac{1}{4}$
   - (C) $\frac{1}{2}$
   - (D) $\frac{6}{12}$

3. In the school chorus, $\frac{2}{12}$ of the students are fourth graders. In simplest form, what fraction of the students in the school chorus are fourth graders?
   - (A) $\frac{4}{12}$
   - (B) $\frac{2}{12}$
   - (C) $\frac{2}{6}$
   - (D) $\frac{1}{6}$

4. Ten of 12 balloons at Jean's party are filled with helium. In simplest form, what fraction of the balloons are filled with helium?
   - (A) $\frac{4}{6}$
   - (B) $\frac{5}{6}$
   - (C) $\frac{10}{12}$
   - (D) $\frac{12}{10}$

Problem Solving REAL WORLD

5. At Memorial Hospital, 9 of the 12 babies born on Tuesday were boys. In simplest form, what fraction of the babies born on Tuesday were boys?

   $\frac{3}{4}$

6. Cristina uses a ruler to measure the length of her math textbook. She says that the book is $\frac{4}{10}$ meter long. Is her measurement in simplest form? If not, what is the length of the book in simplest form?

   No; $\frac{2}{5}$ meter

Lesson 50
COMMON CORE STANDARD CC.4.NF.1
Lesson Objective: Use equivalent fractions to represent a pair of fractions with a common denominator.

Common Denominators

A **common denominator** is a common multiple of the denominators of two or more fractions.

Write $\frac{2}{3}$ and $\frac{3}{4}$ as a pair of fractions with common denominators.

Step 1 Identify the denominators of $\frac{2}{3}$ and $\frac{3}{4}$.	$\frac{2}{3}$ and $\frac{3}{4}$ The denominators are 3 and 4.
Step 2 List multiples of 3 and 4. Circle common multiples.	3: 3, 6, 9, 12, 15, 18 4: 4, 8, 12, 16, 20 12 is a common multiple of 3 and 4.
Step 3 Rewrite $\frac{2}{3}$ as a fraction with a denominator of 12.	$\frac{2}{3} = \frac{2 \times 4}{3 \times 4} = \frac{8}{12}$
Step 4 Rewrite $\frac{3}{4}$ as a fraction with a denominator of 12.	$\frac{3}{4} = \frac{3 \times 3}{4 \times 3} = \frac{9}{12}$
So, you can rewrite $\frac{2}{3}$ and $\frac{3}{4}$ as $\frac{8}{12}$ and $\frac{9}{12}$.	

Write the pair of fractions as a pair of fractions with a common denominator. Possible answers are given.

1. $\frac{1}{2}$ and $\frac{1}{3}$ $\frac{3}{6}, \frac{2}{6}$
2. $\frac{2}{4}$ and $\frac{5}{8}$ $\frac{4}{8}, \frac{5}{8}$
3. $\frac{1}{2}$ and $\frac{3}{5}$ $\frac{5}{10}, \frac{6}{10}$
4. $\frac{1}{4}$ and $\frac{5}{6}$ $\frac{3}{12}, \frac{10}{12}$
5. $\frac{2}{5}$ and $\frac{2}{3}$ $\frac{6}{15}, \frac{10}{15}$
6. $\frac{4}{5}$ and $\frac{7}{10}$ $\frac{8}{10}, \frac{7}{10}$

Lesson 50
CC.4.NF.1

1. Elise is doing her homework. She plans to spend $\frac{1}{2}$ hour on math and $\frac{1}{6}$ hour on spelling words. Which of the following is a common denominator for $\frac{1}{2}$ and $\frac{1}{6}$?
   - (A) 4
   - (B) 12
   - (C) 20
   - (D) 26

2. Miguel walked $\frac{1}{2}$ mile to the library and then $\frac{3}{5}$ mile to the post office. How can he write $\frac{1}{2}$ and $\frac{3}{5}$ as a pair of fractions with a common denominator?
   - (A) $\frac{1}{10}$ and $\frac{3}{10}$
   - (B) $\frac{3}{6}$ and $\frac{3}{5}$
   - (C) $\frac{2}{4}$ and $\frac{15}{25}$
   - (D) $\frac{5}{10}$ and $\frac{6}{10}$

3. Allie jogged for $\frac{1}{2}$ hour on Saturday and for $\frac{3}{4}$ hour on Sunday. Which of the following is a common denominator for $\frac{1}{2}$ and $\frac{3}{4}$?
   - (A) 1
   - (B) 4
   - (C) 6
   - (D) 10

4. Jamal helps in the library. He put away $\frac{1}{3}$ of the returned books on Monday and $\frac{5}{6}$ of the returned books on Tuesday. Which of the following is a common denominator for $\frac{1}{3}$ and $\frac{5}{6}$?
   - (A) 2
   - (B) 3
   - (C) 6
   - (D) 9

Problem Solving REAL WORLD

5. Adam drew two same size rectangles and divided them into the same number of equal parts. He shaded $\frac{1}{3}$ of one rectangle and $\frac{1}{4}$ of other rectangle. What is the least number of parts into which both rectangles could be divided?

   12 parts

6. Mera painted equal sections of her bedroom wall to make a pattern. She painted $\frac{2}{5}$ of the wall white and $\frac{1}{2}$ of the wall lavender. Write an equivalent fraction for each using a common denominator.

   Possible answer: $\frac{4}{10}$ and $\frac{5}{10}$

Answer Key

Lesson 51
COMMON CORE STANDARD CC.4.NF.1
Lesson Objective: Use the strategy make a table to solve problems using equivalent fractions.

Problem Solving • Find Equivalent Fractions

Kyle's mom bought bunches of balloons for a family party. Each bunch has 4 balloons, and $\frac{1}{4}$ of the balloons are blue. If Kyle's mom bought 5 bunches of balloons, how many balloons did she buy? How many of the balloons are blue?

Read the Problem		
What do I need to find?	**What information do I need to use?**	**How will I use the information?**
I need to find how many balloons Kyle's mom bought and how many of the balloons are blue.	Each bunch has 1 out of 4 balloons that are blue, and there are 5 bunches.	I will make a table to find the total number balloons Kyle's mom bought and the fraction of balloons that are blue.

Solve the Problem					

I can make a table.

Number of Bunches	1	2	3	4	5
Total Number of Blue Balloons	1	2	3	4	5
Total Number of Balloons	4	8	12	16	20

Kyle's mom bought 20 balloons. 5 of the balloons are blue.

Make a table to solve. *Check students' tables.*

1. Jackie is making a beaded bracelet. The bracelet will have no more than 12 beads. $\frac{1}{3}$ of the beads on the bracelet will be green. What other fractions could represent the part of the beads on the bracelet that will be green?

$\frac{2}{6}, \frac{3}{9}, \frac{4}{12}$

2. Ben works in his dad's bakery packing bagels. Each package can have no more than 16 bagels. $\frac{3}{4}$ of the bagels in each package are plain. What other fractions could represent the part of the bagels in each package that will be plain?

$\frac{6}{8}, \frac{9}{12}, \frac{12}{16}$

Lesson 51
CC.4.NF.1

1. Malia is making a bracelet with beads. She wants $\frac{1}{4}$ of the beads to be blue. If the greatest number of beads that will fit on the bracelet is 20, what fraction does **not** represent the part of the beads on the bracelet that are blue?

   Ⓐ $\frac{4}{8}$
   Ⓑ $\frac{5}{20}$
   Ⓒ $\frac{4}{16}$
   Ⓓ $\frac{3}{12}$

2. Liam works in a toy store that sells bags of marbles. He puts 10 marbles in each bag, and $\frac{2}{10}$ of the marbles are striped. If Liam makes 3 bags of marbles, how many striped marbles does he use?

   Ⓐ 2
   Ⓑ 6
   Ⓒ 20
   Ⓓ 30

3. Suzanne arranges flowers at her restaurant. She puts 8 flowers in each vase. Three flowers in each vase are yellow. If Suzanne uses 32 flowers, how many are yellow?

   Ⓐ 6
   Ⓑ 9
   Ⓒ 12
   Ⓓ 24

4. Every $\frac{1}{2}$ mile along a hiking path there is a water fountain, every $\frac{1}{4}$ mile there is a bench, and every $\frac{1}{8}$ mile there is a marker. Which of the following will be at $\frac{3}{4}$ mile along the path?

   Ⓐ water fountain, bench, and marker
   Ⓑ water fountain and marker
   Ⓒ water fountain and bench
   Ⓓ bench and marker

5. Sandra is making fruit baskets. She wants $\frac{1}{6}$ of the fruit in each basket to be bananas. If the greatest number of pieces of fruit that will fit in each basket is 24, what fractions represent the possible ways Sandra can have bananas in the fruit basket? Explain how you found your answer.

   Possible answer: $\frac{1}{6}, \frac{2}{12}, \frac{3}{18}, \frac{4}{24}$; *I found equivalent fractions for $\frac{1}{6}$ which have a denominator of 24 or less.*

Lesson 52
COMMON CORE STANDARD CC.4.NF.2
Lesson Objective: Compare fractions using benchmarks.

Compare Fractions Using Benchmarks

A **benchmark** is a known size or amount that helps you understand a different size or amount. You can use $\frac{1}{2}$ as a benchmark.

Sara reads for $\frac{3}{6}$ hour every day after school. Connor reads for $\frac{2}{3}$ hour. Who reads for a longer amount of time?

Compare the fractions. $\frac{3}{6}$ ⬤ $\frac{2}{3}$

Step 1 Divide one circle into 6 equal parts. Divide another circle into 3 equal parts.

Step 2 Shade $\frac{3}{6}$ of the first circle. How many parts will you shade? 3 parts

Step 3 Shade $\frac{2}{3}$ of the second circle. How many parts will you shade? 2 parts

Step 4 Compare the shaded parts of each circle. Half of Sara's circle is shaded. More than half of Connor's circle is shaded.

$\frac{3}{6}$ is less than $\frac{2}{3}$. $\frac{3}{6}$ Ⓒ $\frac{2}{3}$

So, Connor reads for a longer amount of time.

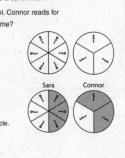

Sara   Connor

1. Compare $\frac{2}{8}$ and $\frac{3}{4}$. Write < or >.

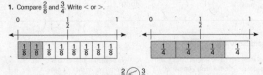

$\frac{2}{8}$ Ⓒ $\frac{3}{4}$

Compare. Write < or >.

2. $\frac{1}{4}$ Ⓒ $\frac{8}{10}$ 3. $\frac{7}{8}$ Ⓒ $\frac{1}{3}$ 4. $\frac{5}{12}$ Ⓒ $\frac{1}{2}$

5. $\frac{2}{8}$ Ⓒ $\frac{8}{12}$ 6. $\frac{4}{6}$ Ⓒ $\frac{4}{8}$ 7. $\frac{7}{12}$ Ⓒ $\frac{2}{4}$

Lesson 52
CC.4.NF.2

1. Asa runs $\frac{2}{5}$ mile. Kim runs $\frac{1}{2}$ mile. Which statement is **true**?

   Ⓐ $\frac{2}{5} > \frac{1}{2}$
   Ⓑ $\frac{1}{2} > \frac{2}{5}$
   Ⓒ $\frac{1}{2} = \frac{2}{5}$
   Ⓓ $\frac{1}{2} < \frac{2}{5}$

2. Carmen has completed $\frac{1}{2}$ of her math homework. Billy has completed $\frac{7}{12}$ of the same assignment. Which statement correctly compares the fractions?

   Ⓐ $\frac{1}{2} > \frac{7}{12}$
   Ⓑ $\frac{7}{12} < \frac{1}{2}$
   Ⓒ $\frac{7}{12} = \frac{1}{2}$
   Ⓓ $\frac{1}{2} < \frac{7}{12}$

3. James and Ella biked around Eagle Lake. James biked $\frac{3}{10}$ of the distance in an hour. Ella biked $\frac{4}{8}$ of the distance in an hour. Which statement correctly compares the fractions?

   Ⓐ $\frac{3}{10} > \frac{4}{8}$
   Ⓑ $\frac{4}{8} = \frac{3}{10}$
   Ⓒ $\frac{3}{10} < \frac{4}{8}$
   Ⓓ $\frac{4}{8} < \frac{3}{10}$

4. Suki rode her bike $\frac{4}{5}$ mile. Claire rode her bike $\frac{1}{3}$ mile. Which statement is **true**?

   Ⓐ $\frac{4}{5} > \frac{1}{3}$
   Ⓑ $\frac{1}{3} > \frac{4}{5}$
   Ⓒ $\frac{1}{3} < \frac{4}{5}$
   Ⓓ $\frac{4}{5} < \frac{1}{3}$

Problem Solving REAL WORLD

5. Erika ran $\frac{3}{8}$ mile. Maria ran $\frac{3}{4}$ mile. Who ran farther?

   Maria

6. Carlos finished $\frac{1}{3}$ of his art project on Monday. Tyler finished $\frac{1}{2}$ of his art project on Monday. Who finished more of his art project on Monday?

   Tyler

Answer Key

Lesson 53
COMMON CORE STANDARD CC.4.NF.2

Compare Fractions

Theo filled a beaker $\frac{2}{4}$ full with water. Angelica filled a beaker $\frac{3}{8}$ full with water. Whose beaker has more water?

Compare $\frac{2}{4}$ and $\frac{3}{8}$.

Step 1 Divide one beaker into 4 equal parts. Divide another beaker into 8 equal parts.

Step 2 Shade $\frac{2}{4}$ of the first beaker.

Step 3 Shade $\frac{3}{8}$ of the second beaker.

Step 4 Compare the shaded parts of each beaker. Half of Theo's beaker is shaded. Less than half of Angelica's beaker is shaded.

$\frac{2}{4}$ is greater than $\frac{3}{8}$.

$\frac{2}{4}$ ⊙> $\frac{3}{8}$

So, Theo's beaker has more water.

1. Compare $\frac{1}{2}$ and $\frac{1}{4}$.

Which is greater? $\frac{1}{2}$

2. Compare $\frac{2}{3}$ and $\frac{3}{6}$.

Which is less? $\frac{3}{6}$

Compare. Write <, >, or =.

3. $\frac{1}{2}$ ⊙< $\frac{3}{4}$
4. $\frac{6}{12}$ ⊙< $\frac{5}{8}$
5. $\frac{2}{3}$ ⊙= $\frac{4}{6}$
6. $\frac{3}{8}$ ⊙> $\frac{1}{4}$

www.harcourtschoolsupply.com © Houghton Mifflin Harcourt Publishing Company 105 Core Standards for Math, Grade 4

Lesson 53
CC.4.NF.2

1. Bill used $\frac{3}{8}$ cup of raisins and $\frac{2}{3}$ cup of banana chips to make a snack. Which statement correctly compares the fractions?
   - (A) $\frac{3}{8} > \frac{2}{3}$
   - (B) $\frac{2}{3} < \frac{3}{8}$
   - (C) $\frac{2}{3} > \frac{3}{8}$
   - (D) $\frac{2}{3} = \frac{3}{8}$

2. Elaine bought $\frac{7}{8}$ pound of potato salad and $\frac{2}{4}$ pound of macaroni salad for a picnic. Which statement correctly compares the fractions?
   - (A) $\frac{7}{8} > \frac{2}{4}$
   - (B) $\frac{7}{8} < \frac{2}{4}$
   - (C) $\frac{2}{4} = \frac{7}{8}$
   - (D) $\frac{2}{4} > \frac{7}{8}$

3. Brad uses $\frac{3}{4}$ cup of milk and $\frac{1}{8}$ cup of yogurt in a recipe. Which statement correctly compares the fractions?
   - (A) $\frac{3}{4} < \frac{1}{8}$
   - (B) $\frac{3}{4} > \frac{1}{8}$
   - (C) $\frac{3}{4} = \frac{1}{8}$
   - (D) $\frac{1}{8} > \frac{3}{4}$

4. In a parade, $\frac{2}{6}$ of the floats have musicians on them. In the same parade, $\frac{4}{12}$ of the floats have animals on them. Which statement correctly compares the fractions?
   - (A) $\frac{2}{6} > \frac{4}{12}$
   - (B) $\frac{2}{6} < \frac{4}{12}$
   - (C) $\frac{4}{12} > \frac{2}{6}$
   - (D) $\frac{4}{12} = \frac{2}{6}$

Problem Solving REAL WORLD

5. A recipe uses $\frac{2}{3}$ cup of flour and $\frac{5}{8}$ cup of blueberries. Is there more flour or more blueberries in the recipe?

   flour

6. Peggy completed $\frac{5}{6}$ of the math homework and Al completed $\frac{4}{5}$ of the math homework. Did Peggy or Al complete more of the math homework?

   Peggy

www.harcourtschoolsupply.com © Houghton Mifflin Harcourt Publishing Company 106 Core Standards for Math, Grade 4

Lesson 54
COMMON CORE STANDARD CC.4.NF.2

Compare and Order Fractions

Write $\frac{3}{8}, \frac{1}{4},$ and $\frac{1}{2}$ in order from least to greatest.

Step 1 Identify a common denominator.
Multiples of 8: 8, 16, 24
Multiples of 4: 4, 8, 16,
Multiples of 2: 2, 4, 6, 8
Use 8 as a common denominator.

Step 2 Use the common denominator to write equivalent fractions.
$\frac{3}{8}$
$\frac{1}{4} = \frac{1 \times 2}{4 \times 2} = \frac{2}{8}$
$\frac{1}{2} = \frac{1 \times 4}{2 \times 4} = \frac{4}{8}$

Step 3 Compare the numerators. $2 < 3 < 4$

Step 4 Order the fractions from least to greatest, using < or > symbols.
$\frac{2}{8} < \frac{3}{8} < \frac{4}{8}$

So, $\frac{1}{4} < \frac{3}{8} < \frac{1}{2}$.

Write the fraction with the greatest value.

1. $\frac{2}{3}, \frac{1}{4}, \frac{1}{6}$ $\frac{2}{3}$
2. $\frac{3}{10}, \frac{1}{2}, \frac{2}{5}$ $\frac{1}{2}$
3. $\frac{1}{8}, \frac{5}{12}, \frac{9}{10}$ $\frac{9}{10}$

Write the fractions in order from least to greatest.

4. $\frac{9}{10}, \frac{1}{2}, \frac{4}{5}$ $\frac{1}{2} < \frac{4}{5} < \frac{9}{10}$
5. $\frac{3}{4}, \frac{7}{8}, \frac{1}{2}$ $\frac{1}{2} < \frac{3}{4} < \frac{7}{8}$
6. $\frac{2}{3}, \frac{3}{4}, \frac{5}{6}$ $\frac{2}{3} < \frac{3}{4} < \frac{5}{6}$

www.harcourtschoolsupply.com © Houghton Mifflin Harcourt Publishing Company 107 Core Standards for Math, Grade 4

Lesson 54
CC.4.NF.2

1. Jeff is making muffins. He combines $\frac{1}{6}$ cup milk, $\frac{1}{8}$ cup raisins, and $\frac{1}{3}$ cup butter. Which list shows the amounts of ingredients in order from **least** to **greatest**?
   - (A) $\frac{1}{8}, \frac{1}{6}, \frac{1}{3}$
   - (B) $\frac{1}{8}, \frac{1}{3}, \frac{1}{6}$
   - (C) $\frac{1}{3}, \frac{1}{6}, \frac{1}{8}$
   - (D) $\frac{1}{1}, \frac{1}{8}, \frac{1}{6}$

2. Shing is wrapping gifts. He has $\frac{5}{6}$ yard of blue ribbon, $\frac{2}{4}$ yard of gold ribbon, and $\frac{5}{12}$ yard of pink ribbon. Which list shows the lengths of the ribbons in order from **least** to **greatest**?
   - (A) $\frac{2}{4}, \frac{5}{12}, \frac{5}{6}$
   - (B) $\frac{5}{12}, \frac{2}{4}, \frac{5}{6}$
   - (C) $\frac{2}{4}, \frac{5}{6}, \frac{5}{12}$
   - (D) $\frac{5}{6}, \frac{2}{4}, \frac{5}{12}$

3. Mr. Adams is driving Betsy, Ed, and Beth home from the mall. Betsy lives $\frac{1}{4}$ mile from the mall. Ed lives $\frac{2}{3}$ mile from the mall, and Beth lives $\frac{1}{2}$ mile from the mall. Which list shows the distances in order from **closest** to **farthest**?
   - (A) $\frac{1}{4}, \frac{2}{3}, \frac{1}{2}$
   - (B) $\frac{1}{4}, \frac{1}{2}, \frac{2}{3}$
   - (C) $\frac{1}{2}, \frac{1}{4}, \frac{2}{3}$
   - (D) $\frac{2}{3}, \frac{1}{2}, \frac{1}{4}$

4. Katie is making necklaces. She has $\frac{1}{3}$ yard of blue ribbon, $\frac{3}{4}$ yard of pink ribbon, and $\frac{7}{8}$ yard of green ribbon. Which list shows the lengths of the ribbons in order from **least** to **greatest**?
   - (A) $\frac{7}{8}, \frac{1}{3}, \frac{3}{4}$
   - (B) $\frac{7}{8}, \frac{3}{4}, \frac{1}{3}$
   - (C) $\frac{1}{3}, \frac{3}{4}, \frac{7}{8}$
   - (D) $\frac{3}{4}, \frac{7}{8}, \frac{1}{3}$

5. Three friends shared a loaf of garlic bread. Ray ate $\frac{2}{6}$ of the loaf, Jay ate $\frac{5}{12}$ of the loaf, and Kay ate $\frac{1}{4}$ of the loaf. List the names in order of **least** to **greatest** amount of the loaf eaten. Explain how you know.

   Kay, Ray, Jay. Possible explanation: I wrote each fraction as an equivalent fraction with a denominator of 12. Then I compared them: $\frac{2}{6} = \frac{4}{12}$ and $\frac{1}{4} = \frac{3}{12}$. $\frac{3}{12} < \frac{4}{12} < \frac{5}{12}$. So Kay ate the least amount of the loaf and Jay ate the greatest amount of the loaf.

www.harcourtschoolsupply.com © Houghton Mifflin Harcourt Publishing Company 108 Core Standards for Math, Grade 4

www.harcourtschoolsupply.com © Houghton Mifflin Harcourt Publishing Company 233 Core Standards for Math, Grade 4

Answer Key

Lesson 55

Name _____

COMMON CORE STANDARD CC.4.NF.3a
Lesson Objective: Understand that to add or subtract fractions, they must refer to parts of the same wholes.

Add and Subtract Parts of a Whole

Justin has $\frac{3}{8}$ pound of cheddar cheese and $\frac{2}{8}$ pound of brick cheese. How much cheese does he have in all?

Step 1 Use fraction strips to model the problem. Use three $\frac{1}{8}$-strips to represent $\frac{3}{8}$ pound of cheddar cheese.

Step 2 Join two more $\frac{1}{8}$-strips to represent the amount of brick cheese.

Step 3 Count the number of $\frac{1}{8}$-strips. There are ___five___ $\frac{1}{8}$-strips. Write the amount as a fraction. Justin has $\frac{5}{8}$ pound of cheese.

Step 4 Use the model to write an equation.

$\frac{3}{8} + \frac{2}{8} = \frac{5}{8}$

Suppose Justin eats $\frac{1}{8}$ pound of cheese. How much cheese is left?

Step 1 Use five $\frac{1}{8}$-strips to represent the $\frac{5}{8}$ pound of cheese.

Step 2 Remove one $\frac{1}{8}$-strip to show the amount eaten.

Step 3 Count the number of $\frac{1}{8}$-strips left. There are ___four___ $\frac{1}{8}$ fraction strips. There is $\frac{4}{8}$ pound left.

Step 4 Write an equation for the model.

$\frac{5}{8} - \frac{1}{8} = \frac{4}{8}$

Use the model to write an equation.

1.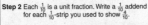

$\frac{1}{5} + \frac{3}{5} = \frac{4}{5}$

2. $\frac{2}{3} - \frac{1}{3} = \frac{1}{3}$

3. $\frac{3}{4} + \frac{1}{4} = \frac{4}{4}$

4. $\frac{5}{6} - \frac{2}{6} = \frac{3}{6}$

Lesson 55

Name _____

CC.4.NF.3a

Use the fraction model for 1–2.

Use the fraction model for 3–4.

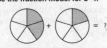

1. Ed cuts a pan of lasagna into 6 equal pieces. He serves 2 of the pieces for dinner. What fraction describes the part of the lasagna Ed serves?

   (A) $\frac{4}{6}$ (C) $\frac{2}{4}$

   (B) $\frac{1}{4}$ (D) $\frac{2}{6}$ ●

2. The next day, Ed serves 3 leftover pieces of lasagna. What fraction describes the part of the lasagna that still remains?

   (A) $\frac{1}{6}$ (C) $\frac{1}{2}$ ●

   (B) $\frac{4}{6}$ (D) $\frac{5}{6}$

3. Which equation represents the shaded parts of the model?

   (A) $\frac{5}{5} + \frac{5}{5} = \frac{10}{5}$

   (B) $\frac{3}{5} + \frac{4}{5} = \frac{5}{5}$

   (C) $\frac{2}{5} + \frac{1}{5} = \frac{3}{5}$ ●

   (D) $\frac{1}{5} + \frac{1}{5} = \frac{2}{5}$

4. For the circle on the left, which equation shows the part of the circle that remains if the gray parts are removed?

   (A) $\frac{5}{5} - \frac{1}{5} = \frac{4}{5}$

   (B) $\frac{5}{5} - \frac{2}{5} = \frac{3}{5}$ ●

   (C) $\frac{5}{5} - \frac{3}{5} = \frac{2}{5}$

   (D) $\frac{10}{5} - \frac{2}{5} = \frac{8}{5}$

5. Look at the fraction models. Write one statement about how the shaded parts are **alike**. Write one statement about how they are **different**.

   Possible answer: both models show a whole divided into 4 equal parts called fourths, with 3 fourths ($\frac{3}{4}$) shaded. They are different because the wholes are not the same size. So, $\frac{1}{4}$ of the circle is not the same size as $\frac{1}{4}$ of the square.

Lesson 56

Name _____

COMMON CORE STANDARD CC.4.NF.3b
Lesson Objective: Decompose a fraction by writing it as a sum of fractions with the same denominators.

Write Fractions as Sums

A **unit fraction** tells the part of the whole that 1 piece represents. A unit fraction always has a numerator of 1.

Bryan has $\frac{4}{10}$ pound of clay for making clay figures. He wants to use $\frac{1}{10}$ pound of clay for each figure. How many clay figures can he make?

Use fraction strips to write $\frac{4}{10}$ as a sum of unit fractions.

Step 1 Represent $\frac{4}{10}$ with fraction strips.

Step 2 Each $\frac{1}{10}$ is a unit fraction. Write a $\frac{1}{10}$ addend for each $\frac{1}{10}$-strip you used to show $\frac{4}{10}$.

$\frac{1}{10} + \frac{1}{10} + \frac{1}{10} + \frac{1}{10}$

Step 3 Count the number of addends. The number of addends represents the number of clay figures Bryan can make.

So, Bryan can make ___4___ clay figures.

Write the fraction as the sum of unit fractions.

1.

$\frac{3}{6} = \frac{1}{6} + \frac{1}{6} + \frac{1}{6}$

2. $\frac{2}{4} = \frac{1}{4} + \frac{1}{4}$

3.  $\frac{4}{8} = \frac{1}{8} + \frac{1}{8} + \frac{1}{8} + \frac{1}{8}$

4. $\frac{5}{5} = \frac{1}{5} + \frac{1}{5} + \frac{1}{5} + \frac{1}{5} + \frac{1}{5}$

Lesson 56

Name _____

CC.4.NF.3b

1. Dillon's dad sells golf balls online. He sells $\frac{4}{5}$ of the golf balls. Which gives the sum of $\frac{4}{5}$?

   (A) $\frac{1}{5} + \frac{1}{5} + \frac{1}{5}$

   (B) $\frac{1}{5} + \frac{1}{5} + \frac{2}{5}$ ●

   (C) $\frac{2}{5} + \frac{2}{5} + \frac{1}{5}$

   (D) $\frac{1}{5} + \frac{1}{5} + \frac{1}{5} + \frac{1}{5} + \frac{1}{5}$

2. Ellie's mom sells toys online. She sells $\frac{7}{10}$ of the toys. Which gives the sum of $\frac{7}{10}$?

   (A) $\frac{1}{10} + \frac{1}{10} + \frac{1}{10} + \frac{1}{10} + \frac{2}{10}$

   (B) $\frac{1}{10} + \frac{2}{10} + \frac{3}{10} + \frac{1}{10}$ ●

   (C) $\frac{2}{10} + \frac{2}{10} + \frac{2}{10} + \frac{2}{10}$

   (D) $\frac{4}{10} + \frac{1}{10} + \frac{1}{10} + \frac{1}{10} + \frac{1}{10}$

3. Santos used a unit fraction to describe how much of his book he has read. Which fraction could Santos have used?

   (A) $\frac{9}{10}$

   (B) $\frac{4}{5}$

   (C) $\frac{5}{8}$

   (D) $\frac{1}{3}$ ●

4. Dawn used a unit fraction to describe how much of her chores she has done. Which fraction could Dawn have used?

   (A) $\frac{7}{8}$

   (B) $\frac{3}{10}$

   (C) $\frac{1}{6}$ ●

   (D) $\frac{3}{24}$

Problem Solving REAL WORLD

5. Miguel's teacher asks him to color $\frac{4}{8}$ of his grid. He must use 3 colors: red, blue, and green. There must be more green sections than red sections. How can Miguel color the sections of his grid to follow all the rules?

   $\frac{1}{8}$ red, $\frac{1}{8}$ blue, and $\frac{2}{8}$ green

6. Petra is asked to color $\frac{6}{6}$ of her grid. She must use 3 colors: blue, red, and pink. There must be more blue sections than red sections or pink sections. What are the different ways Petra can color the sections of her grid and follow all the rules?

   $\frac{3}{6}$ blue, $\frac{2}{6}$ red, $\frac{1}{6}$ pink;
   $\frac{4}{6}$ blue, $\frac{1}{6}$ red, $\frac{1}{6}$ pink;
   $\frac{3}{6}$ blue, $\frac{1}{6}$ red, $\frac{2}{6}$ pink

Lesson 57
COMMON CORE STANDARD CC.4.NF.3b
Lesson Objective: Write fractions greater than 1 as mixed numbers and write mixed numbers as fractions greater than 1.

Name _____

Rename Fractions and Mixed Numbers

A **mixed number** is made up of a whole number and a fraction. You can use multiplication and addition to rename a mixed number as a fraction greater than 1.

Rename $2\frac{5}{6}$ as a fraction.

First, multiply the denominator, or the number of parts in the whole, by the whole number.

$6 \times 2 = 12$

$2\frac{5}{6} = \frac{17}{6}$ total number of parts / number of parts in the whole

Then, add the numerator to your product.

$12 + 5 = 17$

So, $2\frac{5}{6} = \frac{17}{6}$.

You can use division to write a fraction greater than 1 as a mixed number.

Rename $\frac{16}{3}$ as a mixed number.

To rename $\frac{16}{3}$ as a mixed number, divide the numerator by the denominator.

Use the quotient and remainder to write a mixed number.

$\begin{array}{r} 5 \\ 3\overline{)16} \\ -15 \\ \hline 1 \end{array}$

So, $\frac{16}{3} = 5\frac{1}{3}$.

Write the mixed number as a fraction.

1. $3\frac{2}{3} = \frac{11}{3}$ 2. $4\frac{3}{5} = \frac{23}{5}$ 3. $4\frac{3}{8} = \frac{35}{8}$ 4. $2\frac{1}{6} = \frac{13}{6}$

Write the fraction as a mixed number.

5. $\frac{32}{5} = 6\frac{2}{5}$ 6. $\frac{19}{3} = 6\frac{1}{3}$ 7. $\frac{15}{4} = 3\frac{3}{4}$ 8. $\frac{51}{10} = 5\frac{1}{10}$

Lesson 57
CC.4.NF.3b

Name _____

1. Wanda rode her bike $\frac{21}{10}$ miles. Which mixed number shows how far Wanda rode her bike?
   - (A) $1\frac{1}{10}$ miles
   - (B) $1\frac{2}{10}$ miles
   - (C) $2\frac{1}{10}$ miles
   - (D) $2\frac{10}{10}$ miles

2. Ilene is making smoothies. The recipe calls for $1\frac{1}{4}$ cups of strawberries. What is this amount written as a fraction greater than one?
   - (A) $\frac{4}{5}$ cup
   - (B) $\frac{5}{4}$ cups
   - (C) $\frac{6}{4}$ cups
   - (D) $\frac{11}{4}$ cups

3. Lee's vacation is in $3\frac{4}{7}$ weeks. Which shows the number of weeks until Lee's vacation written as a fraction greater than one?
   - (A) $\frac{34}{7}$
   - (B) $\frac{25}{7}$
   - (C) $\frac{24}{7}$
   - (D) $\frac{14}{7}$

4. Derek and his friend shared two small pizzas. Derek ate $\frac{7}{6}$ of the pizzas. Which mixed number shows how much pizza Derek ate?
   - (A) $1\frac{1}{6}$
   - (B) $1\frac{3}{6}$
   - (C) $1\frac{4}{6}$
   - (D) $2\frac{1}{6}$

Problem Solving

5. A recipe calls for $2\frac{2}{4}$ cups of raisins, but Julie only has a $\frac{1}{4}$-cup measuring cup. How many $\frac{1}{4}$ cups does Julie need to measure out $2\frac{2}{4}$ cups of raisins?

   ten $\frac{1}{4}$ cups

6. If Julie needs $3\frac{1}{4}$ cups of oatmeal, how many $\frac{1}{4}$ cups of oatmeal will she use?

   thirteen $\frac{1}{4}$ cups

Lesson 58
COMMON CORE STANDARD CC.4.NF.3c
Lesson Objective: Add and subtract mixed numbers.

Name _____

Add and Subtract Mixed Numbers

Find the sum. $3\frac{1}{4} + 2\frac{1}{4}$

Add the whole number and fraction parts.

- Add the whole numbers: $3 + 2 = 5$
- Add the fractions: $\frac{1}{4} + \frac{1}{4} = \frac{2}{4}$

Write the sum as a mixed number, so the fractional part is less than 1. $3\frac{1}{4} + 2\frac{1}{4} = 5\frac{2}{4}$

Find the difference. $4\frac{5}{8} - 3\frac{1}{8}$

Subtract the fraction and the whole number parts.

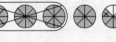

- Subtract the fractions: $\frac{5}{8} - \frac{1}{8} = \frac{4}{8}$
- Subtract the whole numbers: $4 - 3 = 1$

$4\frac{5}{8} - 3\frac{1}{8} = 1\frac{4}{8}$

Find the sum or difference.

1. $3\frac{4}{5} + 4\frac{3}{5} = 8\frac{2}{5}$ 2. $7\frac{2}{3} - 3\frac{1}{3} = 4\frac{1}{3}$ 3. $4\frac{7}{12} + 6\frac{5}{12} = 11$ 4. $12\frac{3}{4} - 6\frac{1}{4} = 6\frac{2}{4}$

5. $2\frac{3}{8} + 8\frac{1}{8} = 10\frac{4}{8}$ 6. $11\frac{9}{10} - 3\frac{7}{10} = 8\frac{2}{10}$ 7. $7\frac{3}{5} + 4\frac{3}{5} = 12\frac{1}{5}$ 8. $8\frac{3}{6} - 3\frac{1}{6} = 5\frac{2}{6}$

Lesson 58
CC.4.NF.3c

Name _____

1. Sue used $2\frac{3}{8}$ cups of walnuts and $1\frac{2}{8}$ cups of almonds to make a nut mix. How many more cups of walnuts than almonds did Sue use?
   - (A) $\frac{1}{8}$ cup
   - (B) $1\frac{1}{8}$ cups
   - (C) $3\frac{1}{8}$ cups
   - (D) $3\frac{5}{8}$ cups

2. Paige hiked $5\frac{5}{6}$ miles. Xavier hiked $2\frac{1}{6}$ miles. How many fewer miles did Xavier hike than Paige?
   - (A) $2\frac{1}{6}$ miles
   - (B) $3\frac{2}{6}$ miles
   - (C) $3\frac{4}{6}$ miles
   - (D) 8 miles

3. Kate has two lengths of ribbon. The pink ribbon is $4\frac{6}{12}$ feet long, and the purple ribbon is $2\frac{4}{12}$ feet long. How much ribbon does Kate have in all?
   - (A) $\frac{10}{12}$ foot
   - (B) $2\frac{2}{12}$ feet
   - (C) $6\frac{10}{12}$ feet
   - (D) $6\frac{11}{12}$ feet

4. Max used $3\frac{7}{8}$ pounds of yellow potatoes and $2\frac{3}{8}$ pounds of sweet potatoes to make a potato salad. How many more pounds of yellow potatoes than sweet potatoes did Max use?
   - (A) $6\frac{4}{8}$ pounds
   - (B) $5\frac{2}{8}$ pounds
   - (C) $1\frac{4}{8}$ pounds
   - (D) $1\frac{2}{8}$ pounds

Problem Solving

5. James wants to send two gifts by mail. The first package weighs $2\frac{3}{4}$ pounds. The other package weighs $1\frac{3}{4}$ pounds. What is the total weight of the packages?

   $4\frac{2}{4}$ pounds

6. Tierra bought $4\frac{3}{8}$ yards blue ribbon and $2\frac{1}{8}$ yards yellow ribbon for a craft project. How much more blue ribbon than yellow ribbon did Tierra buy?

   $2\frac{2}{8}$ yards

Answer Key

Subtraction with Renaming

Fraction strips can help you subtract mixed numbers or subtract a mixed number from a whole number.

Find the difference. $3\frac{1}{3} - 2\frac{2}{3}$

Step 1 Model the number you are subtracting from, $3\frac{1}{3}$.

Step 2 Because you cannot subtract $\frac{2}{3}$ from $\frac{1}{3}$ without renaming, change one of the 1 strips to three $\frac{1}{3}$ strips. Then subtract by crossing out two wholes and two $\frac{1}{3}$ strips.

So, $3\frac{1}{3} - 2\frac{2}{3} = \frac{2}{3}$

Find the difference. $2 - 1\frac{1}{4}$

Step 1 Model the number you are subtracting from, 2.

Step 2 Because you cannot subtract $\frac{1}{4}$ from 1 without renaming, change one of the 1 strips to four $\frac{1}{4}$ strips. Then subtract by crossing out one whole and one $\frac{1}{4}$ strip.

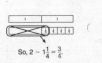

So, $2 - 1\frac{1}{4} = \frac{3}{4}$.

Find the difference.

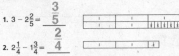

1. $3 - 2\frac{2}{5} = \dfrac{3}{5}$

2. $2\frac{1}{4} - 1\frac{3}{4} = \dfrac{2}{4}$

3. $\begin{array}{r} 3\frac{3}{5} \\ -2\frac{4}{5} \\ \hline \frac{4}{5} \end{array}$

4. $\begin{array}{r} 3\frac{1}{12} \\ -2\frac{11}{12} \\ \hline \frac{2}{12} \end{array}$

5. $\begin{array}{r} 4\frac{5}{8} \\ -2\frac{7}{8} \\ \hline 1\frac{6}{8} \end{array}$

---

1. Thomas got $9\frac{1}{3}$ feet of wood to fix his fence. When he finished, he had $3\frac{2}{3}$ feet of wood left. How much wood did Thomas use to fix his fence?

Ⓐ $5\frac{1}{3}$ feet
Ⓑ $5\frac{2}{3}$ feet
Ⓒ $6\frac{1}{3}$ feet
Ⓓ $6\frac{2}{3}$ feet

2. SuLee has $8\frac{1}{6}$ yards of blue fabric and $4\frac{2}{4}$ yards of green fabric. How much more blue fabric does SuLee have than green fabric?

Ⓐ $3\frac{1}{4}$ yards
Ⓑ $3\frac{3}{4}$ yards
Ⓒ $4\frac{1}{4}$ yards
Ⓓ $4\frac{3}{4}$ yards

3. Alicia had $3\frac{1}{6}$ yards of fabric to make a tablecloth. When she finished the tablecloth, she had $1\frac{1}{6}$ yards of fabric left. How many yards of fabric did Alicia use to make the tablecloth?

Ⓐ $1\frac{3}{6}$ yards
Ⓑ $2\frac{3}{6}$ yards
Ⓒ $2\frac{5}{6}$ yards
Ⓓ $4\frac{5}{6}$ yards

4. Gina has $5\frac{2}{6}$ feet of silver ribbon and $2\frac{4}{6}$ feet of gold ribbon. How much more silver ribbon does Gina have than gold ribbon?

Ⓐ 8
Ⓑ $3\frac{4}{6}$
Ⓒ $3\frac{2}{6}$
Ⓓ $2\frac{4}{6}$

Problem Solving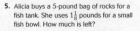

5. Alicia buys a 5-pound bag of rocks for a fish tank. She uses $1\frac{1}{8}$ pounds for a small fish bowl. How much is left?

$3\frac{7}{8}$ pounds

6. Xavier made 25 pounds of roasted almonds for a fair. He has $3\frac{1}{2}$ pounds left at the end of the fair. How many pounds of roasted almonds did he sell at the fair?

$21\frac{1}{2}$ pounds

Algebra • Fractions and Properties of Addition

Properties of addition can help you group and order addends so you can use mental math to find sums.

The **Commutative Property of Addition** states that when the order of two addends is changed, the sum is the same.
$6 + 3 = 3 + 6$

The **Associative Property of Addition** states that when the grouping of addends is changed, the sum is the same.
$(3 + 6) + 4 = 3 + (6 + 4)$

Use the properties and mental math to add $10\frac{3}{8} + 4\frac{7}{8} + 6\frac{5}{8}$

Step 1 Look for fractions that combine to make 1. $10\frac{3}{8} + 4\frac{7}{8} + 6\frac{5}{8}$

Step 2 Use the Commutative Property to order the addends so that the fractions with a sum of 1 are together. $10\frac{3}{8} + 4\frac{7}{8} + 6\frac{5}{8} = 10\frac{3}{8} + 6\frac{5}{8} + 4\frac{7}{8}$

Step 3 Use the Associative Property to group the addends that you can add mentally. $= \left(10\frac{3}{8} + 6\frac{5}{8}\right) + 4\frac{7}{8}$

Step 4 Add the grouped numbers and then add the other mixed number. $= (17) + 4\frac{7}{8}$

Step 5 Write the sum. $= 21\frac{7}{8}$

Use the properties and mental math to find the sum.

1. $\left(3\frac{1}{5} + 1\frac{2}{5}\right) + 4\frac{4}{5}$

$9\frac{2}{5}$

2. $\left(5\frac{7}{10} + 1\frac{4}{10}\right) + 6\frac{3}{10}$

$13\frac{4}{10}$

3. $7\frac{3}{4} + \left(5 + 3\frac{1}{4}\right)$

16

4. $\left(2\frac{5}{12} + 3\frac{11}{12}\right) + 1\frac{7}{12}$

$7\frac{11}{12}$

5. $4\frac{7}{8} + \left(6\frac{3}{8} + \frac{1}{8}\right)$

$11\frac{3}{8}$

6. $9\frac{2}{6} + \left(4\frac{1}{6} + 7\frac{4}{6}\right)$

$21\frac{1}{6}$

---

1. To get the correct color, Johan mixed $3\frac{1}{4}$ quarts of white paint, $1\frac{2}{4}$ quarts of blue paint, and $2\frac{3}{4}$ quarts of green paint. How much paint did Johan mix?

Ⓐ $6\frac{2}{4}$ quarts Ⓒ 7 quarts
Ⓑ $6\frac{3}{4}$ quarts Ⓓ $7\frac{2}{4}$ quarts

2. Kinsey recorded the amount of time she spent swimming during 3 days.

Times Spent Swimming

Day	Mon	Wed	Fri
Time (in hours)	$1\frac{5}{6}$	$2\frac{2}{6}$	$2\frac{1}{6}$

What is the total number of hours Kinsey spent swimming?

Ⓐ $5\frac{2}{6}$ hours Ⓒ $6\frac{2}{6}$ hours
Ⓑ $5\frac{5}{6}$ hours Ⓓ $6\frac{8}{6}$ hours

3. Bobby biked $1\frac{2}{3}$ hours on Monday, $2\frac{1}{3}$ hours on Tuesday, and $2\frac{2}{3}$ hours on Wednesday. What is the total number of hours Bobby spent biking?

Ⓐ $5\frac{2}{3}$ hours Ⓒ $6\frac{1}{3}$ hours
Ⓑ 6 hours Ⓓ $6\frac{2}{3}$ hours

4. Hector recorded the amount of time he spent running during 3 days.

Times Spent Running

Day	Tue	Wed	Thu
Time (in hours)	$1\frac{6}{12}$	$2\frac{1}{12}$	$1\frac{9}{12}$

What is the total number of hours Hector spent running?

Ⓐ $4\frac{4}{12}$ hours Ⓒ $5\frac{5}{12}$ hours
Ⓑ $5\frac{4}{12}$ hours Ⓓ $5\frac{16}{12}$ hours

Problem Solving

5. Nate's classroom has three tables of different lengths. One has a length of $4\frac{1}{2}$ feet, another has a length of 4 feet, and a third has a length of $2\frac{1}{2}$ feet. What is the length of all three tables when pushed end to end?

11 feet

6. Mr. Warren uses $2\frac{1}{4}$ bags of mulch for his garden and another $4\frac{1}{4}$ bags for his front yard. He also uses $\frac{3}{4}$ bag around a fountain. How many total bags of mulch does Mr. Warren use?

$7\frac{1}{4}$ bags

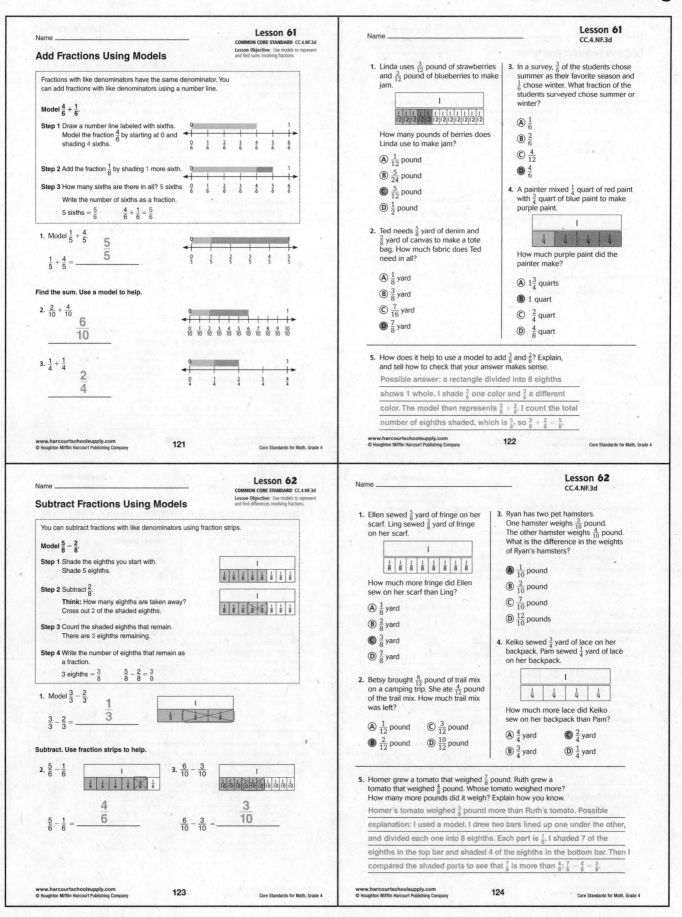

Name _____

Lesson 61
COMMON CORE STANDARD CC.4.NF.3d
Lesson Objective: Use models to represent and find sums involving fractions.

Add Fractions Using Models

Fractions with like denominators have the same denominator. You can add fractions with like denominators using a number line.

Model $\frac{4}{6} + \frac{1}{6}$.

Step 1 Draw a number line labeled with sixths. Model the fraction $\frac{4}{6}$ by starting at 0 and shading 4 sixths.

Step 2 Add the fraction $\frac{1}{6}$ by shading 1 more sixth.

Step 3 How many sixths are there in all? 5 sixths

Write the number of sixths as a fraction.

5 sixths = $\frac{5}{6}$ $\frac{4}{6} + \frac{1}{6} = \frac{5}{6}$

1. Model $\frac{1}{5} + \frac{4}{5}$. $\frac{5}{5}$

$\frac{1}{5} + \frac{4}{5} =$

Find the sum. Use a model to help.

2. $\frac{2}{10} + \frac{4}{10}$ $\frac{6}{10}$

3. $\frac{1}{4} + \frac{1}{4}$ $\frac{2}{4}$

www.harcourtschoolsupply.com
© Houghton Mifflin Harcourt Publishing Company

121

Core Standards for Math, Grade 4

Name _____

Lesson 61
CC.4.NF.3d

1. Linda uses $\frac{3}{12}$ pound of strawberries and $\frac{2}{12}$ pound of blueberries to make jam.

How many pounds of berries does Linda use to make jam?

Ⓐ $\frac{1}{12}$ pound

Ⓑ $\frac{5}{24}$ pound

Ⓒ $\frac{5}{12}$ pound

Ⓓ $\frac{1}{2}$ pound

2. Ted needs $\frac{5}{8}$ yard of denim and $\frac{2}{8}$ yard of canvas to make a tote bag. How much fabric does Ted need in all?

Ⓐ $\frac{1}{8}$ yard

Ⓑ $\frac{3}{8}$ yard

Ⓒ $\frac{7}{16}$ yard

Ⓓ $\frac{7}{8}$ yard

3. In a survey, $\frac{3}{6}$ of the students chose summer as their favorite season and $\frac{1}{6}$ chose winter. What fraction of the students surveyed chose summer or winter?

Ⓐ $\frac{1}{6}$

Ⓑ $\frac{2}{6}$

Ⓒ $\frac{4}{12}$

Ⓓ $\frac{4}{6}$

4. A painter mixed $\frac{1}{4}$ quart of red paint with $\frac{3}{4}$ quart of blue paint to make purple paint.

How much purple paint did the painter make?

Ⓐ $1\frac{3}{4}$ quarts

Ⓑ 1 quart

Ⓒ $\frac{2}{4}$ quart

Ⓓ $\frac{4}{8}$ quart

5. How does it help to use a model to add $\frac{3}{8}$ and $\frac{2}{8}$? Explain, and tell how to check that your answer makes sense.

Possible answer: a rectangle divided into 8 eighths shows 1 whole. I shade $\frac{3}{8}$ one color and $\frac{2}{8}$ a different color. The model then represents $\frac{3}{8} + \frac{2}{8}$. I count the total number of eighths shaded, which is $\frac{5}{8}$, so $\frac{3}{8} + \frac{2}{8} = \frac{5}{8}$.

www.harcourtschoolsupply.com
© Houghton Mifflin Harcourt Publishing Company

122

Core Standards for Math, Grade 4

Name _____

Lesson 62
COMMON CORE STANDARD CC.4.NF.3d
Lesson Objective: Use models to represent and find differences involving fractions.

Subtract Fractions Using Models

You can subtract fractions with like denominators using fraction strips.

Model $\frac{5}{8} - \frac{2}{8}$.

Step 1 Shade the eighths you start with. Shade 5 eighths.

Step 2 Subtract $\frac{2}{8}$.

Think: How many eighths are taken away? Cross out 2 of the shaded eighths.

Step 3 Count the shaded eighths that remain. There are 3 eighths remaining.

Step 4 Write the number of eighths that remain as a fraction.

3 eighths = $\frac{3}{8}$ $\frac{5}{8} - \frac{2}{8} = \frac{3}{8}$

1. Model $\frac{3}{3} - \frac{2}{3}$. $\frac{1}{3}$

$\frac{3}{3} - \frac{2}{3} =$

Subtract. Use fraction strips to help.

2. $\frac{5}{6} - \frac{1}{6}$ $\frac{4}{6}$

$\frac{5}{6} - \frac{1}{6} =$

3. $\frac{6}{10} - \frac{3}{10}$ $\frac{3}{10}$

$\frac{6}{10} - \frac{3}{10} =$

www.harcourtschoolsupply.com
© Houghton Mifflin Harcourt Publishing Company

123

Core Standards for Math, Grade 4

Name _____

Lesson 62
CC.4.NF.3d

1. Ellen sewed $\frac{5}{8}$ yard of fringe on her scarf. Ling sewed $\frac{2}{8}$ yard of fringe on her scarf.

How much more fringe did Ellen sew on her scarf than Ling?

Ⓐ $\frac{1}{8}$ yard

Ⓑ $\frac{2}{8}$ yard

Ⓒ $\frac{3}{8}$ yard

Ⓓ $\frac{7}{8}$ yard

2. Betsy brought $\frac{6}{12}$ pound of trail mix on a camping trip. She ate $\frac{4}{12}$ pound of the trail mix. How much trail mix was left?

Ⓐ $\frac{1}{12}$ pound   Ⓒ $\frac{3}{12}$ pound

Ⓑ $\frac{2}{12}$ pound   Ⓓ $\frac{10}{12}$ pound

3. Ryan has two pet hamsters. One hamster weighs $\frac{3}{10}$ pound. The other hamster weighs $\frac{4}{10}$ pound. What is the difference in the weights of Ryan's hamsters?

Ⓐ $\frac{1}{10}$ pound

Ⓑ $\frac{2}{10}$ pound

Ⓒ $\frac{7}{10}$ pound

Ⓓ $\frac{12}{10}$ pounds

4. Keiko sewed $\frac{3}{4}$ yard of lace on her backpack. Pam sewed $\frac{1}{4}$ yard of lace on her backpack.

How much more lace did Keiko sew on her backpack than Pam?

Ⓐ $\frac{4}{4}$ yard   Ⓒ $\frac{2}{4}$ yard

Ⓑ $\frac{3}{4}$ yard   Ⓓ $\frac{1}{4}$ yard

5. Homer grew a tomato that weighed $\frac{7}{8}$ pound. Ruth grew a tomato that weighed $\frac{4}{8}$ pound. Whose tomato weighed more? How many more pounds did it weigh? Explain how you know.

Homer's tomato weighed $\frac{3}{8}$ pound more than Ruth's tomato. Possible explanation: I used a model. I drew two bars lined up one under the other, and divided each one into 8 eighths. Each part is $\frac{1}{8}$. I shaded 7 of the eighths in the top bar and shaded 4 of the eighths in the bottom bar. Then I compared the shaded parts to see that $\frac{7}{8}$ is more than $\frac{4}{8}$; $\frac{7}{8} - \frac{4}{8} = \frac{3}{8}$.

www.harcourtschoolsupply.com
© Houghton Mifflin Harcourt Publishing Company

124

Core Standards for Math, Grade 4

Answer Key

Name _____

Lesson 63
COMMON CORE STANDARD CC.4.NF.3d
Lesson Objective: Solve word problems involving addition and subtraction with fractions.

Add and Subtract Fractions

You can find and record the sums and the differences of fractions.

Add. $\frac{2}{6} + \frac{4}{6}$

Step 1 Model it.	**Step 2** Think: How many sixths are there in all?	**Step 3** Record it.
	There are 6 sixths.	Write the sum as an addition equation.
	6 sixths = $\frac{6}{6}$	$\frac{2}{6} + \frac{4}{6} = \frac{6}{6}$

Subtract. $\frac{6}{10} - \frac{2}{10}$

Step 1 Model it.	**Step 2** Think: There are 6 tenths. I take away 2 tenths. How many tenths are left?	**Step 3** Record it.
	There are 4 tenths left.	Write the difference as a subtraction equation.
	4 tenths = $\frac{4}{10}$	$\frac{6}{10} - \frac{2}{10} = \frac{4}{10}$

Find the sum or difference.

1. 7 eighth-size parts − 4 eighth-size parts = **3 eighth-size parts**

$\frac{7}{8} - \frac{4}{8} = \underline{\frac{3}{8}}$

2. $\frac{11}{12} - \frac{4}{12} = \underline{\frac{7}{12}}$ 3. $\frac{2}{10} + \frac{2}{10} = \underline{\frac{4}{10}}$ 4. $\frac{6}{8} - \frac{4}{8} = \underline{\frac{2}{8}}$

5. $\frac{2}{4} + \frac{2}{4} = \underline{\frac{4}{4}}$ 6. $\frac{4}{5} - \frac{3}{5} = \underline{\frac{1}{5}}$ 7. $\frac{1}{3} + \frac{2}{3} = \underline{\frac{3}{3}}$

Name _____

Lesson 63
CC.4.NF.3d

1. Mindi planted beans in $\frac{4}{10}$ of her garden and peas in $\frac{5}{10}$ of her garden. What fraction of the garden has beans or peas?

Ⓐ $\frac{1}{10}$
Ⓑ $\frac{9}{20}$
Ⓒ $\frac{8}{10}$
Ⓓ $\frac{9}{10}$

2. Harrison ate $\frac{3}{12}$ of a pizza. Miles ate $\frac{5}{12}$ of the same pizza. How much more of the pizza did Miles eat than Harrison?

Ⓐ $\frac{1}{12}$
Ⓑ $\frac{2}{12}$
Ⓒ $\frac{4}{12}$
Ⓓ $\frac{8}{12}$

3. Miguel is going to sell pet treats at the school fair. He made $\frac{3}{8}$ of the treats for dogs and $\frac{2}{8}$ of the treats for cats. The rest of the treats are for other types of pets. What fraction of the pet treats is for cats or dogs?

Ⓐ $\frac{1}{8}$
Ⓑ $\frac{2}{8}$
Ⓒ $\frac{5}{8}$
Ⓓ $\frac{7}{8}$

4. Teresa planted marigolds in $\frac{1}{6}$ of her garden and petunias in $\frac{4}{6}$ of her garden. What fraction of the garden has marigolds or petunias?

Ⓐ $\frac{6}{12}$
Ⓑ $\frac{5}{6}$
Ⓒ $\frac{5}{12}$
Ⓓ $\frac{1}{6}$

5. Don writes $\frac{6}{10} - \frac{3}{10} = \frac{9}{10}$. Is his answer correct? Explain, and tell how you find the correct answer if Don is wrong.

Don's answer is not correct. Possible explanation: Don used the wrong operation. He added instead of subtracting. I can draw a model showing 10 equal parts and shade 6 parts to show $\frac{6}{10}$. To subtract $\frac{3}{10}$, I would cross out 3 of the parts. The shaded parts left are 3 tenths or $\frac{3}{10}$, so $\frac{6}{10} - \frac{3}{10} = \frac{3}{10}$.

Name _____

Lesson 64
COMMON CORE STANDARD CC.4.NF.3d
Lesson Objective: Use the strategy act it out to solve multistep fraction problems.

Problem Solving • Multistep Fraction Problems

Jeff runs $\frac{3}{5}$ mile each day. He wants to know how many days he has to run before he has run a whole number of miles.

Read the Problem	Solve the Problem
What do I need to find? I need to find _how many days Jeff needs to run $\frac{3}{5}$ mile_ until he has run a whole number of miles.	**Describe how to act it out.** Use a number line. (number line 0 to $\frac{16}{5}$)
What information do I need to use? Jeff runs _$\frac{3}{5}$_ mile a day. He wants the distance run to be a _whole number_.	Day 1: $\frac{3}{5}$ mile Day 2: $\frac{6}{5}$ mile $\frac{3}{5} + \frac{3}{5} = \frac{6}{5}$ 1 whole mile and $\frac{1}{5}$ mile more Day 3: $\frac{9}{5}$ mile $\frac{3}{5} + \frac{3}{5} + \frac{3}{5} = \frac{9}{5}$ 1 whole mile and $\frac{4}{5}$ mile more
How will I use the information? I can use a number line and _patterns_ to _act out_ the problem.	Day 4: $\frac{12}{5}$ mile $\frac{3}{5} + \frac{3}{5} + \frac{3}{5} + \frac{3}{5} = \frac{12}{5}$ 2 whole miles and $\frac{2}{5}$ mile more Day 5: $\frac{15}{5}$ mile $\frac{3}{5} + \frac{3}{5} + \frac{3}{5} + \frac{3}{5} + \frac{3}{5} = \frac{15}{5}$ 3 whole miles So, Jeff will run a total of _3_ miles in _5_ days.

1. Lena runs $\frac{2}{5}$ mile each day. She wants to know how many days she has to run before she has run a whole number of miles.

3 days

2. Mack is repackaging $\frac{6}{8}$-pound bags of birdseed into 1-pound bags of birdseed. What is the least number of $\frac{6}{8}$-pound bags of birdseed he needs in order to fill 1-pound bags without leftovers?

four $\frac{6}{8}$-pound bags

Name _____

Lesson 64
CC.4.NF.3d

1. Ryan's collection is $\frac{3}{6}$ football cards and $\frac{2}{6}$ basketball cards. What part of Ryan's card collection is **not** football or basketball cards?

Ⓐ $\frac{1}{6}$
Ⓑ $\frac{5}{12}$
Ⓒ $\frac{5}{6}$
Ⓓ 1

2. Royce walks $\frac{3}{4}$ mile to school and $\frac{3}{4}$ mile home each day. In how many days will he have walked 3 miles?

Ⓐ 8 days
Ⓑ 6 days
Ⓒ 4 days
Ⓓ 2 days

3. Carson's album is $\frac{8}{12}$ vacation photos and $\frac{3}{12}$ holiday photos. What part of Carson's album is **not** vacation or holiday photos?

Ⓐ 1
Ⓑ $\frac{11}{12}$
Ⓒ $\frac{5}{12}$
Ⓓ $\frac{1}{12}$

4. A quarter is $\frac{1}{4}$ of a dollar. Victor has 32 quarters. How much money does he have?

Ⓐ $16
Ⓑ $8
Ⓒ $6
Ⓓ $5

5. Each day, Mrs. Hewes knits $\frac{1}{3}$ of a scarf in the morning and $\frac{1}{3}$ of a scarf in the afternoon. How many days will it take Mrs. Hewes to knit 2 scarves? Explain how you find the answer.

Possible answer: I keep track of the number of thirds. The first day, she knits $\frac{1}{3} + \frac{1}{3} = \frac{2}{3}$. At the end of day 2, she has knitted $\frac{1}{3} + \frac{1}{3} + \frac{1}{3} + \frac{1}{3} = \frac{4}{3}$. At the end of day 3, she has knitted $\frac{1}{3} + \frac{1}{3} + \frac{1}{3} + \frac{1}{3} + \frac{1}{3} + \frac{1}{3} = \frac{6}{3} = 2$, so it takes 3 days to finish 2 scarves.

Answer Key

Lesson 65

Name _____

COMMON CORE STANDARD CC.4.NF.4a
Lesson Objective: Write a fraction as a product of a whole number and a unit fraction.

Multiples of Unit Fractions

A unit fraction is a fraction with a numerator of 1. You can write a fraction as the product of a whole number and a unit fraction.

Write $\frac{7}{10}$ as the product of a whole number and a unit fraction.

Write $\frac{7}{10}$ as the sum of unit fractions.

$\frac{7}{10} = \frac{1}{10} + \frac{1}{10} + \frac{1}{10} + \frac{1}{10} + \frac{1}{10} + \frac{1}{10} + \frac{1}{10}$

Use multiplication to show repeated addition.

$\frac{7}{10} = \underline{7} \times \frac{1}{10}$

So, $\frac{7}{10} = \underline{7} \times \frac{1}{10}$

The product of a number and a counting number is a multiple of the number. You can find multiples of unit fractions.

List the next 4 multiples of $\frac{1}{8}$.

Make a table and use repeated addition.

$1 \times \frac{1}{8}$	$2 \times \frac{1}{8}$	$3 \times \frac{1}{8}$	$4 \times \frac{1}{8}$	$5 \times \frac{1}{8}$
$\frac{1}{8}$	$\frac{1}{8} + \frac{1}{8}$	$\frac{1}{8} + \frac{1}{8} + \frac{1}{8}$	$\frac{1}{8} + \frac{1}{8} + \frac{1}{8} + \frac{1}{8}$	$\frac{1}{8} + \frac{1}{8} + \frac{1}{8} + \frac{1}{8} + \frac{1}{8}$
$\frac{1}{8}$	$\frac{2}{8}$	$\frac{3}{8}$	$\frac{4}{8}$	$\frac{5}{8}$

The next 4 multiples of $\frac{1}{8}$ are $\frac{2}{8}$, $\frac{3}{8}$, $\frac{4}{8}$, and $\frac{5}{8}$.

Write the fraction as the product of a whole number and a unit fraction.

1. $\frac{2}{5} = \underline{2} \times \frac{1}{5}$ 2. $\frac{5}{12} = \underline{5} \times \frac{1}{12}$ 3. $\frac{7}{2} = \underline{7} \times \frac{1}{2}$

List the next four multiples of the unit fraction.

4. $\frac{1}{4}$ $\frac{2}{4}$ $\frac{3}{4}$ $\frac{4}{4}$ $\frac{5}{4}$ 5. $\frac{1}{6}$ $\frac{2}{6}$ $\frac{3}{6}$ $\frac{4}{6}$ $\frac{5}{6}$

www.harcourtschoolsupply.com
© Houghton Mifflin Harcourt Publishing Company
129
Core Standards for Math, Grade 4

Lesson 65

Name _____

CC.4.NF.4a

1. Aaron made a list of some multiples of $\frac{1}{8}$. Which could be Aaron's list?

   (A) $\frac{1}{8}, \frac{1}{16}, \frac{1}{24}, \frac{1}{32}, \frac{1}{40}$
   (B) $\frac{1}{8}, \frac{2}{9}, \frac{3}{10}, \frac{4}{11}, \frac{5}{12}$
   (C) $\frac{1}{8}, \frac{2}{8}, \frac{3}{8}, \frac{4}{8}, \frac{5}{8}$
   (D) 1, 2, 3, 4, 5

2. Look at the number line. What fraction goes directly below the whole number 2?

   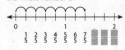

   (A) $\frac{3}{10}$
   (B) $\frac{3}{5}$
   (C) $\frac{8}{5}$
   (D) $\frac{10}{5}$

3. Sandi buys some fabric to make a quilt. She needs $\frac{1}{5}$ yard of each of 9 types of fabric. Sandi writes the following equation. What number goes in the box to make the statement true?

   $$\frac{9}{5} = \boxed{} \times \frac{1}{5}$$

   (A) 9
   (B) 8
   (C) 5
   (D) 4

4. A recipe for one dozen bran muffins needs $\frac{1}{3}$ cup of raisins.

Dozen	1	2	3	4	5	6	7	8
Cup(s) of Raisins	$\frac{1}{3}$	$\frac{2}{3}$	$\frac{3}{3}$					

   How many dozen bran muffins can be made with 2 cups of raisins?

   (A) 2
   (B) 4
   (C) 6
   (D) 8

Problem Solving

5. So far, Monica has read $\frac{5}{6}$ of a book. She has read the same number of pages each day for 5 days. What fraction of the book does Monica read each day?

   $\frac{1}{6}$ of the book

6. Nicholas buys $\frac{3}{8}$ pound of cheese. He puts the same amount of cheese on 3 sandwiches. How much cheese does Nicholas put on each sandwich?

   $\frac{1}{8}$ pound

www.harcourtschoolsupply.com
© Houghton Mifflin Harcourt Publishing Company
130
Core Standards for Math, Grade 4

Lesson 66

Name _____

COMMON CORE STANDARD CC.4.NF.4b
Lesson Objective: Write a product of a whole number and a fraction as a product of a whole number and a unit fraction.

Multiples of Fractions

You have learned to write multiples of unit fractions. You can also write multiples of other fractions.

Write the next 4 multiples of $\frac{2}{5}$.

Make a table.

$1 \times \frac{2}{5}$	$2 \times \frac{2}{5}$	$3 \times \frac{2}{5}$	$4 \times \frac{2}{5}$	$5 \times \frac{2}{5}$
$\frac{2}{5}$	$\frac{2}{5} + \frac{2}{5}$	$\frac{2}{5} + \frac{2}{5} + \frac{2}{5}$	$\frac{2}{5} + \frac{2}{5} + \frac{2}{5} + \frac{2}{5}$	$\frac{2}{5} + \frac{2}{5} + \frac{2}{5} + \frac{2}{5} + \frac{2}{5}$
$\frac{2}{5}$	$\frac{4}{5}$	$\frac{6}{5}$	$\frac{8}{5}$	$\frac{10}{5}$

So, the next 4 multiples of $\frac{2}{5}$ are $\frac{4}{5}$, $\frac{6}{5}$, $\frac{8}{5}$, and $\frac{10}{5}$.

Write $3 \times \frac{2}{5}$ as the product of a whole number and a unit fraction.

Use a number line. Make three jumps of $\frac{2}{5}$.

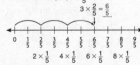
$3 \times \frac{2}{5} = \frac{6}{5}$

$2 \times \frac{1}{5}$ $4 \times \frac{1}{5}$ $6 \times \frac{1}{5}$ $8 \times \frac{1}{5}$

So, $3 \times \frac{2}{5} = \frac{6}{5}$, or $6 \times \frac{1}{5}$.

List the next four multiples of the fraction.

1. $\frac{3}{4}$ $\frac{6}{4}$ $\frac{9}{4}$ $\frac{12}{4}$ $\frac{15}{4}$ 2. $\frac{5}{6}$ $\frac{10}{6}$ $\frac{15}{6}$ $\frac{20}{6}$ $\frac{25}{6}$

Write as the product of a whole number and a unit fraction.

3.
   $3 \times \frac{3}{8} = \underline{9} \times \frac{1}{8}$

4.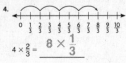
   $4 \times \frac{2}{3} = \underline{8} \times \frac{1}{3}$

www.harcourtschoolsupply.com
© Houghton Mifflin Harcourt Publishing Company
131
Core Standards for Math, Grade 4

Lesson 66

Name _____

CC.4.NF.4b

1. Phil drew a number line showing multiples of $\frac{3}{6}$.

   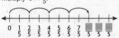

   Which number on the number line shows the product $2 \times \frac{3}{6}$?

   (A) $\frac{2}{6}$
   (B) $\frac{3}{6}$
   (C) $\frac{6}{6}$
   (D) $\frac{9}{6}$

2. Gwen listed the multiples of $\frac{3}{10}$. Which is **not** a multiple of $\frac{3}{10}$?

   (A) $\frac{8}{10}$
   (B) $\frac{9}{10}$
   (C) $\frac{15}{10}$
   (D) $\frac{30}{10}$

3. Oleg drew a number line to help him multiply $4 \times \frac{2}{5}$.

   Which shows $4 \times \frac{2}{5}$ written as the product of a whole number and a unit fraction?

   (A) $4 \times \frac{1}{5}$
   (B) $4 \times \frac{2}{5}$
   (C) $8 \times \frac{1}{5}$
   (D) $8 \times \frac{1}{4}$

4. Alma is making 3 batches of tortillas. She needs to add $\frac{3}{4}$ cup water to each batch. Her measuring cup holds $\frac{1}{4}$ cup. How many times must Alma measure $\frac{1}{4}$ cup of water to have enough for all the tortillas?

   (A) 4
   (B) 6
   (C) 8
   (D) 9

5. Explain how to write the first three multiples of $\frac{4}{9}$.

   Possible explanation: multiply the fraction by the counting numbers. $1 \times \frac{4}{9} = \frac{4}{9}$; $2 \times \frac{4}{9}$ is $\frac{4}{9} + \frac{4}{9}$, which is $\frac{8}{9}$; $3 \times \frac{4}{9}$ is $\frac{4}{9} + \frac{4}{9} + \frac{4}{9}$, which is $\frac{12}{9}$. The first 3 multiples are $\frac{4}{9}, \frac{8}{9}, \frac{12}{9}$.

www.harcourtschoolsupply.com
© Houghton Mifflin Harcourt Publishing Company
132
Core Standards for Math, Grade 4

---

www.harcourtschoolsupply.com
© Houghton Mifflin Harcourt Publishing Company

239

Core Standards for Math, Grade 4

Answer Key

Name _____

Lesson 67
COMMON CORE STANDARD CC.4.NF.4b
Lesson Objective: Use a model to multiply a fraction by a whole number.

Multiply a Fraction by a Whole Number Using Models

You can use a model to multiply a fraction by a whole number.

Find the product of $4 \times \frac{3}{5}$.

Use fraction strips. Show 4 groups of $\frac{3}{5}$ each.

1 group of $\frac{3}{5} = \frac{3}{5}$

2 groups of $\frac{3}{5} = \frac{6}{5}$

3 groups of $\frac{3}{5} = \frac{9}{5}$

4 groups of $\frac{3}{5} = \frac{12}{5}$

So, $4 \times \frac{3}{5} = \frac{12}{5}$.

Multiply.

1.   2.

$2 \times \frac{5}{6} = \dfrac{10}{6}$ $3 \times \frac{7}{8} = \dfrac{21}{8}$

3. $6 \times \frac{2}{3} = \dfrac{12}{3}$ 4. $2 \times \frac{9}{10} = \dfrac{18}{10}$ 5. $5 \times \frac{3}{4} = \dfrac{15}{4}$

6. $4 \times \frac{5}{8} = \dfrac{20}{8}$ 7. $7 \times \frac{2}{5} = \dfrac{14}{5}$ 8. $8 \times \frac{4}{6} = \dfrac{32}{6}$

---

1. Alani uses $\frac{3}{4}$ cup pineapple juice to make one Hawaiian sweet bread. How much pineapple juice will she use to make 5 sweet breads?

Ⓐ $\frac{15}{4}$ cups

Ⓑ $\frac{11}{4}$ cups

Ⓒ $\frac{10}{4}$ cups

Ⓓ $\frac{8}{4}$ cups

2. Jason writes repeated addition to show $4 \times \frac{2}{3}$. Which shows an expression Jason could use?

Ⓐ $4 + \frac{1}{3} + \frac{1}{3} + \frac{1}{3}$

Ⓑ $\frac{2}{12} + \frac{2}{12} + \frac{2}{12} + \frac{2}{12}$

Ⓒ $\frac{2}{3} + \frac{2}{3} + \frac{2}{3} + \frac{2}{3}$

Ⓓ $\frac{1}{3} + \frac{1}{3} + \frac{1}{3} + \frac{1}{3}$

3. Mr. Tuyen uses $\frac{5}{8}$ of a tank of gas each week to drive to and from work. How many tanks of gas does Mr. Tuyen use in 5 weeks?

Ⓐ $\frac{40}{8}$

Ⓑ $\frac{25}{8}$

Ⓒ $\frac{10}{8}$

Ⓓ $\frac{5}{40}$

4. Mark bought 3 packages of grapes. Each package weighed $\frac{7}{8}$ pound. How many pounds of grapes did Mark buy?

Ⓐ $\frac{10}{8}$ pounds

Ⓑ $\frac{21}{8}$ pounds

Ⓒ 10 pounds

Ⓓ 21 pounds

Problem Solving REAL WORLD

5. Matthew walks $\frac{5}{8}$ mile to the bus stop each morning. How far will he walk in 5 days?

$\dfrac{25}{8}$ miles

6. Emily uses $\frac{2}{3}$ cup of milk to make one batch of muffins. How many cups of milk will Emily use if she makes 3 batches of muffins?

$\dfrac{6}{3}$ cups

Name _____

Lesson 68
COMMON CORE STANDARD CC.4.NF.4c
Lesson Objective: Multiply a fraction by a whole number to solve a problem.

Multiply a Fraction or Mixed Number by a Whole Number

To multiply a fraction by a whole number, multiply the numerators. Then multiply the denominators.

A recipe for one loaf of bread calls for $2\frac{1}{4}$ cups of flour. How many cups of flour will you need for 2 loaves of bread?

Step 1 Write and solve an equation.

$2 \times 2\frac{1}{4} = \frac{2}{1} \times \frac{9}{4}$ Write 2 as $\frac{2}{1}$. Write $2\frac{1}{4}$ as a fraction.

$= \frac{2 \times 9}{1 \times 4}$ Multiply the numerators. Then multiply the denominators.

$= \frac{18}{4}$ Simplify.

Step 2 Write the product as a mixed number.

$\frac{18}{4} = \frac{1}{4}+\frac{1}{4}+\frac{1}{4}+\frac{1}{4}+\frac{1}{4}+\frac{1}{4}+\frac{1}{4}+\frac{1}{4}+\frac{1}{4}+\frac{1}{4}+\frac{1}{4}+\frac{1}{4}+\frac{1}{4}+\frac{1}{4}+\frac{1}{4}+\frac{1}{4}+\frac{1}{4}+\frac{1}{4}$

     $1 \quad + \quad 1 \quad + \quad 1 \quad + \quad 1 \quad +\frac{1}{4}+\frac{1}{4}$

$= \frac{4}{4} + \frac{4}{4} + \frac{4}{4}$ Combine the wholes. Then combine the remaining parts.

$= 4\frac{2}{4}$, or $4\frac{1}{2}$ Add. Write the sum as a mixed number.

So, you will need $4\frac{1}{2}$ cups of flour.

Multiply. Write the product as a mixed number.

1. $3 \times \frac{2}{5} = 1\frac{1}{5}$ 2. $4 \times \frac{3}{8} = 1\frac{4}{8}$ 3. $5 \times \frac{1}{3} = 1\frac{2}{3}$

4. $2 \times 1\frac{3}{10} = 2\frac{6}{10}$ 5. $4 \times 1\frac{2}{3} = 6\frac{2}{3}$ 6. $7 \times 1\frac{1}{6} = 8\frac{1}{6}$

---

1. Malak solved a problem that had an answer of $\frac{33}{5}$. How can Malak write $\frac{33}{5}$ as a mixed number?

Ⓐ $6\frac{3}{5}$

Ⓑ $5\frac{3}{5}$

Ⓒ $4\frac{3}{5}$

Ⓓ $3\frac{3}{5}$

2. Bo recorded a basketball game that lasted $2\frac{1}{2}$ hours. Bo watched the game 3 times last week. How many hours did Bo spend watching the game?

Ⓐ $6\frac{1}{2}$ hours

Ⓑ $7\frac{1}{2}$ hours

Ⓒ 9 hours

Ⓓ 10 hours

3. Carrie spends $1\frac{1}{4}$ hours practicing the piano 3 times a week. How much time does Carrie spend practicing the piano in one week?

Ⓐ $4\frac{1}{4}$ hours

Ⓑ 4 hours

Ⓒ $3\frac{3}{4}$ hours

Ⓓ $3\frac{1}{4}$ hours

4. Yasuo always puts $1\frac{1}{2}$ teaspoons of honey in his tea. Yesterday Yasuo drank 5 cups of tea. How much honey did he use in all?

Ⓐ $6\frac{1}{2}$ teaspoons

Ⓑ $7\frac{1}{2}$ teaspoons

Ⓒ 8 teaspoons

Ⓓ $8\frac{1}{2}$ teaspoons

Problem Solving REAL WORLD

5. Brielle exercises for $\frac{3}{4}$ hour each day for 6 days in a row. Altogether, how many hours does she exercise during the 6 days?

$4\frac{2}{4}$ hours

6. A recipe for quinoa calls for $2\frac{2}{3}$ cups of milk. Conner wants to make 4 batches of quinoa. How much milk does he need?

$10\frac{2}{3}$ cups

Answer Key

Lesson 69
COMMON CORE STANDARD CC.4.NF.4c
Lesson Objective: Use the strategy draw a diagram to solve comparison problems with fractions.

Problem Solving • Comparison Problems with Fractions

The Great Salt Lake in Utah is about $\frac{4}{5}$ mile above sea level. Lake Titicaca in South America is about 3 times as high above sea level as the Great Salt Lake. About how high above sea level is Lake Titicaca?

Read the Problem	Solve the Problem
What do I need to find? I need to find about how high above sea level Lake Titicaca is.	Draw a comparison model. Compare the heights above sea level of the Great Salt Lake and Lake Titicaca, in miles. Great Salt Lake $\frac{4}{5}$ Lake Titicaca $\frac{4}{5}$ $\frac{4}{5}$ $\frac{4}{5}$ t
What information do I need to use? The Great Salt Lake is about $\frac{4}{5}$ mile above sea level. Lake Titicaca is about 3 times as high above sea level.	Write an equation and solve. t is the height above sea level of Lake Titicaca, in miles. $t = \frac{3}{1} \times \frac{4}{5}$ Write an equation. $t = \frac{12}{5}$ Multiply. $t = 2\frac{2}{5}$ Write the fraction as a mixed number.
How will I use the information? I can draw a diagram to compare the heights.	

So, Lake Titicaca is about $2\frac{2}{5}$ miles above sea level.

1. Amelia is training for a triathlon. She swims $\frac{3}{5}$ mile. Then she runs about 6 times farther than she swims. About how far does Amelia run?

$3\frac{3}{5}$ miles

2. Last week, Meg bought $1\frac{3}{4}$ pounds of fruit at the market. This week, she buys 4 times as many pounds of fruit as last week. In pounds, how much fruit does Meg buy this week?

7 pounds

137

Lesson 69
CC.4.NF.4c

1. Rudi is comparing shark lengths. He read that a sandbar shark is $4\frac{1}{2}$ feet long. A thresher shark is 3 times as long as that. How long is a thresher shark?

Sandbar Shark $4\frac{1}{2}$

Thresher Shark

- (A) $13\frac{1}{2}$ feet
- (B) 12 feet
- (C) $7\frac{1}{2}$ feet
- (D) 7 feet

2. Cyndi made macaroni salad. She used $1\frac{1}{8}$ cups of mayonnaise. She used 9 times as much macaroni. How many cups of macaroni did Cyndi use?

- (A) $9\frac{2}{3}$ cups
- (B) $10\frac{1}{8}$ cups
- (C) 18 cups
- (D) 81 cups

3. A flight takes $1\frac{1}{4}$ hours to get from Dyson to Hardy. The flight takes 3 times as long to get from Dyson to Williams. How long is the flight from Dyson to Williams?

- (A) $3\frac{3}{4}$ hours
- (B) 4 hours
- (C) $4\frac{1}{4}$ hours
- (D) $4\frac{3}{4}$ hours

4. Paz weighed $5\frac{5}{8}$ pounds when she was born. By age 2, she weighed 4 times as much. If p stands for pounds, which equation could you use to find Paz's weight at age 2?

- (A) $p = 4 + 5\frac{5}{8}$
- (B) $p = (4 \times 5) + \frac{5}{8}$
- (C) $p = 4 \times 5\frac{5}{8}$
- (D) $p = \left(4 \times \frac{5}{8}\right) + 5$

5. A recipe for rice and beans uses $1\frac{1}{2}$ cups of beans and 4 times as much rice. Jess has plenty of beans but only 5 cups of rice. Does she have enough rice to make the recipe? Explain.

No; Possible explanation: I know that 4×1 cup = 4 cups and $4 \times \frac{1}{2} = \frac{4}{2}$, or 2 cups. So Jess needs 4 + 2 or 6 cups of rice. 5 cups is not enough.

138

Lesson 70
COMMON CORE STANDARD CC.4.NF.5
Lesson Objective: Record tenths and hundredths as fractions and decimals.

Equivalent Fractions and Decimals

Lori ran $\frac{20}{100}$ mile. How many tenths of a mile did she run?

Write $\frac{20}{100}$ as an equivalent fraction with a denominator of 10.

Step 1 Think: 10 is a common factor of the numerator and the denominator.

Step 2 Divide the numerator and denominator by 10.

$\frac{20}{100} = \frac{20 \div 10}{100 \div 10} = \frac{2}{10}$

So, Lori ran $\frac{2}{10}$ mile.

Use a place-value chart.

Step 1 Write $\frac{20}{100}$ as an equivalent decimal.

Ones	·	Tenths	Hundredths
0	·	2	0

Step 2 Think: 20 hundredths is 2 tenths 0 hundredths.

Ones	·	Tenths
0	·	2

So, Lori ran 0.2 mile.

Write the number as hundredths in fraction form and decimal form.

1. $\frac{9}{10}$ $\frac{90}{100}$; 0.90

2. 0.6 $\frac{60}{100}$; 0.60

3. $\frac{4}{10}$ $\frac{40}{100}$; 0.40

Write the number as tenths in fraction form and decimal form.

4. $\frac{70}{100}$ $\frac{7}{10}$; 0.7

5. $\frac{80}{100}$ $\frac{8}{10}$; 0.8

6. 0.50 $\frac{5}{10}$; 0.5

139

Lesson 70
CC.4.NF.5

1. Greta lives 0.7 kilometer from the state capitol. Which fraction is equivalent to 0.7?

- (A) $\frac{0}{7}$
- (B) $\frac{1}{7}$
- (C) $\frac{7}{10}$
- (D) $\frac{7}{100}$

2. The U.S. Senate in Washington, D.C., has 100 elected members who make laws for the United States. Last year, 30 senators ran for reelection. Which decimal is equivalent to $\frac{30}{100}$?

- (A) 3.100
- (B) 0.3
- (C) 0.03
- (D) 0.003

3. Which of the following is **not** equivalent to seven tenths?

- (A) $\frac{7}{10}$
- (B) 0.7
- (C) 0.70
- (D) 0.07

4. Matthew walks $\frac{4}{10}$ mile to Zack's house. Which fraction is equivalent to $\frac{4}{10}$?

- (A) $\frac{4}{100}$
- (B) $\frac{40}{100}$
- (C) $\frac{44}{100}$
- (D) $\frac{40}{10}$

Problem Solving REAL WORLD

5. Billy walks $\frac{6}{10}$ mile to school each day. Write $\frac{6}{10}$ as hundredths in fraction form and in decimal form.

$\frac{60}{100}$; 0.60

6. Four states have names that begin with the letter A. This represents 0.08 of all the states. Write 0.08 as a fraction.

$\frac{8}{100}$

140

www.harcourtschoolsupply.com
© Houghton Mifflin Harcourt Publishing Company
241
Core Standards for Math, Grade 4

Answer Key

Name _____

Lesson **71**

COMMON CORE STANDARD CC.4.NF.5
Lesson Objective: Add fractions when the denominators are 10 or 100.

Add Fractional Parts of 10 and 100

Sam uses 100 glass beads for a project. Of the beads, $\frac{35}{100}$ are gold and $\frac{4}{10}$ are silver. What fraction of the glass beads are gold or silver?

Add $\frac{35}{100}$ and $\frac{4}{10}$.

Step 1 Decide on a common denominator. Use __100__.

Step 2 Write $\frac{4}{10}$ as an equivalent fraction with a denominator of 100.

$$\frac{4}{10} = \frac{4 \times 10}{10 \times 10} = \frac{40}{100}$$

Step 3 Add $\frac{35}{100}$ and $\frac{40}{100}$.

$$\frac{35}{100} + \frac{40}{100} = \frac{75}{100} \quad \leftarrow \text{Add the numerators.}$$
$$\leftarrow \text{Use 100 as the denominator.}$$

So, $\frac{75}{100}$ of the glass beads are gold or silver.

Add $0.26 and $0.59.

Step 1 Write each amount as a fraction of a dollar.

$\$0.26 = \frac{26}{100}$ of a dollar $\$0.59 = \frac{59}{100}$ of a dollar

Step 2 Add $\frac{26}{100}$ and $\frac{59}{100}$.

$$\frac{26}{100} + \frac{59}{100} = \frac{85}{100} \quad \leftarrow \text{Add the numerators.}$$
$$\leftarrow \text{100 is the common denominator.}$$

Step 3 Write the sum as a decimal.

$$\frac{85}{100} = 0.85$$

So, $0.26 + $0.59 = __$0.85__

Find the sum.

1. $\frac{75}{100} + \frac{2}{10} = \dfrac{95}{100}$

2. $0.73 + $0.25 = $ __0.98__

$\frac{73}{100} + \frac{25}{100} = \dfrac{98}{100}$

---

1. What is the sum of $\frac{4}{10}$ and $\frac{55}{100}$?
   - (A) $\frac{15}{100}$
   - (B) $\frac{59}{110}$
   - **(C)** $\frac{59}{100}$
   - (D) $\frac{95}{100}$

2. What is the sum of $\frac{4}{10}$ and $\frac{40}{100}$?
   - (A) $\frac{8}{10}$
   - **(B)** $\frac{44}{100}$
   - (C) $\frac{44}{110}$
   - (D) $\frac{8}{100}$

3. Suzi ran for $\frac{4}{10}$ mile. Then she walked for $\frac{16}{100}$ mile. How far did she go in all?
   - (A) $\frac{20}{100}$ mile
   - **(B)** $\frac{56}{100}$ mile
   - (C) $\frac{20}{10}$ miles
   - (D) $\frac{56}{10}$ miles

4. An artist is covering a tabletop with square tiles. So far, she has put blue tiles on $\frac{21}{100}$ of the tabletop and silver tiles on $\frac{3}{10}$ of it. How much of the tabletop has been tiled?
   - (A) $\frac{51}{10}$
   - (B) $\frac{24}{10}$
   - **(C)** $\frac{51}{100}$
   - (D) $\frac{24}{100}$

Problem Solving

5. Ned's frog jumped $\frac{38}{100}$ meter. Then his frog jumped $\frac{4}{10}$ meter. How far did Ned's frog jump in all?

$\dfrac{78}{100}$ meter

6. Keiko walks $\frac{5}{10}$ kilometer from school to the park. Then she walks $\frac{19}{100}$ kilometer from the park to her home. How far does Keiko walk in all?

$\dfrac{69}{100}$ kilometer

Name _____

Lesson **72**

COMMON CORE STANDARD CC.4.NF.6
Lesson Objective: Record tenths as fractions and as decimals.

Relate Tenths and Decimals

Write the fraction and the decimal that are shown by the point on the number line.

Step 1 Count the number of equal parts of the whole shown on the number line. There are ten equal parts.

This tells you that the number line shows tenths.

Step 2 Label the number line with the missing fractions. What fraction is shown by the point on the number line?

The fraction shown by the point on the number line is $\frac{8}{10}$.

Step 3 Label the number line with the missing decimals. What decimal is shown by the point on the number line?

The decimal shown by the point on the number line is 0.8.

So, the fraction and decimal shown by the point on the number line are $\frac{8}{10}$ and 0.8.

Write the fraction or mixed number and the decimal shown by the model.

1. $\dfrac{2}{10}$; 0.2

2. $2\dfrac{6}{10}$; 2.6

---

1. Trisha walked $\frac{9}{10}$ of a mile to school. She shaded a model to show how far she had walked.

   Which decimal shows how far Trisha walked?
   - (A) 0.009 mile
   - (B) 0.09 mile
   - **(C)** 0.9 mile
   - (D) 9.0 miles

2. Denny ran $2\frac{1}{10}$ miles along a marathon route. What is this distance written as a decimal?
   - (A) 21.0 miles
   - **(B)** 2.1 miles
   - (C) 2.01 miles
   - (D) 0.21 mile

3. David hiked $3\frac{7}{10}$ miles along a trail in the state park. What is this distance written as a decimal?
   - (A) 37.10 miles
   - (B) 3.710 miles
   - **(C)** 3.7 miles
   - (D) 3.07 miles

4. The point shown on the number line represents the number of inches Bea's plant grew in one week. What decimal correctly names the point?

   $2\frac{5}{10}$

   - (A) 2.06
   - (B) 2.07
   - **(C)** 2.6
   - (D) 2.7

Problem Solving

5. There are 10 sports balls in the equipment closet. Three are kickballs. Write the portion of the balls that are kickballs as a fraction, as a decimal, and in word form.

$\dfrac{3}{10}$; 0.3; three tenths

6. Peyton has 2 pizzas. Each pizza is cut into 10 equal slices. She and her friends eat 14 slices. What part of the pizzas did they eat? Write your answer as a decimal.

1.4 pizzas

Lesson 73
COMMON CORE STANDARD CC.4.NF.6
Lesson Objective: Record hundredths as fractions and as decimals.

Name _____

Relate Hundredths and Decimals

Write the fraction or mixed number and the decimal shown by the model.

Step 1 Count the number of shaded squares in the model and the total number of squares in the whole model.	Number of shaded squares: 53 Total number of squares: 100
Step 2 Write a fraction to represent the part of the model that is shaded.	$\dfrac{\text{Number of Shaded Squares}}{\text{Total Number of Squares}} = \dfrac{53}{100}$ The fraction shown by the model is $\dfrac{53}{100}$.
Step 3 Write the fraction in decimal form.	**Think:** The fraction shown by the model is $\dfrac{53}{100}$. 0.53 names the same amount as $\dfrac{53}{100}$. The decimal shown by the model is 0.53.

The fraction and decimal shown by the model are $\dfrac{53}{100}$ and 0.53.

Write the fraction or mixed number and the decimal shown by the model.

1. $\dfrac{24}{100}$; 0.24

2. $\dfrac{96}{100}$; 0.96

Lesson 73
CC.4.NF.6

Name _____

1. Manuel read 75 out of 100 pages in his book. He shaded a model to show what part of the book he read.

   Which decimal represents the part of the book Manuel read?

   Ⓐ 0.25   Ⓒ 0.75

   Ⓑ 0.70   Ⓓ 0.80

2. A shark tooth has a mass of $1\frac{6}{100}$ kilograms. Which decimal is equivalent to $1\frac{6}{100}$?

   Ⓐ 0.006

   Ⓑ 0.06

   Ⓒ 1.06

   Ⓓ 1.60

3. Kara made a model for some science data. Which decimal matches the model?

   Ⓐ 0.33

   Ⓑ 1.33

   Ⓒ 1.43

   Ⓓ 10.33

4. The weight of a diamond is measured in carats. Mrs. Wang has a diamond that weighs $1\frac{5}{100}$ carats. Which decimal is equivalent to $1\frac{5}{100}$?

   Ⓐ 1.05

   Ⓑ 1.15

   Ⓒ 1.25

   Ⓓ 1.5

Problem Solving REAL WORLD

5. There are 100 pennies in a dollar. What fraction of a dollar is 61 pennies? Write it as a fraction, as a decimal, and in word form.

   $\dfrac{61}{100}$; 0.61; sixty-one hundredths

6. Kylee has collected 100 souvenir thimbles from different places she has visited with her family. Twenty of the thimbles are carved from wood. Write the fraction of thimbles that are wooden as a decimal.

   0.20

Lesson 74
COMMON CORE STANDARD CC.4.NF.6
Lesson Objective: Translate among representations of fractions, decimals, and money.

Name _____

Relate Fractions, Decimals, and Money

Write the total money amount. Then write the amount as a fraction and as a decimal in terms of a dollar.

Step 1 Count the value of coins from greatest to least. Write the total money amount.

$0.25 → $0.35 → $0.40 → $0.45 → $0.50

Step 2 Write the total money amount as a fraction of a dollar.

The total money amount is $0.50, which is the same as 50 cents.

Think: There are 100 cents in a dollar.

So, the total amount written as a fraction of a dollar is:

$\dfrac{50 \text{ cents}}{100 \text{ cents}} = \dfrac{50}{100}$

Step 3 Write the total money amount as a decimal.

Think: I can write $0.50 as 0.50.

The total money amount is $\dfrac{50}{100}$ written as a fraction of a dollar, and 0.50 written as a decimal.

Write the total money amount. Then write the amount as a fraction or a mixed number and as a decimal in terms of a dollar.

1. $0.80; $\dfrac{80}{100}$; 0.80

2. $1.45; $1\frac{45}{100}$; 1.45

Lesson 74
CC.4.NF.6

Name _____

1. Cora paid $\frac{65}{100}$ of a dollar to buy a postcard from Grand Canyon National Park in Arizona. What is $\frac{65}{100}$ written as a decimal in terms of dollars?

   Ⓐ 0.65   Ⓒ 6.5

   Ⓑ 6.05   Ⓓ 65

2. Maria has these coins.

   What is Maria's total amount as a fraction in terms of a dollar?

   Ⓐ $\dfrac{100}{59}$ Ⓒ $\dfrac{75}{100}$

   Ⓑ $\dfrac{134}{100}$ Ⓓ $\dfrac{59}{100}$

3. Ryan sold a jigsaw puzzle at a yard sale for three dollars and five cents. Which decimal names this money amount in terms of dollars?

   Ⓐ 3.50

   Ⓑ 3.05

   Ⓒ 0.55

   Ⓓ 0.05

4. Rick has one dollar and twenty-seven cents to buy a notebook. Which decimal names this money amount in terms of dollars?

   Ⓐ 0.27

   Ⓑ 1.027

   Ⓒ 1.27

   Ⓓ 12.7

Problem Solving REAL WORLD

5. Kate has 1 dime, 4 nickels, and 8 pennies. Write Kate's total amount as a fraction in terms of a dollar.

   $\dfrac{38}{100}$

6. Nolan says he has $\frac{75}{100}$ of a dollar. If he only has 3 coins, what are the coins?

   three quarters

Answer Key

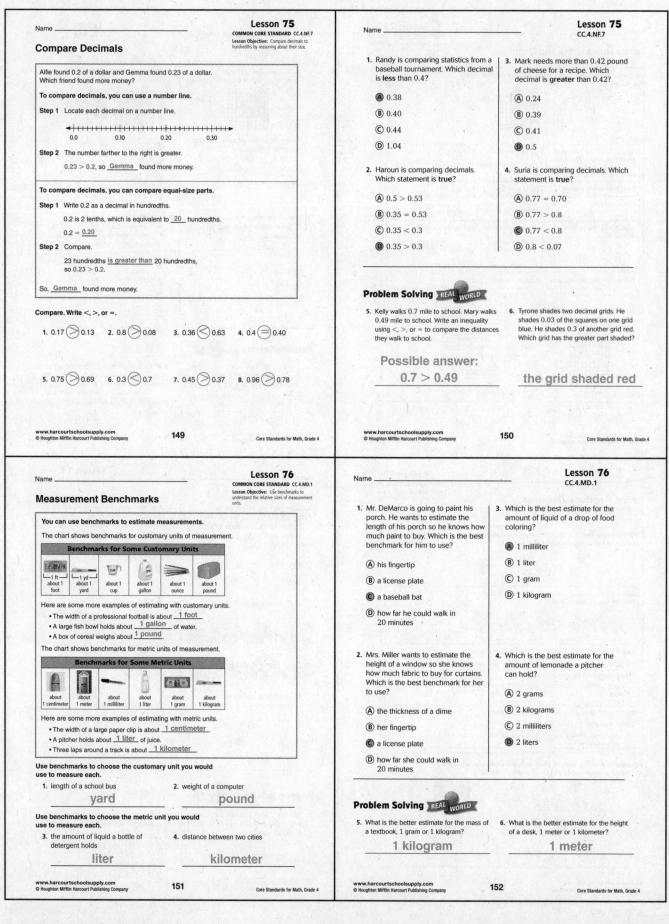

Lesson 75
COMMON CORE STANDARD CC.4.NF.7
Lesson Objective: Compare decimals to hundredths by reasoning about their size.

Name _____

Compare Decimals

Alfie found 0.2 of a dollar and Gemma found 0.23 of a dollar. Which friend found more money?

To compare decimals, you can use a number line.

Step 1 Locate each decimal on a number line.

0.0   0.10   0.20   0.30

Step 2 The number farther to the right is greater.

0.23 > 0.2, so __Gemma__ found more money.

To compare decimals, you can compare equal-size parts.

Step 1 Write 0.2 as a decimal in hundredths.

0.2 is 2 tenths, which is equivalent to __20__ hundredths.

0.2 = __0.20__

Step 2 Compare.

23 hundredths __is greater than__ 20 hundredths, so 0.23 > 0.2.

So, __Gemma__ found more money.

Compare. Write <, >, or =.

1. 0.17 (>) 0.13   2. 0.8 (>) 0.08   3. 0.36 (<) 0.63   4. 0.4 (=) 0.40

5. 0.75 (>) 0.69   6. 0.3 (<) 0.7   7. 0.45 (>) 0.37   8. 0.96 (>) 0.78

www.harcourtschoolsupply.com
© Houghton Mifflin Harcourt Publishing Company
149
Core Standards for Math, Grade 4

Lesson 75
CC.4.NF.7

Name _____

1. Randy is comparing statistics from a baseball tournament. Which decimal is **less** than 0.4?

   Ⓐ 0.38
   Ⓑ 0.40
   Ⓒ 0.44
   Ⓓ 1.04

2. Haroun is comparing decimals. Which statement is **true**?

   Ⓐ 0.5 > 0.53
   Ⓑ 0.35 = 0.53
   Ⓒ 0.35 < 0.3
   Ⓓ 0.35 > 0.3

3. Mark needs more than 0.42 pound of cheese for a recipe. Which decimal is **greater** than 0.42?

   Ⓐ 0.24
   Ⓑ 0.39
   Ⓒ 0.41
   Ⓓ 0.5

4. Suria is comparing decimals. Which statement is **true**?

   Ⓐ 0.77 = 0.70
   Ⓑ 0.77 > 0.8
   Ⓒ 0.77 < 0.8
   Ⓓ 0.8 < 0.07

Problem Solving REAL WORLD

5. Kelly walks 0.7 mile to school. Mary walks 0.49 mile to school. Write an inequality using <, >, or = to compare the distances they walk to school.

   Possible answer:
   __0.7 > 0.49__

6. Tyrone shades two decimal grids. He shades 0.03 of the squares on one grid blue. He shades 0.3 of another grid red. Which grid has the greater part shaded?

   __the grid shaded red__

www.harcourtschoolsupply.com
© Houghton Mifflin Harcourt Publishing Company
150
Core Standards for Math, Grade 4

Lesson 76
COMMON CORE STANDARD CC.4.MD.1
Lesson Objective: Use benchmarks to understand the relative sizes of measurement units.

Name _____

Measurement Benchmarks

You can use benchmarks to estimate measurements.

The chart shows benchmarks for customary units of measurement.

Benchmarks for Some Customary Units					
about 1 foot	about 1 yard	about 1 cup	about 1 gallon	about 1 ounce	about 1 pound

Here are some more examples of estimating with customary units.

• The width of a professional football is about __1 foot__
• A large fish bowl holds about __1 gallon__ of water.
• A box of cereal weighs about __1 pound__

The chart shows benchmarks for metric units of measurement.

Benchmarks for Some Metric Units					
about 1 centimeter	about 1 meter	about 1 milliliter	about 1 liter	about 1 gram	about 1 kilogram

Here are some more examples of estimating with metric units.

• The width of a large paper clip is about __1 centimeter__
• A pitcher holds about __1 liter__ of juice.
• Three laps around a track is about __1 kilometer__

Use benchmarks to choose the customary unit you would use to measure each.

1. length of a school bus
   __yard__

2. weight of a computer
   __pound__

Use benchmarks to choose the metric unit you would use to measure each.

3. the amount of liquid a bottle of detergent holds
   __liter__

4. distance between two cities
   __kilometer__

www.harcourtschoolsupply.com
© Houghton Mifflin Harcourt Publishing Company
151
Core Standards for Math, Grade 4

Lesson 76
CC.4.MD.1

Name _____

1. Mr. DeMarco is going to paint his porch. He wants to estimate the length of his porch so he knows how much paint to buy. Which is the best benchmark for him to use?

   Ⓐ his fingertip
   Ⓑ a license plate
   Ⓒ a baseball bat
   Ⓓ how far he could walk in 20 minutes

2. Mrs. Miller wants to estimate the height of a window so she knows how much fabric to buy for curtains. Which is the best benchmark for her to use?

   Ⓐ the thickness of a dime
   Ⓑ her fingertip
   Ⓒ a license plate
   Ⓓ how far she could walk in 20 minutes

3. Which is the best estimate for the amount of liquid of a drop of food coloring?

   Ⓐ 1 milliliter
   Ⓑ 1 liter
   Ⓒ 1 gram
   Ⓓ 1 kilogram

4. Which is the best estimate for the amount of lemonade a pitcher can hold?

   Ⓐ 2 grams
   Ⓑ 2 kilograms
   Ⓒ 2 milliliters
   Ⓓ 2 liters

Problem Solving REAL WORLD

5. What is the better estimate for the mass of a textbook, 1 gram or 1 kilogram?
   __1 kilogram__

6. What is the better estimate for the height of a desk, 1 meter or 1 kilometer?
   __1 meter__

www.harcourtschoolsupply.com
© Houghton Mifflin Harcourt Publishing Company
152
Core Standards for Math, Grade 4

Name _____

Lesson 77
COMMON CORE STANDARD CC.4.MD.1
Lesson Objective: Use models to compare customary units of length.

Customary Units of Length

A ruler is used to measure length. A ruler that is 1 foot long shows 12 inches in 1 foot. A ruler that is 3 feet long is called a yardstick. There are 3 feet in 1 yard.

How does the size of a foot compare to the size of an inch?

Step 1 A small paper clip is about 1 inch long. Below is a drawing of a chain of paper clips that is about 1 foot long. Number each paper clip, starting with 1.

1 2 3 4 5 6 7 8 9 10 11 12

Step 2 Complete this sentence.

In the chain of paper clips shown, there are ___12___ paper clips.

Step 3 Compare the size of 1 inch to the size of 1 foot.

There are ___12___ inches in ___1___ foot.

So, 1 foot is ___12___ times as long as 1 inch.

Complete.

1. 5 feet = ___60___ inches

2. 3 yards = ___9___ feet

3. 5 yards = ___15___ feet

4. 4 feet = ___48___ inches

5. 6 feet = ___72___ inches

6. 8 yards = ___24___ feet

Name _____

Lesson 77
CC.4.MD.1

1. Kirsten is 5 feet tall. How tall is she in inches?

   (A) 60 inches

   (B) 50 inches

   (C) 48 inches

   (D) 45 inches

2. Shirlee bought 2 yards of fabric. How many inches of fabric did Shirlee buy?

   (A) 24 inches

   (B) 36 inches

   (C) 48 inches

   (D) 72 inches

3. Hank bought 12 yards of computer cable. How many feet of cable is this?

   (A) 4 feet

   (B) 24 feet

   (C) 36 feet

   (D) 144 feet

4. Dwayne bought 5 yards of wrapping paper. How many inches of wrapping paper is this?

   (A) 180 inches

   (B) 60 inches

   (C) 50 inches

   (D) 15 inches

Problem Solving REAL WORLD

5. Carla has two lengths of ribbon. One ribbon is 2 feet long. The other ribbon is 30 inches long. Which length of ribbon is longer? **Explain.**

   30 inches is longer; 2 feet is 24 inches, which is shorter than 30 inches.

6. A football player gained 2 yards on one play. On the next play, he gained 5 feet. Was his gain greater on the first play or the second play? **Explain.**

   The first play; 2 yards is equal to 6 feet, which is greater than 5 feet.

Name _____

Lesson 78
COMMON CORE STANDARD CC.4.MD.1
Lesson Objective: Use models to compare customary units of weight.

Customary Units of Weight

Ounces and **pounds** are customary units of weight. A **ton** is a unit of weight that is equal to 2,000 pounds.

A slice of bread weighs about 1 ounce. Some loaves of bread weigh about 1 pound.

How does the size of 1 ounce compare to the size of 1 pound?

Step 1 You know a slice of bread weighs about 1 ounce. Below is a drawing of a loaf of bread that weighs about 1 pound. Number each slice of bread, starting with 1.

1 2 3 4 5 6 7 8 9 10 11 12 13 14 15 16

Step 2 Complete this sentence.

In the loaf of bread shown above, there are ___16___ slices of bread.

Step 3 Compare the size of 1 ounce to the size of 1 pound.

There are ___16___ ounces in ___1___ pound.

So, 1 pound is ___16___ times as heavy as 1 ounce.

Complete.

1. 2 pounds = ___32___ ounces
   Think: 2 × 16 = 32

2. 2 tons = ___4,000___ pounds

3. 7 pounds = ___112___ ounces

4. 4 pounds = ___64___ ounces

5. 3 tons = ___6,000___ pounds

6. 10 pounds = ___160___ ounces

Name _____

Lesson 78
CC.4.MD.1

1. An elephant living in a wildlife park weighs 4 tons. How many pounds does the elephant weigh?

   (A) 400 pounds

   (B) 800 pounds

   (C) 4,000 pounds

   (D) 8,000 pounds

2. Ayesha's backpack weighs 9 pounds. How many ounces does her backpack weigh?

   (A) 180 ounces

   (B) 144 ounces

   (C) 90 ounces

   (D) 72 ounces

3. Joan is making tomato sauce. She needs 2 pounds of tomatoes. How many ounces of tomatoes does she need?

   (A) 8 ounces

   (B) 16 ounces

   (C) 32 ounces

   (D) 36 ounces

4. An ocean aquarium is home to a gray whale that weighs 35 tons. How many pounds does this gray whale weigh?

   (A) 70,000 pounds

   (B) 35,000 pounds

   (C) 7,000 pounds

   (D) 3,500 pounds

Problem Solving REAL WORLD

5. A company that makes steel girders can produce 6 tons of girders in one day. How many pounds is this?

   12,000 pounds

6. Larry's baby sister weighed 6 pounds at birth. How many ounces did the baby weigh?

   96 ounces

Answer Key

Lesson 79
COMMON CORE STANDARD CC.4.MD.1
Lesson Objective: Use models to compare customary units of liquid volume.

Customary Units of Liquid Volume

Liquid volume is the measure of the space a liquid occupies. Some basic units for measuring liquid volume are **gallons, half gallons, quarts, pints, cups,** and **fluid ounces.** The table at the right shows the relationships among some units of liquid volume.

1 cup = 8 fluid ounces
1 pint = 2 cups
1 quart = 2 pints
1 half gallon = 2 quarts
1 gallon = 4 quarts

How does the size of a gallon compare to the size of a pint?

Step 1 Use the information in the table. Draw a bar to represent 1 gallon.

1 gallon

Step 2 The table shows that 1 gallon is equal to 4 quarts. Draw a bar to show 4 quarts.

1 quart	1 quart	1 quart	1 quart

Step 3 The table shows that 1 quart is equal to 2 pints. Draw a bar to show 2 pints for each of the 4 quarts.

1 pint	1 pint	1 pint	1 pint	1 pint	1 pint	1 pint	1 pint

Step 4 Compare the size of 1 gallon to the size of 1 pint.

There are __8__ pints in __1__ gallon.

So, 1 gallon is __8__ times as much as 1 pint.

Complete. Draw a model to help.

1. 2 quarts = __4__ pints

2. 1 gallon = __16__ cups

3. 1 pint = __16__ fluid ounces

4. 3 pints = __6__ cups

5. 3 quarts = __12__ cups

6. 1 half gallon = __4__ pints

Lesson 79
CC.4.MD.1

1. Randy is making a fruit punch for the class party. He mixes different types of fruit juices to make 1 gallon of punch. How many quarts of punch does Randy make?
   - (A) 1 quart
   - (B) 2 quarts
   - (C) 3 quarts
   - **(D) 4 quarts**

2. Celeste makes 6 quarts of lemonade. How many pints of lemonade does she make?
   - (A) 3 pints
   - (B) 8 pints
   - **(C) 12 pints**
   - (D) 24 pints

3. A carton of cider holds 2 quarts. What is the liquid volume of the carton in cups?
   - (A) 4 cups
   - (B) 6 cups
   - **(C) 8 cups**
   - (D) 12 cups

4. A pitcher can hold 6 cups. What is the liquid volume of the pitcher in fluid ounces?
   - (A) 60 fluid ounces
   - **(B) 48 fluid ounces**
   - (C) 36 fluid ounces
   - (D) 24 fluid ounces

Problem Solving REAL WORLD

5. A chef makes $1\frac{1}{2}$ gallons of soup in a large pot. How many 1-cup servings can the chef get from this large pot of soup?

   __24 1-cup servings__

6. Kendra's water bottle contains 2 quarts of water. She wants to add drink mix to it, but the directions for the drink mix give the amount of water in fluid ounces. How many fluid ounces are in her bottle?

   __64 fluid ounces__

Lesson 80
COMMON CORE STANDARD CC.4.MD.1
Lesson Objective: Use models to compare metric units of length.

Metric Units of Length

Meters (m), decimeters (dm), centimeters (cm), and **millimeters** (mm) are all metric units of length. You can use a ruler and a meterstick to find out how these units are related.

Materials: ruler, meterstick

Step 1 Look at a metric ruler. Most look like the one below.

The short marks between each centimeter mark show millimeters. 1 centimeter has the same length as a group of 10 millimeters.

Step 2 Look at a meterstick. Most look like the one below.

1 decimeter has the same length as a group of 10 centimeters.

Step 3 Use the ruler and the meterstick to compare metric units of length.

1 centimeter = __10__ millimeters   1 decimeter = __10__ centimeters

1 meter = __10__ decimeters   1 meter = __100__ centimeters

Complete.

1. 3 meters = __30__ decimeters

2. 5 meters = __500__ centimeters

3. 4 centimeters = __40__ millimeters

4. 9 decimeters = __90__ centimeters

Lesson 80
CC.4.MD.1

1. Aruna walked 520 meters to her grandmother's house. How many decimeters did Aruna walk to her grandmother's house?
   - (A) 5.2 decimeters
   - (B) 52 decimeters
   - (C) 520 decimeters
   - **(D) 5,200 decimeters**

2. Carol's pencil is 18 centimeters long. How many millimeters long is the pencil?
   - (A) 80 millimeters
   - **(B) 180 millimeters**
   - (C) 1,800 millimeters
   - (D) 18,000 millimeters

3. Jakob plays the violin. His bow is 7 decimeters long. How many centimeters long is Jakob's bow?
   - (A) 0.07 centimeter
   - (B) 0.7 centimeter
   - **(C) 70 centimeters**
   - (D) 700 centimeters

4. Jim's computer screen has a height of 3 decimeters. What is the height of the screen in centimeters?
   - **(A) 30 centimeters**
   - (B) 300 centimeters
   - (C) 3,000 centimeters
   - (D) 30,000 centimeters

Problem Solving REAL WORLD

5. A flagpole is 4 meters tall. How many centimeters tall is the flagpole?

   __400 centimeters__

6. A new building is 25 meters tall. How many decimeters tall is the building?

   __250 decimeters__

Lesson 81 — Metric Units of Mass and Liquid Volume

Name _____

Lesson 81
COMMON CORE STANDARD CC.4.MD.1
Lesson Objective: Use models to compare metric units of mass and liquid volume.

Metric Units of Mass and Liquid Volume

Mass is the amount of matter in an object. Metric units of mass include grams (g) and kilograms (kg). 1 kilogram represents the same mass as 1,000 grams.

One large loaf of bread has a mass of about 1 kilogram. Jacob has 3 large loaves of bread. About how many grams is the mass of the loaves?

3 kilograms = 3 × __1,000__ grams

= __3,000__ grams

Liters (L) and **milliliters** (mL) are metric units of liquid volume. 1 liter represents the same liquid volume as 1,000 milliliters.

A large bowl holds about 2 liters of juice. Carmen needs to know the liquid volume in milliliters.

2 liters = 2 × __1,000__ milliliters

= __2,000__ milliliters

Complete.

1. 4 kilograms = __4,000__ grams 2. 9 liters = __9,000__ milliliters

3. 3 liters = __3,000__ milliliters 4. 7 kilograms = __7,000__ grams

5. 5 kilograms = __5,000__ grams 6. 8 liters = __8,000__ milliliters

www.harcourtschoolsupply.com
© Houghton Mifflin Harcourt Publishing Company
161
Core Standards for Math, Grade 4

Name _____

Lesson 81
CC.4.MD.1

1. Pam saw a koala at the zoo. It had a mass of 7 kilograms. How many grams is 7 kilograms?
   - (A) 70 grams
   - (B) 700 grams
   - (C) 7,000 grams
   - (D) 70,000 grams

2. Koji used 2 liters of water to water his plants. How many milliliters of water did he use?
   - (A) 2,000 milliliters
   - (B) 200 milliliters
   - (C) 20 milliliters
   - (D) 0.2 milliliter

3. June filled the birdbath in her yard with 4 liters of water. How many milliliters of water did she put in the birdbath?
   - (A) .4 milliliters
   - (B) 40 milliliters
   - (C) 400 milliliters
   - (D) 4,000 milliliters

4. A turkey has a mass of 6 kilograms. A bag of sweet potatoes has a mass of 2 kilograms. How many more grams does the turkey weigh than the sweet potatoes?
   - (A) 4 grams
   - (B) 40 grams
   - (C) 400 grams
   - (D) 4,000 grams

5. Harlan went fishing. The sunfish he caught had a mass of 865 grams. The perch he caught had a mass of 1 kilogram. Which fish had the greater mass? Explain your reasoning.

   The perch; possible explanation: I knew I had to compare 1 kilogram and 865 grams. So, I renamed 1 kilogram as 1,000 grams. Since 1,000 > 865, the perch has a greater mass.

www.harcourtschoolsupply.com
© Houghton Mifflin Harcourt Publishing Company
162
Core Standards for Math, Grade 4

Lesson 82 — Units of Time

Name _____

Lesson 82
COMMON CORE STANDARD CC.4.MD.1
Lesson Objective: Use models to compare units of time.

Units of Time

Some analog clocks have an hour hand, a minute hand, and a **second** hand.

There are 60 seconds in a minute. The second hand makes 1 full turn every minute. There are 60 minutes in an hour. The minute hand makes 1 full turn every hour. The hour hand makes 1 full turn every 12 hours.

You can think of the clock as unrolling to become a number line.

hours 0 1 2 3 4 5 6 7 8 9 10 11 12

The hour hand moves from one number to the next in 1 hour.

minutes 0 5 10 15 20 25 30 35 40 45 50 55 60

The minute hand moves from one number to the next in 5 minutes.

Use the table at the right to change between units of time.

Units of Time
1 minute = 60 seconds
1 hour = 60 minutes
1 day = 24 hours
1 week = 7 days
1 year = 12 months
1 year = 52 weeks

1 hour = 60 minutes, or 60 × 60 seconds, or __3,600__ seconds.

So, 1 hour is __3,600__ times as long as 1 second.

1 day = 24 hours, so 3 days = 3 × 24 hours, or __72__ hours.

1 year = 12 months, so 5 years = 5 × 12 months, or __60__ months.

Complete.

1. 3 hours = __180__ minutes 2. 2 years = __104__ weeks

3. 6 days = __144__ hours 4. 5 weeks = __35__ days

5. 8 minutes = __480__ seconds 6. 7 years = __84__ months

www.harcourtschoolsupply.com
© Houghton Mifflin Harcourt Publishing Company
163
Core Standards for Math, Grade 4

Name _____

Lesson 82
CC.4.MD.1

1. The Burke family is taking a 3-week vacation to Alaska. How many days will their vacation last?
   - (A) 7 days
   - (B) 14 days
   - (C) 21 days
   - (D) 30 days

2. Julio's little sister is 3 years old. How many months old is she?
   - (A) 48 months old
   - (B) 36 months old
   - (C) 24 months old
   - (D) 12 months old

3. Fred has been taking guitar lessons for 100 weeks. Nancy has been taking guitar lessons for 3 years. Which statement is true about Fred and Nancy?
   - (A) Fred has been taking lessons a shorter time than Nancy has.
   - (B) Fred has been taking lessons twice as long as Nancy has.
   - (C) Fred has been taking lessons longer than Nancy has.
   - (D) Fred and Nancy have been taking lessons for the same length of time.

4. A candle can burn for up to 600 minutes. Which amount of time is longer than 600 minutes?
   - (A) 1 hour
   - (B) 5 hours
   - (C) 10 hours
   - (D) 12 hours

5. Reese lay down for a nap. He set a timer to ring in 15 minutes to wake him up. Explain how to find the total number of seconds Reese could nap.

   900 seconds; Possible explanation: I know that 1 minute = 60 seconds. So, to find how many seconds in 15 minutes, I multiplied 15 × 60, which is 900.

www.harcourtschoolsupply.com
© Houghton Mifflin Harcourt Publishing Company
164
Core Standards for Math, Grade 4

Answer Key

Name _____

Algebra • Patterns in Measurement Units

Use the relationship between the number pairs to label the columns in the table.

?	?
1	8
2	16
3	24
4	32

Step 1 List the number pairs. _1 and 8; 2 and 16; 3 and 24; 4 and 32_

Step 2 Describe the relationship between the numbers in each pair.

The second number is 8 times as great as the first number.

Step 3 Look for a relationship involving 1 and 8 in the table below.

Length	Weight	Liquid Volume	Time
1 foot = 12 inches	1 pound = 16 ounces	1 cup = 8 fluid ounces	1 minute = 60 seconds
1 yard = 3 feet	1 ton = 2,000 pounds	1 pint = 2 cups	1 hour = 60 minutes
1 yard = 36 inches		1 quart = 2 pints	1 day = 24 hours
		1 gallon = 4 quarts	1 week = 7 days
			1 year = 12 months
			1 year = 52 weeks

So, the label for the first column is ___Cups___
The label for the second column is ___Fluid Ounces___

Each table shows a pattern for two customary units. Label the columns of the table.

1.

Feet	Inches
1	12
2	24
3	36
4	48

2.

Tons	Pounds
1	2,000
2	4,000
3	6,000
4	8,000

Name _____

1. The table shows a pattern for units of time. Which are the best labels for this table?

1	52
2	104
3	156
4	208

Ⓐ Years, Months
Ⓑ Years, Weeks
Ⓒ Weeks, Days
Ⓓ Months, Days

3. The table shows a pattern for units of time. Which are the best labels for this table?

1	24
2	48
3	72
4	96

Ⓐ Years, Weeks
Ⓑ Minutes, Days
Ⓒ Minutes, Seconds
Ⓓ Days, Hours

2. The table shows a pattern for metric units. Which are the best labels for this table?

1	1,000
2	2,000
3	3,000
4	4,000

Ⓐ Centimeters, Meters
Ⓑ Centimeters, Kilometers
Ⓒ Kilograms, Grams
Ⓓ Milliliters, Liters

4. The table shows a pattern for metric units. Which are the best labels for this table?

1	1,000
2	2,000
3	3,000
4	4,000

Ⓐ Centimeters, Meters
Ⓑ Kilometers, Meters
Ⓒ Grams, Kilograms
Ⓓ Milliliters, Liters

5. Mac says the pattern in a table for feet and inches and a table for years and months would look the same without labels. Do you agree? Explain.

Yes; possible explanation: 1 foot = 12 inches and 1 year =
12 months, so the tables could have the same numbers.

Name _____

Problem Solving • Money

Use the strategy *act it out* to solve the problem.

Jessica, Brian, and Grace earned $7.50. They want to share the money equally. How much will each person get?

Read the Problem	Solve the Problem
What do I need to find?	• Show the total amount, _$7.50_, using _7_ one-dollar bills and _2_ quarters.
I need to find the _amount of money each person should get_.	
What information do I need to use?	• Share the one-dollar bills equally.
I need to use the total amount, _$7.50_, and divide it by _3_, the number of people sharing the money equally.	There is _1_ one-dollar bill left.
How will I use the information?	• Change the dollar bill that is left for _4_ quarters. Now there are _6_ quarters.
I will use _dollar bills and coins_ to model the total amount and _act out the problem_.	• Share the quarters equally.
	So, each person gets _2_ one-dollar bills and _2_ quarters, or _$2.50_.

1. Jacob, Dan, and Nathan were given $6.90 to share equally. How much money will each boy get?

_$2.30_

2. Becky, Marlis, and Hallie each earned $2.15 raking leaves. How much did they earn together?

_$6.45_

Name _____

1. Chaz needs $4.77 for new batteries. He has $2.80. How much more money does he need?

Ⓐ $1.97
Ⓑ $2.10
Ⓒ $2.17
Ⓓ $7.57

3. Patty, Helene, and Mira share $0.96 that they found in an old wallet. How much money does each girl get?

Ⓐ $0.48
Ⓑ $0.38
Ⓒ $0.36
Ⓓ $0.32

2. Mrs. Golub wants to share $7.20 equally among her three grandchildren. How much money should each grandchild get?

Ⓐ $1.40
Ⓑ $2.07
Ⓒ $2.40
Ⓓ $4.20

4. Three boys share $1.92 equally. How much money does each boy get?

Ⓐ $0.64
Ⓑ $0.69
Ⓒ $0.72
Ⓓ $5.76

5. Bernie and his two brothers share $8.16 equally. How much money does each boy get? Explain the strategy you use to solve the problem.

$2.72; Possible explanation: I share 8 one-dollar bills;
each boy gets $2, and 2 dollar bills are left. $1 = 10
dimes, so $2 = 20 dimes. 20 dimes shared among 3 boys
gives each boy 6 dimes with 2 dimes left. I change the 2
dimes and 16 cents into pennies, so I have 36 pennies,
which shared among 3 boys is 12 pennies each. So, each
boy has 2 dollar bills + 6 dimes + 12 pennies or $2.00 +
_$0.60 + $0.12 = $2.72._

Name _____

Problem Solving • Elapsed Time

Opal finished her art project at 2:25 P.M. She spent 50 minutes working on her project. What time did she start working on her project?

Read the Problem		
What do I need to find?	**What information do I need to use?**	**How will I use the information?**
I need to find Opal's start time.	End time: __2:25__ P.M. Elapsed time: __50__ minutes	I can draw a diagram of a clock. I can then count back 5 minutes at a time until I reach 50 minutes.

Solve the Problem
I start by showing 2:25 P.M. on the clock.   Then I count back 50 minutes by 5s.   **Think:** As I count back, I go past the 12.   The hour must be 1 hour less than the ending time.   The hour will be __1 o'clock__   So, Opal started on her project at __1:35 P.M.__

Draw hands on the clock to help you solve the problem.

1. Bill wants to be at school at 8:05 A.M. It takes him 20 minutes to walk to school. At what time should Bill leave his house?

   Bill should leave his house at __7:45 a.m.__

2. Mr. Gleason's math class lasts 40 minutes. Math class starts at 9:55 A.M. At what time does math class end?

   Math class ends at __10:35 a.m.__

3. Hannah rode her bike for 1 hour and 15 minutes until she got a flat tire at 2:30 P.M. What time did Hannah start riding her bike?

   Hannah started riding her bike at __1:15 p.m.__

Name _____

1. The tour of the art museum started at 9:35 A.M. It lasted for 1 hour 20 minutes. What time did the tour end?

   (A) 9:55 A.M.
   (B) 10:35 A.M.
   (C) 10:45 A.M.
   (D) 10:55 A.M.

2. The plumber began to fix the leaky sink at 1:45 P.M. He worked on it for 1 hour 45 minutes. What time did the plumber finish the job?

   (A) 2:45 P.M.
   (B) 3:00 P.M.
   (C) 3:20 P.M.
   (D) 3:30 P.M.

3. An author signed copies of her newest book for 57 minutes until the bookstore closed at 5:00 P.M. What time did the author begin signing books?

   (A) 4:03 P.M.
   (B) 4:57 P.M.
   (C) 5:03 P.M.
   (D) 5:57 P.M.

4. Aya was at the library for 48 minutes until it closed at 6:30 P.M. What time did Aya arrive at the library?

   (A) 5:32 P.M.
   (B) 5:42 P.M.
   (C) 5:52 P.M.
   (D) 7:18 P.M.

5. David's gymnastics class ended at 4:15 P.M. It lasted for 46 minutes. Someone asked David what time the class started. Explain how David could find the answer.

   Possible explanation: he could count back 46 minutes starting from 4:15. He could picture a clock face and imagine moving the minute hand back in jumps of 5s for 45 minutes, which is 3:30. Then he could move back 1 more minute to 3:29 p.m.

Name _____

Mixed Measures

Gabrielle's puppy weighs 2 pounds 7 ounces. What is the weight of the puppy in ounces?

Step 1 Think of 2 pounds 7 ounces as 2 pounds + 7 ounces.

Step 2 Change the pounds to ounces.
   Think: 1 pound = __16__ ounces
   So, 2 pounds = 2 × 16 ounces, or __32__ ounces.

Step 3 Add like units to find the answer.
   So, Gabrielle's puppy weighs __39__ ounces.

$$\begin{array}{r} 32 \text{ ounces} \\ + 7 \text{ ounces} \\ \hline 39 \text{ ounces} \end{array}$$

Gabrielle played with her puppy for 2 hours 10 minutes yesterday and 1 hour 25 minutes today. How much longer did she play with the puppy yesterday than today?

Step 1 Subtract the mixed measures. Write the subtraction with like units lined up.
   Think: 25 minutes is greater than 10 minutes.

$$\begin{array}{r} 2 \text{ hr } 10 \text{ min} \\ - 1 \text{ hr } 25 \text{ min} \end{array}$$

Step 2 Rename 2 hours 10 minutes to subtract.
   1 hour = 60 minutes
   So, 2 hr 10 min = 1 hr + 60 min + 10 min, or __1__ hr __70__ min.

$$\begin{array}{r} 1 \quad 70 \\ 2 \text{ hr } 10 \text{ min} \\ - 1 \text{ hr } 25 \text{ min} \\ \hline 0 \text{ hr } 45 \text{ min} \end{array}$$

Step 3 Subtract like units.
   1 hr − 1 hr = 0 hr; 70 min − 25 min = __45 min__

So, she played with the puppy __45__ minutes longer yesterday than today.

Complete.

1. 4 yd 2 ft = __14__ ft   2. 1 hr 20 min = __80__ min   3. 4 qt 1 pt = __9__ pt

Add or subtract.

4. $\begin{array}{r} 2 \text{ gal } 1 \text{ qt} \\ + 3 \text{ gal } 2 \text{ qt} \\ \hline \mathbf{5 \text{ gal } 3 \text{ qt}} \end{array}$

5. $\begin{array}{r} 3 \text{ lb } 12 \text{ oz} \\ - 1 \text{ lb } 8 \text{ oz} \\ \hline \mathbf{2 \text{ lb } 4 \text{ oz}} \end{array}$

6. $\begin{array}{r} 4 \text{ yr } 9 \text{ mo} \\ - 1 \text{ yr } 10 \text{ mo} \\ \hline \mathbf{2 \text{ yr } 11 \text{ mo}} \end{array}$

Name _____

1. Mr. Wallis says he is 6 feet 3 inches tall. How tall is he in inches?

   (A) 75 inches
   (B) 72 inches
   (C) 69 inches
   (D) 33 inches

2. Erin ships a gift through the mail. The gift weighs 8 pounds 11 ounces. She packs the gift in a shipping box with bubble wrap. The package weighs 12 pounds 4 ounces. How much does the shipping box and bubble wrap weigh?

   (A) 4 pounds 7 ounces
   (B) 3 pounds 9 ounces
   (C) 3 pounds 5 ounces
   (D) 3 pounds 3 ounces

3. Adrianna mixed 4 quarts 2 pints of lemonade with 1 pint of grape juice to make party punch. How many pints of party punch does she have?

   (A) 7 pints
   (B) 9 pints
   (C) 10 pints
   (D) 11 pints

4. Mr. Leung told his students that his desk is 4 feet 6 inches long. What is this length in inches?

   (A) 24 inches
   (B) 48 inches
   (C) 54 inches
   (D) 60 inches

Problem Solving REAL WORLD

5. Michael's basketball team practiced for 2 hours 40 minutes yesterday and 3 hours 15 minutes today. How much longer did the team practice today than yesterday?

   __35 minutes__

6. Rhonda had a piece of ribbon that was 5 feet 3 inches long. She removed a 5-inch piece to use in her art project. What is the length of the piece of ribbon now?

   __4 feet 10 inches__

Answer Key

Name _____

Lesson 87
COMMON CORE STANDARD CC.4.MD.3
Lesson Objective: Use a formula to find the perimeter of a rectangle.

Perimeter

Perimeter is the distance around a shape. You can use grid paper to count the number of units around the outside of a rectangle to find its perimeter.

How many feet of ribbon are needed to go around the bulletin board?

5 ft / 3 ft

Step 1 On grid paper, draw a rectangle that has a length of **5** units and a width of **3** units.

Step 2 Find the length of each side of the rectangle. Mark each unit of length as you count.

Step 3 Add the side lengths. $5 + 3 + 5 + 3 = 16$

The perimeter is ___16___ feet.

So, 16 feet of ribbon are needed to go around the bulletin board.

1. What is the perimeter of this square?

$\underline{5} + \underline{5} + \underline{5} + \underline{5} = \underline{20}$ centimeters

5 cm / 5 cm

Find the perimeter of the rectangle or square.

2. 2 m / 6 m   ___16___ meters

3. 3 cm / 3 cm   ___12___ centimeters

4. 4 m / 7 m   ___22___ meters

---

1. Jack plants a vegetable garden. The garden is in the shape of a rectangle. He wants to put fencing around the entire garden.

4 ft / 16 ft

How much fencing does Jack need?

(A) 72 feet (C) 40 feet
(B) 44 feet (D) 22 feet

2. Ian hung a mirror on the wall.

13 cm / 9 cm

What is the perimeter of the mirror?

(A) 22 cm (C) 44 cm
(B) 36 cm (D) 52 cm

3. Mindy puts a rectangular poster of her favorite singer on a wall in her bedroom.

30 in. / 20 in.

What is the perimeter of the poster?

(A) 100 inches (C) 60 inches
(B) 70 inches (D) 50 inches

4. Armando is tiling the top of his kitchen table. Each tile that he is using measures 9 inches along each side. What is the perimeter of a tile?

(A) 9 inches (C) 36 inches
(B) 18 inches (D) 81 inches

Problem Solving REAL WORLD

5. Troy is making a flag shaped like a square. Each side measures 12 inches. He wants to add ribbon along the edges. He has 36 inches of ribbon. Does he have enough ribbon? **Explain.**

No. He needs 48 inches of ribbon.

6. The width of the Ochoa Community Pool is 20 feet. The length is twice as long as its width. What is the perimeter of the pool?

120 feet

Name _____

Lesson 88
COMMON CORE STANDARD CC.4.MD.3
Lesson Objective: Use a formula to find the area of a rectangle.

Area

Area is the number of **square units** needed to cover a flat surface.

Find the area of the rectangle at the right.

8 ft / 14 ft

You can use the formula **Area = base × height**.

Step 1 Identify one side as the base.
The base is ___14___ feet.

Step 2 Identify a perpendicular side as the height.
The height is ___8___ feet.

Step 3 Use the formula to find the area.

$$\text{Area} = \text{base} \times \text{height}$$
$$= 14 \times 8$$
$$= 112$$

So, the area of the rectangle is 112 square feet.

Find the area of the rectangle or square.

1. 6 m / 13 m   ___78 sq m___

2. 19 ft / 7 ft   ___133 sq ft___

3. 30 ft / 30 ft   ___900 sq ft___

4. 14 in. / 3 in.   ___42 sq in.___

---

1. Oscar is cutting a piece of glass that is 3 feet long on each side. What is the area of the glass?

(A) 12 square feet
(B) 9 square feet
(C) 6 square feet
(D) 3 square feet

2. Hiro painted a mural with the dimensions shown.

10 feet / 6 feet

What is the area of Hiro's mural?

(A) 4 square feet
(B) 16 square feet
(C) 32 square feet
(D) 60 square feet

3. Sherry made this arrangement of tiles as part of her art project.

Which of the following is true?

(A) area = 11 square units
(B) area = 14 square units
(C) area = 18 square units
(D) area = 22 square units

4. Laura bought a square canvas to paint a picture of her cat. One side measures 22 centimeters. What is the area of the canvas?

(A) 44 square centimeters
(B) 88 square centimeters
(C) 440 square centimeters
(D) 484 square centimeters

Problem Solving REAL WORLD

5. Meghan is putting wallpaper on a wall that measures 8 feet by 12 feet. How much wallpaper does Meghan need to cover the wall?

96 square feet

6. Bryson is laying down sod in his yard to grow a new lawn. Each piece of sod is a 1-foot by 1-foot square. How many pieces of sod will Bryson need to cover his yard if his yard measures 30 feet by 14 feet?

420 pieces

Name _____

Lesson 89
COMMON CORE STANDARD CC.4.MD.3
Lesson Objective: Find the area of combined rectangles.

Area of Combined Rectangles

Find the area of the combined rectangles.

10 mi
9 mi · 8 mi
18 mi

Step 1 First, find the area of each section of the shape.

LEFT
$A = b \times h$
$= 10 \times 9$
$= 90$

RIGHT
$A = b \times h$
$= 8 \times 8$
$= 64$

Think: $18 - 10 = 8$

Step 2 Add the two areas. $90 + 64 = 154$

So, the total area is __154__ square miles.

Find the area of the combined rectangles.

1.
10 cm
5 cm
4 cm
3 cm

62 sq cm

2.
20 m
6 m
2 m
10 m

80 sq m

3.
9 m 3 m 9 m
9 m   9 m
26 m

210 sq m

4.
13 ft
5 ft
7 ft
4 ft

93 sq ft

5.
24 mi
18 mi   16 mi
9 mi

414 sq mi

6.
7 in.
18 in. 4 in.
7 in.
14 in.

236 sq in.

Name _____

Lesson 89
CC.4.MD.3

1. Mr. Benson built a play area for his children and an office for himself.

15 ft
Play Area
10 ft
Office 10 ft
20 ft

How much carpet does he need to cover the floor in both areas?

(A) 70 square feet
(B) 250 square feet
(C) 300 square feet
(D) 350 square feet

2. Mrs. Ericson is building a new balcony.

6 ft
6 ft   6 ft
2 ft
2 ft 2 ft

What is the area of Mrs. Ericson's new balcony?

(A) 44 square feet
(B) 36 square feet
(C) 32 square feet
(D) 28 square feet

Problem Solving REAL WORLD

Use the diagram for 3–4.
Nadia makes the diagram below to represent the counter space she wants to build in her craft room.

3 ft
15 ft 11 ft 5 ft
Painting 9 ft
Scrapbooking
13 ft

3. What is the area of the space that Nadia has shown for scrapbooking?

52 square feet

4. What is the area of the space she has shown for painting?

25 square feet

Name _____

Lesson 90
COMMON CORE STANDARD CC.4.MD.3
Lesson Objective: Given perimeter or area, find the unknown measure of a side of a rectangle.

Find Unknown Measures

Fred has 30 yards of fencing to enclose a rectangular vegetable garden. He wants it to be 6 yards wide. How long will his vegetable garden be?

?
6 yd

Step 1 Decide whether this problem involves area or perimeter.

Think: The fencing goes *around the outside* of the garden. This is a measure of perimeter.

Step 2 Use a formula for perimeter. The width is 6. The perimeter is 30. The length is unknown.

$P = (2 \times l) + (2 \times w)$
$30 = (2 \times l) + (2 \times 6)$
$30 = 2 \times l + 12$

Step 3 Find the value of l.

$18 = 2 \times l$, so the value of l is 9.

The length of Fred's garden will be 9 yards.

Carol has 120 square inches of wood. The piece of wood is rectangular and has a height of 10 inches. How long is the base?

10 in.
?

Step 1 Decide whether this problem involves area or perimeter.

Think: *Square inches* is a measure of area.

Step 2 Use a formula for area. The height is 10. The area is 120. The length is unknown.

$A = b \times h$
$120 = b \times 10$

Step 3 Find the value of b.

Since $120 = 12 \times 10$, the value of b is 12.

The base of Carol's piece of wood is 12 inches.

Find the unknown measure.

1.
5 in.
?

Perimeter = 40 inches

width = __15 inches__

2.
?
8 feet

Area = 72 square feet

height = __9 feet__

Name _____

Lesson 90
CC.4.MD.3

1. A rectangle has a perimeter of 50 centimeters. If the width of the rectangle is 10 centimeters, what is its length?

(A) 5 centimeters
(B) 15 centimeters
(C) 20 centimeters
(D) 40 centimeters

2. Kelly wants to enclose a rectangular area for her dog with 240 feet of fencing. She wants the width to be 20 feet. What will be the length of the rectangular area?

(A) 24 feet
(B) 100 feet
(C) 110 feet
(D) 200 feet

3. The Hernandez family built a backyard patio.

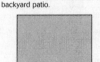

Area = 150 square feet

What could be the dimensions of the patio?

(A) 100 feet long by 50 feet wide
(B) 50 feet long by 25 feet wide
(C) 15 feet long by 10 feet wide
(D) 10 feet long by 5 feet wide

4. A rectangular window has an area of 144 square inches. The height of the window is 9 inches. What is the width of the window?

(A) 16 inches
(B) 20 inches
(C) 135 inches
(D) 153 inches

Problem Solving REAL WORLD

5. Susie is an organic vegetable grower. The perimeter of her rectangular vegetable garden is 72 yards. The width of the vegetable garden is 9 yards. How long is the vegetable garden?

27 yards

6. An artist is creating a rectangular mural for the Northfield Community Center. The mural is 7 feet tall and has an area of 84 square feet. What is the length of the mural?

12 feet

Answer Key

Name _____

Problem Solving • Find the Area

Use the strategy **solve a simpler problem.**

Marilyn is going to paint a wall in her bedroom. The wall is 15 feet long and 8 feet tall. The window takes up an area 6 feet long and 4 feet high. How many square feet of the wall will Marilyn have to paint?

Read the Problem	Solve the Problem
What do I need to find?	First, find the area of the wall.
I need to find how many <u>square feet of the wall</u> Marilyn will paint.	$A = b \times h$ $= 15 \times \underline{8}$ $= \underline{120}$ square feet
What information do I need to use?	Next, find the area of the window.
The paint will cover the wall. The paint will not cover the <u>window</u>. The base of the wall is 15 feet and the height is <u>8 feet</u>. The base of the window is 6 feet and the height is <u>4 feet</u>.	$A = b \times h$ $= \underline{6} \times \underline{4}$ $= \underline{24}$ square feet
How will I use the information?	Last, subtract the area of the window from the area of the wall.
I can solve simpler problems. Find the area of the <u>wall</u>. Then, find the area of the window. Last, <u>subtract</u> the area of the <u>window</u> from the area of the wall.	$\begin{array}{r} 120 \\ -\ 24 \\ \hline \underline{96} \text{ square feet} \end{array}$ So, Marilyn will paint <u>96 square feet</u> of her bedroom wall.

1. Ned wants to wallpaper the wall of his bedroom that has the door. The wall is 14 feet wide and 9 feet high. The door is 3 feet wide and 7 feet high. How many square feet of wallpaper will Ned need for the wall?

105 square

2. Nicole has a rectangular canvas that is 12 inches long and 10 inches wide. She paints a blue square in the center of the canvas. The square is 3 inches on each side. How much of the canvas is NOT painted blue?

111 square inches

Name _____

1. Melanie's blue notebook cover is 20 centimeters by 30 centimeters. She has a sticker for each letter in her name. Each sticker is a square that measures 2 centimeters on each side. If she puts all 7 stickers on her notebook, how much of the blue notebook cover will still be showing?

Ⓐ 596 square centimeters

Ⓑ 586 square centimeters

Ⓒ 572 square centimeters

Ⓓ 544 square centimeters

2. Aidan bought a frame for a photograph that he took.

24 in.
20 in.
8 in.   10 in.

What was the area of the frame that he bought?

Ⓐ 80 square inches

Ⓑ 120 square inches

Ⓒ 160 square inches

Ⓓ 240 square inches

3. Diane made a design using only squares. She shaded the inner square and the outer region.

10 in.   12 in.
3 in.

Find the total area that is shaded. Explain how you found your answer.

53 square inches; Possible answer: I found the area of the 12-inch square, which is 144. Then I subtracted the area of the 10-inch square. Finally I added 9, the area of the 3-inch square.

Name _____

Line Plots

Howard gave a piece of paper with several survey questions to his friends. Then he made a list to show how long it took for his friends to answer the survey. Howard wants to know how many surveys took longer than $\frac{2}{12}$ hour.

Time for Survey Answers (in hours)
$\frac{1}{12}\ \frac{3}{12}\ \frac{1}{12}\ \frac{2}{12}\ \frac{6}{12}\ \frac{3}{12}\ \frac{5}{12}$

Make a line plot to show the data.

Step 1 Order the data from least to greatest.
$\frac{1}{12},\ \frac{1}{12},\ \frac{2}{12},\ \frac{3}{12},\ \frac{3}{12},\ \frac{5}{12},\ \frac{6}{12}$

Step 2 Make a tally table of the data.

Step 3 Label the fractions of an hour on the number line from least to greatest. Notice that $\frac{4}{12}$ is included even though it is not in the data.

Step 4 Plot an X above the number line for each piece of data. Write a title for the line plot.

Step 5 Count the number of Xs that represent data points greater than $\frac{2}{12}$ hour.

There are ___4___ data points greater than $\frac{2}{12}$ hour.

So, ___4___ surveys took more than $\frac{2}{12}$ hour.

Survey	
Time (in hours)	Tally
$\frac{1}{12}$	ll
$\frac{2}{12}$	l
$\frac{3}{12}$	ll
$\frac{5}{12}$	l
$\frac{6}{12}$	l

X   X
X X X   X X
$\frac{1}{12}$ $\frac{2}{12}$ $\frac{3}{12}$ $\frac{4}{12}$ $\frac{5}{12}$ $\frac{6}{12}$
Time for Survey Answers
(in hours)

Use the line plot above for 1 and 2.

1. How many of the surveys that Howard gave to his friends were answered? ___7___

2. What is the difference in hours between the longest time and the shortest time that it took Howard's friends to answer the survey?
$\frac{5}{12}$ hour

Name _____

Use the line plot for 1 and 2.
The line plot shows the distance some students jogged.

X
X
X   X   X
X   X   X   X   X
$\frac{1}{5}$ $\frac{2}{5}$ $\frac{3}{5}$ $\frac{4}{5}$ $\frac{5}{5}$
Distance Students Jogged (in miles)

1. How many students jogged $\frac{3}{5}$ mile?

Ⓐ 4   Ⓒ 2

Ⓑ 3   Ⓓ 1

2. What is the total number of miles the group jogged?

Ⓐ $\frac{4}{5}$ mile   Ⓒ 6 miles

Ⓑ 3 miles   Ⓓ $6\frac{3}{5}$ miles

Use the line plot for 3 and 4.
The line plot shows the distance some students swam during a timed exercise.

X
X   X
X   X   X   X
X   X   X   X   X
$\frac{1}{8}$ $\frac{2}{8}$ $\frac{3}{8}$ $\frac{4}{8}$ $\frac{5}{8}$
Distance Students Swam (in miles)

3. How many students swam $\frac{4}{8}$ mile?

Ⓐ 1   Ⓒ 3

Ⓑ 2   Ⓓ 4

4. What is the total number of miles the group swam?

Ⓐ $4\frac{4}{8}$ miles   Ⓒ $1\frac{7}{8}$ miles

Ⓑ 4 miles   Ⓓ $\frac{1}{2}$ mile

5. The tally table shows how much time students would spend walking home from school if they did not ride the bus. Use the tally table to complete the line plot.

Time Spent Walking Home

Time (in hours)	Tally
$\frac{1}{6}$	llll
$\frac{2}{6}$	lll
$\frac{3}{6}$	ll
$\frac{4}{6}$	l

X
X   X
X   X   X
X   X   X   X
$\frac{1}{6}$ $\frac{2}{6}$ $\frac{3}{6}$ $\frac{4}{6}$

Answer Key

Name _____

Lesson 93
COMMON CORE STANDARD CC.4.MD.5a
Lesson Objective: Relate angles and fractional parts of a circle.

Angles and Fractional Parts of a Circle

Find how many $\frac{1}{6}$ turns make a complete circle.

Materials: fraction circles

Step 1 Place a $\frac{1}{6}$ piece so that the tip of the fraction piece is on the center of the circle. Trace the fraction piece by drawing along the dashed lines in the circle.

Step 2 Shade and label the angle formed by the $\frac{1}{6}$ piece.

Step 3 Place the $\frac{1}{6}$ piece on the shaded angle. Turn it clockwise (in the direction that the hands on a clock move). Turn the fraction piece to line up directly beside the shaded section.

Step 4 Trace the fraction piece. Shade and label it. You have traced __2__ sixths in all.

Step 5 Repeat until you have shaded the entire circle.

There are __six__ angles that come together in the center of the circle.

So, you need __six__ $\frac{1}{6}$ turns to make a circle.

Tell what fraction of the circle the shaded angle represents.

1. $\frac{1}{2}$ 2. $\frac{3}{4}$ 3. $\frac{1}{4}$

Name _____

Lesson 93
CC.4.MD.5a

Use the diagram for 1–2.

1. "Ray" is not used in the lesson. Which statement best describes the shaded turn?
   - (A) $\frac{1}{4}$ turn clockwise
   - (B) $\frac{1}{4}$ turn counterclockwise
   - (C) $\frac{3}{4}$ turn clockwise
   - (D) $\frac{3}{4}$ turn counterclockwise

2. What clockwise turn represents the white part of the circle?
   - (A) 1 full turn
   - (B) $\frac{3}{4}$ turn
   - (C) $\frac{1}{2}$ turn
   - (D) $\frac{1}{4}$ turn

3. Which shaded angle shows $\frac{1}{8}$ of the circle?
   - (A) (B) (C) (D)

4. Which shaded angle shows $\frac{1}{3}$ of the circle?
   - (A) (B) (C) (D)

5. Jack babysat from 4:00 P.M. until 4:45 P.M. Describe the turn the minute hand made, and explain how you know.
   Possible answer: the minute hand made a $\frac{3}{4}$ turn clockwise. I know because the hand started at 12 on the circle and moved $\frac{3}{4}$ of the way around the circle to the 9.

Name _____

Lesson 94
COMMON CORE STANDARD CC.4.MD.5b
Lesson Objective: Relate degrees to fractional parts of a circle by understanding that an angle that measures 1° turns through $\frac{1}{360}$ of a circle.

Degrees

Angles are measured in units called **degrees.** The symbol for degrees is °. If a circle is divided into 360 equal parts, then an angle that turns through 1 part of the 360 measures 1°.

An angle that turns through $\frac{50}{360}$ of a circle measures 50°.

Find the measure of an angle that turns through $\frac{1}{6}$ of a circle.

Step 1 Find a fraction that is equivalent to $\frac{1}{6}$ with 360 in the denominator. **Think:** $6 \times 60 = 360$.

$$\frac{1}{6} = \frac{1 \times 60}{6 \times 60} = \frac{60}{360}$$

Step 2 Look at the numerator of $\frac{60}{360}$.
The numerator tells how many degrees are in $\frac{1}{6}$ of a circle.

So, an angle that turns through $\frac{1}{6}$ of a circle measures __60°__.

Tell the measure of the angle in degrees.

1. 39°   2. 72°
3. 45°   4. 150°

Name _____

Lesson 94
CC.4.MD.5b

1. What term best describes the angle formed by the hands of the clock?
   - (A) acute
   - (B) obtuse
   - (C) right
   - (D) straight

2. How many degrees are in an angle that turns through $\frac{3}{4}$ of a circle?
   - (A) 90°
   - (B) 180°
   - (C) 270°
   - (D) 360°

3. What name is given to an angle that measures 180°?
   - (A) acute angle
   - (B) obtuse angle
   - (C) right angle
   - (D) straight angle

4. In degrees, what is the angle measure of the shaded part?
   - (A) 250°
   - (B) 110°
   - (C) 36°
   - (D) 11°

Problem Solving REAL WORLD

Ann started reading at 4:00 P.M. and finished at 4:20 P.M.

5. Through what fraction of a circle did the minute hand turn?
   $\frac{1}{3}$ turn clockwise

6. How many degrees did the minute hand turn?
   120°

Start   **End**

Answer Key

Lesson 95 (left panel, page 189)

Lesson 95
COMMON CORE STANDARD CC.4.MD.6
Lesson Objective: Use a protractor to measure an angle and to draw an angle with a given measure.

Measure and Draw Angles

A **protractor** is a tool for measuring the size of an angle.

Follow the steps below to measure ∠ABC.

Step 1 Place the center point of the protractor on vertex B of the angle.

Step 2 Align the 0° mark on the protractor with ray BC. Note that the 0° mark is on the outer scale or top scale.

Step 2   Step 1

Step 3 Find where ray BA intersects the same scale.

Step 4

Step 4 Read the angle measure on the scale.

The m∠ABC = __30°__.

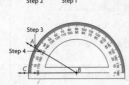

Use a protractor to find the angle measure.

1.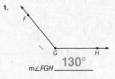

m∠FGH __130°__

2.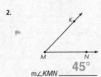

m∠KMN __45°__

Use a protractor to draw the angle. Check students' drawings.

3. 110°

110°

4. 55°

55°

Lesson 95 (right panel, page 190)

Lesson 95
CC.4.MD.6

1. Use a protractor. What is the measure of ∠JKL?

Ⓐ 50°   Ⓒ 110°
Ⓑ 60°   Ⓓ 120°

2. Use a protractor. What is the measure of the angle formed by the hands of the clock?

Ⓐ 115°   Ⓒ 50°
Ⓑ 62°   Ⓓ 25°

Use the diagram for 3–4.

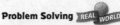

3. Use a protractor. What is the measure of the **largest** angle in the triangle?

Ⓐ 175°   Ⓒ 110°
Ⓑ 130°   Ⓓ 95°

4. Use a protractor. What is the measure of the **smallest** angle in the triangle?

Ⓐ 40°
Ⓑ 30°
Ⓒ 20°
Ⓓ 10°

Problem Solving REAL WORLD

The drawing shows the angles a stair tread makes with a support board along a wall. Use your protractor to measure the angles.

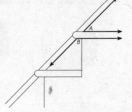

5. What is the measure of ∠A? __45°__

6. What is the measure of ∠B? __135°__

Lesson 96 (left panel, page 191)

Lesson 96
COMMON CORE STANDARD CC.4.MD.7
Lesson Objective: Determine the measure of an angle separated into parts.

Join and Separate Angles

The measure of an angle equals the sum of the measures of its parts.

Use your protractor and the angles at the right.

Step 1 Measure ∠ABC and ∠CBD. Record the measures.

m∠ABC = __35°__; m∠CBD = __40°__

Step 2 Find the sum of the measures.

__35°__ + __40°__ = __75°__

Step 3 Measure ∠ABD. Record the measure.

m∠ABD = __75°__

So, m∠ABC + m∠CBD = m∠ABD.

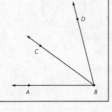

Add to find the measure of the angle. Write an equation to record your work.

1.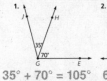

35° + 70° = 105°

m∠EGJ = __105°__

2.

60° + 70° = 130°

m∠KLN = __130°__

3.

45° + 20° = 65°

m∠PRT = __65°__

Use a protractor and the art at the right.

4. Find the measure of each angle. Label each angle with its measure.

5. Write the sum of the angle measures as an equation.

100° + 90° + 140 + 30° = 360°

Lesson 96 (right panel, page 192)

Lesson 96
CC.4.MD.7

1. What is the measure of the unknown angle in the figure?

Ⓐ 15°
Ⓑ 105°
Ⓒ 115°
Ⓓ 165°

2. Which equation shows the sum of the measures of two right angles?

Ⓐ 45° + 45° = 90°
Ⓑ 50° + 50° = 100°
Ⓒ 90° + 90° = 180°
Ⓓ 180° + 180° = 360°

3. What is the measure of the unknown angle in the figure?

Ⓐ 47°   Ⓒ 90°
Ⓑ 57°   Ⓓ 123°

4. Use a protractor. Which equation shows the correct sum of the angle measures in the figure?

Ⓐ 100° + 120° = 220°
Ⓑ 120° + 120° + 120° = 360°
Ⓒ 110° + 120° + 130° = 360°
Ⓓ 100° + 120° + 140° = 360°

Problem Solving REAL WORLD

5. Ned made the design at the right. Use a protractor. Find and write the measure of each of the 3 angles.
50°; 60°; 70°

6. Write an equation to find the measure of the total angle.
50° + 60° + 70° = 180°

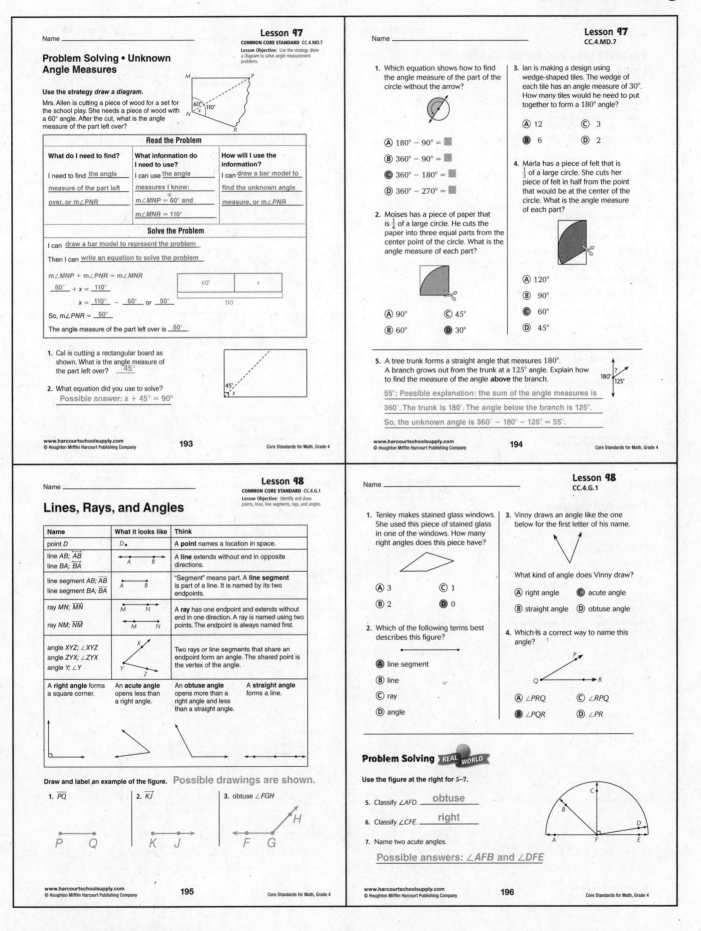

Name _____

Lesson 97

COMMON CORE STANDARD CC.4.MD.7

Lesson Objective: Use the strategy *draw a diagram* to solve angle measurement problems.

Problem Solving • Unknown Angle Measures

Use the strategy *draw a diagram.*

Mrs. Allen is cutting a piece of wood for a set for the school play. She needs a piece of wood with a 60° angle. After the cut, what is the angle measure of the part left over?

Read the Problem

What do I need to find?	What information do I need to use?	How will I use the information?
I need to find _the angle_ _measure of the part left_ _over, or m∠PNR_	I can use _the angle_ _measures I know:_ _m∠MNP = 60° and_ _m∠MNR = 110°_	I can _draw a bar model to_ _find the unknown angle_ _measure, or m∠PNR_

Solve the Problem

I can _draw a bar model to represent the problem_

Then I can _write an equation to solve the problem_

m∠MNP + m∠PNR = m∠MNR

_60°_ + x = _110°_

x = _110°_ – _60°_, or _50°_

So, m∠PNR = _50°_

The angle measure of the part left over is _50°_

1. Cal is cutting a rectangular board as shown. What is the angle measure of the part left over? _45°_

2. What equation did you use to solve? _Possible answer: x + 45° = 90°_

Name _____

Lesson 97

CC.4.MD.7

1. Which equation shows how to find the angle measure of the part of the circle without the arrow?

   Ⓐ 180° – 90° = ▇

   Ⓑ 360° – 90° = ▇

   Ⓒ 360° – 180° = ▇

   Ⓓ 360° – 270° = ▇

2. Moises has a piece of paper that is $\frac{1}{4}$ of a large circle. He cuts the paper into three equal parts from the center point of the circle. What is the angle measure of each part?

   Ⓐ 90°   Ⓒ 45°

   Ⓑ 60°   Ⓓ 30°

3. Ian is making a design using wedge-shaped tiles. The wedge of each tile has an angle measure of 30°. How many tiles would he need to put together to form a 180° angle?

   Ⓐ 12   Ⓒ 3

   Ⓑ 6   Ⓓ 2

4. Marla has a piece of felt that is $\frac{1}{3}$ of a large circle. She cuts her piece of felt in half from the point that would be at the center of the circle. What is the angle measure of each part?

   Ⓐ 120°

   Ⓑ 90°

   Ⓒ 60°

   Ⓓ 45°

5. A tree trunk forms a straight angle that measures 180°. A branch grows out from the trunk at a 125° angle. Explain how to find the measure of the angle **above** the branch.

   55°; Possible explanation: the sum of the angle measures is

   360°. The trunk is 180°. The angle below the branch is 125°.

   So, the unknown angle is 360° – 180° – 125° = 55°.

Name _____

Lesson 98

COMMON CORE STANDARD CC.4.G.1

Lesson Objective: Identify and draw points, lines, line segments, rays, and angles.

Lines, Rays, and Angles

Name	What it looks like	Think
point D		A **point** names a location in space.
line AB; $\overleftrightarrow{AB}$ line BA; $\overleftrightarrow{BA}$		A **line** extends without end in opposite directions.
line segment AB; $\overline{AB}$ line segment BA; $\overline{BA}$		"Segment" means part. A **line segment** is part of a line. It is named by its two endpoints.
ray MN; $\overrightarrow{MN}$ ray NM; $\overrightarrow{NM}$		A **ray** has one endpoint and extends without end in one direction. A ray is named using two points. The endpoint is always named first.
angle XYZ; ∠XYZ angle ZYX; ∠ZYX angle Y; ∠Y		Two rays or line segments that share an endpoint form an angle. The shared point is the vertex of the angle.

A **right angle** forms a square corner.	An **acute angle** opens less than a right angle.	An **obtuse angle** opens more than a right angle and less than a straight angle.	A **straight angle** forms a line.

Draw and label an example of the figure. Possible drawings are shown.

1. $\overline{PQ}$

2. $\overrightarrow{KJ}$

3. obtuse ∠FGH

Name _____

Lesson 98

CC.4.G.1

1. Tenley makes stained glass windows. She used this piece of stained glass in one of the windows. How many right angles does this piece have?

   Ⓐ 3   Ⓒ 1

   Ⓑ 2   Ⓓ 0

2. Which of the following terms best describes this figure?

   Ⓐ line segment

   Ⓑ line

   Ⓒ ray

   Ⓓ angle

3. Vinny draws an angle like the one below for the first letter of his name.

   What kind of angle does Vinny draw?

   Ⓐ right angle   Ⓒ acute angle

   Ⓑ straight angle   Ⓓ obtuse angle

4. Which is a correct way to name this angle?

   Ⓐ ∠PRQ   Ⓒ ∠RPQ

   Ⓑ ∠PQR   Ⓓ ∠PR

Problem Solving REAL WORLD

Use the figure at the right for 5–7.

5. Classify ∠AFD. _obtuse_

6. Classify ∠CFE. _right_

7. Name two acute angles.

   Possible answers: ∠AFB and ∠DFE

Answer Key

Name _____

Lesson 99
COMMON CORE STANDARD CC.4.G.1
Lesson Objective: Identify and draw parallel lines and perpendicular lines.

Parallel Lines and Perpendicular Lines

Parallel lines are lines in a plane that are always the same distance apart. Parallel lines or line segments never meet.

In the figure, lines *AB* and *CD*, even if extended, will never meet. The lines are parallel. Write $\overleftrightarrow{AB} \| \overleftrightarrow{CD}$.
Lines __AD__ and __BC__ are also parallel. So, $\overleftrightarrow{AD} \| \overleftrightarrow{BC}$.

Intersecting lines cross at exactly one point. Intersecting lines that form right angles are **perpendicular.**

In the figure, lines __AD__ and __AB__ are perpendicular because they form right angles at vertex *A*. Write $\overleftrightarrow{AD} \perp \overleftrightarrow{AB}$.
Lines __BC__ and __CD__ are also perpendicular. So, $\overleftrightarrow{BC} \perp \overleftrightarrow{CD}$.

Use the figure for 1–3.

1. Name two sides that appear to be parallel.
   __$\overline{RV}$ and $\overline{ST}$__

2. Name two sides that appear to be perpendicular.
   __$\overline{RV}$ and $\overline{RS}$ or $\overline{RS}$ and $\overline{ST}$__

3. Name two sides that appear to be intersecting, but not perpendicular.
   __$\overline{RV}$ and $\overline{VT}$ or $\overline{TV}$ and $\overline{ST}$__

Name _____

Lesson 99
CC.4.G.1

1. Virginia and Susan are discussing properties of lines during math class. Which best describes intersecting lines?

   Ⓐ They cross each other at one point.
   Ⓑ They always form obtuse angles.
   Ⓒ They only form right angles.
   Ⓓ They never cross each other.

2. Logan draws a map of his neighborhood.

   Which line appears to be parallel to $\overleftrightarrow{GH}$?

   Ⓐ $\overleftrightarrow{AB}$ Ⓒ $\overleftrightarrow{EF}$
   Ⓑ $\overleftrightarrow{CD}$ Ⓓ $\overleftrightarrow{IJ}$

3. Joe drew a figure. Which two sides of the figure are perpendicular?

   Ⓐ $\overline{TU}$ and $\overline{UV}$ Ⓒ $\overline{SV}$ and $\overline{TU}$
   Ⓑ $\overline{ST}$ and $\overline{VU}$ Ⓓ $\overline{TU}$ and $\overline{ST}$

4. Which best describes parallel lines?

   Ⓐ They form four right angles.
   Ⓑ They never cross each other.
   Ⓒ They form four acute angles.
   Ⓓ They form two acute angles and two obtuse angles.

5. Which lines appear to be perpendicular in this figure? Explain your answer.

   Possible answer: $\overleftrightarrow{EF}$ appears to be perpendicular to $\overleftrightarrow{AB}$ and $\overleftrightarrow{CD}$ because the lines appear to form right angles; $\overleftrightarrow{IJ}$ appears to be perpendicular to $\overleftrightarrow{AB}$ and $\overleftrightarrow{CD}$ because the lines appear to form right angles.

Name _____

Lesson 100
COMMON CORE STANDARD CC.4.G.2
Lesson Objective: Classify triangles by the size of their angles.

Classify Triangles

A **triangle** is a polygon with __3__ sides and __3__ angles.
Each pair of sides joins at a vertex.

You can name a triangle by its vertices.

$\triangle PQR$ $\triangle QRP$ $\triangle RPQ$
$\triangle PRQ$ $\triangle QPR$ $\triangle RQP$

There are __3__ types of triangles. All triangles have at least __2__ acute angles.

Obtuse triangle	**Right triangle**	**Acute triangle**
one obtuse angle	one right angle	three acute angles

1. Name the triangle. Tell whether each angle is *acute*, *right*, or *obtuse*. A name for the triangle is __$\triangle XYZ$__

   $\angle X$ is __acute__
   $\angle Y$ is __obtuse__
   $\angle Z$ is __acute__

Classify each triangle. Write *acute*, *right*, or *obtuse*.

2.
   __right__

3.
   __acute__

4.
   __obtuse__

Name _____

Lesson 100
CC.4.G.2

1. A sign is in the shape of an acute triangle. Which of the following could be the shape of the sign?

   Ⓐ
   Ⓑ
   Ⓒ
   Ⓓ

2. How many acute angles does a right triangle have?

   Ⓐ 0   Ⓒ 2
   Ⓑ 1   Ⓓ 3

3. How many acute angles does an obtuse triangle have?

   Ⓐ 0   Ⓒ 2
   Ⓑ 1   Ⓓ 3

4. Janelle made a flag in the shape of a right triangle. Which of the triangles could be Janelle's flag?

   Ⓐ
   Ⓑ
   Ⓒ
   Ⓓ

5. Marla says this figure has a right triangle, an acute triangle, and an obtuse triangle. Do you agree? Explain your answer.

   No; Possible explanation: the figure does not have an obtuse triangle. Triangles *ABC* and *ADC* are acute triangles. Triangles *DEC* and *DEA* are right triangles.

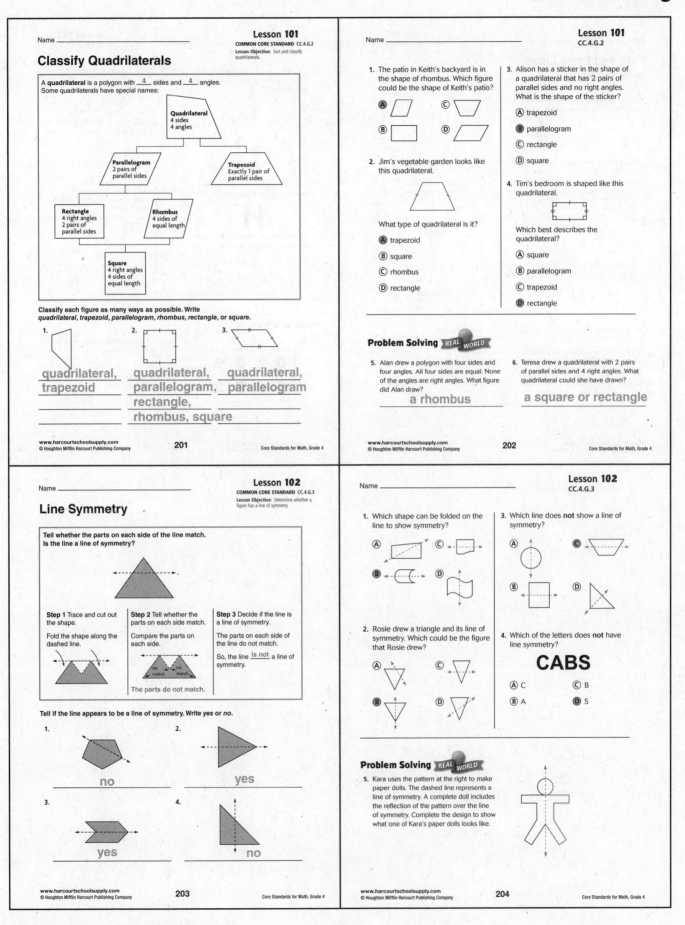

Answer Key

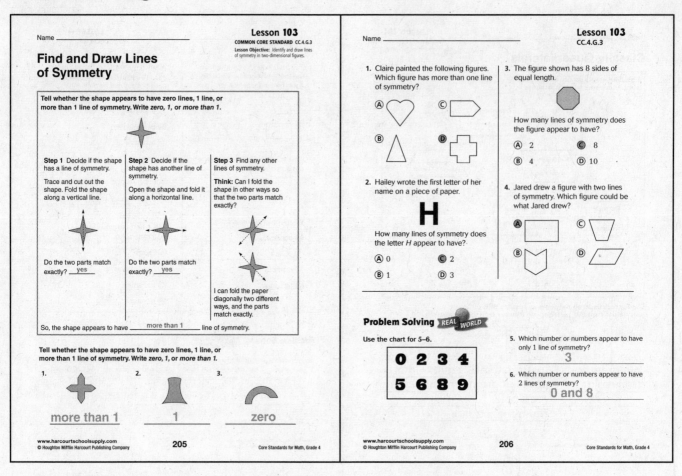

Name _____

Lesson 103
COMMON CORE STANDARD CC.4.G.3
Lesson Objective: Identify and draw lines of symmetry in two-dimensional figures.

Find and Draw Lines of Symmetry

Tell whether the shape appears to have zero lines, 1 line, or more than 1 line of symmetry. Write *zero, 1,* or *more than 1.*

Step 1 Decide if the shape has a line of symmetry.

Trace and cut out the shape. Fold the shape along a vertical line.

Do the two parts match exactly? __yes__

Step 2 Decide if the shape has another line of symmetry.

Open the shape and fold it along a horizontal line.

Do the two parts match exactly? __yes__

Step 3 Find any other lines of symmetry.

Think: Can I fold the shape in other ways so that the two parts match exactly?

I can fold the paper diagonally two different ways, and the parts match exactly.

So, the shape appears to have ___more than 1___ line of symmetry.

Tell whether the shape appears to have zero lines, 1 line, or more than 1 line of symmetry. Write *zero, 1,* or *more than 1.*

1. ___more than 1___

2. ___1___

3. ___zero___

1. Claire painted the following figures. Which figure has more than one line of symmetry?

   Ⓐ Ⓒ
   Ⓑ Ⓓ

2. Hailey wrote the first letter of her name on a piece of paper.

   H

   How many lines of symmetry does the letter *H* appear to have?

   Ⓐ 0   Ⓒ 2
   Ⓑ 1   Ⓓ 3

3. The figure shown has 8 sides of equal length.

   How many lines of symmetry does the figure appear to have?

   Ⓐ 2   Ⓒ 8
   Ⓑ 4   Ⓓ 10

4. Jared drew a figure with two lines of symmetry. Which figure could be what Jared drew?

   Ⓐ Ⓒ
   Ⓑ Ⓓ

Problem Solving REAL WORLD

Use the chart for 5–6.

| 0 | 2 | 3 | 4 |
| 5 | 6 | 8 | 9 |

5. Which number or numbers appear to have only 1 line of symmetry?

   ___3___

6. Which number or numbers appear to have 2 lines of symmetry?

   ___0 and 8___

Operations and Algebraic Thinking CC.4.OA

Use the four operations with whole numbers to solve problems.

1. Interpret a multiplication equation as a comparison, e.g., interpret $35 = 5 \times 7$ as a statement that 35 is 5 times as many as 7 and 7 times as many as 5. Represent verbal statements of multiplicative comparisons as multiplication equations.

2. Multiply or divide to solve word problems involving multiplicative comparison, e.g., by using drawings and equations with a symbol for the unknown number to represent the problem, distinguishing multiplicative comparison from additive comparison.

3. Solve multistep word problems posed with whole numbers and having whole-number answers using the four operations, including problems in which remainders must be interpreted. Represent these problems using equations with a letter standing for the unknown quantity. Assess the reasonableness of answers using mental computation and estimation strategies including rounding.

Gain familiarity with factors and multiples.

4. Find all factor pairs for a whole number in the range 1–100. Recognize that a whole number is a multiple of each of its factors. Determine whether a given whole number in the range 1–100 is a multiple of a given one-digit number. Determine whether a given whole number in the range 1–100 is prime or composite.

Generate and analyze patterns.

5. Generate a number or shape pattern that follows a given rule. Identify apparent features of the pattern that were not explicit in the rule itself.

Common Core State Standards

Number and Operations in Base Ten

Generalize place value understanding for multi-digit whole numbers.

1. Recognize that in a multi-digit whole number, a digit in one place represents ten times what it represents in the place to its right.

2. Read and write multi-digit whole numbers using base-ten numerals, number names, and expanded form. Compare two multi-digit numbers based on meanings of the digits in each place, using >, =, and < symbols to record the results of comparisons.

3. Use place value understanding to round multi-digit whole numbers to any place.

Use place value understanding and properties of operations to perform multi-digit arithmetic.

4. Fluently add and subtract multi-digit whole numbers using the standard algorithm.

5. Multiply a whole number of up to four digits by a one-digit whole number, and multiply two two-digit numbers, using strategies based on place value and the properties of operations. Illustrate and explain the calculation by using equations, rectangular arrays, and/or area models.

6. Find whole-number quotients and remainders with up to four-digit dividends and one-digit divisors, using strategies based on place value, the properties of operations, and/or the relationship between multiplication and division. Illustrate and explain the calculation by using equations, rectangular arrays, and/or area models.

Number and Operations – Fractions

Extend understanding of fraction equivalence and ordering.

1. Explain why a fraction a/b is equivalent to a fraction $(n \times a)/(n \times b)$ by using visual fraction models, with attention to how the number and size of the parts differ even though the two fractions themselves are the same size. Use this principle to recognize and generate equivalent fractions.

2. Compare two fractions with different numerators and different denominators, e.g., by creating common denominators or numerators, or by comparing to a benchmark fraction such as 1/2. Recognize that comparisons are valid only when the two fractions refer to the same whole. Record the results of comparisons with symbols >, =, or <, and justify the conclusions, e.g., by using a visual fraction model.

Build fractions from unit fractions by applying and extending previous understandings of operations on whole numbers.

3. Understand a fraction a/b with $a > 1$ as a sum of fractions $1/b$.

   a. Understand addition and subtraction of fractions as joining and separating parts referring to the same whole.

   b. Decompose a fraction into a sum of fractions with the same denominator in more than one way, recording each decomposition by an equation. Justify decompositions, e.g., by using a visual fraction model.

   c. Add and subtract mixed numbers with like denominators, e.g., by replacing each mixed number with an equivalent fraction, and/or by using properties of operations and the relationship between addition and subtraction.

   d. Solve word problems involving addition and subtraction of fractions referring to the same whole and having like denominators, e.g., by using visual fraction models and equations to represent the problem.

4. Apply and extend previous understandings of multiplication to multiply a fraction by a whole number.

   a. Understand a fraction a/b as a multiple of $1/b$.

   b. Understand a multiple of a/b as a multiple of $1/b$, and use this understanding to multiply a fraction by a whole number.

   c. Solve word problems involving multiplication of a fraction by a whole number, e.g., by using visual fraction models and equations to represent the problem.

Common Core State Standards

Number and Operations – Fractions

Understand decimal notation for fractions, and compare decimal fractions.

5. Express a fraction with denominator 10 as an equivalent fraction with denominator 100, and use this technique to add two fractions with respective denominators 10 and 100.

6. Use decimal notation for fractions with denominators 10 or 100.

7. Compare two decimals to hundredths by reasoning about their size. Recognize that comparisons are valid only when the two decimals refer to the same whole. Record the results of comparisons with the symbols >, =, or <, and justify the conclusions, e.g., by using a visual model.

Measurement and Data

∙∙∙

Solve problems involving measurement and conversion of measurements from a larger unit to a smaller unit.

1. Know relative sizes of measurement units within one system of units including km, m, cm; kg, g; lb, oz.; l, ml; hr, min, sec. Within a single system of measurement, express measurements in a larger unit in terms of a smaller unit. Record measurement equivalents in a two-column table.

2. Use the four operations to solve word problems involving distances, intervals of time, liquid volumes, masses of objects, and money, including problems involving simple fractions or decimals, and problems that require expressing measurements given in a larger unit in terms of a smaller unit. Represent measurement quantities using diagrams such as number line diagrams that feature a measurement scale.

3. Apply the area and perimeter formulas for rectangles in real world and mathematical problems.

∙∙∙

Represent and interpret data.

4. Make a line plot to display a data set of measurements in fractions of a unit $(1/2, 1/4, 1/8)$. Solve problems involving addition and subtraction of fractions by using information presented in line plots.

∙∙∙

Geometric measurement: understand concepts of angle and measure angles.

5. Recognize angles as geometric shapes that are formed wherever two rays share a common endpoint, and understand concepts of angle measurement:

   a. An angle is measured with reference to a circle with its center at the common endpoint of the rays, by considering the fraction of the circular arc between the points where the two rays intersect the circle. An angle that turns through 1/360 of a circle is called a "one-degree angle," and can be used to measure angles.

   b. An angle that turns through n one-degree angles is said to have an angle measure of n degrees.

6. Measure angles in whole-number degrees using a protractor. Sketch angles of specified measure.

7. Recognize angle measure as additive. When an angle is decomposed into non-overlapping parts, the angle measure of the whole is the sum of the angle measures of the parts. Solve addition and subtraction problems to find unknown angles on a diagram in real world and mathematical problems, e.g., by using an equation with a symbol for the unknown angle measure.

Common Core State Standards

Geometry

Draw and identify lines and angles, and classify shapes by properties of their lines and angles.

1. Draw points, lines, line segments, rays, angles (right, acute, obtuse), and perpendicular and parallel lines. Identify these in two-dimensional figures.

2. Classify two-dimensional figures based on the presence or absence of parallel or perpendicular lines, or the presence or absence of angles of a specified size. Recognize right triangles as a category, and identify right triangles.

3. Recognize a line of symmetry for a two-dimensional figure as a line across the figure such that the figure can be folded along the line into matching parts. Identify line-symmetric figures and draw lines of symmetry.